The GMAT For Dummies, 5th Edition

Things to Take with You to the Test

To show up at the test site fully prepared, make sure you bring these three items:

- **Your appointment confirmation letter:** When you schedule an appointment for the GMAT, Pearson VUE sends you a confirmation letter that you should bring with you to the test. It proves you're registered. Don't despair if you can't find yours, though. They'll let you in if you have an appointment.

- **A photo ID:** You have to prove that you're you and not your really smart neighbor who looks a little like you coming in to take the test for you. Any form of identification that doesn't have your picture on it is unacceptable, but government issued picture IDs like driver's licenses, passports, identification cards, and military IDs are great.

- **The names of up to five of your favorite MBA programs:** Pearson VUE sends your GMAT scores to five programs of your choice, so have a list of your five favorites with you on test day.

Tips and Tricks for GMAT Math Questions

Mastering the math is easier when you take these tips to heart:

- Know math formulas before you take the GMAT, because the test doesn't provide them for you.

- Remember that easy questions are worth the same number of points as hard questions, so don't rush through the easy questions and make careless mistakes.

- Eliminate answer choices that don't make sense.

- Memorize the chart for answering data sufficiency questions. As soon as you've determined whether a statement has enough information to answer the question, eliminate answer choices and move on. Don't waste time solving the problem unless you have to do so to make your determination.

- Take advantage of your notepad. Use it to draw pictures, work out formulas, and cross out wrong answer choices.

Tips and Tricks for Critical Reasoning Questions

To fulfill your potential on the critical reasoning questions in the verbal section, remember these techniques:

- Read the question first so you know what kind of question you have to answer before you read the argument.

- For strengthen- or weaken-the-argument questions, determine what type of reasoning the author uses and choose an answer that either helps or hurts that way of reasoning.

- For questions that ask you to draw conclusions, choose an answer that contains an element of all of the author's premises.

- Remember that the correct answer to an inference question usually concerns just one of the argument's premises.

- Assumption questions ask you to choose an answer that states a premise the author assumes to be true but doesn't state directly. The right answer often links the last premise to the conclusion.

- For method-of-reasoning questions, figure out how the author makes the argument. Usually the author uses inductive reasoning, and the GMAT focuses on these specific ways to make an argument through inductive reasoning:

  - Cause and effect

  - Analogy

  - Statistics

The GMAT For Dummies® 5th Edition

Cheat Sheet

Tips and Tricks for Sentence Correction Questions

Correcting sentences in the verbal section is a breeze when you focus on these guidelines:

- Read the sentence and check the pronouns and verbs in the underlined part for agreement. If the verbs and pronouns check out, look for problems with parallelism or word choice.
- If there are no obvious errors, the answer is probably A, but skim through the answer choices just to make sure you didn't miss anything.
- If you spot an error, eliminate answer choices that don't correct the error. Then eliminate answer choices that correct the error but make a new one.
- Reread your answer choice within the sentence to make sure it makes sense before you commit to it.

Tips and Tricks for Reading Comprehension Questions

Heed this advice when answering reading questions in the verbal section:

- Read through the passage before answering the questions.
- As you read, focus on main theme, author's tone, and paragraph topics rather than the specific details of the passage.
- Eliminate answer choices that don't pertain to the information in the passage.
- Remember that the author of a GMAT passage is usually pretty neutral and objective.
- Choose general answers for main theme questions.
- Don't infer too much for inference questions.
- Note that the answers to specific information questions may be a paraphrase of information in the passage.

Tips and Tricks for the Analytical Writing Assessment

Here are some hints for making the most of your analytical essays:

- Choose your thesis immediately. There's no right answer to the question prompts, so don't waste time trying to find it.
- Spend at least two to five minutes constructing a quick outline of your ideas. Make sure you have a general thesis for the essay and a topic statement for each paragraph.
- You should have an introductory paragraph, at least two or three supporting paragraphs, and a conclusion.
- Get specific with your supporting evidence. Draw from your own experience or knowledge. It's okay to get personal.
- Leave a couple minutes at the end to read through your essay and correct any glaring errors.

For Dummies: Bestselling Book Series for Beginners

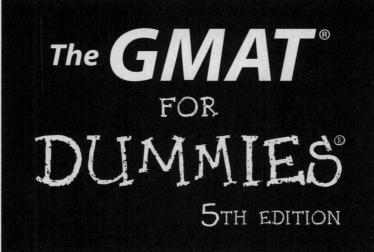

The GMAT® FOR DUMMIES®

5TH EDITION

by Scott Hatch, J.D.
and Lisa Hatch, M.A.

WILEY

Wiley Publishing, Inc.

The GMAT For Dummies® 5th Edition

Published by
Wiley Publishing, Inc.
111 River St.
Hoboken, NJ 07030-5774
www.wiley.com

WILEY

About the Authors

Scott and **Lisa Hatch** have prepared students for college entrance exams for over 25 years. While in law school in the late '70s, Scott Hatch taught LSAT preparation courses throughout Southern California to pay for his education. He was so good at it that after graduation, he went out on his own. Using materials he developed himself, he prepared thousands of anxious potential test-takers for the SAT, ACT, PSAT, LSAT, GRE, and GMAT.

Years ago, Lisa took one of Scott's LSAT preparation courses at the University of Colorado and improved her love life as well as her LSAT score. Lisa's love for instructing and writing allowed her to fit right in with Scott's lifestyle, teaching courses and preparing course materials. They married shortly thereafter.

Since then, Scott and Lisa have taught test preparation to students worldwide. Currently over 300 universities and colleges offer their courses online and through live lectures, and the Hatches have written the curriculum for both formats. The company they have built together, the Center for Legal Studies, provides not only standardized test preparation courses but also courses for those who desire careers in the field of law, including paralegals, legal secretaries, legal investigators, victim advocates, and legal nurse consultants.

Scott has presented standardized test preparation courses since 1979. He is listed in *Who's Who in California* and *Who's Who Among Students in American Colleges and Universities,* and he was named one of the Outstanding Young Men of America by the United States Jaycees. He was a contributing editor to *The Judicial Profiler* (McGraw-Hill) and the *Colorado Law Annotated* (West/Lawyers Co-op) series, and he was editor of several award-winning publications. He received his undergraduate degree from the University of Colorado and his Juris Doctorate from Southwestern University School of Law.

Lisa has been teaching legal certificate and standardized test preparation courses since 1987. She graduated with honors in English from the University of Puget Sound, and she received her master's degree from California State University. She and Scott have co-authored numerous law and standardized test texts, including *Paralegal Procedures and Practices,* published by West Thomson Publishing, and *SAT II U.S. History For Dummies, SAT II Biology For Dummies, SAT II Math For Dummies,* and *Paralegal Career For Dummies,* published by Wiley Publishing.

Dedication

We dedicate our For Dummies books to Alison, Andrew, Zachary, and Zoe Hatch. They demonstrated extreme patience, understanding, and assistance while we wrote this book, and we appreciate them beyond expression.

Authors' Acknowledgments

This book would not be possible without the extensive research and writing contributions of standardized test prep experts David Newland, M.A., J.D, and Benjamin A. Saypol, M.A. Their efforts greatly enhanced our writing, editing, and organization, and we are deeply grateful to them. We'd also like to thank the staff of the Center for Legal Studies, who worked diligently to execute a smooth process in the administrative tasks necessary to bring about this book.

We need to acknowledge the input of the thousands of prospective MBA students and other college applicants who have completed our test preparation courses over the last twenty-six years. The classroom and online contributions offered by these eager learners have provided us with lots of information about which areas require the greatest amount of preparation. Their input is the reason we're able to produce accurate and up-to-date test preparation.

Our meticulous scholarship and attempts at wit were greatly facilitated by the editing professionals at Wiley Publishing. Our thanks go out to Tim Gallan and Natalie Harris for their patience and support throughout the process, David Herzog and Laura Nussbaum for their attention to detail during the editing process, and Kathy Cox for getting the project up and running.

Finally, we wish to acknowledge our literary agent, Margo Maley Hutchinson at Waterside Productions in Cardiff, for her assistance and for introducing us to the innovative For Dummies series. We thrive on feedback from our students and encourage our readers to provide comments and critiques at feedback@legalstudies.com.

Publisher's Acknowledgments

We're proud of this book; please send us your comments through our Dummies online registration form located at www.dummies.com/register/.

Some of the people who helped bring this book to market include the following:

Acquisitions, Editorial, and Media Development

Project Editors: Tim Gallan, Natalie Faye Harris
(Previous Edition: Sherri Fugit)

Acquisitions Editor: Kathy Cox
(Previous Edition: Karen Hansen)

Copy Editors: Laura Peterson Nussbaum,
Danielle Voirol (Previous Edition: Donna Frederick)

Editorial Program Coordinator: Hanna K. Scott

Technical Editor: David Herzog

Editorial Manager: Christine Beck

Editorial Assistants: Erin Calligan, Nadine Bell,
David Lutton

Cartoons: Rich Tennant (www.the5thwave.com)

Composition Services

Project Coordinator: Jennifer Theriot

Layout and Graphics: Carrie A. Foster, Lauren Goddard,
Denny Hager, Joyce Haughey, Stephanie D. Jumper
Lynsey Osborn, Heather Ryan

Proofreaders: Debbye Butler, Jessica Kramer,
Charles Spencer

Indexer: Julie Kawabata

Special Help
Sara Westfall

Publishing and Editorial for Consumer Dummies

Diane Graves Steele, Vice President and Publisher, Consumer Dummies

Joyce Pepple, Acquisitions Director, Consumer Dummies

Kristin A. Cocks, Product Development Director, Consumer Dummies

Michael Spring, Vice President and Publisher, Travel

Kelly Regan, Editorial Director, Travel

Publishing for Technology Dummies

Andy Cummings, Vice President and Publisher, Dummies Technology/General User

Composition Services

Gerry Fahey, Vice President of Production Services

Debbie Stailey, Director of Composition Services

Contents at a Glance

Table of Contents

Introduction

*Y*ou're merrily skimming through the admissions requirements for your favorite MBA programs when all of a sudden you're dealt a shocking blow. Your absolute top choice — you'll die if you don't get in — program requires that you take the Graduate Management Admission Test (GMAT). And you thought your days of filling in little round circles and waking at the crack of dawn on an otherwise sleepy Saturday were over!

Most MBA programs include the GMAT as an admissions requirement, so you'll be in good company on test day. But how do you prepare for such a comprehensive test? What are you going to do? Get out your spiral notebooks from undergraduate courses and sift through years' worth of doodles? Many years may have gone by since you encountered a geometry problem, and we bet your grammar skills have gotten a little rusty since English 101.

Clearly, you need a readable, concisely structured resource. You've come to right place. *GMAT For Dummies,* 5th Edition, puts at your fingertips everything you need to know to conquer the GMAT. We give you complete math and grammar reviews and provide insights into how to avoid the pitfalls that the GMAT creators want you to fall into. We also try to make this book as enjoyable as a book that devotes itself to diagramming equations and critiquing arguments can be.

About This Book

We suspect that you aren't eagerly anticipating sitting through the GMAT, and you're probably not looking forward to studying for it either. Therefore, we've attempted to make the study process as painless as possible by giving you clearly written advice in a casual tone. We realize you have a bunch of things you'd rather be doing, so we've broken down the information into easily digested bites. If you have an extra hour before work or Pilates class, you can devour a chapter or even a particular section within a chapter. (If these eating metaphors are making you hungry, feel free to take a snack break.)

In this book, you can find

- ✔ Plenty of sample questions so you can see just how the GMAT tests a particular concept. Our sample questions read like the actual test questions, so you can get comfortable with the way the GMAT phrases questions and expresses answer choices.

- ✔ Two practice tests. Ultimately, the best way to prepare for any standardized test is to practice on lots of test questions, and this book has about 200 of them.

- ✔ Time-tested techniques for improving your score. We show you how to quickly eliminate incorrect answer choices and make educated guesses.

- ✔ Tips on how to manage your time wisely.

- ✔ Suggestions for creating a relaxation routine to employ if you start to panic during the test.

We've included all kinds of information to help you do your best on the GMAT!

Conventions Used in This Book

You should find this book to be easily accessible, but a few things may require explanation. A few of the chapters may contain sidebars (a paragraph or two in a shaded box). Sidebars contain quirky bits of information that we think may interest you but that aren't essential to your performance on the GMAT. If you're trying to save time, you can skip the sidebars.

The book highlights information you should remember in several ways. Lists are bulleted and marked with a solid bar to the left of the list. Icons appear in the margins to emphasize particularly significant information in the text. You can use these highlighting tools to focus on the most important elements of each chapter.

Foolish Assumptions

Although we guess it is possible that you picked up this book just because you have an insatiable love for math, grammar, and argument analysis, we're betting it's more likely that you're reading this book particularly because you've been told you have to take the GMAT. (We have been praised for our startling ability to recognize the obvious!) And because we're pretty astute, we've figured that this means that you intend to apply to MBA programs and probably are considering working toward a master's of business administration.

Generally, MBA programs are pretty selective, so we're thinking that you're a pretty motivated student. Some of you are fresh out of college and may have more recent experience with math and grammar. Others of you probably haven't stepped into a classroom in over a decade but possess work skills and life experience that will help you maximize your GMAT score despite the time that's passed since college.

If math and grammar are fresh in your mind and you just need to know what to expect when you arrive at the test site, this book has that information for you. If you've been out of school for a while, this book provides you with all the basics as well as advanced concepts to give you everything you need to know to excel on the GMAT.

How This Book Is Organized

The first part of this book introduces you to the nature of the GMAT beast and advises you on how to tame it. An in-depth discussion of how to approach and answer the questions in the verbal section of the test follows. We give you tips on how to succeed on the sentence correction, reading comprehension, and critical reasoning questions you'll encounter there. Then we tell you how to write the analytical essays. Even if you haven't written anything more than a grocery list in a while, you'll be ready to expound come test day. We follow the analytical writing portion with a comprehensive math review, covering everything from number types to standard deviation. Our discussion of each section ends with a mini practice test to prepare you for the two full-length practice tests that follow the math review. Test your knowledge on these two tests and then score yourself to see how you've done.

Part 1: Putting the GMAT into Perspective

Read this part if you want to know more about what kinds of information the GMAT tests and how you can best handle it.

Part II: Vanquishing the Verbal Section

The verbal section of the GMAT includes three different kinds of questions: sentence correction, reading comprehension, and critical reasoning. We show you the types of errors to look for in the sentence correction questions, how to read through a passage quickly and effectively for the reading questions, and how to break apart and analyze arguments for the critical reasoning questions. We end the part with a mini practice test of randomly organized questions of all three types.

Part III: Acing the Analytical Writing Section

The GMAT requires you to write two essays, one that analyzes an issue and one that analyzes an argument. We let you know what the GMAT is looking for in each essay type and give you pointers on writing a well-organized and compelling essay.

Part IV: Conquering the Quantitative Section

This part is for you if you haven't solved equations in a while and if you work with math concepts every day. We cover basic arithmetic and algebra (things you may have forgotten after all these years) and explain more complex concepts like coordinate geometry and standard deviation. You find out how to tackle the data-sufficiency question type that appears only on the GMAT. We tie up the part by giving you a mini practice test that covers all areas of math and both types of GMAT math questions.

Part V: Practice Makes Perfect

After you feel comfortable with your GMAT prowess, you can practice on the two full-length tests found in this part. Each test comes complete with a scoring guide and explanatory answers to help you figure out which areas of the GMAT you have down pat and which ones you need to study more for.

Part VI: The Part of Tens

This part finishes up the fun with a summary of questions you can't miss, writing errors you should avoid, and math formulas you should memorize.

Icons Used in This Book

One exciting feature of this book is the icons that highlight especially significant portions of the text. These little pictures in the margins alert you to areas where you should pay particularly close attention.

This icon highlights really important information that you should remember even after you close the book.

Throughout the book, we give you insights into how you can enhance your performance on the GMAT. The tips give you juicy timesavers and point out especially relevant concepts to keep in mind for the test.

Your world won't fall apart if you ignore our warnings, but your score may suffer. Heed these cautionary pointers to avoid making careless mistakes that can cost you points.

Whenever you see this icon in the text, you know you're going to get to practice the particular area of instruction covered in that section with a question like one you may see on the test. Our examples include detailed explanations of how to most efficiently answer GMAT questions and avoid common pitfalls.

Where to Go from Here

We know that everyone who uses this book has different strengths and weaknesses, so this book is designed for you to read in the way that best suits you. If you're a math whiz and only need to brush up on your verbal skills, you can skim Part IV and focus on Parts I, II, and III. If you've been writing proposals every day for the last ten years, you can probably scan Part III and focus your attention on the math review in Part IV.

We suggest that you take a more thorough approach, however. Familiarize yourself with the general test-taking process in the first two chapters and then go through the complete GMAT review, starting with the verbal section and working your way through the analytical writing and math sections. You can skim through information that you know more about by just reading the Tips and Warnings and working through the examples in those sections.

Some of our students like to take a diagnostic test before they study. This is a fancy way of saying that they take one of the practice tests in Part V before they read the rest of the book. Taking a preview test shows you which questions you seem to cruise through and which areas need more work. After you've taken a practice exam, you can focus your study time on the question types that gave you the most trouble during the exam. Then, when you've finished reading through the rest of the book (Parts I, II, III, and IV), you can take another practice test and compare your score to the one you got on the first test. This way, you can see just how much you improve with practice.

Because the GMAT is a computerized test and we don't have a computer hooked up to this book, you may want to visit the official GMAT Web site at www.mba.com and download the free GMATPrep software there. This software mimics the computerized format of the test and gives you practice on the types of mouse-clicking and eye-straining skills you need to succeed on the exam. At this time, they don't have a version for Mac users, so if you have a Mac machine, see whether you can find a friend to let you use a PC to use this software. That way, you'll experience what it's like to deal with these questions on a computer screen.

We're confident that if you devote a few hours a week to practicing the skills and tips we provide for you in this book, you'll do the best you can when you sit in front of that computer on GMAT test day. We wish you our best for your ultimate GMAT score!

Part I
Putting the GMAT into Perspective

The 5th Wave · By Rich Tennant

"Did any of you fall for that trap in question 7?"

In this part . . .

The first part of this book initiates you to the marvels of the GMAT. The chapters here introduce the format of the test and explain how to take the test seriously (but not too seriously). You may be tempted to skip this part and jump headlong into the reviews. If you do so, we strongly suggest that you come back to this part later. We include information in here that you may not get elsewhere.

Among other things, you find out what to expect on the test, how the test is scored, how the CAT (which stands for computer-adaptive format) works, and what stuff is tested on each of the three test sections (verbal, math, and analytical writing). You also discover some helpful tips for organizing your time and relaxing if you get nervous.

Chapter 1

Getting the Lowdown on the GMAT

Congratulations on deciding to take a significant step in your business career! More than one hundred countries offer the Graduate Management Admission Test (GMAT), and it's used by over 1,800 graduate programs in admissions decisions. But you're probably not taking the GMAT because you want to. In fact, you may not be looking forward to the experience at all!

The GMAT need not be a daunting ordeal. A little knowledge helps calm your nerves, so this chapter shows you how admissions programs use your test score and addresses the concerns you may have about the GMAT's format and testing and scoring procedures.

Knowing Why the GMAT's Important

If you're reading this book, you're probably thinking about applying to an MBA program. And if you're applying to an MBA program, you need to take the GMAT. Almost all MBA programs require that you submit a GMAT score for the admissions process.

Your GMAT score gives the admissions committee another tool to use to assess your skills and compare you with other applicants. The GMAT doesn't attempt to asses any particular subject area that you might've studied, but instead it gives admissions officers a reliable idea of how you'd likely perform in the classes that make up a graduate business curriculum. Although the GMAT doesn't rate your experience or motivation, it does provide an estimate of your academic preparation for graduate business studies.

Not every MBA applicant has the same undergraduate experience, but every applicant takes the same standardized test. Other admissions factors, like college grades, work experience, the admissions essay or essays, and a personal interview are important, but the GMAT is the one admissions tool that admissions committees can use to directly compare you with other applicants.

The most selective schools primarily admit candidates with solid GMAT scores, and good scores will certainly strengthen your application to any program, but you shouldn't feel discouraged if your practice tests don't put you in the 90th percentile. Very few students achieve anything like a perfect score on the GMAT. Even if you don't score as high as you'd like to, you undoubtedly have other strengths in your admissions profile, such as work experience, leadership ability, good college grades, motivation, and people skills. You may want to contact the admissions offices of the schools you're interested in to see how much they emphasize the GMAT. That said, the GMAT is a very important factor in admissions, and because you're required to take the test anyway, you should do everything you can to perform your best!

Timing It Perfectly: When to Take the GMAT (and What to Bring)

Which MBA programs to apply to isn't the only decision you have to make. After you've figured out where you want to go, you have to make plans for the GMAT. You need to determine when's the best time to take the test and what you should bring with you when you do.

When to register for and take the GMAT

When's the best time to take the GMAT? With the computerized test, this question has become more interesting. When the exam was a paper-and-pencil format with a test booklet and an answer sheet full of bubbles, you had a very limited choice of possible test dates — about one every two months. Now you've got much more flexibility when choosing the date and time for taking the test. You can choose just about any time to sit down and click answer choices with your mouse.

Registering when you're ready

The first step in the GMAT registration process is scheduling an appointment, but don't put off making this appointment the way you'd put off calling the dentist (even though you probably would like to avoid both!). Depending on the time of year, appointment times can go quickly. Usually, you have to wait at least a month for an open time. To determine what's available, you can go to the official GMAT Web site, www.mba.com, and select "Take the GMAT." From there, you can choose a testing location and find out what dates and times are available at that location. When you find a date and time you like, you can register online, over the phone, or by mail or fax.

The best time to take the GMAT is after you've had about four to six weeks of quality study time and during a period when you don't have a lot of other things going on to distract you. Of course, if your MBA program application is due in four weeks, put this book down and schedule an appointment right away! If you have more flexibility, you should still plan to take the GMAT as soon as you think you've studied sufficiently. All of the following circumstances warrant taking the GMAT as soon as you can:

✔ **You want to start your MBA program right away.** If you're confident that you'd like to begin business school within the next few semesters, you should consider taking the GMAT in the near future. After you know your score, you'll be better able to narrow down the business schools you want to apply to. Then you can focus on the other parts of your application, and you won't have to worry about having an application due in four weeks and no GMAT score.

- ✔ **You're considering attending business school.** Maybe you don't know whether you want to pursue an MBA. Even so, now's a good time to take the GMAT. Your GMAT score may help you decide that you've got the skills to succeed academically in graduate business school. You may think that you don't have what it takes, but your performance on the GMAT may surprise you! When you do decide to apply to an MBA program, you'll already have one key component of the application under wraps.

- ✔ **You're about to earn (or have just earned) your bachelor's degree.** If you're nearing graduation or have just graduated from college and you think you may want to get an MBA, it's better to take the GMAT now than wait until later. You're used to studying. You're used to tests. And math and grammar concepts are probably as fresh on your mind as they'll ever be.

  You don't have to start an MBA program right away. Your GMAT scores are generally valid for up to five years, so you can take the test now and take advantage of your current skills as a student to get you into a great graduate program later.

Giving yourself about four to six weeks to study provides you with enough time to master the GMAT concepts but not so much time that you forget what you've learned by the time you sit for the test.

Scheduling for success

Whenever you register, there are a few considerations to keep in mind when scheduling a test date and time. Take advantage of the flexibility allowed by the computer format. The GMAT is no longer just an 8:00 a.m. Saturday morning option. You can take the test every day of the week except Sunday, and you can start at a variety of times, ranging from around 8:30 a.m. to about 1:00 p.m. You make the test fit into your life instead of having to make your life fit the test!

If you're not a morning person, don't schedule an early test! If the afternoon is when you're strongest and most able to handle a nonstop, two-and-a-half-hour barrage of questions — not to mention the analytical essays — schedule your test for the afternoon. By choosing the time that works for you, you'll be able to comfortably approach the test instead of worrying whether you set your alarm. We're guessing that you have enough to worry about in life as it is without the added stress of an inconvenient test time.

Study for the test at different times of the day to see when you're at your best. Then schedule your test session for that time. Even if you have to take a few hours away from work or classes, it's worth it to have the advantage of taking the test at a time that's best for you.

While you're thinking about the time that's best for the test, you should think about days of the week as well. For some people Saturday may still be a good day for a test — just maybe not at 8 a.m.! For others, the weekend is the wrong time for that type of concentrated academic activity. If you're used to taking the weekends off, it may make more sense for you to schedule the test during the week.

Choosing the time and day to take the GMAT is primarily up to you. Be honest with yourself about your habits, preferences, and schedule, and pick a time and day when you'll excel.

Things to take to the GMAT (and things to leave at home)

The most important thing you can bring to the GMAT is a positive attitude and a willingness to succeed. However, if you forget your admission voucher or your photo I.D., you won't get the chance to apply those qualities! In addition to the voucher and I.D., you should also bring a list of five schools where you'd like to have your scores sent. You can send your scores to up to five schools for free if you select those schools when entering your pretest information at the test site. You can, of course, list fewer than five schools, but if you decide to send your scores to additional schools later, you'll have to pay. If you can come up with five schools you'd like to apply to, you may as well send your scores for free.

Because you can take two optional five-minute breaks, we recommend you bring along a quick snack like a granola bar and perhaps a bottle of water. You can't take food or drink with you to the testing area, but you are given a little locker that you can access during a break.

There's really nothing else to bring. You can't use a calculator and you'll be provided with an erasable notepad (which is a lot like a mini dry-erase board), which you're required to use instead of pencil and paper.

Forming First Impressions: The Format of the GMAT

The GMAT is a standardized test, and by now in your academic career, you're probably familiar with what that means: lots of questions to answer in a short period of time, no way to cram for or memorize answers, and very little chance of scoring one hundred percent. The skills tested on the GMAT are those that leading business schools have decided are important for MBA students: verbal, quantitative, and analytical writing.

Getting familiar with what the GMAT tests

Standardized tests are supposed to test your academic potential, not your knowledge of specific subjects. The GMAT focuses on the areas that admissions committees have found to be relevant to MBA programs. The sections that follow are an introduction to the three GMAT sections. We devote the majority of the rest of this book to telling you exactly how to approach each one.

Demonstrating your writing ability

You type two original analytical writing samples during the GMAT. The test gives you thirty minutes to compose and type each of the essays. One of the samples asks you to analyze an issue, and the other presents you with an argument to analyze. You're expected to write these essays in standard written English. Although you won't know exactly the nature of the issue and argument you'll get on test day, examining previous topics gives you adequate preparation for the types of topics you're bound to see.

The readers of your GMAT essay score you based on the overall quality of your ideas and your ability to organize, develop, express, and support those ideas.

Validating your verbal skills

The GMAT verbal section consists of 41 questions of three general types: the ubiquitous reading comprehension problem, sentence correction questions, and critical reasoning questions. Reading comprehension requires you to answer questions about written passages on a number of different subjects. Sentence correction questions test your ability to spot and correct writing errors. Critical reasoning questions require you to analyze logical arguments and understand how to strengthen or weaken those arguments.

Quizzing your quantitative skills

The quantitative section is pretty similar to most standardized math sections except that it presents you with a different question format and tests your knowledge of statistics and probability. In the 37-question section, the GMAT tests your knowledge of arithmetic, algebra, geometry, and data interpretation with standard problem-solving questions. You'll have to solve problems and choose the correct answer from five possible choices.

Additionally, GMAT data sufficiency questions present you with two statements and ask you to decide whether the problem can be solved by using the information provided by just the first statement, just the second statement, both statements, or neither statement. We show exactly how to tackle these unusual math questions in Chapter 15.

Understanding the computerized format

The GMAT can be taken only as a *computer-adaptive test* (CAT). The CAT adapts to your ability level by presenting you with questions of various difficulty, depending on how you answer previous questions. If you're answering many questions correctly, the computer gives you harder questions as it seeks to find the limits of your impressive intellect. If you're having a tough day and many of your answers are wrong, the computer will present you with easier questions as it seeks to find the correct level of difficulty for you.

With the CAT format, your score isn't based solely on how many questions you get right and wrong but rather on the average difficulty of the questions. You could miss several questions and still get a very high score, so long as the questions you missed were among the most difficult available in the bank of questions. At the end of each section, the computer scores you based on your level of ability.

Answering in an orderly fashion

With the CAT format, the question order in the verbal and quantitative sections is different from the order on paper exams that have a test booklet and answer sheet. On the CAT, the first ten questions of the test are preselected for you, and the order of subsequent questions depends on how well you've answered the previous questions. So if you do well on the first ten questions, question 11 will reflect your success by being more challenging. If you do poorly on the initial questions, you'll get an easier question 11. The program continues to take all previous questions into account as it feeds you question after question.

Perhaps the most important difference of the CAT format is that because each question is based on your answers to previous questions, you can't go back to any question. You must answer each question as it comes. After you confirm your answer, it's final. If you realize three questions later that you made a mistake, try not to worry about it. After all, your score is based on not only your number of right and wrong answers but also the difficulty of the questions.

Observing time limits

Both the verbal and quantitative sections have a 75-minute time limit. Because the quantitative section has 37 questions, you have about two minutes to master each question. The verbal section has 41 questions, so you have a little less time to ponder those, about a minute and three-quarters per question. You don't have unlimited time in the analytical writing section either; you have to write each of the two essays within 30 minutes, for a total of 60 minutes spent on analytical writing.

These time limits have important implications for your test strategy. As we discuss later in this chapter, your GMAT score depends on the number of questions you're able to answer. If you run out of time and leave questions unanswered at the end of a section, you'll essentially reduce your score by the number of questions you don't answer. In Chapter 2, we present you with an efficient, workable strategy for managing your time and maximizing your score.

Honing your computer skills for the GMAT

Technically challenged, take heart! You need to have only minimal computer skills to take the CAT format of the GMAT test. In fact, the skills you need for the test are far less than those you'll need while pursuing an MBA! Because you have to type your essays, you need basic word-processing skills. For the multiple-choice sections, you need to know how to select answers using either the mouse or the keyboard. That's it for the computer skills you need to take the GMAT.

Knowing Where You Stand: Scoring Considerations

Okay, you know the GMAT's format and how many questions it has and so on. But what about what's really important to you, the crucial final score? Probably very few people take standardized tests for fun, so here's the lowdown on scoring.

How the GMAT testers figure your score

Because the GMAT is a computer-adaptive test, your verbal and quantitative scores aren't based just on the number of questions you get right. The scores you earn are based on three factors:

- ✔ **The difficulty of the questions you answer:** The questions become more difficult as you continue to answer correctly, so getting tough questions means you're doing well on the test.

- ✔ **The number of questions that you answer:** If you don't get to all the questions in the verbal and quantitative sections, your score is reduced by the proportion of questions you didn't answer. So if you fail to answer 5 of the 37 quantitative questions, for example, your raw score would be reduced by 13 percent and your percentile rank may go from the 90th percentile to the 75th percentile.

- ✔ **The number of questions you answer correctly:** In addition to scoring based on how difficult the questions are, the GMAT score also reflects your ability to answer those questions correctly.

GMAT essay readers determine your analytical writing assessment (AWA) score. College and university faculty members from different disciplines read your responses to the essay prompts. Two independent readers score each of the two writing assignments separately on a scale from 1 to 6, with 6 being the top score. Your final score is the average of the scores from each of the readers for each of the essays.

If the two readers assigned to one of your writing tasks give you scores that differ by more than one point, a third reader is assigned to adjudicate. For example, if one reader gives you a 6 and the other gives you a 4, a third reader will also review your essay.

How the GMAT testers report your score

Your final GMAT score consists of separate verbal, quantitative, and analytical writing scores and a combined verbal and quantitative score. When you're finished with the test — or when your time is up — the computer immediately calculates your verbal and quantitative scores. You'll have a separate scaled score of from 0 to 60 for the verbal and quantitative sections. The two scores are added together and converted to a scaled score ranging between 200 and 800. The mean total score falls slightly above 500.

You get your analytical writing assessment scores after the essays have been read and scored. This score will be included in the official score report that's either mailed to you or made available online about twenty days after you take the exam. So although you'll be able to view your verbal, quantitative, and total scores immediately after the test, you'll need to wait three weeks to see how well you did on the AWA.

When you do get your official scores, the AWA score appears as a number between 1 and 6. This number is a scaled score that's the average of the scores for all four of the readings of your responses (two for analysis of an issue and two for analysis of an argument). The final score is rounded to the nearest half point, so a 4.8 average is reported as 5.

Official scores, including the verbal, quantitative, total, and AWA scores, are sent to the schools that you've requested receive them. The score reports that they receive include all the scores listed above, as well as a table showing the percentage of test-takers who scored below you. (For example, if your total score is 670, then about 89 percent of test-takers have a score lower than yours.) You don't have to pay for the five schools you select at the time of the test to receive your scores, and for a fee you can request your scores be sent to any other school at any time up to five years after the test.

Why you should (almost) never cancel your GMAT score

Immediately after you conclude the GMAT test and before the computer displays your scores, you're given the option of canceling your scores. You may see this as a blessing if you've had a rough day at the computer. You may jump at the chance to get rid of all evidence of your verbal, quantitative, and writing struggles.

Canceling your scores is almost always a bad idea. There are several reasons why this is the case:

- ✔ **People routinely overestimate or underestimate their performance on standardized tests.** The GMAT isn't a test on state capitals or chemical symbols, so it's not always easy to know how well you did. So long as you answer most of the questions and are able to focus reasonably well during the test, you'll probably earn scores that aren't too different from the average scores you'd get if you took the test repeatedly. People who retake the GMAT and other standardized tests rarely see their scores change significantly unless they're initially unprepared to take the exam and later attempt it with significant preparation. You're reading this book, so you don't fall into that category of test-taker.

✔ **You may not have time to reschedule.** It may take a while to reschedule the test. If your applications are due right away, you could miss an application deadline because you don't have GMAT scores to submit.

✔ **You'll never know how you did.** If you cancel your scores, you'll never know how you did or what areas you need to work on to improve your score if you decide to retake the test later.

✔ **Your score cancellation will be added to your GMAT record.** Cancelled scores are noted on all official GMAT score reports. Some schools may look on your cancelled score unfavorably.

A few circumstances exist in which you should consider canceling your scores. These situations aren't based on your estimation of how you did, which may be inaccurate, but on extenuating factors:

✔ **You're pretty darn ill during the test.** Waking up on test day with a fever of 101°F or getting sick during the test may warrant canceling a GMAT score.

✔ **You were unable to concentrate during the test.** Unusual personal difficulties, like a death in the family or the demise of a close relationship, could distract you to the point where you freeze up in the middle of the exam.

✔ **You left many questions unanswered.** If you forget the time management techniques we discuss in Chapter 2 and you leave quite a few questions unanswered in the verbal and quantitative sections, you may consider canceling your scores.

Repeating the Process: Retaking the GMAT

Because most programs consider only your top scores, it may be in your best interest to retake the GMAT if you aren't happy with your first score. The GMAT administrators let you take the test quite a few times if you want (that's pretty big of them, considering you have to pay for it every time). If you do retake the GMAT, make sure you take the process and test seriously. You should show score improvement. A college will be much more impressed with a rising score than a falling one.

Most colleges will be turned off if they see that you have taken the GMAT more than two or three times. The key is to prepare to do your best on the first try. Obviously, that's your goal if you've chosen to read this book.

Official GMAT reports contain scores for every time you take the test. So if you take the GMAT twice, both scores appear on your report. It's up to the business program to decide how to use those scores. Some may take the higher score and some may take the average. Keep in mind that your new scores won't automatically be sent to the recipients of previous scores. You'll need to reselect those programs when you take the retest.

Chapter 2

Maximizing Your Score on the GMAT

You enter the test center and stare down the computer. For the next three and a half hours, that machine is your adversary. The GMAT test loaded on it is your nemesis. All you have to aid you in this showdown is an erasable notepad and your intellect. The questions come quickly, and your reward for answering a question correctly is another, usually more difficult question! Why did you give up your precious free time for this torture?

By the time you actually take the GMAT, you'll have already given up hours and hours of your free time studying for the test, researching business schools, and planning for the future. Those three and a half hours alone with a computer represent a rite of passage that you must complete to accomplish the goals you've set for yourself. And because the test is a necessary evil, you may as well get the highest score you're capable of achieving!

This chapter contains the techniques you need to apply to pull together a winning strategy. You already have the brains, and the test center will provide the erasable notepad. We share with you the other tools you need to maximize your score.

Knowing How to Choose: Strategies for Successful Guessing

You may be surprised that we start this chapter by discussing guessing strategies. Your ideal GMAT test day scenario probably involves knowing the answers to most of the questions right away rather than randomly guessing! The reality is that almost no one knows every answer to every question on the GMAT. Think back; did you have to guess at any questions on the ACT or SAT? We bet you did!

The computer made me do it: Forced guessing

Remember that standardized tests aren't like tests in your college courses. If you studied hard in college, you may not have had to do much guessing on your midterms and finals. And you probably couldn't miss too many questions before you fell below the 90 percent level.

On the GMAT, however, almost everyone misses several questions in each section. That's because the GMAT is designed to test the potential of a wide range of future MBA students. Some of the questions have to be ridiculously difficult to challenge that one-in-a-million Einstein who takes the GMAT. Don't worry if you have to guess; just figure out how to guess very effectively!

With the computer-adaptive test (CAT) format, developing a strategy for successful guessing is actually more important than ever. The computer won't allow you to skip questions, so the test requires you to guess. And as you answer questions correctly, the level of difficulty will continue to increase. Even if you do really, really well on the test, you'll probably find yourself guessing eventually. On the GMAT *everyone* guesses!

It's not over 'til it's over: The importance of completing each question

To get the optimum score for the questions you answer correctly, you must respond to all the questions in each section. If you don't answer everything, your score is reduced in proportion to the number of questions you didn't answer. It's important, therefore, to move at a pace that allows you to get to all the questions.

One of the ways you can get into real trouble with the CAT format is by spending too much time early on trying to correctly answer questions that are more difficult. If you're reluctant to guess and therefore spend more than a minute or two on several difficult questions, you may not have time to answer the relatively easy questions at the end.

Answer every question in each section! If you notice that you only have three or four minutes remaining in a section and more than five questions left, spend the remaining minutes marking an answer for every question, even if you don't have time to read them. You always have a 20 percent chance of randomly guessing the right answer to a question, which is better than not answering the question at all. If you have to guess randomly at the end of the section, mark the same bubble for each answer. For example, you may choose to mark the second bubble from the bottom. There's a good chance that at least one in five questions will have a correct answer placed second to the end. Marking the same bubble also saves time because you don't have to choose which answer to mark for each question; you already have your guessing strategy in mind, so you don't have to think about it.

Even the GMAT folks warn of a severe penalty for not completing the test. They claim that if you fail to answer just 5 questions out of the 41 in the verbal section, your score could go from the 91st percentile to the 77th percentile. That's the kind of score reduction that could make a huge difference to your admissions chances!

Winning the Race Against the Clock: Wise Time Management

Random guessing as the clock runs out serves you better than leaving the remaining questions in a section unanswered, but it's not a good way to approach the test in general. Instead, adopt a strategy of good time management that combines proper pacing, an active approach to answering questions, and appropriate guessing.

Giving each question equal treatment

You may have heard that you should spend a lot of time on the first ten questions because your performance on them determines your ultimate score. Although it's true that your performance on the first ten questions does give the computer an initial estimate of your ability, in the end these first questions don't carry greater significance than any other questions. You'll still encounter all the questions in the section eventually, so there's no reason to spend an unreasonable length of time on the first ten.

If you spend too much time on the first ten questions and answer them all correctly, you'll have a limited amount of time in which to answer the 27 remaining quantitative or 31 remaining verbal questions. The computer program would give you a high estimated score after those first ten questions, but that initial estimate would then most likely fall steadily throughout the session as you hurry through questions and guess at those you didn't have time to answer at the end. The worst outcome of all would be if you were unable to finish the section and had your score reduced in proportion to the questions you couldn't answer. You can't cheat the system by focusing on the first few questions. If you could, the very intelligent, highly paid test designers would find a way to adjust the format to thwart you.

Making time for the last ten questions

A much better approach than lavishing time on the *first* ten questions is to allow ample time to answer the *last* ten questions in both the verbal and quantitative sections. Because the best way to score well is to give adequate time to each question, guess when necessary, and complete the entire test, you shouldn't spend a disproportionate amount of time answering the early questions.

Here are the steps to follow for this approach:

1. **Work through the first 55 minutes of the quantitative and verbal sections at a good pace (two minutes per question for quantitative and a little over a minute and a half per question for verbal).**

2. **Don't spend more than three minutes on any question during the first 75 percent of the quantitative and verbal sections.**

3. **When you have ten questions remaining in the section (when you're on question 27 of the quantitative section or question 31 of the verbal section), check the time remaining and adjust your pace accordingly.**

   For example, if you've answered the first 27 quantitative questions in only 50 minutes, you have a total of 25 minutes to work on the last ten questions. That means you can spend about two and half minutes on each of the last ten questions. That extra 30 seconds per question may be what you need to answer a high percentage of those final ten questions correctly. Avoid random guesses on the last unanswered questions of either section.

We're not suggesting that you rush through the first 55 minutes of each section so you can spend lots of time on the last ten questions. Instead, you should stick to a pace that allows you to give equal time to all the questions in a section. You can't spend five or six minutes on a single question without sacrificing your performance on the rest of the test, so stick to your pace.

If you happen to have additional time when you get to the last ten questions, by all means use it. There's a severe penalty for not finishing a section but no prize for getting done early.

When you work steadily and carefully through the first 75 percent of each section, you're rewarded with a score that stabilizes toward the higher end of the percentile and that may rise to an even higher level at the end of the section as you spend any extra time you have getting the last questions right. The last question of the section may be the most difficult you encounter, because you've done well throughout and paid special attention to the last ten questions. Talk about ending on a high note!

Keeping track of your pace

You may think that keeping an even pace throughout the test means a lot of clock watching — but this isn't the case if you go into the test site with a plan. You can conceal the clock on the computer to keep from becoming obsessed with time, but you should periodically reveal the clock to check your progress. For example, you may plan to check your computer clock every time you've answered eight questions. This means revealing the feature about five or six times during each section. You'll spend a second or two clicking on the clock and glancing at it, but it'll be worth using those precious seconds to know that you're on pace.

If you time yourself during practice tests you take at home, you'll probably begin to know intuitively whether you're falling behind. During the actual exam, you may not have to look at your clock as frequently. However, if you suspect that you're using too much time on a question (over three minutes), you should check the clock. If you've spent more than three minutes, mark your best guess from the choices you haven't already eliminated and move on.

Getting Rid of Wrong Answers

We've stressed that the key to success is to move through the test steadily so that you can answer every question and maximize your score. Keeping this steady pace will probably require you to make some intelligent guesses, and intelligent guesses hang on your ability to eliminate incorrect answers.

Eliminating answer choices is crucial on the GMAT. Most questions come with five answer choices, and usually one or two of the options are obviously wrong (especially in the verbal section). As soon as you know that an answer choice is wrong, you should eliminate it. And after you've eliminated that answer, don't waste time reading it again. By quickly getting rid of choices that you know are *wrong,* you'll be well on your way to finding the *right* answer!

Keeping track of eliminated answer choices in the CAT format

You may be thinking that it's impossible to eliminate answer choices on a computerized test. In truth, doing so is more difficult than on a paper test where you can actually cross off the entire answer in your test booklet. However, you can achieve the same results on the computerized test with a little practice. You must train your mind to look just at the remaining choices and not simply read every word that your eyes fall upon. You can't afford to waste time rereading a choice after you've eliminated it. That's why you need a system.

You can use the erasable notepad they give you at the test site to help you with answer elimination. Keep in mind that you don't need your old notes. After you confirm an answer to a question, it's final. Because you can't go back to previous questions to review or change any answers, you can get rid of notes on questions you've already answered.

Here are some simple steps to help you keep track of which answers you've eliminated:

1. **At the beginning of the section (especially the verbal one, where eliminating answer choices is easier to do) quickly write down A, B, C, D, and E in a vertical row on your notepad.**

   A stands for the first answer choice, B for the second, C for the third, and so on, even though these letters don't appear on your computer screen.

2. **When you eliminate an answer choice, literally erase the corresponding letter from your notepad.**

   For example, if you're sure that the second and fifth answers are wrong, erase B and E on your notepad.

3. **If you look at your erasable notepad and see only one remaining answer letter, you've zeroed in on the right answer.**

   You don't need to reread the answer choices to remember which one was correct. It's listed right there on the notepad.

4. **If you can't narrow your choices down to just one answer, eliminating two or three incorrect choices gives you a good chance of guessing correctly between the two or three options that remain.**

5. **Quickly rewrite whatever letters you've erased; repeat the process for the next question.**

Don't forget to replace the answers you've eliminated on your notepad before you go on to the next question.

Practice this technique when you're taking your practice tests. The hard part isn't erasing the letters on your notepad. It's training your eyes to skip the wrong answers on the computer screen. Your brain will want to read through each choice every time you look at the answers. With the paper test booklet, you'd simply cross out the entire answer choice and then skip that choice every time you came to it. With the computerized test, you have to mentally cross out wrong answers. Developing this skill takes time. Mastering it is especially important for the verbal section, which has some long answer choices.

To practice test-taking conditions at home, purchase a small (approximately 8½" by 11") dry erase board with a marker and eraser. Complete your GMAT practice tests using the dry erase board instead of writing on scratch paper or in your book. When test day comes, you'll be used to erasing your calculations after each question and be familiar with ways to use your board for eliminating answer choices. Remember, you can use only one color of marker.

Recognizing wrong answers

So maybe you've mastered the art of the notepad answer elimination system, but you may be wondering how you know which answers to eliminate. Most of the verbal questions are best answered by process of elimination because answers aren't as clearly right or wrong as they may be for the math questions. For many math questions, the correct answer is obvious after you've performed the necessary calculations, but you may be able to answer some math questions without performing complex calculations if you look through answers first and eliminate choices that don't make sense. So by using your common sense and analyzing all the information you have to work with, you can reach a correct answer without knowing everything there is to know about a question.

Using common sense

Reading carefully reveals a surprising number of answer choices that are obviously wrong. In the quantitative section, you may know before you even do a math problem that one or two of the answers are simply illogical. In the verbal section, critical reasoning questions may have answer choices that don't deal with the topic of the argument or some sentence correction answer choices that obviously display poor grammar or faulty sentence construction. You can immediately eliminate these eyesores from contention. If an answer is outside the realm of possibility, you don't ever have to read through it again. For example, consider this sample critical reasoning question found in the GMAT verbal section:

Most New Year's resolutions are quickly forgotten. Americans commonly make resolutions to exercise, lose weight, quit smoking, or spend less money. In January, many people take some action, such as joining a gym, but by February they are back to their old habits again.

Which of the following, if true, most strengthens the argument above?

(A) Some Americans don't make New Year's resolutions.

(B) Americans who do not keep their resolutions feel guilty the rest of the year.

(C) Attempts to quit smoking begun at times other than the first of the year are less successful than those begun in January.

(D) Increased sports programming in January motivates people to exercise more.

(E) People who are serious about lifestyle changes usually make those changes immediately and don't wait for New Year's Day.

Chapter 5 gives you a whole slew of tips on how to answer critical reasoning questions, but without even looking closely at this one, you can eliminate at least two choices immediately. The argument states that people usually don't live up to New Year's resolutions and the question asks you to strengthen that argument. Two of the answer choices have nothing to do with keeping resolutions. These are choices that you can discard right away. Answer A provides irrelevant information. The argument is about people who make resolutions, not those who don't. Answer D brings up a completely different topic, sports programming, and doesn't mention resolutions.

Without even taxing your brain, you've gone from five choices down to three. Psychologically, it's much easier to deal with three answer choices than five. Plus, if you were short on time and had to guess quickly at this question, you'd have a much better chance of answering it correctly than if were to you guess from among all five choices.

Relying on what you know

Before you attempt to solve a quantitative problem or begin to answer a sentence correction question, you can use what you know to eliminate answer choices.

For example, if a quantitative question asks for a solution that's an absolute value, you could immediately eliminate any negative answers choices — absolute value is always positive. (For more about absolute value, read Chapter 10.) Even if you don't remember how to solve the problem, you can at least narrow down the choices and increase your chances of guessing correctly. If you eliminate one or two choices and if you have the time, you may be able to plug the remaining answer choices back into the problem and find the correct answer that way. So if you approach a question with a stash of knowledge, you can correctly answer more questions than you realize.

Letting the question guide you

If you've ever watched a popular TV game show, you know that the clue to the answer can sometimes be found in the question. Although the answers to most GMAT questions aren't as obvious as the answer to "in 1959, the U.S. said 'Aloha' to this 50th state," you can still use clues in GMAT questions to answer them.

In the critical reasoning example on New Year's resolutions in the preceding section, you were left with three answer choices. Paying attention to the wording of the question helps you eliminate one more.

The question asks you to *strengthen* the argument that Americans quickly forget their New Year's resolutions. Choice B seriously *weakens* the argument by indicating that instead of forgetting their resolutions, Americans are haunted by failed resolutions for the rest of the year. Because this answer weakens the argument instead of strengthening it as the question asks, you can eliminate it also. You have only two answers to choose from even though you haven't yet seriously considered the logic of the argument. You can evaluate two answer choices much more thoroughly in a smaller amount of time than five, and even if you guess, you've increased your chances of answering the question correctly to 50-50!

Quickly recognizing and eliminating wrong answers after only a few seconds puts you on the path to choosing a right answer. This strategy works in the quantitative section as well. Consider this problem-solving question example:

If ½ of the air is removed from a balloon every 10 seconds, what fraction of the air has been removed from a balloon after 30 seconds?

(A) ⅛

(B) ⅙

(C) ¼

(D) ⅚

(E) ⅞

You can immediately eliminate any choices with fractions smaller than one-half because the problem tells you that half the air departs within the first ten seconds. So you can discard choices A, B, and C. Without performing any calculations at all, you've narrowed your choices to just two!

Another benefit of eliminating obviously wrong answer choices is that you save yourself from inadvertently making costly errors. The GMAT offers up choices A, B, and C to trap unsuspecting test-takers. If you mistakenly tried to solve the problem by multiplying ½ × ½ × ½, you'd come up with ⅛. But if you'd already eliminated that answer, you would know you'd done something wrong. By immediately getting rid of the answer choices that can't be right, you avoid choosing a clever distracter. By the way, ⅛ is the amount of air remaining in the balloon after thirty seconds, so the amount of air removed in that time is E, ⅞, because 1 − ⅛ = ⅞.

Dealing with questions that contain Roman numerals

The GMAT presents a special type of question that pops up from time to time. This question gives you three statements marked with the Roman numerals I, II, and III and asks you to evaluate their validity. You'll find these questions in the quantitative section and the verbal section. You're supposed to choose the answer choice that presents the correct list of either valid or invalid statements, depending on what the question's looking for.

To approach questions that contain statements with Roman numerals, follow these steps:

1. **Evaluate the validity of the first statement or the statement that seems easiest to evaluate.**

2. **If the first statement meets the qualifications stated by the question, eliminate any answer choices that don't contain Roman numeral I. If it doesn't, eliminate any choices that have Roman numeral I in them.**

3. **Examine the remaining answer choices to see which of the two remaining statements are best to evaluate next.**

4. **Evaluate another statement and eliminate answer choices based on your findings. You may find that you don't have to spend time evaluating the third statement.**

Here's an example from the quantitative section to show how the approach works.

If x and y are different positive whole numbers, each greater than 1, which of the following must be true?

   I. $x + y > 4$

  II. $x - y = 0$

  III. $x - y$ results in an integer

(A) II only

(B) I and II

(C) I, II, and III

(D) I and III

(E) III only

Consider the statements one by one. Start with Roman numeral I and determine whether it's true that $x + y > 4$. Because x and y must be different whole numbers and the smaller of the two must be at least 2, the other number can't be less than 3: $2 + 3 = 5$, so $x + y$ must be at least 5, and the statement is correct.

Don't read statement II yet. Instead, run through the answer choices and eliminate any that don't include I. A and E don't include I, so erase them from your notepad. The remaining choices don't give you any indication which statement is best to evaluate next, so proceed with your evaluation of statement II, which states that $x - y = 0$. This statement can't be correct because x and y are different whole numbers. The only way one number subtracted from another number results in zero is if the two numbers are the same. The difference of two different whole numbers will always be at least one.

Because II isn't right, eliminate choices that include II. You can erase B and C, which leaves you with D. By process of elimination, D has to be right. You don't even need to read statement III, because you know the correct answer. Not all Roman numeral questions are so helpful, but many are, and in those cases, the strategy is a real timesaver!

Playing It Smart: A Few Things You Shouldn't Do When Taking the Test

Most of this chapter focuses on what you should do to maximize your score on the GMAT. There are a few things that you shouldn't do as well. Avoid these mistakes and you'll have an advantage over many other test-takers!

Don't lose your focus

You may be used to the fast-paced world of business or the cooperative world of group presentations that are popular in many business classes. Don't be surprised if 150 minutes of multiple-choice questions peppered with an hour of essay writing gets a little boring. We know the prospect is shocking!

Don't allow yourself to lose focus. Keep your brain on a tight leash and don't let your mind wander. This test is too important. Just remind yourself how important these three and a half hours are to your future. Teach yourself to concentrate and rely on the relaxation tips we give you at the end of the chapter to avoid incessant mind wandering. You'll need those powers of concentration in that MBA program you'll soon be starting!

Don't read questions at lightning speed

We hate to break it to you, but you probably aren't a superhero named "Speedy Reader." You'll be very anxious when the test begins and you may want to blow through the questions at record speed. Big mistake! You don't get bonus points for finishing early, and you have plenty of time to answer every question if you read at a reasonable pace. You may take pride in your ability to speed-read novels, and that skill will help you with the reading comprehension passages, but don't use it to read the questions. You need to read questions carefully to capture the nuances the GMAT offers and understand exactly what it asks of you.

Many people who get bogged down on a few questions and fail to complete a section do so because of poor test-taking techniques, not because of slow reading. Do yourself a favor. Relax, read at a reasonable pace, and maximize your score!

Don't waste all your time on the hardest questions

Although you shouldn't try to work at lightning speed, remember not to get held back by a few hard questions, either. The difficulty of a question depends on the person taking the test. For everyone, even the high scorers, there are a few questions on a test that are just harder than others. When you confront a difficult question on the GMAT, do your best, eliminate as many wrong answers as you can, and then make an intelligent guess. Even if you had all day, you may not be able to answer that particular question. If you allow yourself to guess and move on, you can work on plenty of other questions that you'll answer correctly.

Don't cheat

We aren't sure how you'd cheat on the computerized GMAT, and we won't be wasting our time thinking of ways! Spend your time practicing for the test and do your best. Cheating is futile.

Tackling a Case of Nerves: Relaxation Techniques

All this talk about time management, distracting answer choices, blind guessing, and losing focus may be making you nervous. Relax. After you've read this book, you'll have plenty of techniques for turning your quick intellect and that erasable notepad into a high GMAT score. You may feel a little nervous on the day of the test, but don't worry about it, because a little nervous adrenaline can actually keep you alert. Just don't let anxiety ruin your performance.

You may be working along steadily when suddenly, from out of the blue, a question appears that you don't understand at all. Instead of trying to eliminate answer choices and solve the problem, you may stare at the question as if it were written in a foreign language. You may start to second-guess your performance on the test as a whole. You panic and think that maybe you're just not cut out for a graduate business degree. You're on the verge of freaking out . . . help!

Because you're taking the GMAT on computer, a super-hard question probably means you're doing pretty well. Besides, if you do miss a question, you'll just get an easier question next — unless you're on the last question, in which case you needn't freak out about the final one!

If you do find yourself seizing up with anxiety partway through the test, and if these facts about computerized tests don't ease your tension, try these techniques to get back on track:

- ✔ **Inhale deeply.** When you stress out, you take shallow breaths and don't get the oxygen you need to think straight. Breathing deeply can calm you and supply the air you need to get back to doing your best.

- ✔ **Stretch a little.** Anxiety causes tension, and so does working at a computer. Do a few simple stretches to relax and get the blood flowing. Try shrugging your shoulders toward your ears and rolling your head from side to side. You can put your hands together and stretch your arms up above your head or stretch your legs out and move your ankles up and down (or both!). Last, shake your hands as though you've just washed them and there aren't any towels.

- ✔ **Give yourself a mini massage.** If you're really tense, give yourself a little rubdown. The shoulders and neck usually hold the most tension in your body, so rub your right shoulder with your left hand and vice versa. Rub the back of your neck. It's not as great as getting a full rubdown from a professional, but you can book that appointment for after the test!

- ✔ **Think positive thoughts.** Give yourself a quick break. The GMAT is tough, but don't get discouraged. Focus on the positive; think about the questions you've done well on. If you're facing a tough question, realize that it will get better.

- ✔ **Take a little vacation.** If nothing else is working and you're still anxious, picture a place in your mind that makes you feel comfortable and confident. Visit that place for a few moments and come back ready to take charge!

Part II
Vanquishing the Verbal Section

The 5th Wave   By Rich Tennant

"Excuse me, does anyone know what 'soporific' means?"

In this part . . .

The GMAT verbal section tests a variety of skills using three different question types. This part shows you how to excel on all three of them.

Sentence correction questions challenge your knowledge of the rules of standard written English. Because the questions don't test your knowledge of common *spoken* English, you won't always be able to correct sentence errors based on what sounds right. Don't worry. We provide you with the means to catch and correct the errors the GMAT writers are most fond of throwing at you.

Also included in the verbal section is the customary reading comprehension question. You've seen it before on almost every standardized test you've ever taken. It's not particularly hard to read a passage and answer questions about it, except when you have only a few minutes to do so! That's why this part provides you with techniques to help you move through the passages quickly and focus on only the most important information when you answer questions.

The critical reasoning exercises are like miniature reading comprehension questions, requiring you to read information and answer questions. But these beauties are usually limited to one paragraph and only one question. You can get really good at evaluating the arguments and answering the questions because we show you how to apply our time tested strategy for approaching critical reasoning arguments.

This part covers a lot of information. We make sure you remember it all by ending it with a short version of a GMAT verbal section so you can see how all three question types come together.

Chapter 3

Applying What You Learned (We Hope) in Grammar Class: Sentence Correction

You know you have what it takes to succeed in business, but how long has it been since you've had a course in grammar? And why do they test your knowledge of grammar on the GMAT, anyway? The answer is that success in business depends on a number of diverse skills, and one of the most important of these skills is the ability to communicate effectively.

The GMAT can't test your speaking ability (not yet, anyway), so it focuses on examining your reading and writing skills. In fact, more than half of the GMAT is devoted to reading and writing. And of course, knowing the rules of standard written English is essential to good writing. The GMAT test-makers have developed diabolically effective ways use multiple-choice questions to test your knowledge of written English.

Punctuation, subject-verb agreement, parallel construction, and other keys to good grammar may have you lying awake at night. Take heart. We won't let your dream of attending the business school of your choice die on the sentence correction portion of the GMAT. Fortunately, the kinds of sentence errors that crop up on the GMAT don't change much, so you can focus your study on the common ones.

First, we review the grammar basics you should have down before test day. Then we tell you what sentence correction questions look like, which common errors the GMAT likes to test, and what's the best way to approach the questions.

Building a Solid Foundation: Grammar Basics

Luckily, the rules of grammar are really pretty logical. After you understand the basic rules regarding the parts of speech and the elements of a sentence, you've got it made. Here's what you need to know to do well on sentence correction questions. As an added bonus, this refresher can help you write the GMAT essays.

Getting wordy: The parts of speech

Sentence correction questions consist of, well, sentences. Sentences are made up of words, and each word in a sentence has a function. The parts of speech in the English language that are important to know for GMAT grammar are verbs, nouns, pronouns, adjectives, adverbs, conjunctions, and prepositions.

Acting out: Verbs

Every sentence has a verb, which means that a sentence isn't complete without one. You should be familiar with three types of verbs:

- **Action verbs:** These verbs state what the subject of the sentence is doing. *Run, jump, compile,* and *learn* are examples of action verbs.

- **To be:** The verb *to be* (conjugated as *am, is, are, was, were, been,* and *being*) functions like an equal sign. It equates the subject with a noun or adjective. For example: *Ben is successful* means *Ben = successful. She is a CEO* means *She = CEO.*

- **Linking verbs:** These words join (or link) the subject to an adjective that describes the condition of the subject. Like the verb *to be,* they express a state of the subject, but they provide more information about the subject than *to be* verbs do. Common linking verbs are *feel, seem, appear, remain, look, taste,* and *smell.*

Telling it like it is: Nouns

You've undoubtedly heard nouns defined as persons, places, or things. They provide the "what" of the sentence. A noun can function in a sentence in different ways:

1. The *subject* plays the principal role in the sentence. It's what the sentence is about, or who is doing the action.

2. A *direct object* receives the action of an action verb.

3. An *indirect object* receives the direct object. Sentences with direct objects don't need indirect objects, but you need a direct object before you can have an indirect object.

4. The *object of a preposition* receives a preposition. (See "Joining forces: Conjunctions and prepositions," later in this chapter.)

5. The *object in a verbal phrase* serves as the receiver of the *gerund* (which is a verb form that functions as a noun, like *singing*).

6. *Appositives* clarify or rename other nouns.

7. *Predicate nouns* follow the verb *to be* and regard the subject.

So you can see how these different types of nouns function, we've marked their appearances in these two sentences with the number that corresponds to the list:

> *Being a businesswoman(5) with great leadership abilities(4), Anna Arnold(1), an MBA(6), gave her employees(3) the opportunity(2) to succeed. Anna(1) was a supportive supervisor(7).*

The GMAT won't ask you to define the various noun functions, but being familiar with them helps when we talk about the different types of sentence errors you may encounter.

One of the most important things for you to remember about nouns and verbs on the GMAT is that the subject and verb of a sentence have to agree in number. We go into this in "Pointing Out Mistakes: Common Sentence Correction Errors."

Standing in: Pronouns

Pronouns figure prominently in the sentence correction portion of the GMAT. Pronouns rename nouns and provide a means of avoiding the needless repetition of names and other nouns in a sentence or paragraph. On the GMAT, pronoun errors are common. To correct these errors, you need to be familiar with the three types of pronouns: personal, indefinite, and relative:

- **Personal pronouns:** These words rename specific nouns. They take two forms: subjective and objective.

  - The subjective personal pronouns are *I, you, he, she, it, we,* and *they. Subjective personal pronouns* are used when the pronoun functions as a subject or predicate noun (see the preceding section for info on noun functions).

  - The *objective* personal pronouns are *me, you, him, her, it, us,* and *them. Objective personal pronouns* are properly used when they function as an object in the sentence.

- **Indefinite pronouns:** These pronouns refer to general nouns rather than specific ones. Some common examples are *everyone, somebody, anything, each, one, none,* and *no one.* It's important to remember that most indefinite pronouns are singular, which means they require singular verbs: ***One** of the employees is being laid off.*

- **Relative pronouns:** These words, like *that, which,* and *who,* link adjective clauses to the nouns they describe. *Who* refers to persons; *which* and *that* refer primarily to animals and things: *He is a manager **who** is comfortable leading. The consulting work **that** she does usually saves companies money, **which** makes her a very popular consultant.*

Filling in the details: Adjectives

Adjectives describe and clarify nouns and pronouns. For instance: *The **secretive** culture of the corporation created **discontented** employees. Secretive* defines the kind of culture and *discontented* describes the feeling of the employees. Without the adjectives, the sentence is virtually meaningless: *The culture of the corporation created employees.*

With sentence correction questions, make sure that adjectives are positioned correctly in the sentence so that each adjective modifies the word it's supposed to. For instance, *I brought the slides to the meeting **that I created*** makes it seem that the author of the sentence created the meeting rather than the slides. The adjectival phrase *that I created* is in the wrong place. The better composition is *I brought the slides **that I created** to the meeting.*

Describing the action: Adverbs

Adverbs are like adjectives because they add extra information to the sentence, but adjectives usually modify nouns and adverbs primarily define verbs. Adverbs include all words and groups of words (called *adverb phrases*) that answer the questions *where, when, how,* and *why: The stock market **gradually** recovered from the 1999 crash. Gradually* defines how the stock market recovered.

Some adverbs modify adjectives or other adverbs: *The **extremely** unfortunate plumber yodeled **very well.*** See Chapter 6 for more examples of how adverbs are used in this way.

You'll recognize many adverbs by the *-ly* ending. But not all adverbs end in *-ly*. For example, in *The company's manufacturing moved **overseas,*** the adverb *overseas* reveals where the manufacturing is located. In *The Human Resources director resigned **today***, *today* explains when the director resigned.

Positioning adverbs correctly is important on the GMAT. Separating adverbs from the words they modify makes sentences imprecise.

Joining forces: Conjunctions and prepositions

Conjunctions and prepositions link the main elements of the sentence.

- **Conjunctions:** This part of speech joins words, phrases, and clauses. The three types of conjunctions are *coordinating, correlative,* and *subordinating.* Don't worry about memorizing these terms; just remember that the three types exist.

  - The seven coordinating conjunctions — *and, but, for, nor, or, so,* and *yet* — are the ones most people think of when they consider conjunctions.

  - Correlative conjunctions always appear in pairs: *either/or, neither/nor, not only/ but also.* These conjunctions correlate two similar clauses in one sentence. Therefore, if you use *either* as a conjunction, you have to include *or.*

  - Subordinating conjunctions introduce dependent clauses and connect them to independent clauses. *Although, because, if, when,* and *while* are common examples of subordinating conjunctions. We talk more about clauses in "In so many words: Phrases and clauses."

- **Prepositions:** These words join nouns to the rest of a sentence. We would need several pages to list all the prepositions, but common examples are *about, above, at, for, in, over, to,* and *with.* A preposition can't function within a sentence unless the preposition is connected to a noun, so prepositions always appear in prepositional phrases. These phrases consist of a preposition and noun, which is called the *object of the preposition: The woman* **in the suit** *went* **to the office** *to sit down.* The preposition *in* relates its object, *suit,* to another noun, *woman,* so *in the suit* is a propositional phrase that works as an adjective to describe *woman; to the office* is an adverbial prepositional phrase that describes where the woman went. Note that the word *to* in *to sit down* isn't a preposition; rather, it's part of the infinitive form of the verb *to sit* — the phrase doesn't have an object, so you don't have a prepositional phrase.

Prepositions often play a part in sentence correction questions. The GMAT may provide you with a sentence that contains an improper preposition construction. Here's a simple example: *He watched the flood while sitting in the roof.* The correct preposition is *on,* not *in.* Other types of preposition questions may not be so easy, but we highlight these for you in "Pointing Out Mistakes: Common Sentence Correction Errors."

Pulling together: The parts of a sentence

The parts of speech work together to form sentences. And the thrust of the sentence's information is conveyed by three main elements: the subject, the verb, and the element that links the verb to the subject. To locate the main idea of a sentence, you focus on these three elements. Other information within the sentence is secondary.

Trouble comes in threes: Subject, verb, and third element

The subject is the main character of the sentence; it's the noun that carries out the action of the sentence or whose condition the sentence describes. The verb describes the action or links the subject and predicate. Depending on the verb used, the third important part of the sentence could be a direct object, an adverb, an adjective, or a predicate noun. The third element for a sentence with a *transitive verb* (an action verb that must be followed by a direct object) is always a direct object. *Intransitive verbs* (action verbs that can't be followed by direct objects) may be completed by adverbs. You can follow the verb *to be* with either an adjective or a predicate noun. Recognizing the three main elements of the sentence helps you spot errors in the sentence correction questions.

Not so needy: The functions of dependent clauses

Dependent clauses that function as adverbs begin with subordinating conjunctions and answer the questions *how, when, where,* or *why*. For example: *The woman got the job because she was more qualified.* The bolded portion is a dependent clause explaining *why* the woman got the job. On the other hand, an adjectival clause usually begins with a relative pronoun to provide more infor-

mation about the noun it modifies, like in this sentence: *The judge is a man who requires a silent courtroom.* The bolded clause describes what type of man the judge is. Dependent clauses may also function as nouns: *The insurance company was focusing on how much money the hurricane would cost.* The dependent clause in this sentence is the object of the preposition *on.*

In so many words: Phrases and clauses

In addition to the main elements, a sentence may contain single words, phrases, or clauses that convey more information about the sentence's main message. Phrases and clauses are groups of words that work together to form a single part of speech, like an adverb or adjective. The difference between phrases and clauses is that clauses contain their own subjects and verbs, and phrases don't. A good understanding of both clauses and phrases can help you greatly on the sentence correction portion of the GMAT.

Phrases

The thing you should know about phrases is that they're groups of words that function together as a part of speech. Many tested errors on the GMAT concern phrases, and we discuss these in more depth in "Pointing Out Mistakes: Common Sentence Correction Errors."

Independent and dependent clauses

The distinguishing characteristic of clauses is that they contain subjects and verbs. There are two types: independent and dependent. Recognizing the difference between independent and dependent clauses can help you with many of the sentence correction problems on the GMAT.

- ✔ **Independent clauses:** These clauses express complete thoughts and could stand as sentences by themselves. Here's an example of a sentence that contains two independent clauses: *The firm will go public, and investors will rush to buy stock.* Each clause is a complete sentence: *The firm will go public. Investors will rush to buy stock.*

  Punctuate two independent clauses in a sentence by joining them either with a semicolon or with a comma and a coordinating conjunction.

- ✔ **Dependent clauses:** These clauses express incomplete thoughts and are therefore sentence fragments if left by themselves. Even though they contain a subject and verb, they cannot stand alone as sentences without other information. For instance, in the sentence *After the two companies merge, they'll need only one board of directors,* the dependent clause in the sentence is *after the two companies merge.* The clause has a subject, *companies,* and a verb, *merge,* but it still leaves the reader needing more information; thus, the clause is dependent. To form a complete sentence, a dependent clause must accompany an independent clause.

  Punctuate a beginning dependent clause by placing a comma between it and the dependent clause that comes after it. If the dependent clause follows the independent clause, you don't need any punctuation: *They'll need only one board of directors after the two companies merge.*

When you understand the difference between independent and dependent clauses, you'll be better able to recognize sentence fragments and faulty modification errors (more about those appears in "Pointing Out Mistakes: Common Sentence Correction Errors").

Before we talk about the most commonly tested errors in the sentence correction questions, we need to share one more thing about dependent clauses. Dependent clauses can be classified as either *restrictive* or *nonrestrictive*. Distinguishing between the two can be tricky.

- ✔ **Restrictive clauses are vital to the meaning of the sentence.** Without them, the sentence is no longer true. For example, in *She never wins her cases that involve the IRS,* the restrictive clause *that involve the IRS* provides essential information about the particular type of cases she never wins. The point of the sentence is that she never wins IRS cases.

- ✔ **Nonrestrictive clauses provide clarifying information, but they aren't mandatory for the sentence to make sense.** In the sentence *She never wins her cases, which involve the IRS,* the nonrestrictive clause, *which involve the IRS,* makes a "by the way" statement. It provides additional information about what type of cases she handles. The main point of the sentence is that she never wins a case.

Note that in the preceding examples, the restrictive clause begins with *that* and the nonrestrictive clause begins with *which*. You don't use commas with *that* because it's a restrictive clause and an integral part of the sentence. You should use commas to set the nonrestrictive clause apart from rest of the sentence.

Pointing Out Mistakes: Common Sentence Correction Errors

Sentence correction questions test your ability to edit written material so that it follows the rules of standard written English. The questions provide you with sentences that contain underlined words. From the five provided answer choices, you have to choose the answer that conveys the underlined portion of the sentence in the way that conforms to the dictates of standard written English.

The first answer choice is always the same as the underlined portion of the sentence. So if you think the sentence is fine as is, you should select the first answer. The other four choices present alternative ways of expressing the idea in the underlined passage. Your task is to determine whether the underlined portion of the statement contains an error and, if so, which of the four alternatives best corrects the error.

You correct errors in sentence correction sentences by applying the basic rules of English grammar. The good news is that you won't be asked to define words, spell words, or diagram any sentences! And no question expects you to correct specific punctuation errors, though knowing the rules for placing commas helps you eliminate answer choices in some cases.

The GMAT is a test for admission to business school. Therefore, sentence correction questions center on errors that adversely affect the quality of business writing, such as improper word choices, incomplete or run-on sentences, and verb tense and agreement issues. The kind of errors that you'll be asked to correct on the GMAT are the kind that you should avoid if you want to be successful in business.

Can't we all just get along? Errors in subject-verb and pronoun agreement

One of the most fundamental skills in writing is the ability to make the elements of a sentence agree. If your noun is singular and your verb, plural, you've got a problem! Even in less formal kinds of communication, like quick e-mails, errors in subject-verb or noun-pronoun agreement can obscure the message you hope to communicate. You can be sure that the GMAT sentence correction problems will contain some agreement errors.

Subject-verb agreement

When we say the subjects and verbs agree, we don't mean they're having a meeting of minds. We mean that plural subjects pair with plural verbs and singular subjects require singular verbs. Errors in simple constructions are pretty easy to spot. It just doesn't sound right to say *He attend classes at the University of Michigan.*

When the subject isn't simple or obvious, finding it gets a little more difficult. For example, take a look at this sentence: *His fixation with commodities markets have grown into several prosperous ventures, including a consulting business.* The subject is *fixation,* but the prepositional phrase *with commodities markets* may confuse you into thinking that *markets* is the subject. *Markets* is a plural noun, so it would take a plural verb if it were the subject. But you know that *markets* can't be the subject of the sentence because *markets* is part of a prepositional phrase. It's the object of the preposition *with,* and a noun can't be an object and a subject at the same time. The subject has to be *fixation,* so the verb *has,* rather than *have,* is proper.

Focus on the three main elements of any complex sentence by mentally eliminating words and phrases that aren't essential to the sentence's point. Then you can check the subjects and verbs to make sure they agree. For example, when you remove the prepositional phrase *with commodities markets* from the sample sentence we just discussed, you get *His fixation have grown,* which reveals obvious disagreement between the subject and verb.

Pronoun agreement

Another relationship you need to keep on track is the one between nouns and the pronouns that refer to them. A pronoun must agree in number with the noun (or other pronoun) it refers to. Plural nouns take plural pronouns, and singular nouns take singular pronouns. For example, this sentence has improper noun-pronoun agreement: *You can determine the ripeness of citrus by handling them and noting their color.* *Citrus* is a singular noun, so using plural pronouns to refer to it is incorrect. It would be correct to say *You can determine the ripeness of citrus by handling it and noting its color.*

Another problem with pronouns is unclear references. To know whether a pronoun agrees with its subject, you have to be clear about just what the pronoun refers to. For example, it's not clear which noun the pronoun in this sentence refers to: *Bobby and Tom went to the store, and he purchased a candy bar.* Because the subject of the first clause is plural, the pronoun *he* could refer to either Bobby or Tom or even to a third person. To improve clarity in this case, using the name of the person who bought the candy bar rather than a pronoun is a good idea.

If a GMAT sentence correction question contains a pronoun in the underlined portion, make sure the pronoun clearly refers to a particular noun in the sentence and that it matches that noun in number. Otherwise, you need to find an answer choice that clarifies the reference or corrects the number.

Here's a sample question that contains both types of agreement errors:

Much work performed by small business owners, like managing human relations, keeping track of accounts, and paying taxes, <u>which are essential to its successful operation, have gone virtually unnoticed by their employees.</u>

(A) which are essential to its successful operation, have gone virtually unnoticed by their employees.

(B) which are essential to successful operations, have gone virtually unnoticed by their employees.

(C) which is essential to its successful operation, have gone virtually unnoticed by its employees.

(D) which are essential to successful operation, has gone virtually unnoticed by their employees.

(E) which are essential to successful operation, has gone virtually unnoticed by its employees.

The underlined portion contains several agreement errors, and your job is to locate and fix all of them. To accomplish this task, isolate the three main elements of this sentence:

- The subject is *work*. None of the other nouns or pronouns or noun phrases in the sentence can be the main subject because they're all either objects *(owners, managing, keeping, paying, relations, accounts, taxes, operation, employees)* or subjects of dependent clauses *(that)*.

- The main verb is *have gone*. The other verb *(are)* belongs to the dependent clause, so it can't be the main verb.

- The third element is *unnoticed*.

So the essential sentence states that *work have gone unnoticed*. Well, that doesn't sound right! You know you have to change the verb to the singular *has* to make it agree with the singular subject *work*. Eliminate any answer choices that don't change *have* to *has,* which leaves you with D and E.

You'll notice that both D and E use the verb *are*. That's because the pronoun *which* refers back to *managing, keeping,* and *paying* (which, together, are plural), so the verb that corresponds to *which* has to be plural, too. Also, both choices eliminate *its* before *successful operation* because it's unclear what *its* refers to.

The difference between the two choices is that E changes *their* to *its*. Ask yourself which noun the pronoun before *employees* refers to. Who or what has the employees? The only possibility is *business owners,* which is a plural noun. So the pronoun that refers to it must also be plural. *Their* is plural; *its* is not. Therefore, D is the best answer: *Much work performed by small business owners, like managing human relations, keeping track of accounts, and paying taxes, which are essential to successful operation, has gone virtually unnoticed by their employees.*

Building code violations: Faulty construction

Errors in construction threaten the stability, readability, and even the existence of a sentence! You have, no doubt, often been told to avoid incomplete and run-on sentences. It's equally important to avoid sentences that confuse your reader. Some sentences may not have grammatical errors, but they can be so rhetorically poor as to obscure the point. Both grammatical and rhetorical constructions rely on correct punctuation, ordering of clauses, and parallelism. Major errors often require only minor adjustments. We start with the errors that threaten the existence of a sentence.

Errors in grammatical construction

The most commonly tested errors in grammatical construction are sentence fragments, run-on sentences, and sentences that lack parallel structure. After you get used to them, these errors are pretty easy to spot.

Sentence fragments

Sentence fragments on the GMAT usually show up as dependent clauses pretending to convey complete thoughts or as a bunch of words with something that looks like a verb but doesn't act like one (technically, a *verbal*).

- ✔ **Dependent clauses standing alone are fragments because they don't present complete thoughts.** For example, this clause comes complete with a subject and verb: *Although many companies have failed to maintain consistent profits with downsizing.* However, it begins with a subordinating conjunction, *although,* so it leaves you hanging without additional information.

- ✔ **Phrases with a verbal instead of a verb can appear to be complete if you don't read them carefully.** The verbal phrases in this sentence look like verbs but don't function as verbs: *The peacefulness of a morning warmed by the summer sun and the verdant pastures humming with the sound of busy bees. Warmed* and *humming* can be verbs in other instances, but in this sentence, they're part of phrases that provide description but don't tell what the subjects (peacefulness and pastures) are like or what they're doing.

You get the hang of recognizing sentence fragments with practice. If you read the sentence under your breath, you should be able to tell whether it expresses a complete thought.

Correcting fragments is usually pretty simple. You just add the information that completes the thought or change the verbal phrase to an actual verb. For instance, you could make *although many companies have failed to maintain consistent profits with downsizing* into a complete sentence by adding a comma and *some still try: Although many companies have failed to maintain consistent profits with downsizing, some still try.* To complete *the peacefulness of a morning warmed by the summer sun and the verdant pastures humming with the sound of busy bees,* you could change the verbal phrases: *The peacefulness of a morning is warmed by the summer sun, and the verdant pastures hum with the sound of busy bees.*

Run-on sentences

Run-on sentences occur when a sentence with multiple independent clauses is improperly punctuated. Here's an example: *I had a job interview that morning so I wore my best suit.* Both *I had a job interview* and *I wore my best suit* are independent clauses. You can't just stick a coordinating conjunction between them to make a sentence. Here are the two rules for punctuating multiple independent clauses in a sentence:

- ✔ **Independent clauses may be joined with a comma and a coordinating conjunction.** You could correct the problem by adding a comma, like this: *I had a job interview that morning, so I wore my best suit.*

- ✔ **Independent clauses may be joined by a semicolon.** The sentence could look like this: *I had a job interview that morning; I wore my best suit.*

Of course, you could change one of the independent clauses to a dependent clause, like this: *Because I had a job interview that morning, I wore my best suit.* If you do that, remember to separate the clauses with a comma if the dependent clause precedes the independent one.

The GMAT probably won't give you a run-on sentence to correct, but it may give you an answer choice that looks pretty good except that it makes the original sentence a run-on. Make sure the answer you choose doesn't create a run-on sentence.

Verb tense issues

In addition to checking for subject-verb agreement, make sure that the verbs in the underlined portion of the sentence correction question are in the proper tense. The other verbs in the sentence give you clues to what tense the underlined verbs should be in.

Lack of parallelism

You can count on several sentence correction questions that test your ability to recognize a lack of parallel structure. The basic rule of parallel structure is that all phrases joined by conjunctions should be constructed in the same manner. For example, this sentence has a problem with parallelism: *Ann spent the morning e-mailing clients, responding to voice mails, and wrote an article for the newsletter.*

The problem with the sentence is that the three phrases joined by the coordinating conjunction *(and)* in this sentence are constructed in different ways. *E-mailing* and *responding* both take the gerund (or *-ing*) form, but *wrote* doesn't follow suit. Changing *wrote* to its gerund form solves the problem: *Ann spent the morning e-mailing clients, responding to voice mails, and writing an article for the newsletter.*

Parallel structure is also a factor when you join verbal phrases with a form of the verb *to be.* Because the verb *to be* means *equals,* the two equal parts must be constructed equally. The following sentence lacks parallel structure: *To be physically healthy is as important as being prosperous in your work.* The sentence compares a phrase in the infinitive form, *to be physically healthy,* with a phrase in the gerund form, *being prosperous in your work.* Changing one of the constructions to match the other does the trick: *Being physically healthy is as important as being prosperous in your work.*

When you see a sentence correction question with an underlined list, check for lack of parallelism. Look for phrases joined by coordinating conjunctions. If the phrases or sentence parts exhibit dissimilar constructions, you have to correct the parallelism error.

Here's how the GMAT may question you about parallel structure:

The consultant recommended that the company <u>eliminate unneeded positions, existing departments should be consolidated, and use outsourcing when possible.</u>

(A) eliminate unneeded positions, existing departments should be consolidated, and use outsourcing when possible.

(B) eliminate unneeded positions, consolidate existing departments, and outsource when possible.

(C) eliminate unneeded positions, existing departments should be consolidated, and when possible outsourcing used.

(D) eliminate unneeded positions and departments and use outsourcing when possible.

(E) eliminate unneeded positions, existing departments are consolidated, and outsourcing used when possible.

The underlined portion of this sentence contains a list joined by *and,* which is a pretty good clue that you're dealing with a lack of parallelism issue. You know there's an error, so eliminate A.

Next, eliminate the answers that don't solve the problem. Choice C keeps the same faulty construction as the original statement in the first two recommendations, and it introduces even more awkwardness by changing *use* to *used* and adding it to the end of the third recommendation. You can clearly eliminate C. Get rid of E because it's also worse than the original. Each of the three elements in E has a completely different construction.

Both B and D seem to correct the error by introducing each recommendation with a similar construction, but D creates a new error because it changes the meaning of the sentence. If you choose D, you're stating that some departments are also unneeded and should be eliminated. The original, however, stated that departments should be consolidated. An answer isn't correct if it changes the meaning of the original sentence, so D is wrong.

Choice B solves the problem without changing the original meaning, so it's the one to choose: *The consultant recommended that the company eliminate unneeded positions, consolidate existing departments, and outsource when possible.*

Other construction errors

It may surprise you to know that a GMAT sentence can be grammatically accurate and still need correction. Sentences that exhibit awkward, wordy, imprecise, redundant, or unclear constructions require fixing. The GMAT calls these *errors in rhetorical construction.* The good news is that you can often use your ear to correct these problems. The right answer will often simply sound better to you.

  ✔ **Using passive instead of active voice makes a sentence seem weak and wordy.** Passive voice beats around the bush to make a point, so it lacks clarity. For instance, this passive voice sentence masks the doer of an action: *The speech was heard by most members of the corporation.* The sentence isn't technically incorrect, but it's better to say it this way: *Most members of the corporation heard the speech.* Notice also that the active voice sentence uses fewer words. So if all else is equal, choose active voice over passive voice.

  ✔ **Using repetitive language adds unnecessary words and seems silly.** A sentence shouldn't use more words than it needs to. For example, it's a bit ridiculous to say the following: *The speaker added an additional row of chairs to accommodate the large crowd.* The construction of *added an additional* isn't grammatically incorrect, but it's needlessly repetitive. It's more precise and less wordy to say *The speaker added a row of chairs to accommodate the large crowd.*

The bottom line is that any sentence that uses an excessive number of words to convey its message probably has construction problems. Often, wordiness accompanies another type of error in the underlined part. You want to find the answer that corrects the main error using the fewest words.

Recently, the price of crude oil <u>have been seeing fluctuations with</u> the demand for gasoline in China.

  (A) have been seeing fluctuations with

  (B) have fluctuated with

  (C) fluctuate with

  (D) has fluctuated with

  (E) has changed itself along with

The main error in the sentence concerns subject-verb agreement. The singular subject, *price*, requires a singular verb. Additionally, the underlined portion is needlessly wordy. First eliminate answer choices that don't correct the agreement problem. Then focus on choices that clarify the language.

Both B and C perpetuate the agreement problem by providing plural verbs for the singular subject. Eliminate those along with A, and you're left with D and E.

Choice E is even more awkward than the original construction, so D is the best answer: *Recently, the price of crude oil has fluctuated with the demand for gasoline in China.*

Follow the idiom: Correct use of standard expressions

Idiomatic expressions are constructions English speakers use because, well, those are the expressions they use. In other words, we use certain words in certain ways for no particular reason other than because that's the way we do it. However, even native English speakers often fail to use idiomatic expressions correctly. It's common to hear people use *further* instead of *farther* when they mean distance or *less* instead of *fewer* when they're talking about the number of countable items.

The GMAT tests you on your knowledge of idiomatic expressions because sentences that are idiomatically incorrect can damage your credibility and interfere with the clarity of your message. The only way to know idiomatic constructions is to memorize them. Luckily, you probably know most of them already. To help you along, Table 3-1 lists some commonly tested idioms and how to use them correctly.

Table 3-1	Idiomatically Correct Constructions for the GMAT	
Expression	*Rule*	*Correct Use*
among/ between	Use *among* for comparing three or more things or persons, *between* for two things or persons.	*Between* the two of us there are few problems, but *among* the four of us there is much discord.
as . . . as	When you use *as* in a comparison, use the construction of *as . . . as.*	The dog is *as* wide *as* he is tall.
being	Don't use *being* after *regard as.*	She is *regarded as* the best salesperson on the team. (Not: She is *regarded as being* the best salesperson.)
better/best and worse/ worst	Use b*etter* and *worse* to compare two things, *best* and *worst* to compare more than two things.	Of the two products, the first is *better* known, but this product is the *best* known of all 20 on the market.
but	Don't use *but* after *doubt* or *help.*	He could not *help* liking the chartreuse curtains with the mauve carpet. (Not: He could not *help but* like the curtains.)
different from	Use *different from* rather than *different than.*	This plan is *different from* the one we implemented last year. (Not: This plan is *different than* last year's.)

Expression	Rule	Correct Use
effect/affect	Generally, use *effect* as a noun and *affect* as a verb.	No one could know how the *effect* of the presentation would *affect* the client's choice.
farther/further	Use *farther* to refer to distance and *further* to refer to time or quantity.	Carol walked *farther* today than she did yesterday, and she vows to *further* study the benefits of walking.
hopefully	*Hopefully* is an adverb meaning *with hope* and should never be used to mean *I hope* or *it is hoped.*	*I hope* they offer me the managerial position. (Not: *Hopefully,* they'll offer me the managerial position.)
however	*However* used at the beginning of a sentence (without a comma) means *to whatever extent.*	*However* they try to discourage his antics, he continues to engage in office pranks.
imply/infer	Use *imply* to mean to suggest or indicate, *infer* to mean deduce.	From his *implication* that the car was packed, I *inferred* that it was time to leave.
in regard to	Use *in regard to* rather than *in regards to.*	The memo was *in regard to* the meeting we had yesterday. (Not: The memo was *in regards to* the meeting.)
less/fewer	Use *less* to refer to quantity, *fewer* to number.	That office building is *less* noticeable because it has *fewer* floors.
less/least	Use *less* to compare two things and *least* to compare more than two things.	He is *less* educated than his brother is, but he is not the *least* educated of his entire family.
like/as	Use *like* before simple nouns and pronouns, *as* before phrases and clauses.	*Like* Ruth, Steve wanted the office policy to be just *as* it had always been.
loan/lend	Use *loan* as a noun, *lend* as a verb.	Betty asked Julia to *lend* her a car until she received her *loan.*
many/much	Use *many* to refer to number, *much* to refer to quantity.	*Many* days I woke up feeling *much* anxiety, but I'm better now that I'm reading *GMAT For Dummies.*
more/most	Use *more* to compare two things, *most* to compare more than two things.	Of the two girls, the older is *more* educated, and she is the *most* educated person in her family.
try/come	*Try* and *come* take the infinitive form of a subsequent verb.	*Try to* file it by tomorrow. (Not: *Try and* file it by tomorrow.)

In addition to the expressions listed in Table 3-1, you should also memorize the correlative expressions in Table 3-2, which shows you words that must appear together in the same sentence. To maintain parallel structure, the elements that follow each component of the correlative should be similar. Thus, if *not only* precedes a verb and direct object, the *but also* that follows it should also precede a verb and direct object.

Table 3-2	Correlative Expressions
Expression	*Example*
not only . . . but also	He *not only* had his cake *but also* ate it.
either . . . or	*Either* you do it my way, *or* you take the highway.
neither . . . nor	*Neither* steaming locomotives *nor* wild horses can persuade me to change my mind.

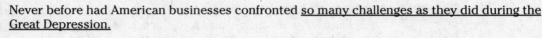

Here's how you may see idioms tested on the GMAT:

Never before had American businesses confronted <u>so many challenges as they did during the Great Depression.</u>

- (A) so many challenges as they did during the Great Depression.
- (B) so many challenges at one time as they did during the Great Depression.
- (C) at once so many challenges as they did during the Great Depression.
- (D) as many challenges as it confronted during the Great Depression.
- (E) as many challenges as they confronted during the Great Depression.

You've memorized that the proper comparison construction is *as . . . as,* so you know that the sentence contains an idiomatically improper construction (it also probably sounded strange to you!). Start by eliminating all answers that don't correct *so many . . . as* to *as . . . as.* Choices A, B, and C retain the improper construction, so cross them out.

Now consider D and E. Both change the original verb, which was in the wrong tense. The sentence compares two different periods of time. The first portion of the sentence refers to the period before the Great Depression, which requires the past perfect verb *had . . . confronted.* The underlined part of the sentence simply requires the past verb *confronted.* Choices D and E both contain the proper verb tense, but D creates a new error in pronoun agreement by using the singular pronoun *it* to refer to the plural noun *businesses.* Choice E is the correct answer: *Never before had American businesses confronted as many challenges as they confronted during the Great Depression.*

Implementing an Approach to Sentence Correction Questions

The key to performing well on sentence correction questions is to approach them systematically:

1. **Determine the nature of the original sentence's error (if there is one).**

   If a sentence has more than one error, focus on one error at a time. If you can, come up with a quick idea of how to fix the error to give yourself an idea of what you're looking for in the answers.

2. **Skim through the answer choices and eliminate any choices that don't correct the error.**

3. **Eliminate answer choices that correct the original error but add a new error or errors.**

You should be left with just one answer that fixes the original problem without creating new errors.

4. **Reread the sentence with the new answer choice inserted just to make sure that you haven't missed something and that the answer you've chosen makes sense.**

As we show you how this process works, we'll refer to this example throughout the next few sections:

Because the company is disorganized, <u>they will never reach their goal.</u>

(A) they will never reach their goal.

(B) it will never reach their goal.

(C) it will never reach its goal.

(D) their goal will never be reached.

(E) its goal will never be reached.

Spotting the error

When you read the sentence correction question, pay particular attention to the underlined portion and look for at least one error.

- ✔ If the underlined section contains verbs, make sure they agree with their subjects and are in the proper tense.

- ✔ Check any pronouns to determine whether they agree in number with the nouns they refer to.

- ✔ Look at lists to confirm that their construction is parallel.

- ✔ Note any tricky idiomatic phrases to verify that they're used correctly.

- ✔ Look for repetitive and otherwise wordy language.

If you don't see any obvious errors, read through the answer choices just to make sure they don't reveal something you may have missed. If you still don't see a problem, choose the first answer choice. About 20 percent of the sentence correction sentences contain no errors.

Don't look for errors in the portion of the sentence that isn't underlined. Even if you find something, you can't correct it!

The underlined portion of the sample question above contains a verb (will reach), but it agrees with its subject and is in the proper tense. There's also a pronoun, *they. They* refers to *company,* but *company* is a singular noun and *they* is a plural pronoun. You can't have a plural pronoun refer to a singular noun. Therefore, the underlined section definitely has a pronoun agreement error.

Eliminating answers that don't correct errors

If you spot an error in the underlined portion, read through the answer choices and eliminate those that don't correct it. If you see more than one error in the underlined portion of the statement, begin with the error that has the more obvious correction. For example, if there's both a rhetorical error and an error in subject-verb agreement, begin with the error in subject-verb agreement. Eliminating answer choices that don't address the agreement is quick and easy. After you've eliminated the choices that don't fix the obvious error, move on to the other error or errors. Comparing rhetorical constructions in answer choices can take a while, so eliminating choices before this step saves you time.

After you've eliminated an answer choice, don't reread it! Chapter 2 gives you tips on how to "erase" wrong answer choices. Follow the guidelines in Chapter 2 to avoid wasting time on answers you've already determined are wrong.

In the example problem, you know there's an error, so you can eliminate A. Now eliminate any choices that don't correct the incorrect pronoun reference. Choice D doesn't; it still uses a plural pronoun *(their)* to refer to a singular subject. Eliminate D, and don't look at it again. The other three choices, B, C, and E, seem to fix that particular pronoun error.

The underlined portion contains another problem with pronoun agreement, though. *Their* in the original sentence is also plural but refers to the singular noun *company*. Although choice B makes the first plural pronoun singular, it retains the second problem pronoun, so you can eliminate B. Only C and E are left.

Eliminating choices that create new errors

The next step is to eliminate answers that create new errors.

A new error in an answer choice usually isn't the same type of error as in the underlined portion of the statement. GMAT writers know you'll look for pronoun errors if there's a pronoun error in the original sentence, so the new error in an answer choice may be an improper expression or a verb tense error.

Check the remaining answer choices for new errors. Choice E doesn't contain an agreement error, but it changes the underlined portion of the sentence to a passive construction. On sentence corrections, active voice is always better than passive voice. Choice C is the answer that corrects the pronoun problem without creating new errors.

You should end up with only one answer choice that corrects the existing errors without creating new ones. If you end up with two seemingly correct answer choices, read them both within the context of the original sentence. One will have an error that you've overlooked.

Rereading the sentence

Don't skip this step! Check your answer by replacing the underlined portion with your answer choice and reading the new sentence in its entirety. Don't just check to see whether the answer sounds good in the sentence; also check for errors that you may not have noticed as you worked through the question.

Missing errors is easy when you focus on the underlined portion of the statement. After you integrate your answer choice with the rest of the statement, errors you've missed may suddenly become obvious. Reading the statement with the answer choice is the best way to check your answer.

When you reread the sentence with answer choice C, you get this: *Because the company is disorganized, it will never reach its goal.* The corrected sentence contains the proper pronoun agreement.

Reviewing the process and guessing on sentence corrections

The approach outlined in this section works well as long as you have time to determine the error in the sentence or recognize that there's no error. If you're running short on time or can't tell whether the statement is correct as written, you may need to guess. Eliminate the choices you know are wrong because they contain their own errors. Then read each of the possible choices in the context of the entire statement. You may find errors that you didn't notice before. If you still can't narrow your choices down to one answer, guess. You won't ruin your score with a few guesses.

Here's another example to review the process:

Most state governors now have the power of line item veto, <u>while the U.S. President does not.</u>

(A) while the U.S. President does not.

(B) a power which is not yet available to the U.S. President.

(C) which the U.S. President has no such power.

(D) the U.S. President does not.

(E) they do not share that with the U.S. President.

Always begin by trying to identify the error in the underlined portion of the statement. The underlined words don't contain any pronouns and the subject and verb agree, so you don't have any agreement errors. Parallel construction doesn't seem to be an issue. Analysis doesn't reveal an error. But just to be sure, read each answer choice in the context of the sentence to see whether doing so reveals an error you may not have recognized. Choice B is an example of poor rhetorical construction (*that* should replace *which,* because the clause is restrictive; the President's lack is essential to the meaning of the sentence). Choice C is awkward. Because D and E are independent clauses, the resulting sentences with these answer choices plugged in would be punctuated incorrectly (you can't join two independent clauses with just a comma). Both of these answer choices would create a run-on sentence. Choice A must be the correct answer.

Remember that about 20 percent of the time, the underlined part contains no error. Don't always assume that the sentences have errors.

While all state governments faced budget problems after the economic downturn of 2000, the problems were <u>worse</u> in states with high-tech industries.

(A) worse

(B) worst

(C) more

(D) great

(E) worsening

This example has only one underlined word, which is nice because you know just what to focus on. If you were to simply go by what sounds good, you may think this example is fine the way it is. You probably hear English speakers use *worse* like this in everyday conversations. But the GMAT doesn't test common spoken English; it tests standard written English.

You use *worse* to compare two entities and *worst* to compare three or more.

The sentence talks about a situation among *all state governments. Worse* would be appropriate for a comparison between two states or two groups of states. But this sentence compares budget problems in all the states, so the superlative form is needed.

Eliminate choices that don't correct the error, which in this case means you can eliminate all but one. You've found an error, so A can't be right. Choices C and D don't use the superlative form, and E uses an incorrect part of speech. You don't use the verb form *worsening* to make comparisons. Choice B provides the correct superlative form of *bad.*

Reread the sentence just to be sure: *While all state governments faced budget problems after the economic downturn of 2000, the problems were worst in states with high-tech industries.*

Chapter 4

Not as Enticing as a Bestseller: Reading Comprehension

In This Chapter

▶ Getting familiar with the format of reading comprehension questions

▶ Reading through passages efficiently

▶ Discovering the kinds of passages that appear on the GMAT

▶ Knowing the four general types of reading questions

*I*f you find yourself reading approximately 350 words about white dwarfs in space, you're probably tackling a reading comprehension problem on the GMAT. The GMAT test-makers have discovered yet another way to poke and prod your intellect. The test presents you with a fairly lengthy reading selection and then asks you several questions about it. The questions may be very specific and focus on highlighted portions of the passage, or they may concern general themes, like the author's main idea.

Reading comprehension questions are designed to test how well you understand unfamiliar reading material. But you're probably less concerned with the reason these passages are included on the GMAT than you are with getting through all that reading and question-answering and still having enough time in the verbal section to confront those pesky sentence correction and critical reasoning problems. After all, you don't want your chances of going to a great business school to diminish because you freeze on a reading passage about the history of the Italian textile industry!

What you need is a proven strategy. We give you one by introducing you to the types of passages and questions you'll encounter and telling you how to deal with them.

Judging by Appearances: What Reading Comprehension Questions Look Like

The verbal section mixes reading comprehension questions with critical reasoning questions and sentence correction questions. So you may correct the grammatical errors in a few sentences and then come to a set of reading comprehension questions. You'll see a split screen with an article on the left and a question with five answer choices on the right. About one-third of the 41 questions in the verbal section are reading questions.

Although every passage has more than one question (there are usually about 5 to 8 questions per passage), only one question pops up at a time. You read the passage (which is never more than 350 words), click on the choice that best answers the question, and confirm your answer. As soon as you confirm your answer, another question pops up on the right side of the screen. The passage remains on the left. Sometimes a question refers to a particular part of the passage. For these questions, the GMAT highlights the portion of the passage you need to focus on to answer the question.

Approaching Reading Passages

Reading comprehension questions don't ask you to do anything particularly unfamiliar. You've probably been reading passages and answering multiple-choice questions about them since you were in elementary school. If you're having difficulty answering reading comprehension questions correctly, it's probably not because you lack reading skills. It's more likely that you're not familiar with the specific way you have to read for the GMAT.

You have less than two minutes to answer each reading question, and that includes the time you spend reading the passage. Generally, you shouldn't spend more than five minutes reading a passage before you answer its question, so you have to read as efficiently as you can. You need a plan for getting through the passage in a way that allows you to answer questions correctly and quickly. When you read a passage, focus on the following elements:

- ✔ The passage's general theme
- ✔ The author's tone
- ✔ The way the author organizes the passage

Unless you have a photographic memory, you won't be able to remember all of a passage's details long enough to answer the questions. Don't spend time trying to figure out the passage's minutiae while you're reading it. If you encounter a question about a little detail, you can go back and reread the relevant section. Instead of sweating the small stuff, make sure you understand the author's main point, the tone the author uses to make it, and the overall way the author presents the information.

Mastering the message: The main point

Generally, people write passages to inform or persuade. Most of the passages on the GMAT are informative rather than argumentative, and even the argumentative ones are pretty tame.

The main point of GMAT passages is often *to discuss a topic, to inform the reader about a phenomenon,* or *to compare one idea to another.* Rarely does a GMAT passage seek to condemn, criticize, or enthusiastically advocate a particular idea or position.

Because most authors present the main theme in the first paragraph or two, you'll probably figure it out in the first few seconds of your reading. If it's not clear in the first paragraphs, it probably appears in the last paragraph, when the author sums up the ideas. After you've figured out what the author's overall theme is, quickly jot down on your notepad a word or two to help you remember the theme. For a passage that describes the differences between the flight patterns of houseflies and horseflies, you could write down *compare flight — house/horse.* Your notation gives you something to refer to when you're asked the inevitable main theme synthesis question (which we discuss in greater detail later in this chapter, in the section "Getting to the point: Main theme questions").

Absorbing the ambiance: Author's tone

In addition to understanding the author's point, you need to know how the author feels about the issue. You get clues to the author's tone or mood by noticing the words he or she uses. GMAT passages either inform the reader about something or try to persuade the reader to adopt the author's viewpoint. Informative passages are often more objective than persuasive ones, so the author's tone is usually neutral. Authors of persuasive passages may exhibit more emotion. You may sense that an author is critical, sarcastic, pessimistic, optimistic, or supportive. When you figure out how the author feels about the topic, write down a short description of the tone on your notepad, like *objective, hopeful,* or *mildly critical.* Knowing the tone of a passage helps you choose answers that exhibit the same tone or level of bias.

Regardless of the author's mood, don't let your personal opinions about a passage's subject matter influence your answer choices. Getting emotionally involved with the content of the passage can cloud your judgment. You may subconsciously rely on your opinions as you answer questions. To avoid doing so, you may find it helpful to remind yourself that correct answers are true *according to the passage* or *according to the author.*

Finding the framework: The passage's outline

Knowing the structure of a passage is much more important than understanding its details. Instead of trying to comprehend everything the author says, focus on how the author lays out the information.

Standard essay format includes an introduction with a thesis, two or three supporting paragraphs, and a conclusion. Many GMAT passages are excerpts from larger works, so they may not exhibit exact standard essay form, but they will contain evidence of all three elements. As you read, determine the passage's overall point and the main points of each of its paragraphs.

You may find it helpful to construct, on your notepad, a mini-outline of the passage as you read it. Underneath the main theme, jot down a word or two that describes the type of information contained in each paragraph. So under *compare flight — house/horse,* you may list a synopsis of each supporting paragraph: *difference in wingspan, size difference — horse 3x bigger, ways flight helps house.* This outline tells you that in the first supporting paragraph, you find information about how the two flies differ in wingspan. The second supporting paragraph is where you find information that explains how the greater size of horseflies affects their flight. And from the third supporting paragraph, you find out how the housefly's flight helps it in everyday life. Although you may not understand all the fascinating details of the author's account, you know where to go in the passage if you have to answer a detail question.

Building an outline in your head or on your notepad helps you know where in the passage you can find answers to questions about particular details. Doing so also helps you answer any questions that ask you *how* an author develops his or her point.

Even though you don't need to read and understand every detail of a passage before you answer its questions, we highly recommend that you read the entire passage before you attempt the questions. You need an idea of what a passage is about and how it's organized before you look at the questions. Any minutes you save by not reading the passage first will be wasted when you have to read and reread paragraphs because you don't know where information is located or what the passage is about.

Sticking to the Subject: Types of Passages

You may think that because the GMAT measures your aptitude for MBA programs, its reading passages would deal with subjects like marketing and economics. You'd be wrong. Although some of the passages do concern business matters, you'll also read about topics from the sciences and humanities. The GMAT wants to see how well you analyze a variety of topics, unfamiliar and familiar, so it presents you with articles about everything from the steel-making process to the quality of artifacts from the Bronze Age.

Experimenting with natural science passages

Physical and biological sciences mean big business. Some of the areas of commerce that depend on science include pharmaceuticals, computers, agriculture, the defense industry, household products, and materials manufacturing (such as plastics and polymers). These industries, taken together, exert a huge influence on American quality of life and the nation's bottom line. Just think of this country without computers and pharmaceuticals, not to mention modern agriculture!

Although you may concede that the natural sciences are important, you may not be eager to confront a chemistry passage halfway through the GMAT verbal section. The good news is that the reading comprehension questions don't assume that you have any previous knowledge in the subject. If you do come across a reading passage on chemistry and it's been 20 years since you've studied the periodic table, relax. The answer to every question is located somewhere in the passage.

You really don't need to know a lot about a passage topic to answer the questions correctly. Although it's true that a chemistry major may read a passage about polymers more quickly than someone who never took a college chemistry course, that doesn't necessarily mean the chemistry expert will answer more questions correctly. The chemistry major may actually be at a disadvantage because he or she may try to answer questions based on outside knowledge instead of using the information stated in the passage.

Reading comprehension questions test your reading skills, not the plethora of details you keep tucked away in your long-term memory. When you come across a passage on a subject that you're pretty familiar with, *don't rely on your outside knowledge to answer the question!* Make sure the answers you choose can be justified by information contained in the passage.

Natural science passages tend to be more objective and neutral than persuasive in tone. So usually, the main theme of a natural science topic is *to explain, describe,* or *inform about* a scientific event. Here's an example of what a nice, neutral natural science passage may look like on the GMAT:

A logarithmic unit known as the decibel (dB) is used to represent the intensity of sound. The decibel scale is similar to the Richter scale used to measure earthquakes. On the Richter scale, a 7.0 earthquake is ten times stronger than a 6.0 earthquake. On the decibel scale, an increase of 10 dB is equivalent to a 10-fold increase in intensity or power. Thus, a

(5) sound registering 80 dB is ten times louder than a 70 dB sound. In the range of sounds audible to humans, a whisper has an intensity of 20 dB; 140 dB (a jet aircraft taking off nearby) is the threshold of immediate pain.

The perceived intensity of sound is not simply a function of volume; certain frequencies of sound appear louder to the human ear than do other frequencies, even at the same volume.

(10) Decibel measurements of noise are therefore often "A-weighted" to take into account the fact that some sound wavelengths are perceived as being particularly loud. A soft whisper is 20 dB, but on the A-weighted scale the whisper is 30 dBA. This is because human ears are particularly attuned to human speech. Quiet conversation has a sound level of about 60 dBA.

(15) Continuous exposure to sounds over 80 dBA can eventually result in mild hearing loss, while exposure to louder sounds can cause much greater damage in a very short period of time. Emergency sirens, motorcycles, chainsaws, construction activities, and other mechanical or amplified noises are often in the 80–120 dBA range. Sound levels above 120 dBA begin to be felt inside the human ear as discomfort and eventually as pain.

(20) Unfortunately, the greatest damage to hearing is done voluntarily. Music, especially when played through headphones, can grow to be deceptively loud. The ear becomes numbed by the loud noise, and the listener often turns up the volume until the music approaches 120 dBA. This level of noise can cause permanent hearing loss in a short period of time, and in fact, many young Americans now have a degree of hearing loss once seen only in much older persons.

This passage is almost exactly 350 words, so it's as long as any passage on the GMAT is going to get. Don't let the unfamiliar scientific concepts worry you. You're probably familiar with the term *decibel,* but you may have never encountered the *A-weighted decibel* or *dBA,* as it's abbreviated. Focus on the main point of the passage, which is to describe dBAs and how human ears perceive them, and what type of information appears in each paragraph.

Gathering in social circles: Social science and humanities passages

In addition to natural science passages, the GMAT presents passages about a different kind of science: social science, which includes topics like law, philosophy, history, political science, archeology, sociology, and psychology. Related passages about the human experience concern literature, film studies, English, religion, and foreign languages. (Don't worry, though — no GMAT reading passages actually appear in a foreign language!)

The good news about social science and humanities passages is that their topics tend to crop up more in the news and in daily conversation than does, for example, physics! So you're more likely to be comfortable, if not necessarily familiar, with them. Although passages about the social sciences and humanities are still mostly descriptive and informative, they're more likely to be persuasive than natural science passages, so you may see more variety in the kinds of tones these passages display. For instance, the personality and opinion of the author of this sample philosophy passage are more apparent than those of the author who wrote the natural science passage:

For most Americans and Europeans, this should be the best time in all of human history to live. Survival—the very purpose of all life—is nearly guaranteed for large parts of the world, especially in the "West." This should allow people a sense of security and contentment. If life is no longer as Thomas Hobbs famously wrote, "nasty, brutish and short," then

(5) should it not be pleasant, dignified and long? To know that tomorrow is nearly guaranteed, along with thousands of additional tomorrows, should be enough to render hundreds of millions of people awe-struck with happiness. *And* modern humans, especially in the West, have every opportunity to be free, even as they enjoy ever-longer lives. Why is it, then, that so many people feel unhappy and trapped? The answer lies in the constant pressure of trying to

(10) meet needs that don't actually exist.

The term "need" has been used with less and less precision in modern life. Today, many things are described as needs, including fashion items, SUV's, vacations, and other luxuries. People say, "I need a new car," when their current vehicle continues to function. People with many pairs of shoes may still say they "need" a new pair. Clearly this careless usage is inac-

(15) curate; neither the new car nor the additional shoes are truly "needed."

What is a need then? The Oxford English Dictionary defines the condition of "need" as "lack of means of subsistence." This definition points the way toward an understanding of what a need truly is: A need is something required for survival. Therefore, the true needs of

life are air, food, water, and in cold climates, shelter. Taken together, this is the stuff of sur-
(20) vival. Since the purpose of life is to survive, or more broadly, to live, then these few modest
requirements are all that a modern human truly needs. Other things make life exciting or
enjoyable, and these are often referred to as "the purpose of life"—but this is surely an exag-
geration. These additional trappings are mere wants and not true needs.

Getting down to business passages

Business reading selections are generated from fields like economics, marketing, resource
management, and accounting, among others. Finally, topics you're familiar with! You can
forego the archeology of New Zealand or an anatomy lesson on the long-horned beetle. This
is business, your chosen field of study. At least it's a topic you're clearly interested in. You'll
probably breeze right through most of these passages. But don't let familiarity with the
topic serve as an excuse to slack off. You need your powers of concentration for every passage topic.

WARNING!

If the passage is on a familiar subject, don't fall into the trap of using your own information
to answer questions. Being familiar with a passage topic is an advantage, but only if you
approach each question reminding yourself that the correct answer is based on information
in the passage and not on what you studied last semester in your marketing courses or discussed last week in your sales meeting.

Business passages may be objective or persuasive. Here's a sample of what you may
encounter. This passage is an excerpt from *Microeconomics Theory and Applications*,
9th edition, by Edgar K. Browning and Mark A. Zupan (Wiley):

In 1980, Washington, D.C., city officials, hard-pressed for tax revenues, levied a 6 percent
tax on the sale of gasoline. As a first approximation (and a reasonable one, it turns out), this
tax could be expected to increase the price of gasoline by 6 percent. The elasticity of demand
is a key factor in the consequences of this action, because the more sharply the sales of
(5) gasoline fall, the less tax revenue the city will raise. Presumably, city officials hoped that
gasoline sales would be largely unaffected by the higher price. Within a few months, however, the amount of gasoline sold had fallen by 33 percent.[1] A 6 percent price increase producing a 33 percent quantity reduction means the price elasticity was about 5.5.
The sharp sales drop meant that tax revenue was not increased. Further indications
(10) were that when consumers had fully adjusted to the tax, tax revenues would actually
decrease. (There had been a 10 cent per gallon tax before the 6 percent tax was added, so
although the 6 percent levy was raising revenue, the gain was largely offset by the loss in
revenue from the initial 10 cent tax following the reduction in sales.) This was not a general
increase in gasoline prices but a rise only within the D.C. city limits. Gasoline sold in the
(15) District of Columbia is a narrowly defined product that has good substitutes — gasoline
sold in nearby Virginia and Maryland. Higher gasoline prices in the District of Columbia,
when the prices charged in Virginia and Maryland are unchanged, indicate high elasticity in
the market.
No economist would be surprised at the results of this tax, but apparently city officials
(20) were. Observed one city councilman: "We think of ourselves here in the District as an island
to ourselves. But we've got to realize that we're not. We've got to realize that Maryland and
Virginia are right out there, and there's nothing to stop people from crossing over the line."
The 6 percent gasoline tax was repealed five months after it was levied.

[1]"Barry Asks Gasoline Tax Repeal," *Washington Post*, November 2, 1980, p. A1.

Approaching Reading Questions

The GMAT verbal section has 41 questions, and you're allotted 75 minutes to answer them. That comes out to under two minutes per question. If you spend too much time answering reading questions, you'll have less time to consider the sentence correction and critical reasoning questions that also comprise the verbal test. So having a system for tackling reading questions is just as important as knowing how to read through the passages. Your approach should include

- ✔ Recognizing the type of question
- ✔ Quickly eliminating incorrect answer choices
- ✔ Knowing how to manage questions that ask for the answer that *isn't* supported by the passage

Identifying the question type

The first step in answering a reading question correctly is identifying what type of question it is. We've found that most reading comprehension questions fall into one of these four categories:

- ✔ Summarizing the main theme
- ✔ Finding specific information
- ✔ Making inferences
- ✔ Assessing the author's tone

Each of the four question types requires a slightly different approach. Main theme and tone questions ask you to make determinations about the passage as a whole, and specific information and inference questions usually ask you to hone in on particular parts of the passage. When you know, for example, that a question is about specific details in the passage, you can focus your attention on the portion of the passage that's relevant to the information in the question.

Getting to the point: Main theme questions

Main theme questions ask you to identify the primary purpose of the whole passage. Almost every passage has at least one question that asks you to identify the thesis of the passage, and often it's the first question you answer for a particular reading passage.

You can identify main theme questions by the language they contain. Here are some examples of the ways main theme questions may be worded:

- ✔ The author of the passage is primarily concerned with which of the following?
- ✔ The author's primary goal (or purpose) in the passage is to do which of the following?
- ✔ An appropriate title that best summarizes this passage is

While you read the passage, look for its main theme because you know you'll probably be asked about it. For instance, as you read through the dBA passage presented in "Experimenting with natural science passages" earlier in this chapter, you recognize that the author is clearly concerned about hearing loss and the effects of loud noises, specifically voluntary exposure to very loud noises through the misuse of headphones. You may state the passage's primary purpose like this: "The author seeks to educate people about the way noise is measured and warn them of the danger of hearing loss from exposure to loud noises." If you're asked a question about the passage's main theme, you'll look for an answer that conveys an idea similar to your statement of the author's purpose.

The best answer to a main theme question is general rather than specific. If an answer choice concerns information that's discussed in only one part of the passage, it probably isn't the correct answer to a main theme question. Here are some other ways to eliminate answer choices for main theme questions:

- Eliminate answer choices that contain information that comes only from the middle paragraphs of the passage. These paragraphs probably deal with specific points rather than the main theme.

- Eliminate any answer choices that contain information that you can't find in the passage. These choices are irrelevant.

- Sometimes you can eliminate answer choices based on just the first words. For example, if you're trying to find the best answer to the author's purpose in an objectively written natural science passage, you can eliminate answers that begin with less objective terms, like *to argue that . . ., to criticize . . .,* and *to refute the opposition's position that. . . .*

And furthermore: Specific information questions

Some GMAT reading questions ask you about specific statements in the passage. These questions are potentially the easiest type of reading question because the information you need to answer them is stated in the passage. You just need to find it. This information may be quantitative, such as years, figures, or numbers, or the information may be qualitative, like ideas, emotions, or thoughts.

Specific information questions are worded in many different ways, but they almost always contain some reference to the passage. For example:

- The passage states that . . .

- According to the passage, . . .

- In the passage, the author indicates that . . .

Sometimes the GMAT highlights in yellow the portion of the passage that discusses the material in question. If the test highlights information for you, you know that you'll be doing more than just finding an answer that duplicates the wording in the passage.

To succeed on specific information questions, read the question carefully and refer to the outline of the passage you've written on your notepad to remind you where the passage addresses certain types of information. And keep in mind that the right answer may paraphrase the passage rather than provide a word-for-word repeat.

Reading between the lines: Inference questions

Inference questions ask you about information that's *implied* by the passage rather than directly stated. These questions test your ability to draw conclusions using evidence that does appear in the passage. On inference questions, you're normally required to do one of these three things:

- Identify a different interpretation of an author's statement

- Infer the intended meaning of a word that's used figuratively in the passage

- Interpret the author's statements one step beyond what is actually written

For instance, suppose you read a passage that compares the flight patterns of houseflies and horseflies. Information in paragraph two may state that horseflies travel south in the winter. Information in paragraph four may say that a Purple Winger is a type of horsefly. From this information, you can infer that the Purple Winger flies south in the winter. This is an example of the third bullet: taking the author's statements one step beyond what is actually written.

The horsefly conclusion doesn't require that you make great leaps of logic. When you're answering an inference question, look for the choice that slightly extends the meaning of the passage. Choices that go beyond the scope of the passage are usually incorrect. Don't choose an answer that requires you to come up with information that isn't somehow addressed by the passage.

Sometimes knowing a great deal about a passage's topic can be a detriment, because you may be tempted to answer questions based on your own knowledge rather than the passage itself. Simply answer the questions as they're asked, and make inferences that can be justified by information in the passage.

The GMAT loves inference questions, so expect to see a lot of them. They're easily recognizable because they usually contain either *infer* or *imply* in the question, like these examples:

- It can be inferred from the passage that . . .
- The passage implies (or suggests) that . . .
- The author brings up southern migration patterns to imply which of the following?

Feeling moody: Questions about the author's tone and style

As you read the passage, you should look for clues to the author's tone as well as his or her purpose. You're bound to see questions that ask you to gauge how the author feels about the topic. Tone and style questions commonly ask you to figure out the author's attitude or complete the logical flow of the author's ideas. The author may be neutral, negative, or positive and may have different attitudes about different types of information within the same passage. It's up to you to determine the nature and degree of the author's feeling from the language used in the passage. With practice, you'll figure out how to distinguish between an enthusiastic author and one who's faking enthusiasm to mock the subject of the passage.

You can recognize questions about tone and style by the way they're worded. Here are some examples of how tone and style questions may appear on the GMAT:

- The author's attitude appears to be one of . . .
- With which of the following statements would the author most likely agree?
- The tone of the passage suggests that the author is most skeptical about which of the following?

When making determinations about the author's style and tone, consider the passage as a whole. You may find one or two examples of praise in an article that is otherwise overwhelmingly critical of a subject. Don't make the mistake of quickly categorizing the passage from a very few words that happen to catch your attention. Instead, determine the main idea of the passage and the author's purpose (you need to do this to answer other questions, anyway) and use that information to help you discern the author's style and tone. For example, if an author's purpose is to argue against a particular point of view, critical words regarding the proponents of that viewpoint reveal an overall critical attitude. However, you wouldn't say the same about an author of a passage that supports a viewpoint overall but includes one or two criticisms about some supporters of the viewpoint.

Style and tone questions may point you to a specific portion of a passage, or they may be about the whole passage. Even if a question does reference a specific part of the text, it'll do so in relation to the passage as a whole. For example, you can usually answer a question that asks you why an author chose to use certain words in a particular sentence only within the context of the entire passage. So if you know the main idea, author's purpose, and tone of the entire passage, you should be able to effectively deal with questions about the use of a particular word or phrase in one part of the passage.

Eliminating answer choices

One of the most effective ways of moving through reading comprehension questions is to eliminate incorrect answer choices. That's because you're looking for the best answer choice, not necessarily the perfect answer choice. Sometimes you'll have to choose the best choice out of five pretty great choices, and other times you'll choose from five really crummy ones. Because the definitive answer usually won't pop right out at you, you have to know how to eliminate obviously wrong choices. Chapter 2 gives you general tips for eliminating answer choices. In this section, we show you how to apply those techniques specifically to reading questions.

Much of the time you can eliminate wrong choices without having to refer back to the passage. As long as you carefully read the passage and have a good idea of the main theme, the author's purpose in writing the selection, and the author's style or tone, you should be able to recognize some wrong answers immediately.

Some common wrong answers include:

- **Choices that concern information that isn't found in the passage:** Some answer choices contain information that's beyond the scope of the passage. Even if the information in these choices is true, you can't choose them. You have to choose answers based on what's stated or implied in the passage. Eliminate these choices, no matter how tempting they may be.

- **Choices that contradict the main theme, author's tone, or specific information in the passage:** After you've read through the passage, you should be able to quickly eliminate most of the choices that contradict what you know about the passage.

- **Choices that go counter to the wording of the question:** You can also eliminate some answer choices by paying careful attention to the wording of the question. For example, a question may ask about a *disadvantage* of something discussed in the passage. If one of the answer choices lists an advantage instead of a disadvantage, you can eliminate that choice without thinking too much about it. Or a question may ask you to choose which answer the author is most optimistic about. If one of the things listed is something the author is negative about, you can eliminate that choice.

The GMAT may try to entice you with answer choices that deal with information directly stated in the passage but don't relate to the actual question at hand. Don't choose an answer just because it looks familiar. Make sure it actually answers the question.

- **Choices that contain *debatable* words:** Question any answer choice that uses absolutes. Examples are *all, always, complete, never, every,* and *none.* An answer choice that contains a word that leaves no room for exception is probably wrong. The GMAT makers don't want you calling them up complaining that you know of a circumstance where, say, not all fire engines are red. ***Beware:*** Usually the rest of an answer choice that includes a debatable word sounds pretty good, so you may be tempted to choose it.

Don't automatically eliminate an answer choice that contains a debatable word. If information in the passage justifies the presence of *all* or *none* in an answer choice, it may be right. For instance, if a passage tells you that all horseflies travel south in the winter, the choice with *all* in it may be accurate.

Putting it all together: Answering sample reading questions

To show you how to eliminate answer choices, this section presents some questions based on the passages from earlier in this chapter.

Social science and humanities passage

This first question refers to the passage in "Gathering in social circles: Social science and humanities passages." Reread the passage now. When you're done, see whether you can immediately eliminate some of the answer choices below based on what you've read.

Which of the following most accurately states the main idea of the passage?

(A) Modern Americans and Europeans feel unhappy and trapped because they don't distinguish true needs from mere wants.

(B) There are no human needs and all so-called needs are merely wants.

(C) Human needs can never be satisfied in this life and therefore people will always be unhappy.

(D) The satisfaction of human needs has resulted in nearly universal happiness for people in the United States and Europe.

(E) There is no difference between needs and wants; the desire for wealth and power are just as real as the need for food and shelter.

First identify the question type. This one's pretty easy because it contains the phrase *main idea* right in the question. You're dealing with a main theme question, so the answer concerns the general idea and purpose of the passage and is probably found in the first or last paragraphs of the passage.

Eliminate any choices that go beyond the scope of the information discussed in the passage. You recall that the passage distinguished *true needs* from *mere wants*. Answer choice C says, "Human needs can never be satisfied in this life. . . ." The reading passage never mentions anything about needs not being satisfied in this life. You may or may not agree with the statement in choice C, but it can be eliminated because it discusses ideas not covered in the passage.

Next, look for choices that contradict what you remember from reading through the passage. Choice B states that there "are no human needs." The passage specifically lists human needs of food, water, shelter, and so on. So B has to be wrong. You may also recall that this list of needs is included in a section in which the author distinguishes between needs and wants. Choice E says that there's no difference between needs and wants; you know that the passage says otherwise, so you can eliminate E.

You're left with choices A and D. If you have trouble choosing between them, consult the reading. Concentrate on the first paragraph that says that although Americans and Europeans should be happy, many are "unhappy and trapped." You can therefore eliminate choice D.

Choice A should be the correct answer. But take a moment to reread A to make sure that it makes sense as the main idea of the paragraph. Choice A says, "Modern Americans and Europeans feel unhappy and trapped because they don't distinguish true needs from mere wants." This statement agrees with the author's questioning of the reasons behind modern unhappiness found in the first paragraph and the author's distinguishing of needs from wants in the last paragraph. Choice A is the correct answer.

Natural science passage

The next two examples come from the passage found in "Experimenting with natural science passages."

The author mentions that "emergency sirens, motorcycles, chainsaws, construction activities, and other mechanical or amplified noises" fall in the 80-120 dBA range. It can be inferred from this statement that these noises

(A) are unwanted, outside intrusions common in urban life

(B) can cause hearing loss with constant exposure

(C) are more dangerous to hearing than sounds of the same dBA level from headphones

(D) are loud enough to cause immediate pain

(E) have no negative impacts

The word *infer* in the question gives you a fairly obvious clue to the type of question you're dealing with. Again, you can rely on the process of elimination to answer it.

Begin by eliminating those choices that rely on outside information. This passage focuses on noise levels and health effects. The passage doesn't mention societal concerns such as the intrusive impacts of a plethora of noise in urban life. Therefore, you can cross out choice A on your notepad. All the other choices have something to do with noise levels and health, so don't eliminate them yet.

Next, look for choices that contradict what you know about the passage. One of the author's purposes in writing the passage seems to be to warn young people of the hearing loss associated with headphone use (or abuse). It would be contradictory, then, to say that the noises mentioned in the question are *more* dangerous than noises at the same decibel level from headphones. Because C is inconsistent with what you find out from the passage, you can eliminate it.

You can use the information in the question to narrow down your choices. The question indicates that the noises mentioned are in the 80–120 dBA range. Even if you don't remember all the specifics of the passage, you probably remember that noises over 100 dBA are very loud. You may even remember that 120 dBA is the threshold for feeling discomfort in the ear. It's therefore not logical to say, as choice E does, that noises in this range would have *no* health effects. Noises that loud have some impact on the ear!

You can also eliminate choice E because it contains an implicit debatable word. *No impacts* in this answer choice suggests *none,* and answer choices that contain the word *none* are almost always wrong because *none* doesn't allow for any exceptions. If the answer were worded a little differently to say "may have no negative impacts," it could be correct. Short exposure to noise may, in fact, have no impact.

You're left with just two answer choices. If you happen to remember that 140 dB is the threshold for immediate pain, you can answer the question without having to refer back to the text. However, if you have any doubt, it's always better to take a few seconds to be sure. Remember, with the computerized test, you can't go back to check your answers. After you confirm an answer, it can't be changed.

The last sentence of the first paragraph indicates that 140 dB is the threshold of immediate pain, and in the third paragraph you learn that 120 dBA can "eventually lead to pain." Therefore, you can eliminate D, so B is probably the answer. Glancing at the passage confirms that it indicates that constant exposure to sounds over 80 dBA can result in hearing loss. Choice B is the correct answer.

In the second paragraph of the passage, the author introduces the concept of the A-weighted decibel scale. For any particular sound, the A-weighted decibel level differs from the unweighted decibel level in that

(A) The A-weighted number is 10 points higher than the unweighted number.

(B) The A-weighted number is based on the way the noise is perceived in the human ear.

(C) The unweighted number is always higher than the A-weighed number.

(D) The A-weighted number is measured by more accurate instruments.

(E) Only on the unweighted scale does a 10 dB increase in sound equal a ten-fold increase in intensity.

On the computerized test, the question would refer to a highlighted part of the passage on the screen instead of quoting it, but for our purposes we'll use the quotation. This problem is probably a specific information question, because it refers to details of the passage without using *infer* or *imply*.

You can eliminate E because the passage doesn't mention a difference between a 10 dB increase and a 10 dBA increase. Choice D also refers to information not covered in the passage. Nowhere does the reading suggest that instruments used to measure A-weighted decibels are more accurate; it just indicates that sounds are measured differently with the A-weighted scale. Cross out D on your notepad. Likewise, C is incorrect because it directly contradicts prominent information from the reading. A whisper registers a higher number on the A-weighted scale, as does quiet conversation, so C can't be correct.

The two choices that are left, A and B, both provide correct information, but only one answers the question. A whisper does register 30 dBA on the A-weighted scale, as opposed to 20 dB on the normal decibel scale, so choice A provides good information. But if you refer back to the passage, you find that some wavelengths are heard more clearly than others. The passage clearly states that the reason for the A-weighted scale is to take into account those noises that are perceived better by the human ear, which is how the A-weighted scale differs from the unweighted scale. Choice B is a better answer than choice A.

Business passage

Try three more questions. They're based on the reading in "Getting down to business passages."

It can be inferred from the passage that the word "elasticity" in the last sentence of the second paragraph refers to

(A) fluctuations in the price of gasoline in Washington, D.C.

(B) fluctuations in the price of gasoline in Virginia and Maryland.

(C) changes in the amount of tax collected at 6 percent.

(D) changes in the number of vehicles in the region.

(E) fluctuations in the demand for gasoline sold in Washington, D.C.

That this is an inference question is pretty obvious. Be careful not to make an inference that goes beyond the scope of what's stated in the passage.

Eliminate incorrect answer choices. Because this is an inference question, it may be hard to recognize answer choices that use outside knowledge. The point of inferring is, after all, to extend the reasoning beyond what's actually written. But one of the choices strays too far from the information in the passage. Choice D mentions changes in the number of vehicles in the region, but the passage says nothing about people getting rid of their cars or not driving through D.C. in reaction to the increase in the price of gas. Eliminate D.

Choice B is inconsistent with the passage as a whole, so you can also cross it off your notepad. The passage is about price increases in Washington, D.C., and specifically *not* about price increases in Maryland and Virginia. This leaves you with three possible answers, each of which could fit with the term *elasticity* in this passage. You need to go back and reread the sentence that's referenced in the question. You should also reread the surrounding sentences in order to understand the sentence's context:

> "This was not a general increase in gasoline prices but a rise only within the D.C. city limits. Gasoline sold in the District of Columbia is a narrowly defined product that has good substitutes — gasoline sold in nearby Virginia and Maryland. Higher gasoline prices in the District of Columbia, when the prices charged in Virginia and Maryland are unchanged, indicate high elasticity in the market."

The sentence clearly doesn't apply to "the amount of tax collected at 6 percent," so you can cross out C. The sentence does mention changes in price in D.C. Yet if you read the entire second paragraph carefully, especially the last two sentences, you'll see that the author discusses lower demand in D.C. because of good substitutes: gas in Maryland and Virginia. The paragraph states outright that prices have gone up in D.C. — but this is an inference question, which means you're looking for an implication. It's not the prices that are elastic, which means A is wrong. *Elasticity* must refer to the demand for gas, because low price and demand are positively related. So E is the best answer to this difficult question.

For which of the following reasons does the second paragraph of the passage mention the original gas tax of 10 cents per gallon?

(A) To show that Washington, D.C., residents were already overtaxed

(B) To distinguish between a straight 10 cent per gallon tax and a percent tax

(C) To explain why residents should not be subjected to different kinds of taxes

(D) To contrast the 10 cent tax that was included in the pump price and the 6 percent sales tax that was added after the sale

(E) To show that with a sufficient decrease in gasoline sales the city would actually lose money despite the higher tax

This question is also an inference one, even though it doesn't contain words that suggest inference. You know it's an inference question because you're asked about the reason the author mentions something, and the passage doesn't directly state the reason.

As usual, start by eliminating obviously incorrect answer choices that don't deal with the subject matter of the passage. The author doesn't mention residents being overtaxed or undertaxed; the article just mentions gas prices and shifting demand. So you can eliminate A. Choice D is incorrect because there's no mention in the passage of collecting the taxes differently or at different times. The article makes no effort to distinguish between the straight 10 cent tax and the percentage tax, so you can also cross out B.

This leaves you with just two choices, C and E. Quickly referring to the second paragraph of the passage reveals that before the authors mention the 10 cent tax, they indicate that lower demand might actually result in lower tax revenue. To show how this could be true, the authors mention that the city was previously collecting 10 cents on each gallon. When less gasoline was sold, the city lost this revenue. Choice E is a better answer than choice C because it pinpoints the authors' reasons for mentioning the earlier tax.

The author is primarily concerned with doing which of the following?

(A) Arguing for increased gas taxes

(B) Arguing against increased gas taxes

(C) Ridiculing all local government officials

(D) Advancing a particular ideology

(E) Explaining certain principles of supply and demand

When you're answering a question about an author's purpose, looking at the beginning words of each answer choice can be helpful. The author doesn't appear to be particularly argumentative or condescending in this piece, so you can probably eliminate A, B, and C right off the bat. Additionally, C contains the debatable word *all*. The author doesn't talk about *all* local officials in D.C., much less *all* local officials in general.

This leaves choices D and E. You can eliminate D because the author doesn't advance "a particular ideology." Instead, the author is stunned that the city council didn't know the basic theory of supply and demand. Choice E is the best answer of the five.

To double-check your answer, read through the answers you eliminated based solely on first words. Choice A is clearly wrong because the author shows that increased taxes actually resulted in decreased revenues. Choice B seems more logical because the author is showing the problems with the gas tax increase in Washington, D.C. But if you check the passage, you'll notice that the author never advocates for lower taxes in the passage. The author explains why the gas tax failed in the unique case of Washington, D.C., but that isn't enough to make B the primary purpose for writing the passage. The author is primarily concerned with explaining the principles of supply and demand using the Washington, D.C., gas tax as a case study. Choice E is the correct choice.

Dealing with exception questions

Most questions ask you to choose the one correct answer, but some questions are cleverly disguised to ask for the one false answer. We call these gems *exception questions*. You'll recognize these questions by the presence of a negative word in all capital letters, usually *EXCEPT* or *NOT*. When you see these words capitalized in a question, you know you're looking for the one answer choice that doesn't satisfy the requirements of the question.

You won't see many exception questions on the GMAT, but when you do see that word in all caps, take a moment to make sure that you know exactly what the question is asking. Don't get confused or rush and automatically choose the first choice that looks good. Remember, the question is asking for the one answer out of five that's false or not part of the information stated or implied in the passage.

Exception questions aren't that difficult if you approach them systematically. Determining that an answer definitely isn't discussed in the passage takes time. You have to carefully look through the passage for the choice and *not* find it — then check again just to be sure. But there's a better way. Instead of determining if an answer isn't discussed, eliminate the four true answers, which leaves you with the one false (and therefore correct) answer.

Identifying those choices that are in the passage is much easier than determining the one choice that isn't in the passage. You may even remember from reading the passage. After you've identified the four correct answers (remember to use your erasable notepad to keep track), you can enter the one false answer as the choice for that question.

Take a look at two exception questions that are based on a fairly difficult natural science passage:

Geologists have proposed the term *eon* for the largest divisions of the geologic time scale. In chronologic succession, the eons of geologic time are the Hadean, Archean, Proterozoic, and Phanerozoic. The beginning of the Archean corresponds approximately to the ages of the oldest known rocks on Earth. Although not universally used, the term *Hadean*
(5) refers to that period of time for which we have no rock record, which began with the origin of the planet 4.6 billion years ago. The Proterozoic Eon refers to the time interval from 2500 to 544 million years ago.

The rocks of the Archean and Proterozoic are informally referred to as *Precambrian.* The antiquity of Precambrian rocks was recognized in the mid-1700s by Johann G. Lehman, a pro-
(10) fessor of mineralogy in Berlin, who referred to them as the "Primary Series." One frequently finds this term in the writing of French and Italian geologists who were contemporaries of Lehman. In 1833, the term appeared again when Lyell used it in his formation of a surprisingly modern geologic time scale. Lyell and his predecessors recognized these "primary" rocks by their crystalline character and took their uppermost boundary to be an unconfor-
(15) mity that separated them from the overlying—and therefore younger—fossiliferous strata.

The remainder of geologic time is included in the Phanerozoic Eon. As a result of careful study of the superposition of rock bodies accompanied by correlations based on the abundant fossil record of the Phanerozoic, geologists have divided it into three major subdivisions, termed eras. The oldest is the Paleozoic Era, which we now know lasted about 300 million
(20) years. Following the Paleozoic is the Mesozoic Era, which continued for about 179 million years. The Cenozoic Era, in which we are now living, began about 65 million years ago.

This passage is excerpted from *The Earth Through Time,* 7th Edition, by Harold L. Levin (Wiley Publishing, 2003).

The passage uses all of the following terms to describe *eons* or *eras* EXCEPT

(A) Archean

(B) Paleozoic

(C) Holocene

(D) Phanerozoic

(E) Cenozoic

The terms in this passage may be unfamiliar to you, but if you read the passage carefully, you should be able to get a general sense of what it's talking about. For this exception question, which tests you on unfamiliar terms, the best way to approach the question is to consult the text and eliminate the four terms that it uses to describe eons or eras.

First, scan the answer choices so you have an idea of the words you're looking for. Then begin at the top of the passage and look for words that resemble the answer choices. You should be especially aware of any lists that occur in the text, as exception questions often focus on lists. It's very difficult for test-makers to come up with a good exception question without a list.

The passage contains three lists. The first one appears in the first paragraph. It names eons of geologic time. The question refers to eons, and uses four terms that certainly resemble the answer choices. Consult this first list and eliminate any choices that appear on it. The terms *Archean* and *Phanerozoic* appear, so you can eliminate choices A and D. In the second paragraph, you see the term *Precambrian* (which isn't an answer choice) and a list of geologists who have mentioned Precambrian rocks. The second paragraph doesn't help with this question, so move quickly to the third paragraph.

The third paragraph also provides a list of eras that are part of the Phanerozoic eon. In this list, you see the terms *Paleozoic, Mesozoic,* and *Cenozoic.* Paleozoic is choice B, and Cenozoic is choice E, so you can eliminate both of these terms. Therefore, the correct answer to this exception question is C, Holocene, which isn't mentioned in the passage and, in fact, is neither an eon nor an era but the epoch in which you're living!

Here's another exception question based on the same passage:

Which of the following terms is NOT used in the passage to describe rocks more than 544 million years old?

(A) Precambrian

(B) Cenozoic

(C) Primary Series

(D) Archean

(E) Proterozoic

This question is more difficult because all the terms appear in the passage, but one of them doesn't apply to rocks that are more than 544 million years old. Begin in the same way you did on the previous question, by scanning the answer choices so you know the kinds of words you're looking for.

When you find a term, don't automatically eliminate it. In this example, you must confirm that it refers to rocks more than 544 million years old before you can cross it off.

The list in the second sentence of the first paragraph doesn't help because it has no corresponding dates for the eons. The next sentence, however, says that *Archean* rocks are the "oldest known rocks on Earth." You can probably eliminate D, but keep reading to be sure. The last sentence of the paragraph says that Proterozoic rocks are 544 million to 2,500 million (2.5 billion) years old. And because Archean rocks are older than that, you can eliminate both D and E.

At the beginning of the second paragraph, you discover that Archean and Proterozoic rocks are both referred to as *Precambrian.* Because both types of rock are older than 544 million years, you can also eliminate A. Finally, in the very next sentence you find out that Precambrian rocks are also called *Primary Series* rocks. So you can eliminate C. Choice B is the correct answer.

You'd also know that B is the correct answer if you happen to look at the last sentence of the passage. That sentence tells you that the Cenozoic era started just 65 million years ago. The question asks for the rocks that are NOT older than 544 million years. Clearly, Cenozoic rocks are, at most, 65 million years old. So B must be the one. You can definitely skip the elimination process if you happen to stumble onto the right information, but this method won't work for all elimination questions. You're better off approaching the question by eliminating the four answers that you find in the passage or that satisfy the criteria and locating the exception by process of elimination.

Elimination questions can take some time, but they're among the easier reading comprehension questions because the answers are right there in the text! So don't get in a hurry and make a mistake. Relax and use the proper approach, and you'll do exceptionally well on exception questions.

Chapter 5

Getting Logical: Critical Reasoning

You're taking the GMAT to go to business school, not to get a Ph.D. in philosophy, so you're probably wondering why you need to be tested in logic and critical reasoning. Don't worry — the critical reasoning section on the GMAT doesn't require any knowledge of formal logic. You won't be constructing syllogisms or using fancy Latin words for logical fallacies, like *ad hominem*. The GMAT tests you on informal logic, which is a lot like the kind of reasoning you use to decide between a chocolate frosted doughnut or a bran muffin when the office pastry cart passes by. The people who run the admissions offices at business schools want to make sure that their future students can think clearly and carefully. That's where the critical reasoning question type comes in.

Critical reasoning questions test your ability to analyze an argument. The good news is that you analyze arguments all the time even though you may not know that's what you're doing. When you see a commercial advertising a new product that claims it'll make your life better, you probably question that claim. If a weight-loss drug helped someone lose 50 pounds, you ask, "Is that a typical result?" If four out of five dentists recommend a chewing gum, you say, "Did they ask only five dentists?" When a mutual fund boasts of its performance, you ask, "Is that better than the market average?" This is the same kind of thinking that you'll use to ace the critical reasoning section on the GMAT.

Keying In on "Critical" Concepts: An Overview

Critical reasoning questions consist of an argument, a question, and five answer choices. You'll encounter short passages from a variety of sources, like speeches, advertisements, newspapers, and scholarly articles. You may see an argument like this: "The local sales tax must be raised to fund city services. Admittedly, this increased sales tax will impose a greater hardship on the poorest citizens. But if the sales tax is not increased, all city services for the poor will have to be cut." The paragraph reflects the type of arguments that you encounter in the news every day.

The structure of the questions

Each critical reasoning question has essentially the same structure. The question begins with a two- to five-sentence paragraph that contains the argument. The question contains all the information you need to answer the question. Don't rely on any outside information! Even if you happen to be an expert in the area a question covers, don't rely on your expertise to answer the question.

The short argument paragraph is followed by a question (or possibly two questions, although the computer displays only one at a time). The questions usually fall conveniently into one of a few types. The question may ask that you weaken or strengthen an argument, draw a conclusion, analyze the structure of an argument, or identify an unstated assumption the author makes. We examine each of these question types in "Getting from point A to point B: Types of reasoning," later in this chapter.

Each question has five possible answer choices, which are often long, sometimes even longer than the argument or question. For this reason, you'll spend most of your time for each question examining the answer choices.

As with most GMAT questions, you can quickly eliminate one or two of the answers that are obviously wrong. The remaining answers will be more difficult to eliminate, so spend your time analyzing these better answer choices.

The basics of how to answer the questions

To break down a critical reasoning question, follow these three steps:

1. **Read the question.**

2. **Read the argument paragraph, focusing on the specific information you need to know to answer the question.**

3. **As you read the argument, look for inconsistencies and/or assumptions in the logic.**

The best way to tackle a critical reasoning question is to read the question first to determine its type. The section "Thinking Inside the Box: Question Types" shows you how to distinguish critical reasoning question types. When you first read the question, don't read all the answer choices; that takes way too much time and clutters your thinking. You need to concentrate just on the information you need to find to answer the question.

After you figure out what kind of question you're dealing with, you can read the paragraph very carefully. Be sure to locate the conclusion of the argument. The conclusion may come at the beginning, middle, or end of the paragraph. When you've identified the conclusion, you can better understand the rest of the paragraph. As you read the paragraph, look for inconsistencies or gaps in the argument that may help you answer the question. Isolating the argument's premises, assumptions, and conclusion helps you determine the method of reasoning.

The argument paragraph usually isn't too complicated, and therefore you may be tempted to read it too quickly. Force yourself to read slowly and carefully so you don't skim over the word or words that provide the keys to the argument. If you read thoroughly enough, you'll be able to eliminate some — or even most — of the answer choices. When you're down to two possible answers, you can then easily refer back to the text to make sure you choose the correct answer.

Thinking It Through: Essentials of Informal Logic

You could score well on the critical reasoning section of the GMAT without any knowledge of logic, but if you understand a few terms and concepts used in logic, you can score even higher. You really just need to know the two basic components of a logical argument and a few methods of coming up with a conclusion.

Fighting fair: The elements of an argument

A logical argument consists of premises and a conclusion, and when you're analyzing arguments, identifying what parts are premises and what makes up the conclusion can help. The *premises* give the supporting evidence that you can draw a conclusion from. You can usually find the *conclusion* in the argument because it's the statement that you can preface with "therefore." The conclusion is often, but not always, the last sentence of the argument. For example, take a look at this simple argument:

All runners are fast. John is a runner. Therefore, John is fast.

The premises in the argument are "All runners are fast" and "John is a runner." You know this because they provide the supporting evidence for the conclusion that John is fast, which is the sentence that begins with "therefore." Not all conclusions in the GMAT critical reasoning arguments will begin with "therefore" or other words like it (like "thus" and "so"), but you can try adding "therefore" to any statement you believe is the conclusion to see whether the argument makes sense. We give you plenty of sample arguments in this chapter, so you can use them to practice identifying premises and conclusions.

Getting from point A to point B: Types of reasoning

Each logical argument has premises and a conclusion, but not every argument comes to a conclusion in the same way. For the purposes of the GMAT, you should be familiar with two basic types of logical reasoning: deductive and inductive. You use both types of reasoning all the time, but now you can apply definitions to your logical genius.

Sure seems Greek to me: Origins of logical thought

Legend has it that a Greek philosopher named Parmenides in the 5th century B.C. had plenty of time on his hands while living in a Greek colony off the west coast of Italy. So he whiled away the hours contemplating logical thought and became one of the first Westerners to record his findings. He penned a philosophical poem in which an unnamed goddess instructs him in the ways of determining truth about the universe. His poem explored the contrast between truth and appearance and portrayed truth to be firm and steadfast, whereas appearance (the way mortal men usually

think) was unstable and wavering. Parmenides's work influenced other great Greek thinkers, like Plato, Aristotle, and Plotinus.

Unfortunately, you won't have a goddess to guide you through the critical reasoning questions of the GMAT, but you can rely on Aristotle's method of developing syllogisms to examine GMAT arguments. He's the one who came up with this famous syllogism: All humans are mortal; Socrates is human; therefore, Socrates is mortal.

Elementary, my dear Watson: Deductive reasoning

In *deductive reasoning,* you come up with a specific conclusion from more-general premises. The great thing about deductive reasoning is that if the premises are true, the conclusion *must* be true! The following is an example of a deductive reasoning argument:

> All horses have hooves. (General premise)
>
> Bella is a horse. (More specific premise)
>
> Therefore, Bella has hooves. (Very specific conclusion)

If the premise that all horses have hooves is true, and if Bella is, in fact, a horse, then it must be true that Bella has hooves. The same holds true for all examples of deductive reasoning. Here's another example:

> All who take the GMAT must complete an analytical essay. (General premise)
>
> You're taking the GMAT. (More specific premise)
>
> Therefore, you have to complete an analytical essay. (Very specific conclusion)

This example shows the relationship between the truth of the premises and that of the conclusion. The first premise is categorically true: The GMAT requires you to write an essay. The second premise, however, may not be true. Certainly, you're thinking of taking the GMAT or you wouldn't be reading this book, but you may still decide not to take the test. This possibility does not affect the logic of the argument. Remember, in deductive reasoning, the conclusion must be true *if* the premises are true. If you take the test, you have to write an essay, so this argument is valid.

When you analyze deductive reasoning arguments for the GMAT, remember that the only way you can prove that a conclusion is true is by showing that all premises are true. The only way to prove that a deductive reasoning conclusion is false is to show that at least one of the premises is false.

Perhaps I'm just generalizing: Inductive reasoning

In deductive reasoning, you draw a specific conclusion from general premises. With *inductive reasoning,* you do just the opposite; you develop a general conclusion from specific premises. These types of reasoning have another very important difference. In an inductive reasoning argument, a conclusion could be false even if all of the premises are true. With inductive reasoning, the conclusion is essentially your best guess. That's because an inductive reasoning argument relies on less-complete information than deductive reasoning does. Consider this example of an inductive argument:

> Bella is a horse and has hooves. (Specific premise)
>
> Smoky is a horse and has hooves. (Specific premise)
>
> Nutmeg is a horse and has hooves. (Specific premise)
>
> Shadow is a horse and has hooves. (Specific premise)
>
> Therefore, it is likely that all horses have hooves. (General conclusion)

Because inductive argument derives general conclusions from specific examples, you can't come up with a statement that "must be true." The best you can say, even if all of the premises are true, is that the conclusion can be or is likely to be true.

Inductive reasoning arguments come in all sorts of flavors, but the folks who create the GMAT tend to favor three types: analogy, statistical, and cause and effect. To excel on the GMAT, you want to get very familiar with these three methods of inductive reasoning:

- ✔ **Cause-and-effect arguments:** A cause-and-effect argument concludes that one event is the result of another. These types of arguments are strongest when the premises prove that the alleged cause of an event is the most likely one and that there are no other probable causes. For example, after years of football watching, you may conclude the following: "Every time I wear my lucky shirt, my favorite team wins; therefore, wearing my lucky shirt causes the team to win." The above example is a weak because it doesn't take into consideration other, more probable reasons (like the team's talent) for the wins.

- ✔ **Analogy arguments:** An analogy argument tries to show that two or more concepts are similar so that what holds true for one is true for the other. The strength of the argument depends on the degree of similarity between the persons, objects, or ideas being compared. For example, in drawing a conclusion about Beth's likes, you may compare her to Alex: "Alex is a student, and he likes rap music. Beth is also a student, so she probably likes rap music, too." Your argument would be stronger if you could show that Alex and Beth have other similar interests that apply to rap music, like hip-hop dancing or wearing bling. If, on the other hand, you show that Alex likes to go to dance clubs while Beth prefers practicing her violin at home, your original conclusion may be less likely.

- ✔ **Statistical arguments:** Arguments based on statistical evidence rely on numbers to reach a conclusion. These types of arguments claim that what's true for the statistical majority is also true for the individual. But because these are inductive reasoning arguments, you can't prove that the conclusions are absolutely true. When you analyze statistical arguments on the GMAT, focus on how well the given statistics apply to the circumstances of the conclusion. For instance, if you wanted people to buy clothing through your Web site, you may make this argument: "In a recent study of the preferences of consumers, 80 percent of shoppers surveyed spent more than six hours a day on the Internet; therefore, you'll probably prefer to buy clothes online." You'd support your conclusion if you could show that there's a positive correlation between the amount of time people spend on the Internet and a preference to buy clothing online. If you can't demonstrate that correlation, the statistics regarding time spent on the Internet have little to do with predicting one's preference for online shopping.

TIP

To do well on the critical reasoning questions, you need to recognize premises and conclusion in arguments, determine whether the argument applies deductive or inductive reasoning (most will be inductive), and if the argument is inductive, figure out the method the author uses to reach the conclusion. As you can induce, knowing a little about logical reasoning is essential to scoring well on the GMAT!

Thinking inside the Box: Question Types

When you were growing up, you probably experienced clichés. You had your jocks, your stoners, the smart kids (that was you!), and various other categories. Labels were important because they gave you clues on how to deal with someone who was a member of a particular group. You knew better than to pick a fight with a jock, and it was a good bet that you could get a match from a stoner. Well, we categorize GMAT questions for the same reason. After you figure out a critical reasoning question's type, you know just how to deal with it. Most of the critical reasoning questions you'll encounter on the GMAT fit into one of the following five categories:

- **Strengthening or weakening arguments:** The argument presents premises and a conclusion and asks you to evaluate the answer choices to determine which one would best strengthen or weaken the author's conclusion.

- **Drawing conclusions from premises:** The argument paragraph consists of a bunch of premises but doesn't provide a conclusion. Your job is to choose the best conclusion for the argument.

- **Seeking assumptions:** This more subtle type of question requires you to discover the premise the author doesn't state directly when reaching a conclusion but without which the conclusion isn't valid.

- **Making inferences:** For these less common question types, you have to surmise information that isn't directly stated, usually about one of the premises rather than the conclusion.

- **Finding the method of reasoning:** In these questions, you'll be asked to find an argument in the answer choices that uses the same method of reasoning as the original given argument.

Because each question type has a best way to handle it, recognizing what type of question you're dealing with before you try to answer it is important. That's why you read the question before you tackle the argument. You'll immediately know what you need to look for when you read the argument from the wording of the question.

Stalking Your Prey: How to Approach Each Question Type

Knowing the types of questions you'll face is valuable only if you know the specialized strategies for dealing with each one. This section gives you the tips you need to make approaching each of the types second nature. You get some practice questions, too, so you'll know just what they look like.

Muscling through questions that ask you to strengthen or weaken arguments

Critical reasoning questions that ask you how to best support or damage an argument are some of the easiest to answer, which is a good thing because they appear the most frequently. You probably analyze ideas every day and think of evidence to attack or defend those ideas. Because you already have the skill to evaluate arguments, it doesn't take much work for you to modify that skill to fit this specific GMAT question format. This question category has two subtypes: One asks you to strengthen an argument, and the other asks you to weaken it. You'll recognize these questions because they include words that mean to strengthen or weaken (like support, bolster, or impair), and they almost always contain an "if true" qualifier.

Here are a couple samples of the ways the questions could be worded:

- ✔ Which of the following statements, if true, would most seriously weaken the conclusion reached by the business owners?
- ✔ Which of the following, if true, provides the most support for the conclusion?

Nearly all of these questions contain the words "if true," but not all questions that have "if true" in them are strengthening-or-weakening-the-argument types. To make sure an "if true" question is really a strengthening-or-weakening question, look for the identifying language that asks you to either strengthen or weaken the argument.

Here are three simple steps to follow when approaching strengthening-or-weakening-the-argument questions:

1. **Read the question very carefully so you know exactly what it is you'll be strengthening or weakening.**

   In most cases, it'll be the conclusion of the main argument. But in less frequent cases, you may be asked to support or impair a different conclusion, like the view of the author's opponent.

2. **Examine the argument to find the premises and conclusion and to determine what method of reasoning the author uses to reach the conclusion.**

   Usually the author uses inductive reasoning, so you'll need to figure out whether the argument relies on analogy, statistics, or cause and effect to arrive at the conclusion. In the upcoming sections, we tell you what to look for in each type of reasoning.

3. **Evaluate the answer choices to determine which choice best fits with the author's conclusion and method of reasoning.**

   Assume all the answer choices are true and then determine which one best either supports or undermines the specific conclusion addressed in the question.

Always assume that all the answers to strengthening-or-weakening-the-argument questions are true. Almost all of these questions include the words "if true" in them to remind you that you're supposed to assume that each answer choice presents a true statement. Don't fall into the trap of trying to evaluate whether answer choices are true or false! Your only job is to determine whether the choices help or hurt the argument. This means that a statement like "humans do not breathe air" could be a correct answer choice even though you know it's not true. Perhaps you're supposed to weaken the conclusion that a company must pump air into an underwater habitat for humans. If humans don't breathe air, pumping in air may not be necessary. Make sure you don't dismiss any answer choices simply because you know they aren't usually true.

Affecting cause-and-effect arguments

Questions that ask you to evaluate arguments often apply cause-and-effect reasoning. If the argument uses cause and effect to make its point, focus on the causes. Almost always, the right answer to a question that asks you to strengthen the conclusion is an answer choice that shows the cause mentioned is the most likely source of the effect. The best answer for a question in which you have to weaken the argument points to another probable cause of the effect. Here's how you'd apply this reasoning to a sample question:

Average hours of television viewing per American have rapidly increased for more than three decades. To fight the rise in obesity, Americans must limit their hours of television viewing.

Which of the following, if true, would most weaken the author's conclusion?

(A) A person burns more calories while watching television than while sleeping.

(B) Over the last 30 years, there has been an increase in the number of fast food restaurants in America.

(C) Americans spend most of their television time watching sports events rather than cooking shows.

(D) Television viewing in Japan has also increased over the past three decades.

(E) Studies show that the number of television commercials that promote junk food has risen over the past ten years.

To tackle this question, first identify the conclusion you're supposed to weaken and the premises the author states or implies to reach that conclusion. The conclusion's pretty easy to spot. The last thought of the argument is that Americans must limit their hours of television viewing to curb the rise in obesity. The author makes this judgment using the following evidence:

✔ The author directly states that the number of television viewing hours has increased over the last 30 years.

✔ According to the author, the number of obese Americans has also increased.

✔ The author implies that television viewing causes obesity.

To weaken the argument that Americans have to reduce their television watching, you have to find the answer choice that shows that there's another cause for the rise in obesity.

You may have been tempted to choose A because it shows that television watching may be less fat-producing than another activity, sleeping. But it doesn't give you another reason for the rise in obesity. Answer A could be right only if it showed that Americans were sleeping more than they were thirty years ago. It doesn't, so move on.

On the other hand, stating that during the same time period the number of fast food restaurants also increased introduces another possible cause of obesity and weakens the conclusion that Americans have to stop watching so much TV to get slimmer. Maybe it's the popularity of fast food that's the culprit! Answer B is a better answer than A, but read through all of the possibilities before you commit. C is wrong because there's nothing in the argument that suggests that the type of television Americans watch affects their obesity; nor does C show that viewing patterns have changed over the last three decades. You can eliminate C from contention. D is also out because it doesn't correlate what's happening in Japan with what's happening in America. You don't know whether Japanese citizens weigh more now than they did 30 years ago, so the information in D is useless.

If the question had asked you to strengthen the conclusion, E would be a good option. It shows a reason that increased television watching could cause obesity. But the question asks you to weaken the conclusion, so B is the best answer. It's the only one that shows another cause for the rise in obesity.

Analyzing analogy arguments

Remember that analogy arguments rely on the similarity of the two persons, things, or ideas being compared. Therefore, if the author uses an analogy to reach a conclusion, answer choices that show similarities between the compared elements will support the conclusion, and choices that emphasize the differences between the elements will weaken the conclusion. Take a look at this example of an analogy argument:

Hundo is a Japanese car company, and Hundos run for many miles on a gallon of gas. Toyo is also a Japanese car company; therefore, Toyos should get good gas mileage, too.

The author's conclusion would be best supported by which of the following?

(A) All Japanese car manufacturers use the same types of engines in their cars.

(B) British cars run for as many miles on a tank of gas as Hundos do.

(C) The Toyo manufacturer focuses on producing large utility vehicles.

(D) Toyo has been manufacturing cars for over 20 years.

(E) All Japanese cars have excellent service records.

Recognizing the premises and conclusion in this argument is simple. The author states directly that Hundo cars are Japanese and get good gas mileage and that Toyo cars are Japanese; therefore, Toyos also get good gas mileage. Your job is to find the answer that perpetuates the similarity between Hundos and Toyos.

You can generally eliminate answer choices that introduce irrelevant information, like B, D, and E. The author compares Japanese cars, so what British cars do has nothing to do with the argument. The length of time that Toyo has been in business tells you nothing about how similar its cars are to Hundo's. And the question is talking about gas mileage, not service records, so don't spend too much time considering E.

Answer C tells you the focus of Toyo producers, but it doesn't give you any information about how that compares to Hundo, so the best answer is A. If all Japanese manufacturers supply their cars with the same engines and Hundo and Toyo are both Japanese manufacturers, it's more likely that Toyos will achieve a gas mileage similar to that experienced by Hundos.

Stabbing at statistical arguments

If you see statistics used to promote an argument, you're looking for an answer that shows whether the statistics actually relate to the topic of the conclusion. If they do, you'll strengthen the conclusion. On the other hand, an answer choice that shows the statistic is unrelated to the conclusion significantly weakens that conclusion. The following is an example of a statistical argument critical reasoning question you could find on the GMAT:

In a survey of 100 pet owners, 80 percent said that they would buy a more expensive pet food if it contained vitamin supplements. Consequently, CatCo's new premium cat food should be a top-seller.

Which of the following best demonstrates a weakness in the author's conclusion?

(A) Some brands of cat food contain more vitamin supplements than CatCo's does.

(B) CatCo sells more cat food than any of its competitors.

(C) Some of the cat owners surveyed stated that they never buy expensive brands of cat food.

(D) Ninety-five of those pet owners surveyed did not own cats.

(E) Many veterinarians have stated that vitamin supplements in cat food do not greatly increase health benefits.

Because the argument hinges on statistics, eliminate answers that don't directly address the statistical evidence. Those surveyed stated they would pay more for cat food with vitamin supplements, but they didn't provide information on whether the amount of vitamin supplements was important. So even though A may entice you, it isn't the best answer because it doesn't address the statistics used in the argument. B doesn't regard the survey results either, and it seems to support the conclusion rather than weaken it. The argument has nothing at all to do with veterinarians, so E can't be right. Only C and D deal with the survey the author uses to reach the conclusion that CatCo's premium cat food will be a big seller.

You can eliminate answer choices that show there's an exception to the statistical evidence. Exceptions don't significantly weaken a statistical argument.

Therefore, C is wrong and D is the best answer because it demonstrates a weakness in the statistics the author uses to support the conclusion. The preferences of dog or bird owners isn't a good indicator of the habits of cat owners.

Dabbling in deductive reasoning arguments

Rarely will you see a strengthen-or-weaken-the-argument question that uses deductive reasoning to reach a conclusion. It's just too hard to come up with challenging answer choices for weakening deductive arguments, because the only way to weaken them is to question the accuracy of the evidence, and correct answers are pretty easy to spot. The only way to strengthen a deductive argument is to reinforce the validity of the premises, which seems sort of silly. Even though GMAT creators don't want to make things too easy for you, one or two deductive arguments may crop up. To weaken an argument with a conclusion that must be true, look for an answer choice that shows that one of the premises is untrue. For instance, you may see a question with the following argument:

All horses have tails. Nutmeg is a horse. Therefore, Nutmeg must have a tail.

The only way to weaken this argument is to question one of the two premises. Answer choices like "Scientists have recently developed a breed of horses that has no tail" or "Although Nutmeg looks like a horse, she's really a donkey" would weaken the conclusion.

Examining a sample weakening-the-argument question

To review the approach to strengthening-or-weakening-the-argument questions, here's another sample question:

It seems that Americans are smarter than they were 50 years ago. Many more Americans are attending college now than in the past, and the typical entry-level job in business now requires a college degree.

Which of the following statements, if true, would most weaken the argument above?

(A) High school courses are more rigorous now than they were in the past.

(B) Tuition at colleges and universities has more than tripled in the past 25 years.

(C) High school class sizes have gotten smaller, and computers have introduced a more individualized curriculum.

(D) Businesses are not requiring as high a level of writing or math skills as they did in past decades.

(E) Many of the skills and concepts taught in high school 50 years ago are now taught in college.

Read the question first so you know what to focus on in the passage. Because this question asks you to weaken the conclusion, you know you'll need to figure out what the conclusion is and what kind of reasoning the author uses in moving from the premises to the conclusion.

When you examine the argument, you may notice that the conclusion actually comes first. The author concludes that Americans are smarter than they were 50 years ago and does so by contrasting current college participation and entry-level job requirements with those of the past. The method of reasoning is similar to analogy, except instead of showing similarities between Americans now and 50 years ago, the author shows the differences. To weaken the conclusion that Americans are smarter today, you need to find the answer choice that shows that things really aren't all that different today than they were 50 years ago.

First, eliminate answer choices with irrelevant information. Neither college tuition rates nor high class size and curriculum have anything to do with levels of intelligence, so B and C are wrong. Plus, you're looking for an answer that shows that things aren't much different between now and yesterday, and B and C demonstrate more differences.

Then get rid of any answer that tends to strengthen rather than weaken the conclusion that Americans are smarter. Harder high school courses seems to indicate that Americans may indeed be smarter, so disregard A. This leaves you with D and E, and your job is to choose the one that shows that now and then aren't all that different. Not only does D demonstrate a difference between the eras, but it also refutes the premise that businesses are looking for the higher skill levels of a college education.

The correct answer must be E. If skills that were part of the high school curriculum 50 years ago are now offered in college, actual education hasn't changed all that much from then to now. Americans must now attend college to acquire the high school skills of earlier times, and businesses need to require college degrees to know their employees have the same skills as high school students in the past. If the skill levels are the same, Americans aren't really any smarter than they were 50 years ago.

You must know precisely what a paragraph is arguing before you can strengthen or weaken that argument. Take the time to understand the premises, conclusion, and method of reasoning so you can quickly eliminate answer choices and accurately select the best answer. When you really understand the argument, attacking or defending it is fairly easy.

Delving into drawing conclusions

Another common critical reasoning question type tests your ability to draw logical conclusions (or hypotheses). The GMAT gives you a series of premises (the evidence), and you choose an answer that best concludes the information. Questions that ask you to draw conclusions from premises may be worded like this:

✔ Which of the following conclusions is best supported by the information above?

✔ Assuming the statements above are true, which of the following must also be true?

✔ The experimental results listed above support which of the following hypotheses?

As you read through the premises, think of a logical conclusion of your own making. Then look through the answer choices to see whether one listed comes close to what you've thought up.

The key to correctly answering drawing-conclusions questions is to look for an answer choice that addresses all the information contained in the premises. Eliminate any choices that are off topic or incomplete. A conclusion that addresses only part of the information may be plausible, but it probably isn't be the best answer. For example, consider the following premises:

> Five hundred healthy adults were allowed to sleep no more than five hours a night for one month. Half of the group members were allowed 90-minute naps in the afternoon each day; the remaining subjects were allowed no naps. Throughout the month, the subjects of the experiment were tested to determine the impact of sleep deprivation on their performance of standard tasks. By the end of the month, the group that was not allowed to nap suffered significant declines in their performance, while the napping group suffered more moderate declines.

The best conclusion for these premises would have to address all of the following:

- ✔ The nightly sleep deprivation of healthy adults
- ✔ The allowance for naps for half of the study group
- ✔ The smaller decline in performance of standard tasks for the group who took naps

Any conclusion that fails to address all three points isn't the best conclusion. For example, the statement "Sleep deprivation causes accumulating declines in performance among healthy adults" would not be the best conclusion because it fails to address the effect of naps. A better conclusion would be "Napping helps reduce the declines in performance caused by nightly sleep deprivation among healthy adults."

You'll often see more than one plausible conclusion among the answer choices. Your task is to identify the best choice. Don't fall for the trap of choosing an answer that just restates one of the premises. Answer choices that restate a premise may entice you because they echo part of the information in the argument, but the best choice must contain an element of each of the pieces of information presented in the question.

The process is pretty simple, really. Try this sample question to see for yourself:

Over the last eight years, the Federal Reserve Bank has raised the prime interest rate by a quarter-point more than ten times. The Bank raises rates when its Board of Governors fears inflation and lowers rates when the economy is slowing down.

Which of the following is the most logical conclusion for the paragraph above?

(A) The Federal Reserve should be replaced with regional banks that can respond more quickly to changing economic conditions.

(B) The Federal Reserve has raised the prime rate in recent years to try to control inflation.

(C) The economy has entered a prolonged recession caused by Federal Reserve policies.

(D) The monetary policy of the United States is no longer controlled by the Federal Reserve.

(E) The Federal Reserve has consistently raised the prime rate over the last several years.

You know from the language that this is a drawing-conclusions question, so you don't have to look for a conclusion in the argument. Just read through the premises and formulate a quick conclusion, something like "Because the Federal Reserve has raised interest rates more than once a year over the last eight years, it must fear inflation."

Eliminate answer choices that aren't relevant or that contain information not presented by the premises. The argument says nothing about regional banks or the termination of the Federal Reserve's control over U.S. monetary policy, so you can disregard A and D. Then get rid of any choices that don't take all premises into consideration. E just reiterates the first premise, so it's wrong. You're left with B and C, but C contradicts the information in the premises. The problem says the Federal Reserve responds to the economy, not the other way around, so it would be wrong to say the Federal Reserve causes a recession. B is clearly the best answer. It takes into consideration the information that the Federal Reserve has raised rates and that raising rates is its response to inflation.

Be careful to avoid relying on outside knowledge or opinions when answering drawing-conclusions questions. You may have studied the Federal Reserve Bank and have opinions about monetary policy. Answer choices A, C, and D reflect some possible current opinions about the Federal Reserve. Don't get trapped into choosing an answer because it supports your opinion.

Spotting those sneaky assumptions

Some GMAT critical reasoning questions ask you to identify a premise that isn't there. For these types of questions, the author directly states a series of premises and provides a clear conclusion, but in getting to that conclusion, the author assumes information. Your job is to figure out what the author assumes to be true but doesn't state directly in drawing the conclusion to the argument. Seeking-assumptions questions may look like these:

- ✔ The argument in the above passage depends on which of the following assumptions?

- ✔ The conclusion reached by the author of the above passage is a questionable one. On which of the following assumptions did the author rely?

- ✔ The above paragraph presupposes which of the following?

Words like *assume, rely, presuppose, depend on,* and their derivatives usually indicate seeking-assumptions questions. Remember, these questions ask you to look for the ideas the author relies on but doesn't state.

As you read seeking-assumptions questions, look for information that's necessary to the argument but isn't stated by the author. In these questions, the author always takes for granted something on which the entire argument depends. You just need to identify what that is. To do so effectively, choose an answer that links the existing premises to the conclusion. The assumption you're seeking always bears directly on the conclusion and ties in with one or more premises, often with the last premise. Therefore, the best answer often contains information from both the last premise and the conclusion. Try on this one for size:

Women receive fewer speeding tickets than men do. Women also have lower car insurance rates. It is clear that women are better drivers than men.

The conclusion above is based on which of the following assumptions?

   I. Men and women drive cars equal distances and with equal frequency.

  II. Lower car insurance rates are a sign of a better driver.

 III. Speeding tickets are equally awarded for violations without any gender bias on the part of police officers.

(A) I only

(B) III only

(C) I and III only

(D) II and III only

(E) I, II, and III

As always, read the question first. Because it contains "assumptions" in it, we bet you figured out pretty quickly that it's a seeking-assumptions question.

Next, read through the argument and try to figure out the assumption or assumptions the author makes in reaching the conclusion that women are better drivers. The author moves from the premises to the conclusion pretty quickly and assumes that fewer speeding tickets and lower car insurance rates indicate better driving skills. The author also assumes that men and women have equal driving experiences. Use this information to examine each of your options.

Look at I first. It fits with your second observation that men and women experience equal driving situations, so eliminate any answer choices that *don't* include I. This means you can get rid of B and D. This leaves you with A, C, and E.

Before you continue reading through your options, take some time to examine the remaining answer choices. You'll see that it's best to examine II next, because if it's true, you won't even have to read III; you'll know the answer is E. You have to read III only if you determine that II isn't an assumption. (For more about strategies for answering Roman numeral questions, see Chapter 2.)

The information in II links the author's last premise, that women have lower insurance rates, to the conclusion that women are better drivers. Thus, II is also correct. You can eliminate A and C, and by process of elimination, the answer must be E. If you read through III, you'll confirm that it, too, is an assumption the author makes about men and women having an equal playing field in the driving game.

If you find seeking-assumption questions to be tricky, try arguing the opposite position. For example, in the sample question, you could've taken the opposing view, that men are better drivers. This means you'll be looking for ways to undermine the conclusion. If you assume the premises to be true, the best way to attack the conclusion is to show that the author assumes things that aren't true. For instance, you may argue that men have more accidents because they drive more, they get more tickets because police are less forgiving with male speeders, and they have higher car insurance rates because they drive more expensive cars. Those counterarguments expose the author's assumptions!

Using your noggin to make inferences

You may see only one or two inference questions on the GMAT, so don't spend too much time figuring out how to answer them. But we know you want to do your very best, so here are a few tips. These types of questions ask you to make an inference (using inductive reasoning) based on the argument in the passage. Making-inferences questions are pretty easy to recognize because they usually include the word "infer."

- ✔ Which of the following statements can be correctly inferred from the passage above?
- ✔ Which of the following can be inferred from the above statements?

The key to answering these questions correctly is to know that they usually ask you to make an inference about one of the premises in the argument rather than about the entire argument or the conclusion. Because these questions usually deal with the premises and not the conclusion, you should choose an answer that makes a plausible inference about one or more of the premises. Like the correct answer choices for the drawing-conclusions questions, the best answers to this type of question don't go beyond the scope of the information provided in the paragraph. Here's what one looks like:

The highest rated television shows do not always command the most advertising dollars. Ads that run during shows with lower overall ratings are often more expensive because the audience for those shows includes a high proportion of males between the ages of 19 and 34. Therefore, ads that run during sporting events are often more expensive than ads running during other types of programs.

Which of the following can properly be inferred from the passage above?

- (A) Advertisers have done little research into the typical consumer and are not using their advertising dollars wisely.
- (B) Sports programs have higher overall ratings than prime time network programs.
- (C) Advertisers believe males between the ages of 19 and 34 are more likely to be influenced by advertisers than are other categories of viewers.
- (D) Advertising executives prefer sports programs and assume that other Americans do as well.
- (E) Ads that run during the biggest sporting events are the most expensive of all ads.

You know you're dealing with an inference question before you read through the argument because you've read the question first and it contains "inferred." Focus on the premises of the argument as you read it. Then look through the answer choices and eliminate any that don't address one of the premises or that present inferences that require additional information.

The argument says nothing about advertising research or whether the particular advertising practice is wise, so you can eliminate A immediately. You're stretching beyond the scope of the information if you infer that advertisers are unwise. Likewise, D mentions the preferences and assumptions of advertisers, but none of the premises discuss advertisers, so you can get rid of D. The inference in E relates to the conclusion rather than any of the premises, so you can probably eliminate it right away. Furthermore, just because sporting events ads are "often more expensive" than other ads doesn't necessarily mean that they're always the most expensive. This leaves you with B and C.

Answer B contradicts information in the argument. The author implies that some sporting events have lower overall ratings even though they have higher advertising rates. You're left with C. You need an explanation for the information in the second sentence that states that advertising is often more expensive for lower rated shows viewed by males who are between 19 and 34. This practice would be logical only if males of these ages were more susceptible to advertising than other groups. It makes sense that C is the correct answer.

Remember to check your outside knowledge about the critical reasoning subjects at the door! You may know that Super Bowl ads are the most expensive ads, which may tempt you to choose E. Using your own knowledge rather than what's expressly stated in the test questions will cause you to miss questions that someone with less knowledge might answer correctly.

Making your way through method-of-reasoning questions

Method-of-reasoning questions are the rarest form of GMAT critical reasoning question types. This type of question either directly asks you what type of reasoning the author uses to make an argument or, more often, asks you to choose an answer that uses the same method of reasoning as the argument does. You may see method-of-reasoning questions phrased like these:

- Which of the following employs the same method of reasoning as the above argument?
- The author's point is made by which method of reasoning?
- David's argument is similar to Katy's in which of the following ways?

The two types of method-of-reasoning questions may seem different, but each of them asks for you to do the same thing: to recognize the type of reasoning used in the argument. Remember that for the purposes of the GMAT, the methods of reasoning are as follows:

- Deductive, which is reaching a specific conclusion from general premises
- Inductive, which is drawing a general conclusion from specific premises and includes the following methods:
  - Cause and effect, which shows that one event resulted from another
  - Analogy, which shows that one thing is sufficiently similar to another thing such that what holds true for one is true for the other
  - Statistics, which uses population samples (surveys) to reach conclusions about the population as a whole

Questions that ask you to specifically choose what kind of reasoning the author uses are straightforward, so we focus on the other type of question, which asks you to choose an answer that mimics the reasoning method of the given argument. When you know you're dealing with this type of question, you just need to focus on the way the author makes the argument to make sure you choose an answer that follows the logic most exactly.

Don't choose an answer just because it deals with the same subject matter as the given argument. These choices are often traps to lure you away from the answer that more exactly duplicates the author's logic but addresses another topic.

It doesn't matter whether the argument makes sense. If the given argument isn't logical, pick an answer choice that isn't logical in the same way.

You may focus on the method of reasoning better if you substitute letters for ideas in the argument. For instance, say you're presented with this argument: "Balloons that contain helium float. Jerry's balloon doesn't float, so it contains oxygen rather than helium." You could state this logic with letters like this: "All A (helium balloons) are B (floaters). C (Jerry's balloon) isn't B (a floater), so C isn't A." Then you can apply that formula to your answer choices to see which one matches best.

Some of the reasoning methods may be as obscure as the one in this sample question:

A teacher told the students in her class, "The information that you read in your history book is correct because I chose the history book and I will be creating the test and assigning your grades."

The reasoning in which of the following statements most closely resembles that of the above argument?

(A) The decisions made by the Supreme Court are just because the Court has the authority to administer justice.

(B) The people who have fame are famous because they deserve to be famous.

(C) Those who play sports get better grades because of the link between the health of the body and the health of the mind.

(D) Since my favorite teacher chooses to drive this kind of car, I should as well.

(E) Of 100 professors surveyed, 99 agree with the conclusions reached by the scientist in his paper on global warming.

Reading the question first tells you that you'll have to analyze the way the author reaches the conclusion in the argument. As you read, you find that this illogical cause-and-effect argument states that information is correct because someone in a position of authority (the teacher) says so, so you need to find an equally illogical argument based on power and authority.

Because this is a cause-and-effect argument, you can eliminate any choices that don't use cause and effect to reach a conclusion. All choices seem to contain an element of cause and effect except D, which presumes an analogy between a favorite teacher and the writer, and E, which uses statistical evidence. (Note that just because D also concerns a teacher, it isn't automatically the right answer.) Disregard D and E and examine the other three choices.

Among A, B, and C, the only choice that uses power to justify a cause-and-effect relationship is A. B is faulty because it uses circular reasoning, which means it uses its conclusion as a premise, instead of using power to advance its position. C doesn't work because its logic isn't necessarily faulty. Instead, it relies on a logical correlation between physical health and intellectual prowess. Therefore, A is the answer that most nearly matches the kind of reasoning in the original argument.

With practice, you'll probably find that critical reasoning questions become some of the easiest question types to master on the GMAT. For more critical reasoning practice, check out the practice verbal section in Chapter 6 and the full-length practice tests in Chapters 17 and 19.

Chapter 6

Bringing It Together: A Practice Mini Verbal Section

....

In This Chapter

▶ Practicing sentence correction, reading comprehension, and critical reasoning questions

▶ Finding out why right answers are right and wrong answers are wrong

....

*L*ike the real GMAT verbal section, the practice test in this chapter has an equal distribution of each of the three types of verbal questions. It contains seven reading comprehension questions, seven sentence correction questions, and seven critical reasoning questions. The total of 21 questions makes this test just about half the size of the 41-question GMAT verbal section. To get more practice, take the full-length practice exams in Chapters 17 and 19.

If you're the competitive type and want to subject yourself to a timed test, give yourself just a little over a half-hour to complete the 21 questions. We can't simulate a computer in this book, but don't let that deter you. Just mark the answers right in the book, and try not to look at the answers until after you've answered the questions.

To best mimic the computer experience during this practice test, answer each question in sequence and don't go back and change any of your answers after you've moved on to the next question. You won't have a test booklet to write in, so try not to write anything except your answers on the pages of this book. To keep your notes and record eliminated answers, use a single sheet of paper and a sharp pencil with an eraser to simulate the erasable notepad you'll use on test day. Or to really set the stage, purchase a small dry erase board and some dry erase markers of your very own.

Take the time to read through the answer explanations, even for the questions that you got right. The explanations apply the techniques covered in the other chapters of this book and show you why a certain answer is a better choice than the others.

You probably know the directions for the three verbal question types, but here's a review before you begin:

✔ Sentence correction questions give you a sentence that has one portion underlined. Choose the answer choice that best phrases the underlined portion of the sentence according to the rules of standard English. The first answer choice duplicates the phrasing of the underlined portion; if you think the sentence is best with its original wording, choose the first answer. The other four answers provide alternative phrasings. Choose the one that rephrases the sentence in the clearest, most grammatically correct manner.

- ✔ Answer reading comprehension questions based on what the passage states directly or implicitly. Choose the best answer to every question.

- ✔ Critical reasoning questions present you with an argument and a question about the argument. Pick the choice that best answers the question.

When you're ready, jump right in!

1. A study of energy consumption revealed that homeowners living within 100 miles of the Gulf of Mexico used less energy from November 1 to April 30 than did homeowners in any other region of the United States. The same study found that from May 1 to October 31, those same homeowners used more energy than any other homeowners.

Which of the following, if true, would most contribute to an explanation of the facts above?

(A) People who own homes near the Gulf of Mexico often own second homes in cooler locations, where they spend the summers.

(B) Air conditioning a home is a more energy efficient process than heating a similarly sized home.

(C) Homes near the Gulf of Mexico require very little heating during the warm winters, but air conditioners must run longer in the summer to cool the warm, humid air.

(D) The average daily temperature is lower year-round near the Gulf of Mexico than in other areas of the United States.

(E) Because of the large number of refineries located in the Gulf region, the price of energy there is less than in any other area of the country.

This critical reasoning question asks you to strengthen the argument by providing a piece to the cause-and-effect pattern. With cause-and-effect questions, you select the answer choice that could logically cause the effects noted in the premises. So for this problem, you have to decide which of the five choices helps explain why Gulf Coast homes use little energy in the winter *and* a great deal of energy in the summer. Without even looking at the answer choices, you may conclude that the Gulf Coast climate is milder than other parts of the nation in the winter and perhaps hotter in the summer. The correct answer probably addresses that issue.

Eliminate A — if most Gulf Coast residents spend the summer elsewhere, their vacant homes would use less energy during summer months rather than more. This answer would produce the opposite effect of that explained in the argument. You can also eliminate B, because it doesn't provide a way of comparing energy use in the Gulf region to energy use in the rest of the country. It may provide a reason why summer energy use would be lower than winter use, but that's not the issue in this argument.

Answer C gives a reason why the Gulf region would have lower energy use in winter and higher use in summer, which may explain why it's different from the rest of the country as a whole. This is probably the correct answer, but read through the remaining two choices just to be sure.

D doesn't work because a region that's cool year-round would have high energy consumption in the winter for heat and low consumption in the summer. And you can eliminate E because the argument is about energy consumption, not energy price. *Correct answer:* C.

2. A conservation group is trying to convince Americans that the return of gray wolves to the northern United States is a positive development. Introduction of the wolf faces significant opposition because of the wolf's reputation as a killer of people and livestock. So that the wolf will be more acceptable to average Americans, the conservation group wants to dispel the myth that the wolf is a vicious killer.

Which of the following, if true, would most weaken the opposition's claim?

(A) Wolves are necessary for a healthy population of white-tailed deer because wolves kill the weaker animals and limit the population to sustainable numbers.

(B) In a confrontation, black bears are much more dangerous to humans than wolves are.

(C) Wolves are superb hunters, operating in packs to track down their prey and kill it.

(D) There has never been a documented case of a wolf killing a human in the 500-year recorded history of North America.

(E) Wolves occasionally take livestock because domestic animals are not equipped to protect themselves the way wild animals are.

This critical reasoning question asks you to weaken the opposition's statement that the wolf is vicious, so look for a statement that shows that the wolf isn't a danger to people or livestock. Begin by eliminating answers that don't address the appropriate conclusion. Choice A deals with the beneficial impact of wolves on the ecosystem but doesn't talk about their propensity toward viciousness, so eliminate it. You can also eliminate C, because the hunting prowess of the wolf isn't the issue, and this choice may actually strengthen the contention that wolves are dangerous. Choice E also doesn't weaken the conclusion in question; it seems to argue that wolves may threaten livestock. This leaves you with B and D. Choice B compares the danger posed by wolves with the danger posed by black bears. Even if a wolf is less dangerous than a bear, that doesn't mean a wolf isn't dangerous. The best answer is D, because it provides a statistic that weakens the opposition's argument that wolves are dangerous to humans. *Correct answer:* D.

Questions 3–5 refer to the following passage:

It is hard for us to imagine today how utterly different the world of night used to be from the daylight world. Of course, we can still re-create something of that lost mystique. When we sit around a campfire and tell ghost stories, our goose bumps (and our children's) remind us of the terrors that night used to hold. But it is all too easy for us to pile in the car at the
(5) end of our camping trip and return to the comfort of our incandescent, fluorescent, floodlit modern word. Two thousand, or even two hundred, years ago there was no such escape from the darkness. It was a physical presence that gripped the world from sunset until the cock's crow.

"As different as night and day," we say today. But in centuries past, night and day really
(10) were different. In a time when every scrap of light after sunset was desperately appreciated, when travelers would mark the road by piling up light stones or by stripping the bark off of trees to expose the lighter wood underneath, the Moon was the traveler's greatest friend. It was known in folklore as "the parish lantern." It was steady, portable, and—unlike a torch—entailed no risk of fire. It would never blow out, although it could, of course, hide behind a
(15) cloud.

Nowadays we don't need the moon to divide the light from the darkness because electric lights do it for us. Many of us never even see a truly dark sky. According to a recent survey on light pollution, 97 percent of the U.S. population lives under a night sky at least as bright as it was on a half-moon night in ancient times. Many city-dwellers live their entire lives
(20) under the equivalent of a full moon.

This passage is excerpted from *The Big Splat, or How Our Moon Came to Be,* by Dana Mackenzie (Wiley Publishing, 2003).

3. The primary purpose of this passage is to

    (A) compare and contrast nighttime in the modern world with the dark nights of centuries past

    (B) explain why the invention of the electric light was essential to increasing worker productivity

    (C) lament the loss of the dark nights and the danger and excitement that moonless nights would bring

    (D) describe the diminishing brightness of the moon and the subsequent need for more electric lights

    (E) argue for an end to the excessive light pollution that plagues 97 percent of the U.S. population

For a primary purpose reading comprehension question, remember that you're looking for the reason the author wrote the passage. Focus on the passage as a whole and not on any particular portion. You usually can find clues to the main theme and the author's purpose in the first and last paragraphs of the passage. The main idea of this passage is that night was very different in centuries past than it is in current times, and the author's purpose is to show how this is true. So look for an answer that reflects this purpose.

You can start by eliminating answers based on their first words.

Compare and contrast, explain, and *describe* reflect the author's purpose, but *lament* and *argue* imply more emotion on the part of the author than is displayed in the passage, so eliminate C and E. Worker productivity has nothing to do with showing how our ancestors perceived night differently, so you can eliminate B. Choice D is simply wrong; the author doesn't maintain that the moon is actually getting darker, just that it's become overshadowed by electric lights. *Correct answer:* A.

4. The passage mentions all of the following as possible ways for travelers to find the path at night EXCEPT:

    (A) piles of light-colored stones

    (B) the moon

    (C) a torch

    (D) railings made of light wood

    (E) trees with the bark stripped off

This specific information exception question asks you to refer to the text to eliminate answers that *are* ways in the passage that travelers can find a path at night. The second paragraph specifically mentions A, light-colored stones; B, the moon; C, torches; and E, trees with the bark stripped off. Railings aren't mentioned anywhere in the passage. *Correct answer:* D.

5. The author includes the statistic "97 percent of the U.S. population lives under a night sky at least as bright as it was on a half-moon night in ancient times" to primarily emphasize which of the following points?

   (A) Modern humans have the luxury of being able to see well at night despite cloud cover or a moonless night.

   (B) Most modern people cannot really understand how important the moon was to people in centuries past.

   (C) Americans are unique among the people of the world in having so much artificial light at night.

   (D) A full moon in ancient times was brighter than modern electric lights, which are only as bright as a half-moon.

   (E) Light pollution is one of the most important problems facing the United States in the 21st century.

   This question asks you about the use of a specific statistic. To answer this question correctly, keep in mind the author's purpose for writing the passage, which you've already considered in the third question. Find the choice that links the statistic to the author's purpose of comparing nighttime now and nighttime in centuries past. Eliminate C because the author compares time periods, not modern countries. Because the passage doesn't indicate that the moon is brighter than electric lights, you can eliminate D. Although the 97 percent statistic may lead you to conclude that light pollution is a big problem, that's not the author's reason for using the statistic, so eliminate E. A is a little more plausible, but B is better because the author is more concerned with showing how night skies are different now than with showing that the modern well-lit sky is a luxury. *Correct answer:* B.

6. The sugar maples give us syrup in March, a display of beautiful flowers in spring, and <u>their foliage is spectacular in October.</u>

   (A) their foliage is spectacular in October.

   (B) spectacularly, their foliage changes color in October.

   (C) has spectacular foliage in October.

   (D) spectacular foliage in October.

   (E) October foliage that is spectacular in orange and red.

   This sentence correction question has a parallelism problem. You know this because the underlined portion is a part of a list of elements joined by a conjunction and not all the elements in the list exhibit the same construction. The third element is expressed as a clause, and the other elements are noun phrases. Because the sentence contains an error, you know A is wrong. B, C, and E do not change the clause to a phrase. *Correct answer:* D.

7. The Industrial Revolution required levels of financing <u>which were previously unknown</u>; for instance, Florence had eighty banking houses that took deposits, made loans, and performed many of the other functions of a modern bank.

   (A) which were previously unknown

   (B) that were previously unknown

   (C) unknown before that time

   (D) which had been unknown in earlier times

   (E) that was previously unknown

This sentence correction question has an improperly used pronoun. You use *which* to introduce nonessential clauses. Because the information after the *which* is essential to the meaning of the sentence, you have to use *that* instead. You can eliminate A and D because both keep the *which* construction. C uses too many words to mean previously unknown, and E changes *which* to *that* but presents a new problem because *that* refers to *levels,* which is plural, so it requires the plural verb *have.* Thus, B is the only answer that corrects the problem without creating new ones. *Correct answer:* B.

8. His efforts to learn scuba diving, a major goal Bob had set for himself for the coming year, has not significantly begun, seeing as how his fear of claustrophobia is triggered anytime he is underwater.

   (A) has not successfully begun, seeing as how

   (B) have not successfully begun, seeing as how

   (C) have not been successful because

   (D) has not been successful because

   (E) have not yet met with success, on account of

The underlined portion of this sentence correction question has problems with agreement and rhetorical construction. The plural subject *efforts* doesn't work with the singular verb *has.* Because you find an error, you automatically eliminate A. D doesn't correct the agreement error. This leaves you with B, C, and E, all of which correct the agreement problem, but *because* is a better, clearer construction than *seeing as how* and *on account of. Correct answer:* C.

Questions 9 and 10 are based on the following information:

Tom: The unemployment rate has dropped below five percent, and that is good news for America. A lower unemployment rate is better for almost everyone.

Shelly: Actually, a low unemployment rate is good for most workers but not for everyone. Workers are certainly happy to have jobs, but many businesses are negatively affected by a low unemployment rate because they have fewer applicants for jobs, and to expand their workforce, they have to hire workers they would not usually hire. The wealthiest Americans also privately complain about the inability to get good gardeners, housecleaners, and nannies when most Americans are already employed. So a low unemployment rate is not, in fact, good for America.

9. Which of the following, if true, would most weaken the argument that a low unemployment rate is bad for business?

   (A) Businesses must pay skilled or experienced workers higher salaries when the unemployment rate is low.

   (B) The states don't have to pay unemployment compensation to as many workers when unemployment is low.

   (C) Higher unemployment generally means higher enrollment levels in college and graduate school.

   (D) Inflation can increase with low unemployment, making capital more expensive for any business seeking to expand.

   (E) Low unemployment rates generally mean that Americans have more money to spend on the goods and services created by American businesses.

This critical reasoning question requires you to weaken Shelly's argument that a low unemployment rate is bad for business. A and D give two examples of how low unemployment hurts businesses, so they actually strengthen the argument instead of weakening it. Eliminate them along with B and C, because these statements are basically off topic; they deal with government and universities, not businesses. E is the correct answer, because employed American workers' buying more American products provides a significant advantage for businesses. *Correct answer:* E.

10. Shelly's conclusion that "a low unemployment rate is not, in fact, good for America" relies on the assumption that

   (A) What is bad for businesses owners and the wealthy is bad for America.

   (B) Fluctuations in the unemployment rate affect the number of applicants for job openings.

   (C) Wealthy Americans rarely employ other Americans to clean their houses or as nannies for their children.

   (D) Business owners always want what is best for their workers even when it negatively impacts the bottom line.

   (E) Low unemployment hurts some workers because they would prefer to stay at home and collect unemployment checks.

   This critical reasoning question asks you to identify an assumption that Shelly relied on in making her conclusion that a low unemployment rate is not "good for America."

   REMEMBER

   When you're asked to find an assumption, look for a statement that supports the conclusion but isn't actually stated in the argument.

   Eliminate choices that don't support the conclusion. Whether businesses favor workers over the bottom line may affect the unemployment rate, but it doesn't show how low unemployment isn't good for America, so D is incorrect. E doesn't support the conclusion, either. The conclusion is about what's good for America in general, not a select few disinclined workers.

   A person's assumption wouldn't contradict a stated premise, so C can't be right. B may support the conclusion, but it's actually stated in the given premises and therefore can't be an unstated assumption. A is the correct answer because it links Shelly's premises about businesses and wealthy Americans to her conclusion about America in general. *Correct answer:* A.

11. A particular company makes a system that is installed in the engine block of a car and, if that car is stolen, relays the car's location to police via satellite. The recovery rate of stolen cars with this device is ninety percent. This system helps everyone because it is impossible for a thief to tell which cars it is installed on. For these reasons, insurance companies try to encourage customers to get this system by offering lower rates to those who have the system. Competing systems include brightly colored steel bars that attach to the steering wheel and loud alarms that go off when the car is tampered with. These systems simply encourage thieves to steal different cars, and when cars with these devices are stolen, the police rarely recovery them.

   Which of the following is the most logical conclusion to the author's premises?

   (A) Insurance companies should give the same discount to car owners that have any protective system because their cars are less likely to be stolen.

   (B) The police shouldn't allow car owners to install the loud sirens on their cars because everyone simply ignores the sirens anyway.

   (C) Car owners with the system that relays location to the police should prominently advertise the fact on the side window of their cars.

   (D) Thieves should simply steal the cars with loud alarms or bright steel bars because those cars probably wouldn't also have the more effective system installed.

   (E) Insurance companies should give less of a discount, or no discount at all, to the siren and steering wheel systems because they aren't as effective as the relay system.

This critical reasoning question requires you to draw a conclusion from the premises included in the argument.

Look for an answer choice that addresses all the information in the premises. You can eliminate conclusions that are off topic or incomplete.

Eliminate choices that don't include all the elements of the argument. Neither B, C, nor D mention the insurance companies that are the subject of one of the premises. This leaves you with A and E, which offer nearly opposite conclusions. The premises indicate that one of the reasons insurance companies like the engine-block system is that thieves don't know which cars it's installed on. A concludes that cars with any protective system, including alarms and steering wheel bars, should get a discount because those cars are less likely to be stolen. This conclusion doesn't flow logically from the premises, however, because the reasons given for the insurance discounts are a high recovery rate of stolen vehicles and the general deterrent to all car thefts. Neither of these advantages comes from the alarms or steering wheel bars. E addresses all the premises and logically concludes the argument. *Correct answer:* E.

12. The managers were asked to rate <u>their depth of knowledge having been increased</u> as a result of the emergency simulation, and in each area, they reported large gains.

    (A) their depth of knowledge having been increased

    (B) how much their depth of knowledge had increased

    (C) if they had more knowledge

    (D) how deep their knowledge is

    (E) their knowledge depth

The underlined portion in this sentence correction question is passive, so you can eliminate A. Neither C, D, nor E addresses both the knowledge increase *and* the knowledge depth, so you can eliminate them, too. The best answer is B. It makes the construction active and includes both the increase and depth of knowledge. *Correct answer:* B.

13. Keeping the nose of her kayak directly into the wind, she paddled fiercely toward the safety of the harbor <u>through the seeming endless waves, each of those larger than the last.</u>

    (A) through the seeming endless waves, each of those larger than the last.

    (B) through the seeming endless waves, each larger than the last.

    (C) through the seemingly endless waves, each of those larger than the last.

    (D) through the seemingly endless waves, each larger than the last.

    (E) through waves that seemingly have no end, each larger than the last.

You probably first noticed that the underlined portion of the sentence correction question contains a modification error. Adjectives like *seeming* modify nouns and pronouns. They can't modify other adjectives like *endless*. Adverbs must be used for that. Instead of *seeming*, you can use the adverb *seemingly*. Therefore, you know you can disregard A. You can also eliminate B because it doesn't make the change to *seeming*. C, D, and E change *seeming* to *seemingly*. There's also a problem with redundancy. *Each* refers sufficiently to *waves*; *of those* isn't necessary. C doesn't fix this error, so it's wrong. This leaves you with D and E. Both fix each of the errors, but E creates another. The sentence is past tense, so the verb *have* should be in past tense like this: *seemingly had no end*. D corrects both original errors and doesn't introduce more, so it's the correct answer. *Correct answer:* D.

14. Companies X and Y have the same number of employees working the same number of hours per week. According to the records kept by the human resources department of each company, the employees of company X took nearly twice as many sick days as the employees of company Y. Therefore, the employees of company Y are healthier than the employees of company X.

    Which of the following, if true, most seriously weakens the conclusion above?

    (A) Company X allows employees to use sick days to take care of sick family members.

    (B) Company Y offers its employees dental insurance and company X doesn't.

    (C) Company X offers its employees a free membership to the local gym.

    (D) Company Y uses a newer system for keeping records of sick days.

    (E) Both companies offer two weeks of sick days per year.

    This critical reasoning question asks you to weaken the conclusion that the employees of company Y are healthier than the employees of company X. The author draws the conclusion that Y's employees are healthier than X's employees based on the cause-and-effect argument that more sick days means sicker employees.

    To weaken cause-and-effect arguments, look for an answer choice that shows another cause is possible for the effect.

    Choice E doesn't distinguish between the two companies, so it can't show another cause for the different number of sick days, and therefore it can't be right. Choice D differentiates between the two companies' record keeping, but it doesn't explain how company Y's new records system accounts for fewer sick days. Dental insurance shouldn't affect the number of sick days, so B doesn't work. Choice C doesn't address the issue of company X's greater number of sick days, so free gym memberships don't matter. The best answer is A because it provides a reason other than employee health for the greater number of sick days that X's employees take. *Correct answer:* A.

    Questions 15–18 refer to the following passage:

    For millennia, the circulation of music in human societies has been as free as the circulation of air and water; it just comes naturally. Indeed, one of the ways that a society constitutes itself as a society is by freely sharing its words, music, and art. Only in the past century or so has music been placed in a tight envelope of property rights and strictly monitored for
    (5) unauthorized flows. In the past decade, the proliferation of personal computers, Internet access, and digital technologies has fueled two conflicting forces: the democratization of creativity and the demand for stronger copyright protections.

    While the public continues to have nominal fair use rights to copyrighted music, in practice the legal and technological controls over music have grown tighter. At the same time,
    (10) creators at the fringes of mass culture, especially some hip-hop and remix artists, remain contemptuous of such controls and routinely appropriate whatever sounds they want to create interesting music.

    Copyright protection is a critically important tool for artists in earning a livelihood from their creativity. But as many singers, composers, and musicians have discovered, the bene-
    (15) fits of copyright law in the contemporary marketplace tend to accrue to the recording industry, not to the struggling garage band. As alternative distribution and marketing outlets have arisen, the recording industry has sought to ban, delay, or control as many of them as possible. After all, technological innovations that provide faster, cheaper distribution of music are likely to disrupt the industry's fixed investments and entrenched ways of doing business.
    (20) New technologies allow newcomers to enter the market and compete, sometimes on superior terms. New technologies enable new types of audiences to emerge that may or may not be compatible with existing marketing strategies.

No wonder the recording industry has scrambled to develop new technological locks and broader copyright protections; they strengthen its control of music distribution. If (25) metering devices could turn barroom singalongs into a market, the music industry would likely declare this form of unauthorized musical performance to be copyright infringement.

This passage is excerpted from *Brand Name Bullies: The Quest to Own and Control Culture*, by David Bollier (Wiley Publishing, 2005).

15. Which of the following most accurately states the main idea of the passage?

   (A) Only with the development of technology in the past century has music begun to freely circulate in society.

   (B) The recording industry is trying to develop an ever-tighter hold on the distribution of music, which used to circulate freely.

   (C) Copyright protection is an important tool for composers and musicians who earn their living from their music.

   (D) Technology allows new distribution methods that threaten to undermine the marketing strategies of music companies.

   (E) If music is no longer allowed to flow freely through the society, then the identity of the society itself will be lost.

This reading comprehension question asks for the main idea of the passage.

Answers to main theme questions are usually more general than specific in their wording.

Choices C and D each focus on sub-themes in the passage but not the main idea. Copyright protection and technology are specific subjects covered in the passage, but they aren't the main idea, which is that the music industry is trying to control distribution of music. You can eliminate A because it's not supported by any part of the passage. The passage clearly states that music has circulated freely in society for millennia. Choice E is wrong because it goes beyond what's stated in the passage. The author may well imply that without the free flow of music society will lose its identity, but this isn't the passage's main idea. *Correct answer:* B.

16. Given the author's overall opinion of increased copyright protections, what is his attitude toward "hip-hop and remix artists" mentioned in paragraph 2?

   (A) wonder that they aren't sued more for their theft of copyright-protected music

   (B) disappointment that they don't understand the damage they are doing to society

   (C) envy of their extravagant lifestyle and increasing popularity

   (D) approval of their continued borrowing of music despite tighter copyright controls

   (E) shock at their blatant sampling of the music of other artists

This reading comprehension question asks about the author's attitude toward *hip-hop and remix artists* as specifically mentioned in the second paragraph. This phrase would be high-lighted in yellow for you on the real GMAT. You've already answered a question about the main idea, so you know the author's concerned about the tightening grip the recording industry has on the distribution of music. Because the hip-hop and remix artists defy the music industry, they will likely meet with the author's approval. Although A may express a valid opinion, you can eliminate it because it isn't supported by the passage. The author probably approves of hip-hop and remix artists, so he or she doesn't think they're doing damage — B is completely off-base. Envy and shock are usually too strong emotions for GMAT passages, so rule out C and E. *Correct answer:* D.

17. According to the passage, new technology has resulted (or will result) in each of the following EXCEPT:

    (A) new locks on music distribution

    (B) newcomers' competing in the music market

    (C) better music

    (D) democratization of creativity

    (E) faster, cheaper distribution of music

    Here's another specific-information reading comprehension question looking for an exception. Examine the text and eliminate the answers you find there. The one that remains is your correct answer. In connection with technology, the passage mentions A, new locks on music distribution; B, newcomers' competing in the market; D, democratization of creativity; and E, faster, cheaper distribution of music. The author certainly doesn't mention better music. *Correct answer:* C.

18. The final sentence of the passage seems to imply what about the executives of the record industry?

    (A) They have found ways to make money from any performance of any music at any time.

    (B) They are boldly leading the music industry into a new technological era of vastly increased profits.

    (C) They want their music to be performed as often as possible by the maximum number of people to create greater exposure for artists.

    (D) They don't actually like music or know anything about music and are attempting to limit the society's exposure to music.

    (E) No performance of music anywhere is safe from their attempts to control the distribution of all music.

    For this reading comprehension inference question, you need to determine what the final sentence implies about recording-industry executives. The final sentence mentions that if it were possible, executives would try to stop unauthorized singalongs. This shows that the author thinks that executives will go to any length to control the distribution of music. Choices B and C paint the executives in a positive light, which is certainly not warranted by the last sentence. You can also eliminate D because the last sentence has nothing to do with whether executives like or dislike music. Choice A is closer, but the sentence doesn't talk about making money from singalongs so much as stopping them altogether. *Correct answer:* E.

19. Five new loon pairs successfully raised chicks this year, <u>bringing</u> to twenty-four the number of pairs actively breeding in the lakes of Massachusetts.

    (A) bringing

    (B) and brings

    (C) and it brings

    (D) and it brought

    (E) and brought

    This sentence correction question tests your knowledge of verb forms and grammatical construction. You're not dealing with word choice, because all the answer choices include a form of the verb *to bring*. Choices C and D introduce the pronoun *it,* which has no clear reference, and so they're not right. Choice A applies a singular verb to a plural subject. Choice E includes *and,* which would make the comma in the non-underlined part of the sentence improper. The sentence is best as is. *Correct answer:* A.

20. New laws make it easier to patent just about anything, from parts of the human genome to a peanut butter and jelly sandwich. Commentators are concerned about the implications of allowing patents for things that can hardly be described as "inventions." However, the U.S. Patent and Trademark Office believes that allowing for strong copyright and patent protections fosters the kind of investment in research and development needed to spur innovation.

Which of the following can be properly inferred from the statements above?

(A) It was not possible in the past to patent something as common as a peanut butter and jelly sandwich.

(B) The U.S. Patent and Trademark Office is more interested in business profits than in true innovation.

(C) Investment in research and development is often needed to spur innovation.

(D) The human genome is part of nature and shouldn't be patented.

(E) Commentators who are concerned about too many patents aren't very well informed.

This critical reasoning question asks you to draw an inference from the passage. Inference questions generally focus on a premise rather than on a conclusion. The passage implies that the patent office wants to promote invention, so B doesn't work. Choices D and E express opinions that aren't presented in the passage. Although you may agree that the genome shouldn't be patented or that people who are concerned about patents aren't well-informed, the question doesn't ask you for your opinion.

Don't choose answer choices to critical reasoning questions just because you agree with them. Base your answers on the opinions stated or implied by the paragraph.

Because C is actually stated in the passage, it can't be an inference. The answer must be A, because it flows logically from the first premise and isn't stated in the passage. *Correct answer:* A.

21. Despite the fact that they were colonists, <u>more Americans thought of themselves as British citizens</u>, and throughout the early years of the American Revolution, more than half of all Americans were loyal to Britain.

(A) more Americans thought of themselves as British citizens

(B) fewer Americans felt that they were British citizens

(C) most Americans thought of themselves as British citizens

(D) many of them felt like British citizens

(E) most Americans believed we were British citizens

The final sentence correction question has an improper comparison. The term *more* requires a comparison between two things (more Americans thought of themselves as British citizens than what?). The sentence doesn't offer a comparison. Because there's an error, eliminate A. Choice B uses the term *fewer,* which also requires a comparison, and this answer choice changes the meaning of the sentence. Choice D gets rid of *more* but introduces the pronoun *them,* which doesn't have a clear reference and therefore can't be right. Choice E also contains a pronoun error: its inclusion of the first person pronoun *we. We* weren't around during the American revolution, so E is incorrect. Choice C changes *more* to *most,* so it eliminates the comparison problem and is the correct answer. *Correct answer:* C.

Part III

Acing the Analytical Writing Section

The 5th Wave   By Rich Tennant

"I always get a good night's sleep the day before a test so I'm relaxed and alert the next morning. Then I grab my pen, eat a banana and I'm on my way."

In this part . . .

The GMAT expects you to write not one but two essays! We guess MBA programs want to know that their potential students can communicate. For some folks, the analytical writing section is the most intimidating of the three sections. If you're one of them, this part can put your mind at ease.

We give you a complete description of the types of topics you'll have to write about and let you know exactly what the GMAT readers look for when they score your essays. Then we tell you how to write what they're looking for by giving you tips on how to avoid grammar and mechanics errors and by providing techniques for organizing your thoughts.

Chapter 7

Analyze This: What to Expect from the Analytical Writing Assessment (AWA)

- -

In This Chapter

▶ Getting to know the AWA

▶ Envisioning the format

▶ Differentiating between the two essay question types

▶ Considering the way they score the AWA

- -

The analytical writing assessment (or AWA, as it's affectionately known) can be intimidating. You're required to write two analytical essays on topics that the computer reveals to you just as your time begins to tick away. To earn the top score, you're expected to provide excellent analyses and insightful examples and demonstrate a mastery of standard written English. Did we mention that you're supposed to do this in only 30 minutes per essay? If it seems a little overwhelming, relax. You can do it, and we show you how.

First, you need to know what you're up against, so we walk you through the AWA and let you know what to expect. Then, we give you a sneak peak at the two types of writing tasks required of you. Finally, we get to the part that interests you most — how the analytical writing assessment is scored.

Fitting in the AWA with the Rest of the GMAT

The AWA is a standalone addition to the GMAT test. The GMAT reports your analytical writing score separately from your quantitative and verbal scores. In other words, your combined total score (with a maximum of 800 points) reflects only how well you do on the multiple-choice sections of the test. So you could leave the essay portion of the test blank and still earn an 800 on the other portions of the test (but we certainly don't recommend that strategy!).

Each business program determines the importance of the analytical writing section. Some schools may give it the same weight as your combined quantitative and verbal score. Other schools may assign it less weight. If you have concerns over how your business programs of choice use the analytical writing score in their admissions decisions, check with the specific schools you're interested in attending. The bottom line is that regardless of how a business program uses your essay score, it will be reported. So it's to your advantage to do as well on the AWA as you can.

Another reason to be prepared for this section is that you start your GMAT with the two analytical writing essays and then move to the quantitative and verbal sections. If you feel that you did well on the analytical writing assessment, this confidence may sustain you through the rest of the test. If you're unprepared for the AWA and have a difficult time completing the essays, your bad start could have a negative impact on your entire test session.

Calling 411: How the AWA is Laid Out

The analytical writing assessment consists of two essay prompts; the GMAT folks refer to them as *tasks*. Each task requires you to write an analytical essay within a 30-minute time limit. For both tasks, you use the computer keyboard to type your response. At the end of the 30 minutes, your task is complete and only what you've actually typed into the computer contributes to your score. Any handwritten notes or great ideas in your head that don't make it into the computer don't count!

You'll be able to use typical word-processing functions like cut, copy, paste, undo, and redo. You can access these word-processing functions with the mouse or by using special keystrokes that the GMAT specifies for you before you begin the test. You can also use your erasable notepad to take notes as you plan your response.

Some word-processing features you may be accustomed to using won't be available:

- ✔ **Automatic corrections:** If you regularly use a program like Word or WordPerfect, you probably don't even notice the automatic corrections anymore. You type in "comittment" and your computer displays "commitment" without your even realizing it. The GMAT won't automatically correct your mistakes.

- ✔ **Spelling and grammar check:** You know that spelling-and-grammar-check function that has saved you from turning in some truly hideous college papers? The function tells you, for example, that you have just written a passive sentence with subject-verb agreement problems and three misspelled words. Spelling and grammar check won't be available, either!

- ✔ **Synonym finder:** You won't have access to that groovy built-in thesaurus that helped you find different words for six of your seven uses of the word *cool* (one of which is *groovy*).

You also won't be able to use your friend, Jean, who edits all of your papers, that dictionary by your desk, or the Internet. On this task, it's all up to you! So when you take your practice tests, turn off the automatic spellchecker and keep your fingers off the thesaurus macro.

Two's Company? The Two Essay Question Types

You may think that the GMAT folks are cruel to require you to write two analytical essays. But the truth is that the two essays require two different analytical skills, and both types of skills are necessary in business. You have to adopt different approaches and techniques for both of the task types if you want to generate the highest scores.

In the analysis of an issue task, you're required to state and defend your own opinion on a given topic. In the analysis-of-an-argument task, you're analyzing the strengths and weaknesses of someone else's argument. These are the kinds of skills you'll need to have for your MBA studies and for your business career.

You're entitled to an opinion: Analysis of an issue

We all have opinions. And some of us seem to have too many of them! So what's so hard about stating your opinion on a given topic? The hard part isn't having an opinion (and you won't be scored on whether your opinion is right or wrong); the hard part is supporting your opinion with well-chosen, well-developed examples and persuasive reasoning — in just 30 minutes.

To paraphrase the directions for the analysis of an issue task, you're supposed to do the following:

- Analyze the issue presented and explain your views on it. There isn't a correct response to the task, so consider various perspectives as you put together your position on the issue.

- Think for a few minutes about the issue and organize your response before you start writing. Leave time for revisions when you're finished.

You'll be scored based on your ability to accomplish these tasks:

- Organize, develop, and express your thoughts about the given issue.

- Provide pertinent supporting ideas with examples.

- Apply the rules of standard written English.

Those are the directions; now here's an example of an analysis of an issue prompt:

> "Corporations exist to make a profit for shareholders; therefore, the primary duty of the corporation is not to employ workers or to provide goods and services but to make as much money as possible."

> From your perspective, how accurate is the above statement? Support your position with reasons and/or examples from your own experience, observations, or reading.

Everyone's a critic: Analysis of an argument

In the analysis of an argument task, the GMAT doesn't want your opinion on a topic. Instead, you're supposed to critique the way someone else reaches an opinion. To score well on this task, you need to analyze the reasoning behind the argument and write a critique of the argument. First, you need to briefly explain what kind of reasoning the author uses (for more about kinds of reasoning, consult Chapter 5). Next, you point out the strengths and weaknesses of the argument. Finally, you consider the validity of the assumptions that the author makes and what effect alternative explanations would have on the author's conclusion.

A paraphrase of the directions for the analysis of an argument task follows:

- Write a critique of the argument presented, but do not provide your own opinion on the matter.

- Think for a few minutes about the argument and organize your response before you start writing. Leave time for revisions when you're finished.

You'll be scored based on your ability to accomplish these tasks:

- ✔ Organize, develop, and express your thoughts about the given argument.
- ✔ Provide pertinent supporting ideas with examples.
- ✔ Apply the rules of standard written English.

Now that you have the directions down, here's an example of an analysis of an argument prompt:

> The following is an excerpt written by the head of a governmental department:
>
> "Stronger environmental regulations are not necessary in order to provide clean air and water. We already have lots of regulations on the books and these are not being adequately enforced. For example, the Clean Air Act amendments, adopted in 1990, have never been fully enforced and, as a result, hundreds of coal-burning power plants are systematically violating that law on a daily basis. The Clean Water Act is also not being enforced. In the state of Ohio alone there were more than 2,500 violations in just one year. Instead of passing new regulations that will also be ignored, this department should begin by vigorously enforcing the existing laws."
>
> Examine this argument and present your judgment on how well reasoned it is. In your discussion, analyze the author's position and how well the author uses evidence to support the argument. For example, you may need to question the author's underlying assumptions or consider alternative explanations that may weaken the conclusion. You can also provide additional support for or arguments against the author's position, describe how stating the argument differently may make it more reasonable, and discuss what provisions may better equip you to evaluate its thesis.

Racking Up the Points: How the GMAT Scores Your Essays

According to the folks who make the GMAT, the analytical writing assessment is designed to measure two things:

- ✔ Your ability to think
- ✔ Your ability to communicate your ideas

To assess how well you do in each of these areas, the GMAT employs the services of two separate readers for each of the essays. Based on their analysis of your written masterpieces, these readers individually assign you a score between 0 and 6.

Getting to know your readers

Two independent readers judge each of your two analytical writing tasks, and each of the readers assigns your essays a score from 0 to 6. If the two readers who are scoring one of your essays differ by more than a single point, a third reader will adjudicate. This means that the third reader's score will be used in conjunction with the other scores.

For example, if one reader assigns your essay a 3 and the other reader gives it a 5, a third reader is brought in. If the third reader also gives your essay a 5, then the 3 would be discarded and your two scores for that essay would be 5 and 5. If however, the third reader splits the difference and assigns you a 4, you'd have two 4's.

One reader who happens to assign you an unfairly low score won't be able to sabotage your analytical writing assessment score.

To obtain your overall score, the GMAT averages the four scores from the two tasks (two from the issues essay and two from the argument essay). Then it rounds the average to the nearest half-point (quarter points and three-quarter points round up instead of down). For example, if your two scores for the analysis of an issue task were 5 and 5 and your two scores for the analysis of an argument task were 5 and 6, your final score would be a 5.5. (You can figure this out because you know all about finding averages from studying for the quantitative section! $5 + 5 + 5 + 6 = 21$; $21/4 = 5.25$, which rounds up to 5.5.)

College and university faculty members from a variety of academic disciplines score your essays. Some of these faculty members are from business management programs, but you can't expect that the particular readers who score your tasks will have any special knowledge of business. Avoid using jargon or assuming that your reader has had all the same business classes that you've had.

An automated scoring program may also score your essay. This program is designed to reflect the judgment of expert readers. One of the things a computer program does best is check for grammatical errors. If you've used a word-processing program, you know that a computer can quickly and accurately identify many grammatical errors. In Chapter 8, we tell you how to avoid common writing errors.

Readers look for two things when they take on your essays: clear analysis and good writing. In order for an essay to earn a score of 5 or 6, it must clearly analyze the issue (or argument), demonstrate good organization, and provide specific, relevant examples and insightful reasons. The paper must demonstrate clear control of language and apply a variety of sentence structures. The essay can have some minor flaws in the use of standard written English but not too many.

This is a tough order in 30 minutes per essay. To help you through it, consult Chapter 8, where we discuss strategies for analyzing issues and arguments quickly and effectively and go over the most common errors that test-takers make when they write under pressure.

Interpreting the scores

The GMAT reports your AWA score as a number from 0 to 6 in half-point increments. A score of 6, the highest possible score, puts you in the 96th percentile, meaning that 96 people out of every 100 test-takers received a lower score. A score of 6 is obviously difficult to earn, because only about 4 percent of the test-takers achieve this score! A score of 5 puts you in the 75th percentile, 4.5 the 57th percentile, 4.0 the 36th percentile, and 3.5 the 19th percentile. The full chart is available on the GMAT Web site at (www.mba.com).

Approximately 60 percent of GMAT test-takers receive a final score on the AWA from 4.0 to 5.5. The typical essay, therefore, falls somewhere between 4 (adequate) and 5 (strong). A number of papers fall into the 3 (limited) category or lower, and the cream of the crop is recognized with a 6 (outstanding). To make sure your score surfaces to the creamy top, practice writing a bunch of essays using the techniques we provide for you in Chapter 8.

Chapter 8

Present Perfect Paragraphs: How to Write a GMAT Essay

Knowing what to expect from the analytical writing assessment gives you an advantage on the GMAT, but if you want to earn a high score, you need to know what you're expected to do and how to do it. To perform well on the two analytical writing tasks, you have to combine good analysis with a good writing style. If you lack either of these key components, your score will suffer. In this chapter, we start with common writing errors that you should avoid and then discuss the steps to writing your analysis.

Avoiding Grammar, Punctuation, and Mechanics Errors

One of the aspects of the analytical writing assessment that causes the most trouble for test takers is the requirement that they demonstrate a good control of standard written English. Standard written English isn't so standard anymore, and it doesn't mirror the way most Americans speak. Spoken phrases are often sentence fragments, and you don't have to worry about things like spelling and punctuation when you speak. Because you can't always rely on what sounds right to you, you have to know the writing rules.

We've identified a few common mistakes that plague GMAT test takers. Writers everywhere seem to repeat these same writing errors. The essay readers will notice these errors, and their presence in your essay will affect your score. If you identify the errors you make most often, you can begin to eliminate them now. Don't wait until test day to isolate your writing issues! In addition to the information we give you in this chapter, you can find more info on applying the rules of grammar and punctuation and on correcting writing problems in Chapter 3 and in *English Grammar For Dummies* (Wiley Publishing).

Punctuation errors

The role of punctuation is to guide the reader through sentences and paragraphs. Without proper punctuation, your reader won't know where one thought ends and another begins. Punctuation errors are among the most common mistakes test takers make on the essay portion of the GMAT.

Many people confuse colons and semicolons. Semicolons join independent clauses when the thoughts they convey are related enough to keep them in the same sentence: *It's almost test day; I need to write a practice essay this weekend.* (Independent clauses can stand alone as complete sentences. For more information on the difference between independent and dependent clauses, see Chapter 3.) On the other hand, you primarily use colons to introduce lists or to precede an example.

The most common punctuation errors involve commas. You use commas to separate items in a series, to replace omitted words, and to set off clauses and parenthetical expressions. You also use them to separate parts of the sentence:

✔ Insert a comma before the coordinating conjunction *(for, and, nor, but, or, yet,* or *so)* that joins two independent clauses.

✔ Include a comma between a beginning dependent clause and an independent clause. (But don't put a comma between the clauses if the independent clause comes first.)

Two of the most common comma errors GMAT essay writers make are comma splices and run-on sentences.

✔ Comma splices occur when you join two independent clauses with just a comma and no coordinating conjunction, like this: *Harold made several errors in his GMAT essay, one was a comma splice.* To correct a comma splice, you make the independent clauses two separate sentences *(Harold made several errors in his GMAT essay. One was a comma splice.),* substitute a semicolon for the comma *(Harold made several errors in his GMAT essay; one was a comma splice.),* or add a coordinating conjunction after the comma *(Harold made several errors in his GMAT essay, and one was a comma splice.).*

✔ You make a run-on sentence when you join together two independent clauses with a coordinating conjunction and no comma: *Harold made several punctuation errors in his GMAT essay and one was a run-on sentence that made his writing seem needlessly wordy.* To correct a run-on, you just add a comma before the conjunction *(Harold made several punctuation errors in his GMAT essay, and one was a run-on sentence that made his writing seem needlessly wordy.).*

Sentence structure problems

Here are two problems with sentence structure that commonly occur in GMAT essays:

✔ **Sentence fragments:** You may be able to blame your propensity for sentence fragments on e-mail communication, but you can't translate your e-mail style to the GMAT essays. A sentence must have a subject and a verb and convey a complete thought. Watch out for dependent clauses masquerading as complete sentences. Even though they contain subjects and verbs, they can't stand alone as sentences without other information. Here are some examples:

• **A sentence and a fragment:** I will return to the workforce. After I earn my MBA.

• **Complete sentence:** I will return to the workforce after I earn my MBA.

✔ **Modifier errors:** Modifiers are words and phrases that describe other words. The rule of thumb is to place modifiers as close as possible to the words they modify:

• **Sloppy:** The assistant found the minutes for the meeting held on Saturday on the desk.

• **Better:** The assistant found Saturday's meeting minutes on the desk.

Faltering in forming possessives?

Another set of errors commonly seen on the GMAT involves forming possessives:

- **Standard issue nouns:** Use the possessive form of a noun when the noun is immediately followed by another noun that it possesses. Most possessives are formed by adding *'s* to the end of a singular noun: *Steve's boss.* This is true even if the noun ends in "s": *Charles's test score.* If the possessive noun is plural and ends in "s," you just add an apostrophe to the end of the word: *The brothers' dogs; many clients' finances.*

- **Pronouns:** The possessive forms of personal pronouns are *my, his, her, your, its, our* and *their* for pronouns that come before the noun and *mine, his, hers, yours, its, ours,* and *theirs* for possessive pronouns that occur at the end of a clause or that function as a subject.

None of the possessive personal pronouns contains an apostrophe. *It's* is a contraction of *it is,* not the possessive form of *its.* As opposed to proper pronouns, possessive indefinite pronouns do contain apostrophes: *Somebody's dog has chewed my carpet.* For information on indefinite and personal pronouns, see Chapter 3.

Spelling out spelling issues

If you're like most people in America, you've come to rely on your word processing program to correct your errors in spelling. The spell-check feature is one of the most popular and useful tools available because it allows you to take your mind off of spelling and concentrate on what you're writing. And if you use an autocorrect feature on your word processing program, you may not even realize how often your computer corrects your misspelled words.

The bad news is that you won't have a spell-check function available when you write your essays on the GMAT. This means that when you take the GMAT, you'll be responsible for correcting your own spelling, perhaps for the first time in years! One or two spelling errors may not be enough to lower your score, but in conjunction with any of the other errors discussed, a few spelling mistakes could make the difference between one score and the next higher.

A good way to avoid potential spelling errors is to steer clear of unfamiliar words. If you've never used a word before and have any doubt about its meaning or how it's spelled, avoid using it. If you use unfamiliar words, you risk not only misspelling the word but also using it inappropriately. Stick to what you know when you write your analytical essays. If you have enough time before the test, you can always broaden your vocabulary. Developing an extensive vocabulary will pay off in your career as well as on the GMAT.

More dos and don'ts

Here are a few more things to keep in mind when preparing for your essay:

- **Use simple, active sentences.** To increase your score, keep your sentences simple and active. The more complex your sentences, the greater your chances of making mistakes in grammar. You may think that long sentences will impress your readers, but they won't. Furthermore, they may cause you to make writing errors more easily.

  Another important characteristic of strong persuasive sentences is the use of active voice. Active voice is clearer and more powerful than passive voice.

- ✔ **Provide clear transitions.** Use transitions to tell the reader where you're going with your argument. You need only a few seconds to provide your readers with words that signal whether the next paragraph is a continuation of the previous idea, whether it refutes the last paragraph, or whether you're moving in a new direction. Transitions are key to good organization.

- ✔ **Use precise descriptions.** Use descriptive words to keep your readers interested and informed. If you use specific, well-chosen words to clearly illustrate your points and examples, your writing will have more impact and you'll earn a higher score.

- ✔ **Avoid slang expressions.** Stick to formal English and avoid contractions and slang. Your readers are professors and should be familiar with formal English, so they expect you to use it in your essays. Using sentence fragments and slang is okay when e-mailing a friend, but on the GMAT, employ a more professional style.

Practice makes perfect!

You can practice writing in GMAT style in creative ways. For example, if you write a lot of e-mails, practice writing them more formally. When your friends send you unpunctuated e-mails full of misspellings and grammatical errors, respond with proper punctuation, superior spelling, good grammar, and perfect paragraphs.

You can't prepare for the GMAT with e-mails alone, so here are some things to think about when writing your practice essays:

- ✔ Write your essays under test conditions. Give yourself a 30-minute time limit and study in a quiet environment.

- ✔ Use only those items you'll have available on the test. Type on your word processor but disable your automatic spell correction, use an erasable board or a single sheet of paper for scratch, and don't use reference books.

- ✔ Take your practice essays seriously (practice the way that you want to perform).

Building a Better Essay: Ten Steps to a Higher Score

If you're going to write well, you need something to write about. Remember that your analytical writing scores are based on the quality of your arguments as well as the quality of your writing. Even though you've been writing for years in college or in the workplace, you probably haven't had to produce very many analytical essays in just 30 minutes. We'll take you through a ten-step process to help you create better essays in less time.

With a plan in mind, you can use your essay time more efficiently and earn a better score. Using part of your 30 minutes to develop a plan means you'll be more organized than someone who just starts writing whatever comes to mind. In fact, you'll likely type for only about 20 minutes during each 30-minute task because you'll spend 5 minutes outlining your argument, about 20 minutes typing it, and 5 minutes proofreading what you've typed.

Work out your timing during your practice tests and note the amount of time that you generally need for each part of the task. Remember that you have only 30 minutes, so you'll never have all the time that you want for any of the three stages, but with practice you'll find the formula that fits your strengths. For example, you may be an excellent typist who can write very fast when you get started. In that case, you can afford a little more time for pre-writing and will need additional time for proofreading all that text you typed. If, on the other hand, you write or type fairly slowly, you'll need to spend at least 20 minutes to get your great ideas on the computer screen and saved for posterity. Here are the ten steps you should follow during each of your 30-minute analytical writing tasks:

1. **Read the specific analytical writing prompt carefully before you begin writing.**

   Although this step may seem obvious, you may hurry through reading the prompt in your rush to start the essay and may miss important elements of your assignment. Take enough time to truly understand the issue or argument you're to analyze. Read the prompt more than once; read it quickly the first time to get an idea of the subject matter and then read it more slowly to catch all the details. Some of your best arguments and examples will come to you when you're reading the topic carefully.

2. **Don't waste time reading the directions.**

   You can make up some of the time that you spend carefully reading the prompt by skimming over the directions that follow. We've paraphrased the instructions for each essay type several times in Chapters 7, 17, and 19, so you know what you're supposed to do. Express your opinion when you conduct an analysis of an issue and critique the way an argument is made when you analyze an argument. The most you need to do is skim the directions to make sure nothing's changed and move on.

3. **Plan your essay format ahead of time.**

   Knowing how to structure your essay can help you plan it. We recommend that you include five paragraphs in each of your analytical essays: an introduction that discusses the issue and presents your position (or *thesis*), three supporting paragraphs that use examples and arguments to persuade others to take your position (and perhaps one other that presents the opposing viewpoint and shows why it isn't sound), and a conclusion that briefly summarizes what you've said in the four previous paragraphs. You may write an essay with four paragraphs or six if that fits your analysis of the issue or argument. Just be sure that you know what you're going to write about before you begin writing.

4. **Use the erasable notepad.**

   Brainstorm and write down your thoughts so you don't forget them. Don't rely on your memory; that's what the notepad is for. Jotting down a word or two can preserve your idea until you're ready to write about it.

5. **Write a brief thesis statement.**

   Pick a position immediately based on your initial preference for one side or another. The side you choose doesn't matter; your readers won't score you on the position you take but on how well you support it. Take the position that you can best support with strong arguments and examples in the short time you're given.

   Write a brief thesis statement indicating which side you support and why. We recommend that you actually type this statement on the computer because it's the key sentence of your introductory paragraph.

   For instance, Chapter 7 presents the following prompt for an analysis of an issue: "Corporations exist to make a profit for shareholders; therefore, the primary duty of the corporation is not to employ workers or to provide goods and services but to make as much money as possible." This prompt helps you form the thesis statement, so if you choose to support that position, you just need to restate a version of the prompt. An example of a opposing thesis statement in opposition could say, "Although a major duty of corporations is to earn money for shareholders, corporations have other responsibilities, like a duty to care for the consumer and an obligation to perform research, that supercede the dangerous desire to make as much money as possible."

6. **Create a quick outline based on your thesis.**

   After you've created your thesis and have typed it into the computer, return to your notepad and make a brief outline. Because your ideas are already on the notepad, out-lining is a very simple process. Select the best arguments and examples to support your thesis. Decide in what order you want to address these ideas and number them "1," "2," and "3" for use as the topic sentences for the three supporting paragraphs of your essay. Under each topic, list several examples and anecdotes that you'll use to support your topic.

7. **Write your introduction.**

   Move from a general statement to more specific ones and end with your thesis. In fact, your introduction may consist of only two sentences: a general introduction to the topic and your thesis statement. A complete introduction for the shareholder duty topic could consist of an introductory sentence stating that many corporations put duty to shareholders above other considerations; the paragraph would conclude with the thesis.

8. **Write your supporting paragraphs.**

   After you've put together an outline and written the introduction, you've completed the hardest parts of the task. Then you just need to write your supporting paragraphs clearly with as few errors as possible. Begin with the idea you designated as "1." Introduce the paragraph with a topic sentence, provide a few supporting examples, and conclude your point. The first supporting paragraph of your corporate essay may state that corporations have a duty of care to consumers and then provide examples from the business world to support the position. Repeat the process for your remain-ing points. Devote a few statements, or even a full paragraph, to addressing the oppos-ing viewpoint and showing why your position is better.

9. **Write a brief conclusion.**

   End your essay with a simple summary of the points you've already made. Provide a synopsis of the conclusions you reached in each of your supporting paragraphs and end with a restatement of your thesis. Move from specific statements to more general ones. Many people try to make too much out of their conclusions, but this paragraph isn't the place to introduce new ideas or argue your position. Instead, just remind the reader of your supporting points and thesis.

10. **Proofread.**

    When you've finished writing, make sure you have time left over to read through what you've written. Look for spelling and punctuation errors and other careless mistakes that you may have made in your rush to complete the assignment on time. Concentrate on errors that you can correct in a few seconds, and don't try to rewrite entire paragraphs.

If you follow these steps in your practice writings and on test day, you'll come away with an AWA score to be proud of.

Chapter 9

Deconstructing Sample GMAT Essays

This chapter defines analytical writing assessment (AWA) scores for you and provides you with some sample GMAT AWA essays so you can see what these babies look like and apply some elements of the examples to your own writing. If you deconstruct essays to figure out what makes for a great essay, you'll have a much better chance of constructing great essays of your own.

Defining GMAT AWA scores

The difference between an essay that's simply adequate and one that's outstanding comes down to a few important factors. Here's how the GMAT differentiates among essays that score 4, 5, and 6, based on analysis and organization:

- ✔ An outstanding essay (score 6) explores the ideas on both sides of the issue and then logically develops a position. The analysis recognizes the complexity of the issue and demonstrates insight in explaining it. The analysis is supported by persuasive examples and reasoning and follows a well-organized outline.

- ✔ A strong essay (score 5) logically develops a position but may not take the time to explore both sides of the issue first. The analysis is still well developed but may not be as insightful as in an outstanding essay. The analysis is supported by well-chosen examples and reasoning and is also well organized, though it's not as tightly organized as an outstanding essay.

- ✔ An adequate essay (score 4) offers a competent analysis of the issue. This essay develops a position and supports it with relevant examples. The analysis and support aren't particularly well-developed, but the fact that the essay at least develops a position and tries to support it distinguishes this essay from lower-scoring essays.

Here's how the GMAT distinguishes among the top three scores based on quality of writing:

- ✔ An outstanding essay demonstrates superior control of the language and employs a variety of grammatically accurate and detailed sentences. This essay uses effective transitions. Although the essay may have a few minor errors, it generally reflects a superior ability in grammar, usage, and mechanics of standard written English.

✔ A strong essay is similar to an outstanding essay, but the sentences may not have quite as much variety and the choice of words may not convey as much detail. This essay employs transitions but not as effectively as an outstanding essay. This essay may have a few minor errors but reflects a facility for grammar, usage, and mechanics.

✔ An adequate essay lacks sentence variety and, although the diction may be accurate, the word choice isn't particularly detailed or precise. This essay may employ transitions, but they're likely to be somewhat abrupt. The adequate essay reflects a familiarity with standard written English but may contain several minor errors or a few more-serious flaws.

In addition to the top three possible scores, four lower scores reflect flaws of differing magnitudes. We give less time to describing these categories, because after you've read Chapters 7 and 8 and practiced writing essays for the exam, you aren't likely to produce one of these lower scores on the GMAT:

✔ A limited essay (score 3) is like an adequate paper in most respects, but it's clearly flawed in one or more areas. This paper may fail to take a position, lack organization, fail to present relevant examples, have problems in sentence structure, or contain errors in grammar, usage, and mechanics numerous enough to interfere with conveying meaning.

✔ A seriously flawed essay (score 2) demonstrates more-significant errors than a limited essay. It may be seriously limited in discussing the issue, lack any semblance of organization, fail to provide any examples, have serious problems with language or sentence structure, and contain errors in grammar, usage, or mechanics that seriously interfere with meaning.

✔ A fundamentally deficient essay (score 1) provides little evidence of the ability to develop a coherent response to the prompt. This essay may also have grave and pervasive writing errors that seriously interfere with the meaning of the essay.

✔ A no-score essay (score 0) is blank, completely off topic, or not written in English.

You've Got Issues: Deconstructing the Analysis of an Issue Essay

In this section, we look at two sample analysis-of-an-issue essays based on the following prompt. If you have 30 minutes to spare, you may find it helpful to write your own essay based on the prompt before looking at the sample essays. It's true that each of the two practice tests includes analytical writing tasks, but taking advantage of this opportunity to get a little more practice may be a good idea. Even if you can't spare a half hour, take about five minutes and go through steps 1–6 discussed in Chapter 8 to create a quick outline based on the prompt. After you've analyzed the prompt or written your own essay, read the samples and try to determine what kind of scores they'd receive. Here's the prompt:

"The most important factor in choosing a career should be the potential salary."

Discuss whether you agree or disagree with the opinion stated above. Provide supporting evidence for your views and use reasons and/or examples from your own experiences.

Sample essay #1

I agree, because money is very important for having a good life. A job with a good salary will let you pay your bills and have a nice house and a nice car to drive. If you don't have a good salary, you will be poor and not be able to buy the things that you want. Everyone should try to get the career that will pay the most that they can, even if maybe it is harder to get that job. High-paying jobs like doctors, lawyers, and architects are important to society and well respected and they also pay well. So those are the kinds of jobs that you should try to get. There are some other careers that are also important to society, but that don't have a very high salary, for example, teachers. I think that people should recognize the importance of educating our children, and pay teachers more.

Some people would say that you should try to have a career doing something that you enjoy and this sounds like a good idea. Otherwise you might get bored or frustrated with your job, and then not do your job very well, and then you might even get fired. But the problem comes if the career that you want to have won't pay very good and then you are unhappy because you are struggling to pay your bills. So I think the very best thing to do is to find a career that pays well so you don't have to worry about financial problems and that you at least like a little bit, and if not then you can always spend your weekends doing the things you like to do because you will have the money to afford luxuries.

Discussion of sample essay #1

How did you score this essay? We bet you eliminated scores 6 and 5 right off the bat. This essay is neither strong nor outstanding. It also isn't so deficient as to earn a 1 or 0. So you need to decide if this essay is a 2, 3, or 4. In order for this essay to be considered fundamentally deficient (score 2), it would have to show very limited analysis, fail to provide examples, or have major language errors that interfere with meaning. Although this essay has problems, it's not fundamentally deficient.

This essay would probably earn a score of either 3 or 4. For it to be scored adequate (score 4), it would need to take a position and support that position with examples and reasoning. This essay takes a position, but it's quite short and doesn't really develop the examples. Its biggest lack is in organization. It fails to come up with two or three clear reasons why salary is most important and then discuss each one in a separate paragraph with supporting evidence. Therefore, the author is prone to tangents, like the sentence on how teachers should get paid more.

The essay reflects a rudimentary command of the English language. It contains several errors (like saying *pay good* instead of *well*) but no major flaws. The discussion of a limited essay (score 3) indicates that it's like an adequate essay except that it's clearly flawed in at least one respect. This essay is generally adequate, but it clearly lacks organization and proper development of the position. This essay would probably garner a 3 instead of a 4.

Sample essay #2

There are many factors to consider when selecting your career, including potential salary, but I don't think this is the most important one. It is important to make enough money to cover all your bills and to support yourself and your family, but I believe it is even more important to be happy with your job. In reality, you don't need a huge house, expensive cars, meals at fancy restaurants, a housecleaner, and regular trips to Europe. You only need to make enough money to pay for food, housing, and other necessities, and this will amount too much less than you think it will be. Beyond basic expenses, it's all either for fun or to make yourself look better compared to others.

As I said already, I think the most important thing about your career is to be happy with it. It is important to be excited about you're job and interested in your job and to think that your job is worthwhile. If you dislike your job or are bored with your job, you will not be inspired to do it well, and you will not like getting up to go to work every day. If, on the other hand, you enjoy your job, it will give you something to look forward to everyday. And your work performance will probably be better if you like the job and this means that you might get a promotion, that would then pay you a higher salary so you get the best of both worlds!

If everyone chose a profession based on potential salary, I suppose we would be a nation of actors and professional athletes. These professions have a high potential salary! Movie stars can make tens of millions of dollars per movie and some TV stars make $1 million per episode. Professional athletes also make millions of dollars, including the highest paid women athletes, tennis player. Does this mean that all women, regardless of athletic ability should try to become professional tennis players? Of course not, because even though professional athletes and actors have a high potential salary, very few people succeed in these professions. It is better to choose a profession based on the likelihood of success rather than the extreme of the highest potential salary.

I have had a lot of jobs in the past that did not pay very much, but I still did them because I was interested in the work and I thought it was a fun job. I have also had jobs that paid a lot more, but was really boring for me and this problem made it harder for me to want to be at work every day. Having experienced it both ways, I believe that it is more important to have the career that is exciting to you than to go for a particular career just because it has a good salary.

Discussion of sample essay #2

This essay is better than sample essay #1. It takes a firm position and supports that position with relevant examples. You probably recognize that this essay could receive a 4 or 5 but probably not a 6. In order for this essay to be considered outstanding (score 6) it would need to explore both sides of the issue before logically developing a position. This essay briefly acknowledges that potential salary is a consideration and that a person should choose a career that at least allows the person to pay the bills, but it doesn't fully consider opposing points and then refute them.

An outstanding essay demonstrates insight, is supported by persuasive examples and reasoning, and is clearly well organized. The second paragraph of sample essay #2 offers a line of reasoning in support of the position that potential salary shouldn't be the first consideration when choosing a career. The reasoning is that if you choose a career that you like rather than the one with the highest salary, you can do well in that career, enjoy it more, and even get promoted, therefore earning a higher salary! This is convincing reasoning that is supported well; however, the point could be developed better with more specific word choice. Both the introduction and the second paragraph are more indicative of an adequate essay (score 4) than an outstanding essay.

The third paragraph contains an example of choosing a career as a movie star or athlete. This example takes the issue to its logical conclusion: If careers were chosen based just on potential salary, then everyone would try to become a movie star or pro athlete. This paragraph argues that some professions have a high salary but a low likelihood of success, but it doesn't make the point until the end of the paragraph. The author argues that going with the higher likelihood of success is better. It's a good argument, but it isn't fully developed. The essay lacks the level of clarity that would make it an outstanding essay.

This essay has very few errors, and the command of the English language is good, but the word choice lacks a certain amount of precision. The first paragraph offers the most specific examples — expensive cars and fancy restaurants — but in the second and last paragraphs, the word *job* is used repeatedly without any attempt to offer the kind of specifics that would give the writing more presence. This is an adequate, and possibly strong, essay, but it's certainly not outstanding. The essay would probably earn a 4 or 5.

You've Got Your Reasons: Deconstructing the Analysis of an Argument Essay

The task for the second essay is to analyze an argument rather than an issue. If you have an extra 30 minutes just lying around, you can take the time to analyze the prompt in this section and write a full essay before you read the sample. If not, at least take five minutes to create a quick outline using steps 1–6 from Chapter 8. Read the instructions following the argument very carefully, because this assignment asks something different from you than the first essay does. Here's the prompt:

> The following appeared as part of an editorial in a business newsletter:

> "Gasoline prices continue to hover at record levels, and increased demand from China and India assures that the days of one dollar per gallon gasoline are over. Continued threat of unrest in the oil-producing regions of the Middle East, Africa, and South America means a perpetual threat to the U.S. oil supply. American leaders have acknowledged the need for new sources of power to fuel the hundreds of millions of cars and trucks in America. Despite this acknowledgment, the U.S. government has yet to provide substantial funding for this important research. Officials are relying on private industry and university researchers to undertake this research that is vital to the economy and national security. Given the long interval before new technologies are likely to become profitable and the tremendous cost, research into new fuels will be successful only if funded by the U.S. government using taxpayer funds."

> Examine this argument and present your judgment on how well reasoned it is. In your discussion, analyze the author's position and how well the author uses evidence to support the argument. For example, you may need to question the author's underlying assumptions or consider alternative explanations that may weaken the conclusion. You can also provide additional support for or arguments against the author's position, describe how stating the argument differently may make it more reasonable, and discuss what provisions may better equip you to evaluate its thesis.

Sample essay #3

The author of this editorial clearly supports the idea that the development of new technology for fueling the automobiles of America is an absolutely necessary project. Substantial evidence is provided to support this claim, for example, the rising price of gasoline, the swelling demand for oil in overseas markets, and warning signs of turbulence and instability in oil-producing countries. However, the author has not provided much evidence or reasoning behind the statement that the U.S. government should fund this research.

The editorial states that it will take a long time and a lot of expense to develop these new technologies, but the argument fails to include evidence of this. The author is making the assumption that readers will know that private companies and universities have been working for decades on projects such as hydrogen fuel cells, bio-diesel, ethanol, and electric cars. The editorial would be much stronger if it included one or two sentences on the fact that each of these technologies is feasible and that with increased funding could be brought rapidly to market.

Furthermore, it is suggested that the development of new fuel technologies is "vital to the economy and national security" of the U.S., but this statement is neither explained nor substantiated. It seems to me that if a greater amount of government funding is dedicated to scientific research, the budgets of other programs and departments will have to be cut, which could have serious negative impacts on national security, and possibly also the economy. If the editorial were to compare the hundreds of millions needed to fund research into alternatives to oil with the hundreds of billions spent each year on national security, then the argument would be stronger.

Clearly, the author of this editorial has made several assumptions about his/her readers, the most important probably being that readers of this business newsletter are familiar with this issue and will be able to provide the details of government funding and alternative fuel research lacking in the editorial. The evidence that the author does provide is strong. The editorial's conclusions seem valid. However, the editorial lacks the necessary foundation of facts and reasoning that would demonstrate, for example, why funding alternative fuel research now will allow new fuel technologies to gradually replace dependence on oil before a crisis hits.

This editorial discusses a very important issue and raises the critical subject of government funding for research into alternative fuels. However, the author has not provided much evidence or reasoning behind the conclusion that the U.S. government should fund this research.

Discussion of sample essay #3

This response is well developed and clearly articulated. The essay begins with a very strong introductory paragraph that develops the position, credits the editorial's strong points, and then clearly states the thesis that the author has made too many assumptions and not provided the necessary evidence. From the start, this essay appears to merit a 5 or 6.

The middle three paragraphs provide specific examples of assumptions that the editorial makes and indicate how the author could strengthen the argument. The first example is the assumption that the reader will know that alternative fuel technologies take a long time to develop. This essay provides the specific examples that the editorial itself lacked. The next paragraph discusses the claim that the economy and national security depend on alternative fuels. This is probably the weakest paragraph in the essay. The essay sidesteps the editorial's point when the essay turns to the issue of reducing the budgets of other programs. Still, this is a well-written paragraph that does offer valid suggestions for strengthening the editorial. The fourth paragraph ties everything together by pointing out the specific assumptions that the editorial is making about its readers. This paragraph demonstrates the sophistication of the essay by pointing out the editorial's intended audience, the weaknesses of the assumptions it makes, its strengths, and finally, ways to make the editorial better.

This essay is strong or outstanding because it's specific and well developed. The essay singles out particular points in the editorial and explains not only the weaknesses of those points but also ways to make them stronger. It provides a clear introduction and thesis statement. The conclusion is brief and fulfills it purpose of restating the thesis. The diction used in this essay is precise and descriptive. The sentences are simple but varied, and they mostly demonstrate active rather than passive voice. There are no obvious errors in grammar, usage, or mechanics. This essay overall is outstanding and would likely garner a 6, definitely nothing lower than a 5.

Now that you know how to score essays and what makes an essay merely adequate or absolutely outstanding, you're ready to write some outstanding essays of your own.

Part IV

Conquering the Quantitative Section

In this part . . .

Here it is — the long-awaited math review! And we give you a thorough going-over of all the important and most commonly tested math concepts on the GMAT. We start with the basics, like fundamental operations, fractions, and exponents, because you don't want to miss the easy points. Then we take you on a trip down memory lane with good old algebra. Remember quadratic equations and functions? If not, don't despair. They're covered here.

The GMAT plane and coordinate geometry questions ask you to measure lines, angles, arcs, and the shapes they create, like rectangles and triangles. We remind you of the formulas for finding area and perimeter, and we give you timesaving tips for finding side lengths of triangles. Speaking of formulas, we also review the ones you need to find the distance between points on the coordinate plane and the slope of a line. After reading this part, you'll be in good shape for the geometry problems on the GMAT.

It is decidedly probable that a good percentage of your GMAT quantitative section will cover statistics and probability, so this part provides you with the highlights of data interpretation, probability, and sets, from the essential concepts of mean and mode to more complex calculations of standard deviation and probability.

And you may be surprised to see that the GMAT math questions come in two varieties: the standard five-answer, multiple-choice, problem-solving kind and something called data sufficiency. Data sufficiency questions can be a bit tricky if you've never seen them before, but this part tells you exactly how to handle them like a pro.

Our computations predict that you'll have a high degree of success on math questions after you study Part IV, and to prove it, we end this part with a mini test so you can see how much you've learned.

Chapter 10

Getting Back to Basics: Numbers and Operations

Those of you who majored in math in college probably look at the math section of the GMAT like an old friend. Those of you who haven't stepped into a math class since high school are more likely dreading it. You know who you are! Don't worry, this chapter will take you back to the beginning with a review of the concepts you've learned through the years but may have temporarily forgotten. You'll see problems that test your knowledge of the math building blocks, like types of numbers, basic operations, exponents and radicals, fractions, and ratios. These concepts form the foundation of more complicated math problems, so this stuff is important to know. For instance, you could end up with a completely wrong answer if you solve for whole numbers when the question asked for integers. Some GMAT takers may end up kicking themselves (and that just looks plain odd) for missing relatively simple problems because they were unfamiliar with some basic terminology. To avoid this unfortunate (and awkward) position, make sure you're well heeled in math basics.

Just Your Type: Kinds of Numbers

Since the Stone Age, humans have found it necessary to rely on numbers in order to get through daily living. In hunter/gatherer cultures, the people made notches in bones to count, for example, the number of days in a lunar cycle or perhaps to indicate how long the nomadic tribe spent in a particular location until they got food. But humankind soon realized over the millennia that these numbers would become large and unwieldy, especially if a cave-woman were to ask the Neanderthal of the house to bring home two dozen carcasses of elk while she went out and drew eight gallons of water from the pond. Things would have gotten downright silly.

In a sense, modern numbers and arithmetic have simplified matters. Although mathematical operations may have burst prehistoric man's cerebral cortex, number systems may have made more sense to them in the long run, and they'll surely come easily for you. For the GMAT, you need to know the more common types of numbers, like natural numbers, integers, real numbers, and prime numbers. And it's good to be able to identify some of the less common types, like rational, irrational, and imaginary numbers.

Counting on it: Natural numbers

Where the cave man made notches on bones to note the passing of the days in the month, the modern day kindergartner counts on her fingers. *Natural numbers* are the numbers you use to count things with, starting with 1, 2, 3, 4, 5, and so on. You may also see natural numbers referred to as *positive integers*. Because they're positive, they *don't* include zero, which is neither positive nor negative. The set of counting numbers that includes zero is the set called *whole numbers*. In other words, whole numbers are all numbers in the following series: 0, 1, 2, 3, 4, 5, and so on. Whole numbers can also be referred to as non-negative integers. It'd be great if everything else in the math sections were as easy as 1-2-3!

Taking the negative with the positive: Integers

Integers belong to the set of all positive and negative whole numbers with zero included. Integers aren't fractions or decimals or portions of a number, so they really have it all together, which gives them their integrity. Integers include –5, –4, –3, –2, –1, 0, 1, 2, 3, 4, and 5 and continue infinitely on either side of zero. Integers greater than zero are called natural numbers or positive integers. Integers less than zero are called negative integers. And zero is neither positive nor negative.

Digging the division: Rational numbers

Rational numbers are expressed as the *ratio* of one integer to another; that is, they're numbers that are expressed as fractions. Rational numbers include all positive and negative integers, plus fractions and decimal numbers that either end or repeat. For example, the fraction $\frac{1}{3}$ can be expressed as 0.33333... . Rational numbers don't include numbers like π or radicals like $\sqrt{2}$ because such numbers can't be expressed as fractions consisting of only two integers.

Keeping it real: Real numbers

Real numbers cast the widest net of all. They include all numbers that you normally think of and deal with in everyday life. Real numbers belong to the set that includes all whole numbers, fractions, and rational as well as irrational numbers. You can think of real numbers as those numbers represented by all the points on a number line, either positive or negative. Real numbers are also those numbers you use to measure length, volume, or weight. In fact, it's hard to imagine a number that isn't a real number (for more on imaginary numbers, see "Using your head: Irrational and imaginary numbers"). When you think of almost any number, assume it's a real number. When the GMAT asks you to give an answer expressed in terms of real numbers, just solve the problem as you normally would.

An irrational feat with an irrational number

Recently, a team of computer engineers in Japan calculated π out to over 1.24 *trillion* decimal digits. It still didn't end, meaning that π is truly irrational. And it may be irrational to attempt to prove otherwise! Thankfully, the GMAT won't ask you to attempt this task or anything remotely like it.

Getting primed for success: Prime numbers

Prime numbers are all of the positive integers that can be divided by only themselves and 1. One isn't a prime number. Two is the smallest of the prime numbers, and it also carries the distinction of being the only even prime number. This doesn't mean that all odd numbers are prime numbers, though. Zero can never be a prime number because you can divide zero by every natural number there is. To determine prime numbers, just think of this series of numbers: 2, 3, 5, 7, 11, 13, 17, 19, 23, 29, and so on. What makes these numbers unique is that the only two factors for these numbers are 1 and the number itself.

You probably won't encounter this term on the GMAT, but in case it comes up at cocktail parties, natural numbers that aren't prime numbers are call *composite numbers*. A composite number is composed of more than two factors. It is the product of more than simply itself and the number 1. The lonely number 1 doesn't get to be included in this set of numbers either.

Prime numbers appear fairly frequently in GMAT math sections. Here's a sample of what you may see:

EXAMPLE

Which of the following expresses 60 as a product of prime numbers?

(A) $2 \times 2 \times 3 \times 5$

(B) $2 \times 2 \times 15$

(C) $2 \times 3 \times 3 \times 5$

(D) $2 \times 3 \times 5$

(E) $1 \times 2 \times 5 \times 6$

This question tests your knowledge of prime numbers. Because the correct answer has to be a series of prime numbers, eliminate any choice that contains a composite (or non-prime) number. This means that B and E are out (even though the product of both is 60) because 15, 1, and 6 aren't prime numbers. Then eliminate any answers that don't equal 60 when you multiply them. C is 90 and D is 30, so the answer must be A. It's the correct answer because it contains only prime numbers and they equal 60 when you multiply them together.

Using your head: Irrational and imaginary numbers

The GMAT won't test you directly about irrational and imaginary numbers, but you should know their definitions for some of the more abstract math problems you'll encounter. Here they are in a nutshell:

✔ **An irrational number is any real number that isn't a rational number.** In other words, just take the definition of rational number and consider its opposite. You'll figure out that an irrational number is one that can't be expressed as a fraction or ratio of one integer to another. Irrational numbers are numbers like π or any radical such as $\sqrt{2}$ that can't be simplified any further. An irrational number, if expressed as a decimal, goes on forever without repeating itself.

✔ **An imaginary number is any number that isn't a real number.** Therefore, an imaginary number is a number like $\sqrt{-2}$. Think about it: You know when you square any positive or negative real number, the result is a positive number. This means you can't find the square root of a negative number unless it's simply not a real number. So imaginary numbers include square roots of negative numbers or any number containing the number i, which represents the square root of –1. Won't you be a fascinating conversationalist at your next soiree!

It's Not Brain Surgery: Basic Operations

Now that you're a bit more comfortable with the terms, it's time to take a stab at manipulating numbers. Figuring out how to do operations is pretty simple, almost as simple as 1-2-3. And playing with numbers can be even more interesting than hearing about the numbers themselves. It doesn't take a brain surgeon to open your mind to endless possibilities.

Figuring with the fabulous four: Adding, subtracting, multiplying, and dividing

You're probably pretty familiar with the standard operations of addition, subtraction, multiplication, and division. But even these math basics have some tricky elements that you may need to refresh your memory on.

Putting two and two together: Addition

Adding's pretty simple. Addition is just the operation of combining two or more numbers to get an end result called the sum. For instance, here's a simple addition problem:

$$3 + 4 + 5 = 12$$

But addition also has two important properties that you may remember from elementary school: the associative property and the commutative property. It's important that you understand these simple concepts for the GMAT math questions:

✔ **The associative property states that the order in which you choose to add up three or more numbers doesn't change the result.** It shows how numbers can group differently with one another and still produce the same answer. So regardless of whether you add 3 and 4 together first and then add 5 or add 4 and 5 together followed by 3, you'll still get an answer of 12.

$$(3 + 4) + 5 = 12$$
$$3 + (4 + 5) = 12$$

✔ **The commutative property states that it doesn't matter what order you use to add the same numbers.** Regardless of what number you list first in a set of numbers, they always produce the same sum. So 2 + 3 = 5 is the same as 3 + 2 = 5.

Depleting the supply: Subtraction

Subtraction, as you probably know, is the opposite of addition. You take away a value from another value and end up with the difference. So if 3 + 4 = 7, then 7 – 4 = 3.

But in subtraction, unlike addition, order does matter, so neither the associative property nor the commutative property applies. You get completely different answers for 3 – 4 – 5 = ? depending on what method you use to associate the values. Here's what we mean.

$$(3 - 4) - 5 = -6$$

but

$$3 - (4 - 5) = 4$$

The order of the values counts in subtraction, too. 3 – 4 is not the same as 4 – 3. 3 – 4 is –1, but 4 – 3 is 1.

Increasing by leaps and bounds: Multiplication

Think of multiplication as repeated addition with an end result called the *product*. 3×5 is the same as 5 + 5 + 5. They both equal 15.

In the GMAT questions, you may see several signs that represent the multiplication operation. A multiplication sign could be designated by $\times$ or simply with a dot, $\cdot$. And in many instances, especially when variables are involved (for more about variables, see Chapter 11), multiplication can be indicated by just putting the factors right next to each other. So ab means the same thing as $a \times b$, and $2a$ is the same as $2 \times a$. One of these back-to-back factors may appear in parentheses: 2(3) means 2×3.

Multiplication is like addition in that the order of the values doesn't matter. So it obeys the commutative property:

$$a \times b = b \times a$$

And the associative property:

$$(a \times b) \times c = a \times (b \times c)$$

There's even another property associated with multiplication, and that's the distributive property. So you may encounter this multiplication problem:

$$a (b + c) =$$

You solve it by distributing the a to b and c, which means that you multiply a and b to get ab and then a and c to get ac, and then you add the results together like this: $a (b + c) = ab + ac$.

Sharing the wealth: Division

Finally, there's division, which you can consider to be the opposite of multiplication. With division, you split one value into smaller values. The end result is called the *quotient*. So whereas $3 \times 5 = 15$, $15 \div 5 = 3$ and $15 \div 3 = 5$.

As in subtraction, order matters in division, so it doesn't follow either the commutative or associative properties. Also, just so you're familiar with any terms you may encounter on the GMAT, the number at the beginning of any equation using division (15 in the last expression) is called the *dividend* and the number that goes into the dividend is the *divisor* (3 in the last expression).

The division sign may be represented by a fraction bar. For more information on fractions, see "Splitting Up: Fractions, Decimals, and Percentages," later in this chapter.

Checking out the real estate: Properties of real numbers

In addition to basic operations, the GMAT will expect you to know the fundamental properties of the numbers you're working with. These include absolute values, evens and odds, and positives and negatives.

Absolutes do exist: Absolute value

To simplify things, just think of the absolute value of any real number as that same number without a negative sign. It's the value of the distance a particular number is from zero on a number line. The symbol for absolute value is $|\ |$, so the absolute value of 3 would be written mathematically as $|3|$. And because the number 3 sits three spaces from zero on the number line, $|3| = 3$. Likewise, because -3 sits three spaces from zero on the number line, its absolute value is also 3: $|-3| = 3$.

The GMAT loves to trip students up when dealing with multiple numbers and absolute values. Remember that absolute value pertains only to the value contained within the absolute value bars. So if you see a negative sign outside the bars, the resulting value is negative. For instance, $-|-3| = -3$ because although the absolute value of -3 is 3, the negative sign outside the bars makes the end result a negative.

A balancing act: Even and odd numbers

We're pretty sure you know that *even numbers* are integers divisible by two: 2, 4, 6, 8, 10, and so on.

And *odd numbers* are those whole numbers that aren't divisible by two: 1, 3, 5, 7, 9, 11, and so on.

You're probably with us so far, but what's important to remember for the GMAT is what happens to even or odd numbers when you add, subtract, or multiply them by one another.

Here are the rules regarding evens and odds for addition and subtraction:

- When you add or subtract two even integers, your result is an even integer.
- When you add or subtract two odd integers, your result is also even.
- If you add or subtract an even integer and an odd integer, your result is an odd integer.

Here's what you should know about multiplying even and odd integers:

- When you multiply an even number by even number, you get an even number.
- When you multiply an odd number by even number, you also get an even number.
- The only time you get an odd number is when you multiply an odd number by another odd number.

Division rules are a little more complex because the quotients aren't always integers; sometimes they're fractions. But there are still a few rules to know:

- ✔ When you divide an even integer by an odd integer, you get an even integer or a fraction.

- ✔ An odd integer divided by another odd integer results in an odd integer or a fraction.

- ✔ An even integer divided by another even integer could result in either an odd or even quotient, so that's not very helpful.

- ✔ When you divide an odd integer by an even one, you always get a fraction; because fractions aren't integers, the quotient for this scenario is neither odd nor even.

You may be wondering why you need to know this. Here's why: Memorizing these rules can be a big timesaver when it comes to eliminating answer choices. For instance, if you have a multiplication problem involving large even numbers, you know you can eliminate any odd-number answer choices without even doing the math! Here's a sample question that shows you just how valuable knowing the rules can be.

If *a* and *b* are different prime numbers, which of the following numbers must be odd?

(A) *ab*

(B) $4a + b$

(C) $a + b + 3$

(D) $ab - 3$

(E) $4a + 4b + 3$

To solve this number theory question, think of numbers for *a* and *b* that represent their possible values. Then substitute these values into the answer choices to eliminate all that could be even. When considering values for *a* and *b*, make sure to include two because it's the only even prime number. Neither one nor zero is an option because neither is prime.

Substitute 2 for *a* or *b*, in A and you'll see that it could be even because the rules tell you that any time you multiply an even number by another number, you get an even number. You also know that B could be even because 4 (an even number) times any number is an even number. If $b = 2$ and you added that to $4a$, you'd be adding two even numbers, which always gives you an even sum. Again, if $b = 2$ in C, then *a* would have to be an odd prime number. You add *a* (odd) to *b* (even) to get an odd sum. Then you add that odd number to the odd number 3, which results in an even number. D could be even if both *a* and *b* are odd. An odd number times an odd number is an odd number. When you subtract an odd number, like 3, from another odd number, you get an even number.

By process of elimination, the answer must be E. It doesn't matter whether *a* or *b* in E is even or odd. $4a$ and $4b$ will always be even, because anytime you multiply an even number another number, you get an even number. When you add two evens, you get an even number, so $4a + 4b$ is an even number. And because an even number plus an odd number is always odd, when you add that even result to 3, you'll get an odd number, always. The correct answer is E.

Half empty or half full: Positive and negative numbers

Positive and negative numbers have their own set of rules regarding operations, and they're even more important to remember than those for even and odd integers. Here's what you need to know for multiplying and dividing:

- When you multiply or divide two positive numbers, the result is positive.
- When you multiply or divide two negative numbers, the result is also positive.
- Multiplying or dividing a negative number by a positive number gives you a negative result (as does dividing a positive number by a negative number).

As you may expect, there are also some things you need to know about adding and subtracting positives and negatives:

- When you add two positive numbers, your result is a positive number.
- If you subtract a negative number from another number, you end up adding it to that number. For instance, $x - (-3)$ is the same thing as $x + 3$.

Using Little Numbers for Big Values: Bases and Exponents

As multiplication can be thought of as repeated addition, you can think of exponents as repeated multiplication; you multiply a number times itself. This means that 4^3 is the same as $4 \times 4 \times 4$ or 64.

In the example, you refer to 4 as the *base* and the superscript 3 as the *exponent*. If you add a variable into this mix, such as $4b^3$, then the base becomes b and the 4 becomes known as the *coefficient*. In our example, the coefficient 4 is simply multiplied by b^3.

As a high school algebra teacher used to scream (usually when he caught his students napping): "The power governs only the number immediately below it!" (that is, the base). So the exponent doesn't affect the coefficient. Only the base gets squared or cubed or whatever the exponent says to do.

This brings up some fascinating properties regarding positive and negative bases and even and odd exponents:

- A positive number taken to an even or odd power remains positive.
- A negative number taken to an odd power remains negative.
- A negative number taken to an even power becomes positive.

What all of this means is that any number taken to an even power either remains or becomes positive and any number taken to an odd power keeps the sign it began with. Another interesting tidbit to digest is that any term with an odd power that results in a negative number will have a negative root, and this is the only possible root for the expression. For example, if $a^3 = -125$, then $a = -5$. That is, the cubed root of -125 is -5.

On the other hand, anytime you have an exponent of 2, there are two potential roots, one positive and one negative, for the expression. For example, if $a^2 = 64$, then $a = 8$ or -8. So there are two possible square roots of 64, either 8 or -8.

Adding and subtracting exponents

The only catch to adding or subtracting exponents is that the base and exponent of each term must be the same. So you can add and subtract like terms such as $4a^2$ and a^2 like this: $4a^2 + a^2 = 5a^2$ and $4a^2 - a^2 = 3a^2$. Notice that the base and exponent remain the same and that the coefficient is the only number that changes in the equation.

Multiplying and dividing exponents

The rules regarding multiplying and dividing exponents are pretty numerous, so to keep them straight, we've set up Table 10-1 for you. The table describes each rule and then gives you an example or two.

Table 10-1	Rules for Multiplying and Dividing Exponents
Rule	**Examples**
To multiply terms with exponents and the same bases, add the exponents.	$a^2 \times a^3 = a^5$ $a \times a^2 = a^3$
If the expression contains coefficients, multiply the coefficients as you normally would.	$4a^2 \times 2a^3 = 8a^5$
When you divide terms with exponents, just subtract the exponents.	$a^5 \div a^3 = a^2$ $a^5 \div a = a^4$
Any coefficients are also divided as usual.	$9a^5 \div 3a^3 = 3a^2$
To multiply and divide exponential terms with different bases, first make sure the exponents are the same. If they are, multiply the coefficients and maintain the same exponent.	$4^3 \times 5^3 = 20^3$ $a^5 \times b^5 = (ab)^5$
Follow the same procedure when you divide exponents with different bases but the same exponents.	$20^3 \div 5^3 = 4^3$ $(ab)^5 \div b^5 = a^5$
When you raise a power to another power, multiply the exponents.	$(a^3)^5 = a^{15}$ $(5^4)^5 = 5^{20}$
If your expression includes a coefficient, take it to the same power.	$(3a^3)^5 = 243a^{15}$

Figuring out the powers of zero and one

Exponents of zero and one have special properties that you'll have to commit to memory:

- The value of a base with an exponent of zero power (like 7^0) is always 1.
- The value of a base with an exponent of one (like 3^1) is the same value as the base ($3^1 = 3$).

Proving the special powers of one and zero

For those skeptics out there, we'll show you why the rules regarding exponents of zero and one are true by plugging some values into equations and following the rules back in Table 10-1. First consider an exponent of zero using this equation:

$4^4 \div 4^4 = ?$ (Divide 4^4 by 4^4 by subtracting the exponents and keeping the base the same.)

$4^4 \div 4^4 = 4^0$ (Substitute 1 for 4^0)

$4^4 \div 4^4 = 1$

To check the equation, solve for the exponents.

$4^4 \div 4^4 = 4^0$

$256 \div 256 = 1$

A base to the zero power does indeed equal one.

Now consider an exponent of one using this equation:

$4^4 \div 4^3 = ?$ (Divide 4^4 by 4^3 by subtracting the exponents and keeping the base the same.)

$4^4 \div 4^3 = 4^1$

$4^4 \div 4^3 = 4$

Check the equation by solving for the exponents.

$4^4 \div 4^3 = 4^1$

$256 \div 64 = 4$

The value of a base to the power of one is the same as the value of that base.

The rules check out! Ain't math grand?

Dealing with fractional exponents

If you see a problem with an exponent in fraction form, consider the top number of the fraction (the *numerator*) as your actual exponent and the bottom number (the *denominator*) as the root. So to solve $256^{1/4}$, simply take 256 to the first power (because the numerator of the fraction is one), which is 256. Then take the fourth root of 256 (because the denominator of the fraction is four), which is 4, and that's your answer. Here's what it looks like mathematically:

$$256^{1/4} = \sqrt[4]{256^1} = \sqrt[4]{256} = 4$$

The GMAT may also present you with a variable coefficient and a fractional exponent. You handle those the same way, like this:

$$a^{2/3} = \sqrt[3]{a^2}$$

This is what you get when you take *a* to the second power and then find its cube root.

Working with negative exponents

A negative exponent works very much like a positive exponent, but the end result is, for the most part, a number that's a lot smaller than you began with. A negative exponent takes the positive exponent and then flips it around so that the exponent becomes its reciprocal, like this:

$$3^{-3} = \frac{1}{3^3} = \frac{1}{27}$$

To see how this works, check out a sample problem in which you'd divide two exponential expressions. Remember that when you divide powers having the same base, you subtract the exponents.

$$3^3 \div 3^6 = 3^{-3} = \tfrac{1}{27}$$

When you work with negative exponents, don't fall for the trick of assuming that the negative exponent somehow turns the original number into a negative number. It ain't a gonna happen! For example, $3^{-5} \neq -243$ or $-\tfrac{1}{243}$ or $-\tfrac{1}{15}$ or anything like them.

Checking Out the Ancestry: Roots

If you like exponents, you'll *love* roots. Roots are simply the opposite of exponents. Another name for them is *radicals*. This means that if $3 \times 3 = 9$ or if $3^2 = 9$ or if 3 squared is equal to 9, then the square root of 9 is 3, or $\sqrt{9} = 3$. In this case, the square root, 3, is the number that you'd square to get the number 9. What could be simpler?

There are as many roots as there are powers. Most of the time, the GMAT will have you work with square roots, but you may also see some other roots. That won't intimidate you, though. If you come upon a cube root or fourth root, you'll know what it is by the radical sign.

For example, a cube root might be expressed as $\sqrt[3]{27}$ or written out as the cube root of 27. This expression is asking what number, when raised to the third power, equals 27. Of course, the answer is 3 because 3 cubed is equal to 27, or $3^3 = 27$.

Radicals, even the seemingly ugly ones, can often be simplified. For example, if you see a number such as $\sqrt{98}$, don't panic! Just determine the factors of 98 to find values that you *can* determine the square root of.

To factor $\sqrt{98}$, consider that $98 = 49 \times 2$. Put these factors under the radical sign and you get a much prettier and more manageable $\sqrt{49 \times 2}$. Because 49 is the perfect square of 7, you can extract the 49 from under the radical sign. You know that 49 is 7^2, so you can remove the 7 and place it outside the radical sign. This leaves you with this simplified expression: $\sqrt{98} = 7\sqrt{2}$. See how you may encounter this situation on the GMAT:

If $\sqrt[n]{512} = 4\sqrt[n]{2}$, then $n = ?$

(A) 1

(B) 2

(C) 3

(D) 4

(E) 5

You can solve this equation most easily by simplifying the radical. The n root of 512 is equal to 4 times the n root of 2. $512 = 2 \times 256$, and $256 = 4 \times 4 \times 4 \times 4$ or 4^4. So the fourth root of 512 equals 4 times the fourth root of 2. $n = 4$, and D is the correct answer.

Because roots are the opposite of exponents, they obey the same rules when it comes to performing operations with them. You can add and subtract roots as long as the roots are of the same order (that is, square root, cube root, and so on) and the roots are of the same number. Here are a couple examples:

$$5\sqrt[3]{7} + 6\sqrt[3]{7} = 11\sqrt[3]{7}$$

$$11\sqrt{a} - 5\sqrt{a} = 6\sqrt{a}$$

When you need to multiply or divide radicals, make sure the roots are of the same order and you're good to go! For multiplication, just multiply what's under the radical signs, like this:

$$\sqrt[3]{9} \times \sqrt[3]{3} = \sqrt[3]{9 \times 3} = \sqrt[3]{27} = 3$$

Divide what's under the radical signs like this:

$$\sqrt[4]{7} \div \sqrt[4]{3} = \sqrt[4]{7/3}$$

And here's how a question regarding operations with roots may appear on the GMAT:

$$\sqrt{16 + 9} = ?$$

(A) 5

(B) 7

(C) 12½.

(D) 25

(E) 625

When you add radicals, pay attention to the values underneath the radical. In this question, the line of the square root symbol extends over the entire expression, so you're supposed to find the square root of 16 + 9, not $\sqrt{16} + \sqrt{9}$. It's a subtle but major difference!

Order of Operations: Please Excuse My Dear Aunt Sally

Basic arithmetic requires that you perform the operations in a certain order from left to right. Okay, so maybe you don't have an aunt named Sally, but the acronym in the title is a helpful mnemonic for the order you use when you have to perform several operations in one problem. What that means is that if you have an expression that contains addition, subtraction, multiplication, division, exponents (and roots), and parentheses to boot, then it helps to know which operation you perform first, second, third, and so on.

The acronym, **P**lease **E**xcuse **M**y **D**ear **A**unt **S**ally can help you remember to perform operations in the following order:

- **P**arentheses

- **E**xponents (and roots)

- **M**ultiplication and **D**ivision

- **A**ddition and **S**ubtraction

Here's an example:

$$20(4 - 7)^3 + 15(\tfrac{9}{3})^1 = x$$

First, evaluate what's inside the parentheses:

$$20 \cdot (-3)^3 + 15(3)^1 = x$$

Then evaluate the exponents:

$$20 \cdot (-27) + 15(3) = x$$

Then multiply:

$$-540 + 45 = x$$

Finally, do the addition and subtraction from left to right:

$$-495 = x$$

First add the values under the radical sign: 16 + 9 = 25. The square root of 25 is 5, so A is the correct answer. If you chose 7, you determined the square root of each of the values before you added them together. $\sqrt{16}$ (or 4) plus $\sqrt{9}$ (or 3) is 7. For 7 to be the correct answer, your problem should have been written with two separate square root signs, one over the 16 and one over the 9.

Splitting Up: Fractions, Decimals, and Percentages

Fractions, decimals, and percentages are interrelated concepts that generally work very well with one another. They all represent parts of a whole. It's likely that you'll need to convert from one form to the other to solve several problems on the GMAT math.

Fractions are really answers to division problems. If you divide the number *a* by the number *b*, then you get the fraction $\frac{a}{b}$. So $1 \div 4 = \frac{1}{4}$.

To convert the fraction to a decimal, you simply perform the division indicated by the fraction bar: $\frac{1}{4} = 1 \div 4 = 0.25$

To convert a decimal back to a fraction, you first count the digits to the right of the decimal point; then divide the original number over a 1 followed by the same number of zeroes as there were digits to the right of the decimal. Then you simplify. So $0.25 = \frac{25}{100}$, which simplifies to $\frac{1}{4}$; $0.356 = \frac{356}{1,000}$, which is $\frac{89}{250}$ in its simplest form.

Changing a decimal to a percent is really pretty easy. Percent simply means per one hundred, or $\div 100$. To perform the conversion, you move the decimal two places to the right. Then you write the resulting number as a percent. For example, 0.25 = 25%, and 0.925 = 92.5%.

To turn a percent back into a decimal, you follow the procedure in reverse. You move the decimal point two spaces to the left and lose the percent sign, like this: 1% = 0.01

Converting takes a little practice, so we give you an exercise in Table 10-2. Provide the proper conversion for the missing information in the table. You can find the solutions in a box at the end of this chapter if you need them.

Table 10-2	Practice Exercise for Converting Fractions, Decimals, and Percentages	
Fraction	**Decimal**	**Percent**
½	0.5	50%
		7.8%
	5.2	
$\frac{7}{16}$		
	0.37	

The GMAT probably won't specifically ask you to express answers in all three formats (fractions, decimals, and percentages), but you need to know that answer choices can appear in any one of the three formats when you're dealing with percentage problems.

You may encounter a GMAT problem that asks you to find the portion of garbage that's paper when you know that 215 million tons of garbage are generated every year and about 86 million tons of the yearly total garbage are paper products. You should be able to express the answer as a fraction, decimal, and percent:

- As a fraction: $^{86}/_{215}$ or $^{2}/_{5}$
- As a decimal: $^{2}/_{5}$ = $^{4}/_{10}$ or 0.4
- As a percent: 0.4 = 40%

Defining numerators, denominators, and other stuff you need to know about fractions

GMAT questions may refer to the numerator or the denominator or some other such verbiage that you may have studied at one time but may have forgotten when you began to learn how to ride a bike. Remember that fractions are just an expression of the value of a part as compared to the whole. This word problem provides an illustration.

Picture a cherry pie sliced into eight equal pieces and a hungry family of seven, each of whom has a slice after dinner (or before dinner if they're sneaky). Figure 10-1 gives you a picture of the yummy pie.

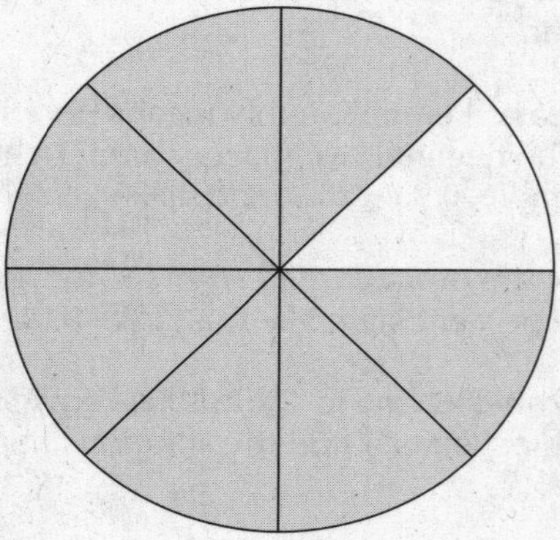

Figure 10-1: Fraction of a pie.

The shaded pieces of pie in Figure 10-1 show how much of the dessert was gobbled up by the family; the unshaded piece shows what's left of the pie when the family is finished.

To put this pie into terms of a fraction, the total number of pieces in the pie to begin with (the whole) represents the denominator, and the number of pieces that were eaten up (the part of the whole) is represented by the numerator. In this case, the number of pieces that were eaten made up $^{7}/_{8}$ of the total pie, so 7 is the numerator and 8 is the denominator. To look at the scenario another way, you could say that the fraction of pie that was left is $^{1}/_{8}$ of what you started with. The numerator and denominator are also known as the *terms* of the fraction.

Proper fractions are those fractions in which the numerator is less than the denominator. Examples of proper fractions are $^{3}/_{4}$, $^{7}/_{8}$, and $^{13}/_{15}$.

Improper fractions are those fractions in which the numerator is either greater than or equal to the denominator. Here are some examples of fractions that aren't fit for proper society: $^{15}/_{2}$, $^{5}/_{3}$, and $^{8}/_{5}$.

You can also show an improper fraction as a mixed fraction, which is made up of a whole number and a fraction. Examples of mixed fractions are $1\frac{1}{2}$, $7\frac{3}{4}$, and $2\frac{2}{3}$.

When you work with fractions on the GMAT, you may have to substitute mixed fractions for improper fractions and vice versa. You'll find that it's often easier to change a mixed fraction into an improper fraction before you perform operations. To change a mixed fraction to an improper fraction, you multiply the whole number by the denominator, add the numerator, and put that value over the original denominator, like this:

$$2\frac{2}{3} = \frac{8}{3}$$

In other words, multiply the whole number (2) by the denominator (3) to get 6; add the numerator (2), which gives you 8; and place that value over the original denominator.

To convert an improper fraction to a mixed number, you divide the numerator by the denominator and put the remainder over the denominator, like this:

$$\frac{31}{4} = 7\frac{3}{4}$$

Divide 31 by 4. 4 goes into 31 seven times with a remainder of 3 ($4 \times 7 = 28$ and $31 - 28 = 3$). Put the remainder over the original denominator, and place that fraction next to the whole number, 7.

Another handy tip for working with fractions involves simplifying fractions. You're probably thinking that these fractions are simple enough, that it just can't get any easier. Simplifying a fraction means reducing it to its simplest terms. Anytime you can take greater terms in a fraction and make them smaller, you're simplifying the fraction. All you do is take the larger terms and make them smaller by dividing both the numerator and denominator by the same number. Here's an example of reducing or simplifying a fraction:

$\frac{12}{36}$ = ? (Both 12 and 36 are divisible by 12: $12 \div 12 = 1$, and $36 \div 12 = 3$)

$\frac{12}{36} = \frac{1}{3}$

Not only will you need to reduce fractions, but you'll also need to make the terms of the fraction bigger for some problems on the GMAT. This happens when you have to add or subtract fractions with different denominators. To make the terms of a fraction larger, you just multiply the numerator and denominator by the same value. Even though the numerator and denominator of the new fraction are larger than the original fraction, the two fractions still represent the same value.

Trading places: Reciprocals

A reciprocal is just the flip-flop of a fraction, a fraction in reverse order. To get the reciprocal of a whole number, you simply divide one by your number. So the reciprocal of 5 is $1 \div 5$ or simply $\frac{1}{5}$. The reciprocal of a fraction is the flipside of its numerator and denominator. So the reciprocal of $\frac{3}{5}$ is $\frac{5}{3}$. If you're working with variables, you need to know that the reciprocal of a variable, like a, is $\frac{1}{a}$, just as long as $a \neq 0$. You won't need to know this for the GMAT, but for the sake of accumulating meaningless information, we'll let you know that the reciprocal of a number is also known as the *multiplicative inverse*.

Adding and subtracting fractions

Because fractions are parts of whole numbers, they're not as easy to put together as 2 + 2. To add or subtract fractions, all the fractions have to have the same denominator. Then all you do is either add or subtract the numerators and put that value over the original denominator, like this:

$\frac{2}{5} + \frac{3}{5} = \frac{5}{5}$

$\frac{5}{5} - \frac{3}{5} = \frac{2}{5}$

But you won't always be asked to add and subtract fractions with the same denominators. You may see something like this: $\frac{2}{3} + \frac{3}{4} = x$

The key is to find the least common denominator when adding and subtracting fractions with different denominators. Because your denominators here are 3 and 4, you need to find a number that both 3 and 4 will go into evenly. If you multiply 3 by 4, you get the number 12, so you know that both 3 and 4 go into 12 and that just so happens to be the least common denominator. Convert $\frac{2}{3}$ to $\frac{8}{12}$ by multiplying the numerator and denominator by 4. Convert $\frac{3}{4}$ to $\frac{9}{12}$ by multiplying both terms by 3. Add up the two new fractions, and you have your answer:

$\frac{8}{12} + \frac{9}{12} = \frac{17}{12}$ or $1\frac{5}{12}$

Multiplying and dividing fractions

Multiplying fractions is easy. Just multiply the numerators by each other, and then do the same with the denominators. Reduce if you have to:

$\frac{4}{5} \times \frac{5}{7} = (4 \times 5)/(5 \times 7) = \frac{20}{35} = \frac{4}{7}$

An even easier and faster (and faster is better on the GMAT) way to perform this task would be to simply cancel out those fives that appear in the denominator of the first fraction and the numerator of the second one. Here's what that looks like:

$$\frac{4}{\underset{1}{\cancel{5}}} \times \frac{\cancel{5}^{1}}{7}$$

$$\frac{4}{1} \times \frac{1}{7} = \frac{4}{7}$$

Dividing fractions is pretty much the same as multiplying them except for one very important additional step. First, find the reciprocal of the second fraction in the equation (that is, turn the second fraction upside down). Then multiply (yes, multiply) the numerators and denominators of the resulting fractions. Here's how:

$\frac{2}{7} \div \frac{3}{5} = x$

$\frac{2}{7} \times \frac{5}{3} = x$

$\frac{10}{21} = x$

Here are few sample problems for which you need to know how to multiply fractions to solve:

$\frac{1}{2} + (\frac{3}{8} \div \frac{2}{5}) - (\frac{5}{6} \times \frac{7}{8}) = ?$

(A) $\frac{1}{8}$

(B) $\frac{15}{16}$

(C) $\frac{17}{24}$

(D) $\frac{13}{6}$

(E) $\frac{5}{6}$

To solve this problem, you need to do all four operations with fractions. First, figure out the operations inside the parentheses:

$\frac{3}{8} \div \frac{2}{5} = \frac{3}{8} \times \frac{5}{2} = \frac{15}{16}$

$\frac{5}{6} \times \frac{7}{8} = \frac{35}{48}$

Now the equation reads like this:

$\frac{1}{2} + \frac{15}{16} - \frac{35}{48}$

The common denominator is 48. To convert the denominator 2 in the first fraction to 48, you multiply by 24. $1 \times 24 = 24$, so $\frac{1}{2}$ is the same as saying $\frac{24}{48}$.

To convert the denominator 16 in the second fraction to 48, you need to multiply by 3. $3 \times 15 = 45$, so $\frac{15}{16} = \frac{45}{48}$.

Now you have the following expression:

$\frac{24}{48} + \frac{45}{48} - \frac{35}{48} = \frac{34}{48}$

$\frac{34}{48}$ is not one of your options in this problem, so you need to simplify the fraction. Divide the numerator and denominator by 2 to get $\frac{17}{24}$, which is C.

What is 75% of $7\frac{1}{4}$?

(A) $\frac{37}{130}$

(B) $5\frac{3}{4}$

(C) $5\frac{7}{16}$

(D) $7\frac{3}{4}$

(E) $21\frac{3}{16}$

This question asks you to determine a percent of a fraction. Note that the answers are in fraction form rather than decimal form. You need to work out the problem so that it ends up as a fraction rather than a decimal.

Whenever you see the word *of* in a word problem, you know it means *multiply*. Therefore, you're multiplying 75 percent by $7\frac{1}{4}$. Converted to a fraction, 75 percent is $\frac{3}{4}$, so you're trying to find the answer to $\frac{3}{4} \times 7\frac{1}{4}$. Converting $7\frac{1}{4}$ to a mixed fraction gives you $\frac{29}{4}$, so the answer is $\frac{3}{4} \times \frac{29}{4}$, or $\frac{87}{16}$.

There's no answer choice for $\frac{87}{16}$, so you need to convert it to a mixed fraction. $\frac{87}{16} = 5\frac{7}{16}$, which is C.

You can easily eliminate D and E. Obviously, 75% of $7\frac{1}{4}$ has to be less than $7\frac{1}{4}$.

Calculating percent change

Percent change is the amount a number increases or decreases expressed as a percentage of the original number. For instance, if a store normally sells tennis shoes for $72 and has them on sale for $60, what is the percent of the markdown? To get the percent decrease, simply take the difference in price, which is $12, and divide that number by the original price:

$12 \div 72 = 0.1667$ or $16\frac{2}{3}\%$

If the store increases the marked down price by $16\frac{2}{3}\%$, you may think the price returns to its original value. But that's not right. If you increase the lower price of $60 by 0.1667, you get just about a $10 increase. The price goes from $60 to just about $70:

$60 \times 1.1667 = 70.002$

How can that be? The reason the numbers don't seem to add up is because when you drop the price the first time, you take $16\frac{2}{3}\%$ of $72, which is a bigger number to take a percent of than when you multiply that same percent by the lower sale price.

So what percent of the marked down price of $60 must you increase the price by in order to get the original price of $72? To find out, take the difference in price, $12, and determine what percent that is of the sale price of $60:

$12 \div 60 = \frac{12}{60} = 0.20 = 20\%$

So it's a 20% increase from 60 to 72.

If you know what the percent increase or decrease of an original number is and want to find out how that increase or decrease changes the original number, keep these two important details in mind:

✔ To find the amount of increase, multiply the original number by 1 plus the rate.

✔ To find the amount of decrease, multiply the original number by 1 minus the rate.

For instance, if you increase 100 by 5 percent, you multiply 100 by (1 + 0.05):

$100 \times (1 + 0.05) = 100 \times 1.05 = 105$

If you decrease 100 by 5 percent, you multiply 100 by (1 – 0.05).

$100 \times (1 - 0.05) = 100 \times 0.95 = 95$

Try same sample percent change problems.

A file cabinet that originally cost $52 is on sale at 15% off. If the sales tax on office furniture is 5% of the purchase price, how much would it cost to buy the file cabinet at its sale price?

(A) $7.80

(B) $40.00

(C) $44.20

(D) $46.41

(E) $48.23

This word problem asks you how to deal with two percentages, the subtraction of the percentage discount and the addition of the percentage sales tax. First, calculate the discount.

You can figure 15% in your head by knowing that 10% of 52 is 5.20 and half of that (5 percent) is 2.60, so the discount is $7.80. Now subtract the discount from the original price. $52.00 – $7.80 = $44.20. The discount price for the cabinet is $44.20.

You still need to calculate the sales tax, so don't choose C! 5 percent of 44.20 is half of 4.42 (10 percent), or 2.21. You add $2.21 to $44.20. The only answer that ends in 1 is D. You can do the math to verify your guess, but D is the correct answer. $44.20 + $2.21 = $46.41. Not a bad price for some much needed organization!

Thirty of the seventy male employees in the corporation work part-time. Thirty of the fifty female employees work part-time. What percentage of the employees work part-time?

(A) 40%

(B) 50%

(C) 42⅔%

(D) 60%

(E) 66⅔%

The trick to solving this word problem is to determine the total number of people from which the percentage is derived. You know that there are 70 males and 50 females, so there's a total of 120 employees in the corporation. Thirty males and 30 females (60 total) work part-time. What percentage of 120 is 60? If it isn't immediately obvious, you can determine the answer like this:

Evaluate the question: What percentage of 120 is 60?

- *What* means ? (the unknown), or what you're trying to find out.
- *Percentage* means %.
- *Of* means multiply.
- *Is* means equals.

So the following equation results from the question:

$$?\% \times 120 = 60$$
$$?\% = {}^{60}\!/_{120}$$
$$?\% = 0.50$$
$$? = 50\%$$

The correct answer is B.

Taking it further: Repeated percent change

Now suppose you want to show a percent change repeated over a period of time. One occasion in which this concept is used is when you want to figure out how much interest accrues on a bank account after several years.

Suppose you have $100 in a bank account at the end of 1992 and you want to know how much money is in that same account at the end of 2002 at an interest rate of 5 percent. No fair pulling it out when the stock market is making a bull run! One way to figure this out is by using the percentage increase formula. The first step would look something like this:

$$100 \times (1 + 0.05) = 105$$

So you have $105 at the end of the first year. Then, all you have to do is multiply by 10 and you get $1,050 right? Nope! This type of question will try to trap anyone who isn't paying attention every time.

To get the correct answer, take the same formula and tweak it a bit by adding an exponent. The exponent will be the number of times the original number changes. The formula looks like this, where n is the number of changes:

final amount = original number $\times (1 + \text{rate})^n$

Plug the numbers into the formula and solve:

$$100 \times (1 + 0.05)^{10} =$$
$$100 \times 1.05^{10} =$$
$$100 \times 1.6289 = 162.89$$

So after 10 years, you'd have $162.89 in the bank.

To show a repeated percent *decrease* over time, you'd use this similar formula, where n is the number of changes:

final amount = original number $\times (1 - \text{rate})^n$

Making Comparisons: Ratios and Proportions

A ratio is the relation between two like numbers or two like values. A ratio may be written as a fraction ($\frac{3}{4}$), as a division expression ($3 \div 4$), or with a colon (3:4), or it can be stated as "3 to 4."

Because a ratio can be regarded as a fraction, multiplying or dividing both terms of a ratio by the same number does not change the value of the ratio. So $\frac{1}{4} = \frac{2}{8} = \frac{4}{16}$. To reduce a ratio to its lowest terms, treat the ratio as a fraction and reduce the fraction to its lowest terms.

Ratios often crop up in word problems. Suppose an auto manufacturer ships a total of 160 cars to two dealerships, and the ratio of cars to the two dealers is 3:5. To determine how many cars each dealership receives, add the terms of ratio, or 3 + 5, to get the total number of fractional parts each dealership will get: 3 + 5 = 8. The first dealership will receive $\frac{3}{8}$ of 160 cars, or $\frac{3}{8} \times 160$, which equals 60. The second dealership receives $\frac{5}{8}$ of 160 cars, or 100. As long as the total number of *things* in this type of problem can be evenly divided by the total number of fractional parts, then the answer is workable.

A proportion is a relationship between two equal ratios. It may be written as the proportion sign "::" or with an equal sign. So 1:4 :: 2:8, which you can read as "1 is to 4 as 2 is to 8."

In a proportion, the first and last terms are called the *extremes,* and the second and third terms are called the *means.* If you multiply the means together, multiply the extremes together, and then compare the products, you find that the products are the same:

$$1 \times 8 = 2 \times 4$$

Anytime you know three terms of a proportion, you can find the missing term first by multiplying either the two means or the two extremes (depending on which are known) and then dividing the product by the remaining term.

Here's what a GMAT ratio problem may look like:

If the ratio of $4a$ to $9b$ is 1 to 9, what is the ratio of $8a$ to $9b$?

(A) 1 to 18

(B) 1 to 39

(C) 2 to 9

(D) 2 to 36

(E) 3 to 9

This problem may appear to be more difficult at first than it actually is. If $4a$ is to $9b$ is a 1 to 9 ratio, then $8a$ to $9b$ must be a 2 to 9 ratio, because $8a$ is 2 times $4a$. If $4a = 1$, then $8a$ must $= 2$. The answer is therefore C.

To find a missing value in a ratio, you just set the ratios equal to each other and cross multiply, like this:

$$\tfrac{3}{4} = \tfrac{6}{x}$$
$$4 \times 6 = 3 \times x$$
$$24 = 3x$$
$$8 = x$$

It's very important to remember to keep the elements of your ratios and proportions consistent. For instance, if your proportion is 3 is to 4 as 5 is to x, you must set up the problem in the following manner:

$$\tfrac{3}{4} = \tfrac{5}{x}$$

and not

$$\tfrac{3}{4} = \tfrac{x}{5}$$

Playing the Numbers: Scientific Notation

Scientific notation is simply the way you write out humongous (technical term) or teensy weensy (another technical term) numbers so they're more manageable. You express a number in scientific notation by writing it as the product of a number and a power of 10. Simply move the decimal point so that all digits except one are to the right of the decimal point; then multiply that decimal number times 10 raised to an exponent that equals the number of places you moved the decimal point. If you're working with a large number and you moved the decimal point to the left, the exponent is positive:

$$1,234,567 = 1.234567 \times 10^6$$

$$20 \text{ million } (20,000,000) = 2.0 \times 10^7$$

For very small numbers, you have to move the decimal point to the right. When you move the decimal point to the right, the exponent on the 10 is negative. In this example, the decimal point moved six places to the right:

$$0.0000037 = 3.7 \times 10^{-6}$$

A typical scientific notation problem may appear on the GMAT like this:

The number of organisms in a liter of water is approximately 6.0×10^{23}. Assuming this number is correct and exact, how many organisms are in a covered Petri dish that contains $\frac{1}{200}$ liter of water?

(A) 6.9

(B) 3.0×10^{21}

(C) 6.0×10^{22}

(D) 3.0×10^{23}

(E) 1.2×10^{26}

This question uses many words to ask you to the find the answer to 6.0×10 to the 23rd power divided by 200. If a liter of water contains a certain number of organisms, $\frac{1}{200}$ liter of water would contain the same number of organisms divided by 200. Try not to let the wording of the question confuse you.

6.0 divided by 200 equals 0.03. The answer is 0.03×10 to the 23rd power. None of the answer choices provides this possibility, but if you move the decimal point two places to the right, you have to change the power by decreasing it by two (remember that when you move the decimal point to the right, the exponent is negative, so you subtract). The answer is B, 3.0×10 to the 21st power.

Solution to the Practice Exercise in Table 10-2

If you took the time to complete the exercise on converting fractions, decimals, and percentages in Table 10-2 and would like to know the correct answers, here they are!

Fraction	Decimal	Percent
$\frac{1}{2}$	0.5	50%
$\frac{39}{500}$	0.078	7.8%
$5\frac{1}{5}$	5.2	520%
$\frac{7}{16}$	0.4375	43.75%
$\frac{37}{100}$	0.37	37%

Chapter 11

Considering All the Variables: Algebra

lgebra is the study of properties of operations carried out on sets of numbers. That may sound like mumbo-jumbo, but the idea is that algebra's really just a form of arithmetic in which symbols, usually letters, stand for numbers. You use algebra to solve equations and to find the value of a variable. For example, how often have you heard the command "Solve the equation for x"?

The algebra concepts tested on the GMAT are limited to the ones you'd use in a first-year algebra course, so you're at no disadvantage if you've never taken Algebra II. But you will see many GMAT math problems that involve basic algebra, and this chapter provides you with what you need to know to excel on all of them.

Defining the Elements: Algebraic Terms

Before we jump into solving algebra problems, we'll take the time to define some terms. Although the GMAT won't specifically test you on the meaning of words like *variable, constant,* and *coefficient,* it will expect you to know these concepts when they crop up in the questions.

Braving the unknowns: Variables and constants

You'll see a lot of *variables* in algebra problems. They're the symbols that stand for numbers. Usually the symbols take the form of letters and represent specific numeric values. True to their name, variables' values can change depending on the equation they're in.

Think of variables as abbreviations for discrete things. For example, if a store charges different prices for apples and oranges and you buy two apples and four oranges, the clerk couldn't simply ring them up together by adding 2 + 4 to get 6. That would be incorrectly comparing apples and oranges! So in algebra, you'd use variables to stand in for the price of apples and oranges, something like this: $2a$ and $4o$.

In contrast to variables, *constants,* as their name implies, are numbers with values that don't change in a specific problem. Letters may also be used to refer to constants, but they don't change their value in an equation as variables do (for instance, *a, b,* and *c* stand for fixed numbers in the formula $y = ax^2 + bx + c$).

Coming together: Terms and expressions

Single constants and variables or constants and variables grouped together form terms; *terms* are any set of variables or constants you can multiply or divide to form a single unit in an equation. You can combine these single parts in an equation that applies addition or subtraction. For example, the following algebraic expression has three terms: $ax^2 + bx + c$. The first term is ax^2, the second term is $bx,$ and the third term is c.

Terms often form expressions. An algebraic *expression* is a collection of terms that are combined by addition or subtraction and are often grouped by parentheses, such as $(x + 2)$, $(x - 3c)$, and $(2x - 3y)$. Although an expression can contain just one term, it's more common to think of expressions as combinations of two or more terms. So in the apples and oranges scenario we presented earlier, you can make an expression for combining two apples and four oranges — it may look something like this: $2a + 4o$.

A *coefficient* is a number or symbol that serves as a measure of a property or characteristic. In $2a + 4o$, the variables are a and $o,$ and the numbers 2 and 4 are the coefficients of the variables. This means that the coefficient of the variable a is 2 and the coefficient of the variable o is 4.

In an algebraic expression, terms involving the same variable, even if they have different coefficients, are called *like terms.* For example, in this expression, $3x + 4y - 2x + y,$ $3x$ and $-2x$ are like terms because they both contain the single x variable; $4y$ and y are also like terms because they both contain the y variable and only the y variable.

The variables must be exact matches with the same powers: for instance, $3x^3y$ and x^3y are like terms, but x and x^2 aren't like terms, and neither are $2x$ and $2xy$.

You can combine (add/subtract) like terms together, but you can't combine unlike terms. So in the sample expression, you can subtract the terms with the common x variable: $3x - 2x = x$. And you can add the like terms with the common y variable: $4y + y = 5y$ (if a variable has no visible numerical coefficient, it's understood that its coefficient is 1; therefore, y is understood to be $1y$). All this combining results in the final expression of $x + 5y$, which is a much simpler expression to work with. We work with many more algebraic expressions in "Maintaining an Orderly Fashion: Algebraic Operations" later in this chapter.

Knowing the nomials: Kinds of expressions

Expressions carry particular names depending on how many terms they contain. On the GMAT you'll work with monomials and polynomials.

A *monomial* is an expression that contains only one term, such as $4x$ or ax^2. A monomial is therefore also referred to as a term in an algebraic expression.

Poly means *many*, so we bet you've already figured out that a *polynomial* is an expression that has more than one term. These multiple terms can be added together or subtracted from one another. Here are a couple of examples of polynomials:

$$a^2 - b^2$$
$$ab^2 + 2ac + b$$

Polynomials can have more specific designations, depending on how many terms they contain. For instance, a *binomial* is a specific kind of polynomial, one that contains two terms, such as $a + b$ or $2a + 3$. And a *trinomial* is a polynomial with three terms, like this: $4x^2 + 3y - 8$.

A famous trinomial that you should be very familiar with for the GMAT is the expression known as a *quadratic* polynomial. The classic form of a quadratic polynomial is this trinomial expression:

$$ax^2 + bx + c$$

We'll discuss this very important expression later in "Solving quadratic equations."

Maintaining an Orderly Fashion: Algebraic Operations

Symbols like $+, -, \times, \div, \sqrt{}$ are common to arithmetic and algebra. They symbolize the operations you perform on numbers. Whereas arithmetic uses numbers with known values, such as $5 + 7 = 12$, in its operations (visit Chapter 10 for more on basic arithmetic operations), algebraic operations deal with unknowns, like the following expression: $x + y = z$. This algebraic equation can't produce an exact numerical value because you don't know what x and y represent, let alone z. But that doesn't stop you from solving algebra problems as best you can with the given information.

Adding to and taking away

From arithmetic, you know that 3 dozen plus 6 dozen is 9 dozen, or

$$(3 \times 12) + (6 \times 12) = (9 \times 12)$$

In algebra, you could write a somewhat similar equation using a variable to stand in for the dozen: $3x + 6x = 9x$. And you can subtract to get the opposite result: $9x - 6x = 3x$.

Notice that you can add and subtract like terms. You simply add or subtract the coefficients in the expression and keep the variable the same. But you can't combine terms with different variables in this manner. So if you have this expression, $3x + 5y$, you can't combine or simplify it any further unless you know the actual value of either x or y.

Remember to combine positive and negative numbers according to the rules of arithmetic (see Chapter 10 if you need a refresher). If you add two or more numbers in an expression, they keep the positive sign. If you add a positive to a negative number, it's as though you're subtracting.

For example, to tackle this expression, $7x + -10x + 22x$, you find the sum of the two positive numbers ($7x$ and $22x$) and then subtract the value of the negative number (because adding a negative is the same as subtracting a positive), like this:

$$7x + -10x + 22x$$
$$= 29x - 10x$$
$$= 19x$$

That's fine for adding and subtracting like terms, you may say, but what about working with unlike terms? You can't combine terms with different symbols or variables the same way you can when the symbols are the same. For instance, take a look at this example:

$$7x + 10y + 15x - 3y$$

If you simply combine the whole expression by adding and subtracting without accounting for the different variables, you'd come up with a wrong answer, something like $29xy$. (And you can bet the GMAT will offer this incorrect figure as one of your answer options to try to trap you.) Instead, you first separate the x's from the y's and add and subtract to get something more manageable like this:

$$7x + 15x = 22x$$
$$10y - 3y = 7y$$

This gives you this final expression.

$$22x + 7y$$

Now suppose you want to get tricky and add two or more expressions. You can do that by setting them up just like you may set up an addition problem in arithmetic. Remember, only like terms can be combined together this way.

$$3x + 4y - 7z$$
$$2x - 2y + 8z$$
$$\underline{-x + 3y + 6z}$$
$$4x + 5y + 7z$$

Here's how an algebra problem may look on the GMAT:

For all x and y, $(4x^2 - 6xy - 12y^2) - (8x^2 - 12xy + 4y^2) = ?$

(A) $-4x^2 - 18xy - 16y^2$

(B) $-4x^2 + 6xy - 16y^2$

(C) $-4x^2 + 6xy - 8y^2$

(D) $4x^2 - 6xy + 16y^2$

(E) $12x^2 - 18xy - 8y^2$

The easiest way to approach this problem is to distribute the negative sign to the second expression. Then combine the two expressions with like terms together, like this:

1. **Distribute the negative sign (multiply each term in the second expression by –1).**

   Remember that subtracting is the same as adding a negative number. So your problem is really $(4x^2 – 6xy – 12y^2) + –(8x^2 – 12xy + 4y^2)$. Distributing the negative sign changes the second expression to $–8x^2 + 12xy – 4y^2$, because a negative times a positive makes a negative and two negatives make a positive.

2. **Combine the expressions with like terms together, like this: $4x^2 – 8x^2 – 6xy + 12xy – 12y^2 – 4y^2$.**

3. **Add and subtract like terms: $4x^2 – 8x^2 = –4x^2$; $–6xy + 12xy = 6xy$; $–12y^2 – 4y^2 = –16y^2$.**

4. **Put the terms back into the polynomial: $–4x^2 + 6xy – 16y^2$.**

So the answer is $–4x^2 + 6xy – 16y^2$, which is B. If you choose any of the other answers, you either distributed the negative sign improperly or you added and subtracted the like terms incorrectly.

After you've combined like terms, double-check that you used the correct signs, particularly when you change all the signs like you did in the second expression. The other answer choices for the sample problem are very similar to the correct choice. They're designed to trap you in case you make an addition or subtraction error. Add and subtract carefully, and you won't fall for these tricks.

Multiplying and dividing expressions

Multiplying and dividing two or more variables works just as though you were performing these same operations on numbers with known values. So, if $2^3 = 2 \cdot 2 \cdot 2$, then $x^3 = x \cdot x \cdot x$. Likewise, if $2^2 \times 2^2 = 2^4$, then $x^2 \times x^2 = x^4$. Similarly, if $2^6 \div 2^4 = 2^2$, then $y^6 \div y^4 = y^2$.

The process is pretty simple for monomials, but polynomials may be a little more complicated. There are a few methods for multiplying and dividing polynomials.

Distributing terms

You can distribute terms in algebra just like you do in arithmetic. For instance, when you multiply a number by a binomial, you multiply the number by each term in the binomial. In this example, you multiply $4x$ by each term inside the parentheses.

$$4x(x – 3) = 4x^2 – 12x$$

With division, you do the same operation in reverse.

$$(16x^2 + 4x) \div 4x = 4x + 1$$

Here are some examples of GMAT questions that you can use distribution to answer:

For all x, $12x – (–10x) – 3x(–x + 10) = ?$

(A) $10x$

(B) $–3x^2 – 10x$

(C) $3x^2 – 52x$

(D) $3x^2 + 8x$

(E) $3x^2 – 8x$

This question tests your ability to add, subtract, and multiply terms in an algebraic expression. First, use distribution to multiply $-3x$ by $(-x + 10)$.

$$-3x \times -x = 3x^2$$
$$-3x \times 10 = -30x$$
$$-3x\,(-x + 10) = 3x^2 - 30x$$

So the full expression looks like this when you put those numbers in the original equation:

$$12x - (-10x) + 3x^2 - 30x = ?$$

You can add those terms that contain the x variable:

$$12x + 10x - 30x = -8x$$

The answer to the equation is E: $3x^2 - 8x$

EXAMPLE

What is the sum of all the solutions of the equation: $\dfrac{2x}{(4+2x)} = \dfrac{6x}{(8x+6)}$

(A) -3

(B) 0

(C) 2

(D) 3

(E) 6

This question is a little more complex. The easiest way to solve it is to make the numerators equal to each other. To do this, multiply the first fraction by ⅗ (or 1), which won't change its value. The result is the following equation:

$$\frac{6x}{3\,(4+2x)} = \frac{6x}{(8x+6)}$$

Because the two numerators are equal, the denominators must also be equal to each other. So you can just place the two denominators equal to each other and solve for x:

$$3(4+2x) = 8x + 6$$
$$12 + 6x = 8x + 6$$
$$6x = 8x - 6$$
$$-2x = -6$$
$$x = 3$$

The correct answer is D.

TIP

You could also solve this by cross-multiplying opposite numerators and denominators, but that's more complicated and time-consuming. You're in a race against the clock on the GMAT, and using shortcuts like this will give you the edge.

Stacking terms

One easy way to multiply polynomials is to stack the two numbers to be multiplied on top of one another. Suppose you have this expression: $(x^2 + 2xy + y^2) \times (x - y)$.

You can calculate this expression just like an old-fashioned arithmetic problem. Just remember to multiply each of your terms in the second line by each term in the first line.

$$
\begin{array}{r}
x^2 + 2xy + y^2 \\
x - y \\
\hline
x^3 + 2x^2 y + xy^2 \\
- x^2 y - 2xy^2 - y^3 \\
\hline
x^3 + x^2 y - xy^2 - y^3
\end{array}
$$

It helps to line up your numbers during the first round of multiplication as in the above example so that like terms match up before add your first two products together.

The GMAT may ask you to divide a polynomial by a monomial. Simply divide each term of the polynomial by the monomial.

$$
\begin{aligned}
\frac{60x^4 - 20x^3}{5x} &= \frac{60x^4}{5x} - \frac{20x^3}{5x} \\
&= \frac{60}{5} \times \frac{x^4}{x} - \frac{20}{5} \times \frac{x^3}{x} \\
&= 12x^{4-1} - 4x^{3-1} \\
&= 12x^3 - 4x^2
\end{aligned}
$$

By dividing the numbers out, you get rid of that ugly fraction bar; plus, the equation's so much simpler to work with when the numbers are more manageable.

Taking a shine to the FOIL method

When you multiply binomials, it's a cinch to use the FOIL method. *FOIL* is an acronym for *first, outer, inner, last,* and that's exactly the order you multiply the terms from one binomial by the terms of the second binomial before adding their products. Take a look at this example:

$$(4x - 5)(3x + 8) =$$

Multiply the *first* terms in each binomial — $4x$ and $3x$.

$$4x \times 3x = 12x^2$$

Then multiply the *outer* terms ($4x$ and 8) to get $32x$ and the *inner* terms ($3x$ and -5) together to get $-15x$. You can add the products at this point because they're like terms.

$$32x - 15x = 17x$$

Last but not least, multiply the *last* terms.

$$-5 \times 8 = -40$$

Now that you've multiplied the terms, you can add the products.

$$12x^2 + 17x - 40$$

You may recognize this expression as the quadratic polynomial we discussed earlier in "Knowing the nomials: Kinds of expressions."

If you're able to keep track of the terms, you can use FOIL to multiply terms in the proper order without taking the time to stack them. The FOIL method comes in handy for solving GMAT problems like this one.

EXAMPLE

When the polynomials $3x + 4$ and $x - 5$ are multiplied together and written in the form $3x^2 - kx - 20$, what is the value of k?

(A) 2

(B) 3

(C) −5

(D) −11

(E) −20

This question asks you for the middle term of the quadratic expression formed by multiplying $3x + 4$ and $x - 5$. Remember with FOIL, you multiply the first, outer, inner, and last. The problem gives you the first term: $3x^2$. The last is also there: −20. Because the problem provides you with the product of the first terms and last terms, all you have to do to get the middle term is multiply the outer and inner numbers of the two expressions and then add them together.

1. **Multiply the outer numbers:**

    $3x \times -5 = -15x$

2. **Multiply the inner numbers:**

    $4 \times x = 4x$

So the middle term of the quadratic is $-15x + 4x = -11x$. The variable k must equal −11, which is D.

To save time on the GMAT, you may wish to commit the following factors and their resulting equations to memory:

$$(x + y)^2 = x^2 + 2xy + y^2$$
$$(x - y)^2 = x^2 - 2xy + y^2$$

So if you're asked to multiply $(x + 3)(x + 3)$, you know without using FOIL that the answer is $x^2 + 2(3x) + 3^2$ or $x^2 + 6x + 9$. And $(x - 3)(x - 3) = x^2 - 6x + 9$.

Extracting Information: Factoring Polynomials

Factors are two or more numbers multiplied together that result in a product. So factoring means you write a bigger number as its factors multiplied by each other. For the GMAT, knowing how to pull out the common factors in expressions and the two binomial factors in a quadratic polynomial is useful.

Something in common: Finding common factors

You can use division to take out common factors from an expression or equation to simplify polynomials for complex problems. (This is the opposite of distributing terms, which we discuss earlier in this chapter.) For instance, see how many common factors you can find in this expression.

$$-14x^3 - 35x^6$$

1. **Because –7 is common to both –14 and –35, take this factor out of the expression by dividing both terms by –7.**

   Then put the remaining expression in parentheses with the common factor outside, like this: $-7(2x^3 + 5x^6)$.

2. **Because x^3 or a multiple of it is common to both terms, divide both terms in parentheses by x^3, multiply x^3 by the other common factor (–7), and put the remaining expression in parentheses: $-7x^3(2 + 5x^3)$.**

So $-14x^3 - 35x^6 = -7x^3(2 + 5x^3)$.

Two by two: Factoring quadratic polynomials

You also need to know how to factor quadratic polynomials for the GMAT. To accomplish this task, you have to perform multiplication in reverse to find the two binomial factors of the quadratic, which means you need to get rid of the exponents, combined terms, and so on, to come up with a couple of binomial factors that look something like this: $(x + a)(x + b)$.

For example, look at the following quadratic polynomial.

$$x^2 + 5x + 6$$

To find its factors, draw two sets of parentheses, like this: ( )( ). The first terms of the two factors have to be x and x because x^2 is the product of x and x. So you can add x as the first term for both sets of parentheses, like this.

$$(x \quad)(x \quad)$$

To find the second terms for the two factors, ask yourself which two numbers have a product of 6 (the third term of the quadratic) and add up to the number 5 (the coefficient of the quadratic's second term). The only two factors that meet these two criteria are 2 and 3. The other factors of 6 (6 and 1, –6 and –1, –2 and –3) don't add up to 5. So the binomial factors of the quadratic equation are $(x + 2)$ and $(x + 3)$.

You may have noticed that by factoring the terms of this equation, you do just the opposite of what you do when you multiply binomials using the FOIL method. You can use the FOIL method to check the binomial factors to make sure they result in the original quadratic when you multiply them together.

There's a timesaving way to factor binomials that are made up a difference of two terms, both of which are perfect squares. Here are some examples of these types of terms:

$$x^2 - 4$$
$$x^2 - 9$$
$$x^2 - 16$$

Factors for these types of quadratic polynomials result the following form:

$$(x - a)(x + a)$$

The variable x is the square root of the first term, and a is the square root of the second term.

In these sample expressions, the first perfect square term is x^2, and the second perfect square term is 4, 9, or 16, respectively. In this case, x is the square root of the first terms, and 2, 3, and 4, respectively, are the square roots of the second terms.

The three sample expressions, then, factor like this:

$(x - 2)(x + 2)$

$(x - 3)(x + 3)$

$(x - 4)(x + 4)$

This factoring technique is very easy to memorize and can help you answer some algebra questions much more quickly than if you were to take the time to carry out long calculations. For example, if you had to multiply these factors, $(x - 5)(x + 5)$, you could use the FOIL method to figure out the answer, but it's much faster to spot that the correct answer will be the difference of two perfect squares. You know the correct answer is $x^2 - 25$ without performing time-consuming calculations.

Likewise, if you need to factor $x^2 - 25$, all you do is figure the square root of x and the square root of 25 and enter those values into the proper factoring form for perfect square quadratics. You know right away that the factors are $(x - 5)(x + 5)$.

When you break down the quadratic polynomial, you'll be able to solve quadratic equations. For more about how to do this, see "Solving quadratic equations," later in this chapter.

Not all the factoring problems on the GMAT will be so straightforward or come with such nice, round numbers. However, you may be pleasantly surprised that mastering these simple little tricks can give you the confidence you need to solve most of the problems that come your way.

Putting On Your Thinking Cap: Problem Solving

Here's what you've been waiting for and what algebra on the GMAT is all about. The test will present all sorts of problems that require you to solve for x in equations or inequalities. You can manipulate expressions quite easily by applying the concepts we've discussed so far in this chapter.

Reading between the lines: Word problems

The GMAT may format algebra and arithmetic problems as word problems, which means you have to translate the language of the words in those problems into numbers that are arranged in a way that makes algebraic sense, whether you're setting up an equation, an inequality, or whatever. (You'll probably see a few geometry word problems, too, but algebra is more common on the GMAT.)

To help you with the translation, Table 11-1 provides you with some of the more common words you'll encounter in word problems and tells you what they look like in math symbols.

Table 11-1	Common Words and Their Math Equivalents
Plain English	*Math Equivalent*
More than, increased by, added to, combined with, total of, sum of	Plus (+)
Less than, fewer than, decreased by, diminished by, reduced by, difference between, taken away from	Minus (−)
Of, times, product of, times	Times (×)
Ratio of, per, out of, quotient	Divide (÷ or /)
What percent of	÷ 100
Is, are, was, were, becomes, results in	Equals (=)
How much, how many	Variable (x, y)

Isolating the variable: Linear equations

A *linear equation* has an unknown variable to solve for and contains no exponent greater than 1. In other words, you don't have to work with squared or cubed variables, so these equations are rather easy to deal with.

In its simplest form, a linear equation can be expressed as $ax + b = 0$, where x is the variable and a and b are constants. An easy way to look at this is to plug in some numbers for the constants and solve the equation for x. Here are two things to keep in mind when you're solving linear equations:

- Isolate the variable in the equation or inequality you're trying to solve, which means you work to get it all by itself on one side of the equation.

- Whatever operation you perform on one side of the equation, you must do to the other side.

An easy example might look like this:

If $4x + 10 = -38$, what is the value of x?

(A) −12

(B) −7

(C) 0

(D) 7

(E) 12

You solve for x by isolating it to one side of the equation.

1. **Eliminate 10 from the left side of the equation by subtracting it.**

    (And remember that if you do something to one side of the equation, you need to do the same thing to the other side. Otherwise, your math teacher is liable to rap you on the knuckles with a slide rule.) Here's what happens when you subtract 10 from both sides:

$$4x + 10 - 10 = -38 - 10$$
$$4x = -48$$

2. **Next, divide both sides by 4, and you have your answer.**

$$4x \div 4 = -48 \div 4$$
$$x = -12$$

The value of x is -12, so the correct answer is A. If you ended up with any of the other answers, you performed the operations incorrectly.

You tackle division problems the same way. So if you're asked to solve for x in this problem, $\frac{x}{4} = -5$, you know what to do. Isolate x to the left side of the equation by multiplying both sides of the equation by 4:

$$\frac{x}{4} \times 4 = (-5) \times 4$$
$$x = -20$$

If your equation includes multiple fractions, you can simplify things and save precious time by eliminating the fractions. Just multiply each fraction by the *least common denominator* (which is the lowest positive whole number that each fraction's denominator divides into evenly). For instance, you may have to solve for x in this problem.

$$\tfrac{3x}{5} + \tfrac{8}{15} = \tfrac{x}{10}$$

The lowest number that 5, 15, and 10 go into evenly is 30, so that's your least common denominator. So multiply each fraction by a fraction equivalent to 1 that will give you 30 in the denominators, like this:

$$\tfrac{3x}{5} \times \tfrac{6}{6} + \tfrac{8}{15} \times \tfrac{2}{2} = \tfrac{x}{10} \times \tfrac{3}{3}$$
$$\tfrac{18x}{30} + \tfrac{16}{30} = \tfrac{3x}{30}$$

Multiplying both sides of the equation by 30, you get this:

$$18x + 16 = 3x$$

Isolate x on the left side by first subtracting $3x$ and 16 from both sides and combining like terms:

$$18x + 16 = 3x$$
$$18x + 16 - 3x = 3x - 3x$$
$$15x + 16 = 0$$
$$15x + 16 - 16 = 0 - 16$$
$$15x = -16$$

The final step is to solve for x by dividing both sides by 15:

$$15x = -16$$
$$\tfrac{15x}{15} = -\tfrac{16}{15}$$
$$x = -\tfrac{16}{15} \approx -1.0667$$

Bringing in the substitution: Simultaneous equations

You can solve an equation that contains two different variables as long as you have another equation that contains at least one of the variables. The two equations are called *simultaneous equations,* or a *system of equations*. You just solve one of the equations for one of the variables and then plug the answer into the other equation and solve. Here's a simple example. The GMAT may give you these two equations and ask you to solve for *x*.

$4x + 5y = 30$ and $y = 2$

Because the second equation simply tells you that *y* is 2, just substitute 2 for the value of *y* in the first equation and you're on your way:

$$4x + 5y = 30$$
$$4x + 5(2) = 30$$
$$4x + 10 = 30$$
$$4x + 10 - 10 = 30 - 10$$
$$4x = 20$$
$$x = 5$$

The equations may not always be that simple, though. For instance, you may have to solve for *x* given these two equations: $4x + 5y = 30$ and $x + \frac{y}{2} = 10$. First, solve for *y* in one of the equations and then substitute this solution for *y* in the other equation, like this:

1. **Solve for *y* in the second equation by subtracting *x* from each side and then multiplying by 2 on both sides.**

$$x + \frac{y}{2} = 10$$
$$\frac{y}{2} = 10 - x$$
$$y = (10 - x)2$$
$$y = 20 - 2x$$

2. **Substitute 20 − 2*x* for *y* in the first equation.**

$$4x + 5y = 30$$
$$4x + 5(20 - 2x) = 30$$

3. **Distribute the 5, combine like terms, and solve for *x*.**

$$4x + 100 - 10x = 30$$
$$-6x + 100 = 30$$
$$-6x = -70$$
$$x = \frac{70}{6} \text{ or } \frac{35}{3} \text{ or } 11\frac{2}{3}$$

That's all there is to it!

You can also solve simultaneous linear equations by combining the equations and eliminating one variable at a time. This works when you have a group of two or more equations that must be true at the same time and you have as many equations as you have variables to solve for. Also, you don't want any numbers with powers of 2 or more.

$$6x + 4y = 66$$
$$-2x + 2y = 8$$

If you look carefully at these equations, you'll see that if you multiply the entire second equation by three, you'll be able to eliminate the x terms ($-2x \times 3 = -6x$, and $6x - 6x = 0$). Eliminating one of the variables saves you a bunch of time. This procedure is legal because you're multiplying the entire equation by 3, which means the value of the new equation is the same as the value of the old one. Here's what the new second equation looks like: $3(-2x + 2y) = 3(8)$ or $-6x + 6y = 24$. Now you can combine the two equations, eliminate the x terms, and solve for y, like this:

$$6x + 4y = 66$$
$$\underline{-6x + 6y = 24}$$
$$0 + 10y = 90$$
$$y = 9$$

Now you can substitute 9 for the value of y in one of the equations to solve for x. We'll plug it into the original second equation.

$$-2x + 2y = 8$$
$$-2x + 2(9) = 8$$
$$-2x + 18 = 8$$
$$-2x = -10$$
$$x = 5$$

Therefore, the solutions, or roots, to the simultaneous equations are $x = 5$ and $y = 9$

Not playing fair: Inequalities

An inequality is a statement such as "x is less than y" or "x is greater than or equal to y."

In addition to the symbols for add, subtract, multiply, and divide, mathematics also applies standard symbols to show how the two sides of an equation are related. You're probably pretty familiar with these symbols, but a little review never hurts. Table 11-2 gives you a rundown of the symbols you'll deal with on the GMAT.

Here are some of the more common symbols used in algebra to signify equality and inequality.

Table 11-2	Mathematical Symbols for Equality and Inequality
Symbol	**Meaning**
=	Equal to
≠	Not equal to
≈	Approximately equal to

Symbol	Meaning
>	Greater than
<	Less than
≥	Greater than or equal to
≤	Less than or equal to

Performing operations with inequalities

For the most part, you treat inequalities a lot like equations. Isolate the variable to one side and perform the same operations on both sides of the inequality. The only wrinkle in that last statement is that if you multiply or divide by a negative number, you need to reverse the direction of the inequality sign.

To see how inequalities work, look at a couple samples. Start with this inequality: $5 > 2$. If you multiply both sides by 5, your inequality still remains true:

$$5 > 2$$
$$5 \times 5 > 2 \times 5$$
$$25 > 10$$

But something happens with you multiply the numbers by a negative number like –3:

$$5 > 2$$
$$-3 \times 5 < -3 \times 2$$
$$-15 > -6$$

–15 is *not* greater than –6, so you have to reverse the sign to make this inequality true:

$$-15 < -6$$

You add and subtract simple inequalities just like you do in equations:

$$x + 5 < 0$$
$$(x + 5) - 5 < 0 - 5$$
$$x < -5$$

Here's how you may be asked to deal with inequalities on the GMAT:

If $x^2 - 1 \le 8$, what is the smallest real value x can have?

(A) –9

(B) –6

(C) –3

(D) 0

(E) 3

This problem asks you to determine the smallest real value of x if $x^2 - 1$ is less than or equal to 8. Solve the inequality for x:

$$x^2 - 1 \le 8$$
$$x^2 - 1 + 1 \le 8 + 1$$
$$x^2 \le 9$$
$$x \le \sqrt{9}$$

Remember that the square root of a number may be positive or negative. The square root of 9 is either 3 or –3. Because –3 is less than 3, –3 must be the smallest real value of x.

To make sure you're right, you can eliminate answer choices using common sense. –9 in A would make x^2 equal 81, and B, –6, would make x^2 equal 36. So neither could be a solution for x. In D, 0 is a solution for x, but it's not the smallest solution, because you know that –3 is a possibility. E can't be right because it's larger than two other possible solutions, –3 and 0. C is the correct answer.

Working with ranges of numbers

You can also use inequalities to show a range of numbers rather than just one single value. For instance, the GMAT may show the range of numbers between –6 and 12 as an algebraic inequality, like this:

$$-6 < x < 12$$

To show the range between –6 and 12 including –6 and 12, you'd use the $\le$ sign:

$$-6 \le x \le 12$$

You can add or subtract with ranges. For instance, you can add 5 to each part of $-6 < x < 12$, like this:

$$-6 < x < 12$$
$$(-6) + 5 < (x) + 5 < (12) + 5$$
$$-1 < x + 5 < 17$$

The inequality keeps all its values intact. To find the sum of two ranges, follow these two steps:

1. **Add the smallest values of each range.**

2. **Add the largest values of each range.**

You can use these steps to answer this problem: if $4 < x < 15$ and $-2 < y < 20$, then what is the range of values of $x + y$?

The smallest values of each of the ranges are 4 and –2, so add those together:

$$4 + (-2) = 2$$

Add the largest values of both ranges:

$$15 + 20 = 35$$

The sum of these two ranges is thus greater than 2 (the smallest sum) and less than 35 (the largest sum), displayed algebraically as:

$$2 < x + y < 35$$

You can also subtract and multiply ranges in the same way. If you subtract the values of end-points of two ranges, the lowest and highest end results give you the new range of the difference between the two ranges. If you multiply the values of the endpoints of the ranges as you did with adding or subtracting them, the product of the ranges will run between the lowest and highest numbers you end up with.

Burning the midnight oil: Work problems

Work problems ask you to find out how much work gets done in a certain amount of time. You use this formula for doing algebra work problems.

production = rate of work × time

Production means the amount of work that gets done. Because you get that quantity by multiplying two other numbers, you can say that production is the product of the rate times the time.

Here's how you'd apply the formula on a GMAT work problem:

There are two dock workers, Alf and Bob. Alf can load 16 tons of steel per day, and Bob can load 20 tons per day. If they each work 8-hour days, how many tons of steel can the two of them load in one hour, assuming they maintain a steady rate?

(A) 2.5

(B) 4.5

(C) 36

(D) 160

(E) 320

This question asks you to find the amount of production and gives you the rate and the time. But to calculate the rate properly, you must state the hours in terms of days. Because a workday is eight hours, one hour is $\frac{1}{8}$ of a day. Figure out how much Alf loads in one hour ($\frac{1}{8}$ of a day) and add it to what Bob loads in one hour.

total production = Alf's production + Bob's production

total production = $(16 \times \frac{1}{8}) + (20 \times \frac{1}{8})$

total production = 2 + 2.5

total production = 4.5

So Alf and Bob load 4.5 tons of steel in one hour ($\frac{1}{8}$ of a day), which is answer B. If you choose C, you figured out the total production for one day rather than one hour.

Going the distance: Distance problems

Distance problems are a lot like work problems. The formula for computing distance or speed problems is this:

distance = rate × time

Any problem involving distance, speed, or time spent traveling can be boiled down to this equation. The important thing is that you have your variables and numbers plugged in properly. Here's an example:

Abby can run a mile in seven minutes. How long does it take her to run ¹⁄₁₀ of a mile at the same speed?

(A) 30 seconds

(B) 42 seconds

(C) 60 seconds

(D) 360 seconds

(E) 420 seconds

Before you do any calculating, you can eliminate E. 420 seconds is 7 minutes, and you know it takes Abby less time to run ¹⁄₁₀ of a mile than it does for her to run a mile.

The problem tells you that Abby's distance is ¹⁄₁₀ of a mile. You can figure her rate to be ¹⁄₇ because she runs 1 mile in 7 minutes. The problem is asking how long she runs, so you need to solve for time. Plug the numbers into the distance formula:

distance = rate × time

$$\tfrac{1}{10} = \tfrac{1}{7} \times t$$

You need to isolate t on one side of the equation, so divide both sides by ¹⁄₇ or multiply both sides by 7. It's faster to multiply:

$$(\tfrac{1}{10}) \times 7 = t$$

$$\tfrac{7}{10} = t$$

So Abby runs ¹⁄₁₀ of a mile in ⁷⁄₁₀ of a minute. ⁷⁄₁₀ isn't an answer choice, so you have to convert minutes to seconds. There are 60 seconds in a minute, and ⁷⁄₁₀ × 60 seconds is 42 seconds. The correct answer must be B.

Here's another example of a distance problem:

Joe must travel a total of 225 kilometers to visit his aunt. He rides his bike 5 kilometers to the bus station. He travels by bus to the train station. He then takes the train 10 times the distance he traveled by bus. How many kilometers did Joe travel by bus?

(A) 20

(B) ²²⁷⁄₁₁

(C) 22

(D) ⁴⁴⁷⁄₁₀

(E) ²²⁷⁄₁₀

The trick here is that this question is not asking you to determine rate or time.

Joe travels a total of 225 kilometers:

225 =

Part of the trip consists of a 5-kilometer bike ride:

225 = 5 +

Joe travels by bus, but we don't know what distance. Go ahead and designate the bus distance with the unknown x:

$225 = 5 + x$

He then takes a train for 10 times the distance he traveled by bus (x):

$225 = 5 + x + 10x$

Now, solve for x:

$225 = 5 + x + 10x$

$220 = x + 10x$

$220 = 11x$

$20 = x$

Joe traveled 20 kilometers by bus. The answer is A.

The GMAT may also ask you to determine average rate of travel. To get the average rate of travel, use the following formula:

average rate = total distance ÷ total time

These types of problems may be worded something like this:

John drives 50 miles to work each day and returns by the same route in the evening. He is able to drive only 25 miles per hour during rush hour in the morning. He decides to come home early and take advantage of the light traffic in the early afternoon. He makes it back home in half the usual rush-hour time. What is his average speed to and from work that day?

(A) 25 mph

(B) 30⅓ mph

(C) 33⅓ mph

(D) 37.5 mph

(E) 50 mph

Don't be fooled by D. The answer seems like it could be 37.5 miles an hour because that's the midpoint between 25 miles an hour in the morning and 50 miles an hour in the afternoon, but that's not how you figure average rate.

The total distance of 100 miles is given to you. But you have to calculate the total time. If John drives 50 miles in the morning at a speed of 25 mph, then it would take him 2 hours to get to work. You probably know this without using the distance formula, but here it is in mathematical terms:

$$50 = (25) \times t$$

Divide both sides by 25:

$$\tfrac{50}{25} = t = 2 \text{ hours}$$

So you know that it takes him one hour to drive home in the afternoon (half the time as in the morning). This means his total driving time for the day is three hours (2 + 1 = 3). Apply this information to the formula for average speed of travel.

average rate = total distance ÷ total time

average rate = 100 ÷ 3

= 33⅓ mph

The answer is C.

Solving quadratic equations

When you set a quadratic polynomial equal to zero, you get what's called a quadratic equation. An example of the classic quadratic form is $ax^2 + bx + c = 0$, where a, b, and c are constants and x is a variable that you have to solve for. Notice that 0 is on one side of the equation and all non-zero terms are on the other side.

Quadratic equations may appear in slightly different forms. For instance, all of the following equations are quadratic equations because they contain a squared variable and equal zero:

$$x^2 = 0$$
$$x^2 - 4 = 0$$
$$3x^2 - 6x + 5 = 0$$

Factoring to find x

The GMAT may give you a quadratic equation and ask you to solve for x. Generally, x will have two roots or solutions. A good way to solve a quadratic equation is to try to factor the equation into two binomials, just like we did earlier in "Two by two: Factoring quadratic polynomials."

$$x^2 - 6x + 5 = 0$$

To factor this trinomial, consider what numbers multiply together to become 5 that also have a sum of –6.

The two factors of 5 are 5 and 1 or –5 and –1. To get a sum of –6, you'll need to go with the negative values. This gives these two binomial factors: $(x - 5)$ and $(x - 1)$. So the resulting equation is

$$(x - 5)(x - 1) = 0$$

To solve for x, you set each of the binomial factors equal to zero. You can do so because you know that one of the factors must equal zero if their product is zero.

$$x - 5 = 0$$
$$x = 5$$

and

$$x - 1 = 0$$
$$x = 1$$

Now the solutions (or roots) to the equation are clear: $x = 1$ and $x = 5$. Both 1 and 5 are possible solutions for x in this quadratic equation.

Determining solutions for the difference of perfect squares

Finding the solution set for a quadratic equation made up of the difference of perfect squares (like $x^2 - y^2 = 0$) is simple if you remember that $x^2 - y^2 = (x + y)(x - y)$. If the GMAT presents you with the task of solving for x when given this type of equation, you know that x equals the positive and negative values of the square root of y^2 (which is the second term).

To find the solution set for $x^2 - 49 = 0$, you'd determine the square root of the second term (49), which is 7. The factors, then, are $(x + 7)$ and $(x - 7)$. If you set each factor equal to zero and solve for x for both equations, you get $x = -7$ and $x = 7$. It's true that the solutions (or roots) for the difference of perfect squares are the positive and negative values of the second term's square root!

Using the quadratic formula

Solving quadratic equations is easy when the solutions come out to be nice, round numbers. But what if the ultimate solutions are harsh looking radicals or perhaps not even real roots? When you can't simply solve a quadratic equation by factoring, you may have to use the quadratic formula, which is a rearrangement of the classic equation: $ax^2 + bx + c = 0$. It looks like this:

$$x = \frac{-b \pm \sqrt{b^2 - 4ac}}{2a}$$

Although this formula may look mighty unmanageable, it may be the only way to find the solution to x for some GMAT quadratic equations that aren't easily factored. Here's how you'd apply the formula when asked to solve $3x^2 + 7x - 6 = 0$ for x. In this equation, $a = 3$, $b = 7$, an $c = -6$. Plug these numbers into the quadratic formula:

$$x = \frac{-7 \pm \sqrt{7^2 - 4(3)(-6)}}{2(3)}$$
$$x = \frac{-7 \pm \sqrt{49 + 72}}{6}$$
$$x = \frac{-7 \pm \sqrt{121}}{6}$$
$$x = \frac{-7 \pm 11}{6}$$
$$x = \frac{-18}{6} = -3 \text{ and } x = \frac{4}{6} = \frac{2}{3}$$

The solutions for x are $\frac{2}{3}$ and -3. Whew! Luckily, the GMAT won't give you too many quadratic equations that require you to apply this formula. But you'll know what to do if you encounter one of the few.

Minding Your Ps and Qs: Functions

Some of the GMAT math questions involve functions. Simply put, *functions* are relationships between two sets of numbers; each number you put into the formula will give you only one possible answer. Functions may sound complicated, but they're really pretty simple. A function problem looks something like this: $f(x) = 2x^2 + 3$. What is $f(2)$?

But before we show you how to solve function problems, you should know a few definitions. Table 11-3 gives you the terms we'll use when we discuss functions.

Table 11-3	Defining Terms for Functions
Term	*Definition*
Function	A rule that turns each member of one set of numbers into a member of another set.
Independent variable (input)	The number you want to find the function of; the x in $f(x)$.
Dependent variable (output)	The result of substituting the independent value into the function, $f(x)$. (This is like your y variable.)
Domain	The set of all possible values of the independent variable.
Range	The set of all possible values of the dependent variable.

Standing in: Understanding the symbols used for functions

Functions can be displayed in any number of ways on the GMAT. Most of the time, you'll see characters like the letters f, F, g, G, and Π. For example, $f(x)$ is used to indicate the function of x, and it simply means "f of x."

F, g, and Π are the most commonly used function symbols, but any type of letter or symbol can represent a function. So you could see symbols like these used to signify functions: $\#(x)$, $\$(x)$, $\&(x)$, and other even stranger ones like other letters from the Greek alphabet.

Don't let these unusual symbols confuse you. The GMAT uses these red herrings to throw you off balance. Regardless of what symbol appears, all you really have to do is substitute for x in the value indicated in the function.

Don't think that the parentheses in the function notation mean multiplication like they do in algebraic operations. The expression $f(x)$ doesn't mean $f \times x$.

To see how functions work, consider the earlier example:

$f(x) = 2x^2 + 3$. What is $f(2)$?

The initial expression is nothing more than a way of saying that the function of x is to square x, multiply the result by 2 and then add 3. To calculate the function exercise with the number $f(2)$, you just substitute for the x with 2.

$$f(2) = 2(2)^2 + 3$$
$$f(2) = 2(4) + 3$$
$$f(2) = 8 + 3$$
$$f(2) = 11$$

That's all there is to it! The function notation is really just a fancy way of telling you to perform a substitution.

Here's another example:

If $g(x) = 2x^2 + 17$, what is $g(12)$?

(A) 12

(B) 17

(C) 100

(D) 288

(E) 305

If you quickly consider the situation, you can eliminate A, B, and C right away. If you substitute 12 for x in the function, you'll be squaring 12, which is 144. The answer then results from multiplying by and adding to that number, so you know the result will be greater than 100. If you look deeper, you'll see that D, 288, is just 2×144. You still have to add 17, so the answer probably isn't D either. Without much calculation, you can eliminate enough answers to determine that E is correct. But to do the calculations, just substitute 12 for x and solve, like this:

$$g(12) = 2(12)^2 + 17$$
$$g(12) = 288 + 17$$
$$g(12) = 305$$

The answer is definitely E.

That was a pretty simple problem. But they can get more complicated on the GMAT. Try these next two examples.

If $\Pi(x) = (x - 2)^2$, find the value of $\Pi(2x - 2)$.

(A) $4x^2 - 4$

(B) $4x^2 + 4$

(C) $4x^2 - 8x + 16$

(D) $4x^2 - 16x + 16$

(E) $4x^2 - 16x - 16$

Just don't try to do this one in your head. Begin by plugging in $(2x - 2)$ for x. Then solve.

$$\Pi(2x - 2) = (2x - 2 - 2)^2$$
$$= (2x - 4)^2$$
$$= (2x - 4)(2x - 4)$$
$$= 4x^2 - 8x - 8x + 16$$
$$= 4x^2 - 16x + 16$$
$$= 4x^2 - 16x + 16, \text{ which is D.}$$

$$h(r) = \begin{cases} 4|r| \text{ if } r \geq 2 \\ -|r| \text{ if } r < 2 \end{cases}$$

Given the above, evaluate $h(-r)$ if $r = -7$.

(A) -28

(B) -14

(C) -7

(D) 7

(E) 28

Don't make the mistake of letting the negative signs mess you up. If $r = -7$, then $h(-r)$ is the same as saying $h(7)$, because $-(-7)$ is 7.

Because 7 is greater than 2, you'll look to the first rule of the function $h(r)$. You want to find the solution to $h(r) = 4$ times the absolute value of 7, or simply 4×7. Your answer for this one, then, is E. You can see that if you messed up the signs, you'd come up with the negative version of the correct answer, which is A. You'd get the other answer choices if you picked the incorrect rule.

Taking it to the limit: Domain and range of functions

The *domain of a function* is the set of all numbers that could possibly be an input of a function. The *range of a function* is the set of all numbers that could possibly be an output of a function. In other words, if you think of the domain as the set of all possible independent variables you can put into a function, the range is the set of all possible dependent variables that can come out of any particular function. Domain and range questions aren't difficult, but you need to be aware of some basic rules to determine the proper limits of the domain and range. The GMAT also tests you on graphing functions on the coordinate plane, but we discuss that in Chapter 13.

Mastering the territory: Domain

The domain of a function includes all real numbers, which means that the only numbers that aren't included in the domain are numbers that aren't real (see Chapter 10 for more info on imaginary and real numbers). Here are some properties of numbers that *aren't* real and therefore can't be part of the domain of a function:

✔ A real number can't be a fraction with a denominator of zero, because then the number would be undefined.

✔ A real number can't be an even-numbered root of a negative number. Even numbered roots of negatives aren't real numbers because any number that's squared or has an even-numbered power can't result in a negative number. So that makes the number imaginary.

For instance, there is no such thing as $\sqrt{-4}$ because there's no one number that you can square that results in −4. −2 × −2 will always equal 4.

To see how domain fits in the GMAT, look at this function:

$$f(x) = \frac{x+4}{x-2}$$

Normally, the domain of x in a function can contain an unlimited number of values. In the above example, though, you have a fraction in the function, which puts the variable x in the denominator. Because your denominator can't add up to zero, the denominator of $x - 2$ can't be equal to zero. This means that x can't equal 2. In terms of functions, the domain of $f(x)$ is $\{x \neq 2\}$. That's all there is to it!

Here's a function involving an even-numbered root:

$$g(n) = 3\sqrt[4]{n+2}$$

In the above function, you have an even-numbered radical sign with the variable n under it. You know that the root of an even-numbered radical, in this case, the 4th root, can't be a negative number. Otherwise, you wouldn't have a real number as your final answer. Therefore, the number under the radical sign can't be less than 0. So n must be greater than or equal to −2. The result is that the domain of the function $g(n)$ is $\{n \geq -2\}$.

On the GMAT, you may see a question like this one:

Determine the domain of the function $f(x) = \dfrac{4}{x^2 - x - 2}$.

(A) $\{x \neq -1, 2\}$

(B) $\{x \neq 1, -2\}$

(C) $\{x = -1, 2\}$

(D) $\{x = -4, 2\}$

(E) $\{x \neq -4, 2\}$

This problem involves simple algebra. You know the denominator can't equal zero, so solve for x in the trinomial. You find the numbers that don't work by factoring:

$$(x^2 - x - 2) = 0$$
$$(x + 1)(x - 2) = 0$$
$$x = -1, 2$$

You're not finished! If you picked C as your answer, your factoring would have been absolutely right, but your answer would be 100 percent wrong. C gives you only the *factors* in the polynomial expression in the denominator.

−1 and 2 are the values of x that make the denominator equal to 0, and therefore, they can't be values in the domain. So the correct answer is A. If you chose B, you had the factors switched around with the incorrect sign in front of them. If you chose D, you found the correct factors of the denominator and then divided the numerator by each root of the denominator. And if you chose E, you divided the numerator by the roots of the denominator and stated that your domain is equal to either of those numbers, which misses the point that the roots of the denominator are the numbers you need to exclude from the domain.

Roaming the land: Range

Just as the domain of a function is limited by certain laws of mathematics, so too is the range.

- ✔ An absolute value of a real number can't be a negative number.

- ✔ An even exponent or power can't produce a negative number.

Check out some situations where these rules come into play. Look at the following functions:

$$g(x) = x^2$$

$$g(x) = |x|$$

Each of these functions can result only in an output that's a positive number. So in each case, the range of the function of g is greater than or equal to zero. The GMAT may express this particular range in one of several ways:

- ✔ The range of $g(x)$ is $\{g(x) \geq 0\}$
- ✔ The range of $g(x)$ is $\{g: g \geq 0\}$
- ✔ The range of $g(x)$ is $\{y: y \geq 0\}$

What is the range of the function $g(x) = 1 - \sqrt{x - 2}$?

- (A) $g(x) \geq -2$
- (B) $g(x) \leq -2$
- (C) $g(x) \geq 2$
- (D) $g(x) \geq -1$
- (E) $g(x) \leq 1$

First, make sure you figure out how to make the radical a real number. You must have at least zero under the square root sign to be a real number, so x must be at least 2. If x is 2, then the function would be $1 - 0$, or simply 1. Any higher value for x results in a lower value for the output of the function. Thus, $g(x) \leq 1$, and the correct answer is E.

It's very easy to get confused and look for the domain when you should be finding the range. If you chose C, you were thinking about the range of x. If you chose A or B, you're hung up trying to make the number under the radical a positive number. If you chose D, you somehow got the number 2 out of the radical and subtracted 1.

Chapter 12

Getting the Angle on Geometry: Planes and Solids

- -

In This Chapter

▶ Looking at lines and angles

▶ Taking a crack at triangles

▶ Questing after quadrilaterals

▶ Pondering polygons

▶ Circumnavigating circles

▶ Reaching out to touch three-dimensional figures

- -

Geometry starts with the basics — plane geometry — which is the study of lines and shapes in two dimensions. From that foundation, geometry constructs increasingly complex models to more accurately portray the real world. Three-dimensional geometry, or solid geometry, puts some depth to the plane. Three-dimensional geometry is almost as simple as plane geometry, with the added dimension of depth.

Despite how fascinating geometry is, in recent years the GMAT test-makers have decreased the number of math questions about planes and solids. This may come as a relief to those of you who aren't particularly fond of manipulating shapes and figures. But 20 percent of GMAT math questions still cover geometry concepts, and this chapter is designed to prepare you for all of 20 percent of them.

Fishing for the Answers: Lines and Angles

The building blocks for geometric forms are lines and angles, so we start by defining these fundamental elements. Although the definitions aren't directly tested, understanding the meanings of these terms is an important part of solving problems on the GMAT. Here are the common terms that pop up on the test:

✔ **Line:** A straight path of points that extends forever in two directions. A line does not have any width or thickness. Arrows are sometimes used to show that the line goes on forever. See line AB in Figure 12-1.

✔ **Line segment:** The set of points on a line between any two points on the line. Basically it's just a piece of a line from one point to another that contains those points and all the points between. See line segment CD in Figure 12-1.

✔ **Ray:** A ray is like half of a line; it starts at an endpoint and extends forever in one direction. You can think of a ray as a ray of light extending from the sun (the endpoint) and shining as far as it can go. See ray EF in Figure 12-1.

✔ **Midpoint:** The point halfway (equal distance) between two endpoints on a line segment.

✔ **Bisect:** To cut something exactly in half, such as when a line segment cuts another line segment or an angle or a polygon into two equal parts. A *bisector* is a line that divides a line segment, an angle, or a polygon into two equal parts.

✔ **Intersect:** Just like it sounds — *intersect* simply means to cross; that is, when one line or line segment crosses another line or line segment.

✔ **Collinear:** A set of points that lie on the same line.

✔ **Vertical:** Lines that run straight up and down.

✔ **Horizontal:** Lines that run straight across from left to right.

✔ **Parallel:** Lines that run in the same direction, always remaining the same distance apart. Parallel lines never cross one another.

✔ **Perpendicular:** When two lines intersect to form a square corner. The intersection of two perpendicular lines forms a right, or 90°, angle.

✔ **Angle:** The intersection of two rays (or line segments) sharing a common endpoint. The common endpoint is called the *vertex*. The size of an angle depends on how much one side rotates away from the other side. An angle is usually measured in degrees or radians.

✔ **Acute angle:** Any angle measuring less than 90°. Like an acute, or sharp, pain, the acute angle has a sharp point. See Figure 12-2.

✔ **Right, or perpendicular, angle:** An angle measuring exactly 90°. It makes up a square corner. See Figure 12-3.

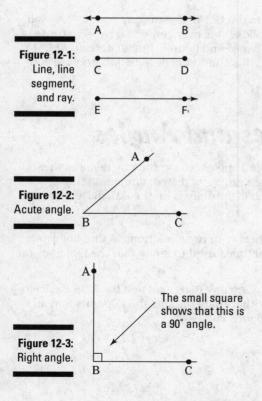

Figure 12-1:
Line, line segment, and ray.

Figure 12-2:
Acute angle.

Figure 12-3:
Right angle.

The small square shows that this is a 90° angle.

✔ **Obtuse angle:** An angle that measures more than 90° but less than 180°. The opposite of an acute angle, an obtuse angle is dull rather than sharp. See Figure 12-4.

✔ **Straight angle:** An angle that measures exactly 180°. A straight angle appears to be a straight line or line segment.

✔ **Complementary angles:** Angles that add together to total 90°. Together, they form a right angle.

✔ **Supplementary angles:** Angles that add together to total 180°. They form a straight angle.

✔ **Similar:** Objects that have the same shape but different sizes.

✔ **Congruent:** Objects that are equal in size and shape. Two line segments with the same length, two angles with the same measure, and two triangles with corresponding sides of equal lengths and angles that have equal degree measures are congruent.

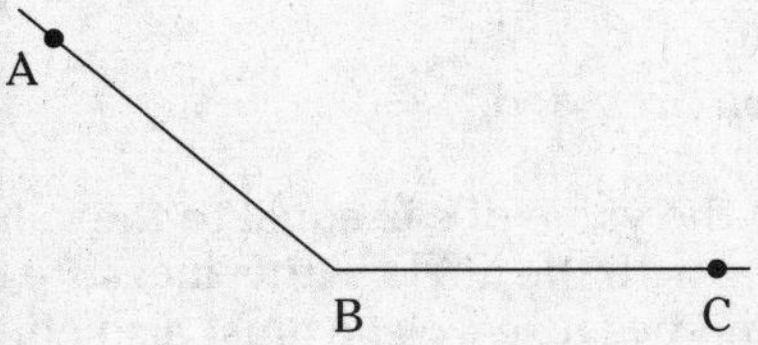

Figure 12-4:
Obtuse
angle.

Two important rules for lines and angles arise from these basic definitions. You can read all about them in Table 12-1.

Table 12-1	Rules for Lines and Angles	
Condition	*Rule*	*Sample Figure*
Intersecting lines	When two lines intersect, the opposite angles (across from each other) are always congruent or equal, and the adjacent angles are always supplementary. Opposite angles are also known as *vertical* angles. Adjacent angles have a common side, so they're right next to each other. In the sample figure, ∠ABC and ∠DBE are congruent; ∠ABC and ∠CBD form a straight line and are therefore supplementary.	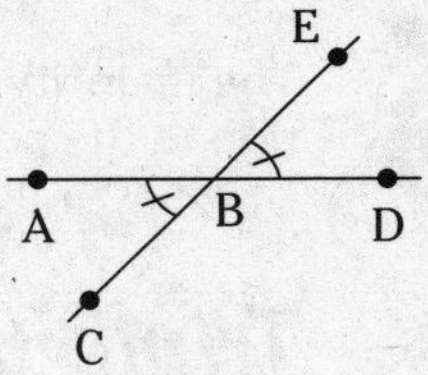
Parallel lines intersected by a transversal	When parallel lines are crossed by a third line that's not perpendicular to them (called a *transversal*), the resulting small and large angles share certain properties. Each of the small angles is equal; the large angles are also equal to each other. The measurement of any small angle added to that of any large angle equals 180°.	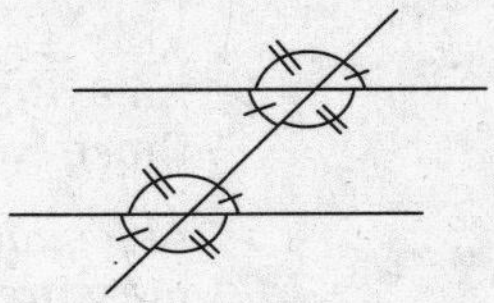

Here's how lines and angles may be tested on the GMAT math section:

In the following figure, line *m* is parallel to line *n* and line *t* is a transversal crossing both lines *m* and *n*. Given the information contained in this figure, what is the value of *e?*

(A) 30°

(B) 60°

(C) 100°

(D) 120°

(E) It cannot be determined from the information provided.

Because lines *m* and *n* are parallel, you know that the value of *e* is equal to the value of *c.* The angle with a value of *c* lies along a straight line with the angle with a measure of *a,* so *a* + *c* = 180°. Because *a* = 60°, *c* must equal 120°. And because *c* = *e,* *e* must also equal 120°. The correct answer is D.

Trusting Triangles

Lines and angles form figures, and one of the most popular GMAT figures is the triangle. A triangle has three sides, and the point where two of the sides intersect is called a vertex. We name triangles by their vertices, so a triangle with vertices A, B, and C is called △ABC.

The majority of geometry questions on the GMAT involve triangles, so pay particular attention to the properties and rules of triangles.

Triple treat: Properties of triangles

Just as lines and angles have rules that apply to lots of situations, triangles have rules that apply to all triangles. But some triangles are so special that some rules exist just for them:

- An *isosceles triangle* has two equal sides, and the measures of the angles opposite those two sides are also equal to each other.

- An *equilateral triangle* has three sides of equal lengths and three angles of equal measure.

- A *right triangle* has one angle that measures 90°. The side opposite the right angle is called the *hypotenuse.*

The measures of the three angles of any triangle always add up to 180°.

Here's an example of how this information may be tested on the GMAT:

In the following figure, line SA is parallel to line TB. If the measure of ∠BTU is 60°, what is the measure of ∠ATB?

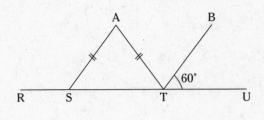

(A) 30°

(B) 40°

(C) 50°

(D) 60°

(E) 80°

Line RU traverses the parallel lines SA and TB. Therefore, ∠BTU equals ∠AST. Because the value of ∠BTU is 60°, ∠AST must also be 60°.

It is important to recognize that because line SA equals line TA, △SAT is isosceles, and the angles opposite these two lines have the same measure.

One of these angles is ∠AST. ∠AST measures 60°; ∠STA has the same measurement as ∠AST; therefore, ∠STA also measures 60°. You know that the measures of the angles along a straight line add up to 180°, so the measure of ∠ATB = 180° – the value of ∠BTU – the value of ∠ATS. ∠BTU and ∠ATS each measure 60°, so the measure of ∠ATB = 180° – 60° – 60°, which is also 60°. The correct answer is D.

Triangles have great proportions. As you can see in Figure 12-5, the side that's opposite of a given angle in a triangle is proportionate to that angle. So the smallest angle faces the shortest side of the triangle. If two or more angles have the same measurement, their opposite sides are also equal.

Figure 12-5:
Angles of a
triangle are
in propor-
tion to their
opposite
sides.

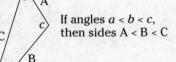

If angles $a < b < c$,
then sides A < B < C

The area of a triangle

The GMAT will probably ask you to determine the area of a triangle, so you better be ready. Memorize this formula:

$A = \frac{1}{2}bh$

A stands for (what else) area, *b* is the length of the base or bottom of the triangle, and *h* stands for the height (or altitude), which is the distance that a perpendicular line runs from the base to the angle opposite the base. For a visual, check out Figure 12-6.

Figure 12-6: The base and height of a triangle.

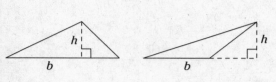

Notice that, as shown in Figure 12-6, the height or altitude is always perpendicular to the base and that the height can be placed either inside or outside the triangle.

The Pythagorean theorem and other cool stuff about right triangles

You can solve GMAT problems for the lengths of the sides of right triangles by using a groovy little formula called the Pythagorean theorem and by memorizing some common right triangle side lengths.

Digging Pythagoras and his theorem

The Pythagorean theorem simply states that the sum of the squares of the legs of a right triangle is equal to the square of the hypotenuse, or $a^2 + b^2 = c^2$, where *a* and *b* represent the two sides or legs of the right triangle and *c* is the hypotenuse. The legs of a right triangle are simply the sides that form the right angle, and the hypotenuse is the side opposite it. (It's always the biggest side of the right triangle.) If you know the length of two sides of a right triangle, you can easily find the length of the other side by using this handy formula.

Keep in mind that the Pythagorean theorem works only with right triangles. You can't use it to find the lengths of sides of triangles that don't have a right angle in them.

Which of the following is the length, in inches, of the remaining side of a right triangle if one side is 7 inches long and the hypotenuse is 12 inches long?

(A) $\sqrt{5}$

(B) 5

(C) 7

(D) 12

(E) $\sqrt{95}$

You may find it helpful to draw a right triangle on your paper to visualize the problem, but doing so isn't necessary. If the hypotenuse is 12 inches and one side is 7 inches, you figure the measurement of the remaining side by applying the formula:

$$a^2 + b^2 = c^2$$
$$7^2 + b^2 = 12^2$$
$$49 + b^2 = 144$$
$$b^2 = 95$$

You know that b^2 is 95, but the question asks for the value of b, not b^2. That means the measurement of the remaining side is the square root of 95, which is answer E.

Getting hip to the common ratios of right triangles

You may find it handy to memorize some ratios based on the Pythagorean theorem. That way, you don't have to work out the whole theorem every time you deal with a right triangle.

The most common ratio of the three sides of a right triangle is 3:4:5 (3 is the measure of the short leg, 4 is the measure of the long leg, and 5 is the measure of the hypotenuse). Related multiples are 6:8:10, 9:12:15, and so on. As soon as you recognize that two sides fit the 3:4:5 ratio or a multiple of the 3:4:5 ratio, you'll automatically know the length of the third side.

Other proportions of right triangles you should try to remember are 5:12:13, 8:15:17, and 7:24:25. Knowing these proportions may allow you to more quickly solve problems like this one on the GMAT:

In the following figure, AB is 6 units long, AC is 8 units long, and BD is 24 units long. How many units long is CD?

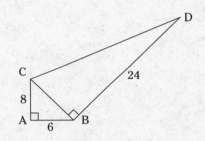

(A) 26

(B) 32

(C) 80

(D) 96

(E) 100

This problem would be very time consuming to solve if you didn't know the common ratios of right triangles. To determine the length of line segment CD, you first need to know the length of CB. You could use the Pythagorean theorem, but you know an easier, faster way. Because AB = 6 and AC = 8, △ABC is a 3:4:5 triangle times two — a 6:8:10 triangle. Therefore, the length of the hypotenuse, BC, is 10.

This makes △BCD a 5:12:13 triangle times two — a 10:24:26 triangle. So, the length of CD = 26, and the correct answer is A.

Knowing what's neat about the 30°:60°:90° triangle

Some other handy right triangles exist. One is the 30°:60°:90° triangle. When you bisect any angle in an equilateral triangle, you get two right triangles with 30°, 60°, and 90° angles. In a 30°:60°:90° triangle, the hypotenuse is two times the length of the shorter leg, as shown in Figure 12-7. The ratio of the three sides is $s : s\sqrt{3} : 2s$, where s = the length of the shortest side.

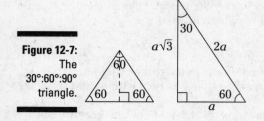

Figure 12-7:
The
30°:60°:90°
triangle.

Feeling the equilibrium of a 45°:45°:90° triangle

If you bisect a square with a diagonal line, you get two triangles that both have two 45° angles. Because the triangle has two equal angles (and therefore two equal sides), the resulting triangle is an isosceles right triangle, or 45°:45°:90° triangle. Its hypotenuse is equal to $\sqrt{2}$ times the length of a leg. It's important to recognize this also means that the length of a leg is equal to the length of the hypotenuse divided by $\sqrt{2}$. The ratio of sides in an isosceles right triangle is, therefore, $s:s:s\sqrt{2}$ (where s = the length of one of the legs) or $\frac{s}{\sqrt{2}}:\frac{s}{\sqrt{2}}:s$ (where s = the length of the hypotenuse). Figure 12-8 shows the formula.

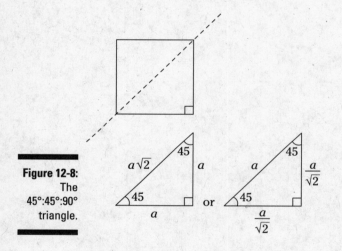

Figure 12-8:
The
45°:45°:90°
triangle.

This example shows just how helpful your knowledge of special triangles can be:

In △STR, ∠TSR measures 45° and ∠SRT is a right angle. If SR is 20 units long, how many units is TR?

(A) 10

(B) $10\sqrt{2}$

(C) 20

(D) $20\sqrt{2}$

(E) 40

You could draw the triangle, but with what you know about 45°:45°:90° triangles, you don't need to.

Because ∠SRT is a right angle, you know that the triangle in this question is a right triangle. If ∠TSR measures 45°, then ∠RTS must also measure 45°, and this is a 45°:45°:90° triangle. So SR must equal TR. The length of line segment SR = 20, so TR = 20. The correct answer is C.

A striking resemblance: Similar triangles

Triangles are *similar* when they have exactly the same angle measures. Similar triangles have the same shape, even though their sides are different lengths. The corresponding sides of similar triangles are in proportion to each other. The heights or altitudes of the two triangles are also in proportion. Figure 12-9 provides an illustration of the relationship between two similar triangles.

Knowing the properties of similar triangles helps you answer GMAT questions like this one:

△RTS and △ACB in the following figure are similar right triangles with side lengths that measure as indicated. What is the area of △ACB?

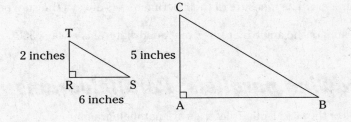

(A) 10

(B) 15

(C) 30

(D) 37.5

(E) 75

To find the area of △ACB, you need to know the measurements of its base and its height. The figure gives you the length of its height (5), so you need to find the length of its base.

Because the two triangles are similar (and proportionate to each other), you can use what you know about △RTS to find the base measurement of △ACB. TR is proportionate to CA, and RS is proportionate to AB. Set up a proportion with x representing the measure of AB, cross multiply, and solve:

$$\tfrac{2}{5} = \tfrac{6}{x}$$

$$2x = 30$$

$$x = 15$$

The base of △ACB is 15 inches.

Don't stop there and choose B. The question asks for the area of △ACB, not the length of AB.

Substitute the base and height measurements for △ACB into the formula for the area of a triangle (½ of the base times the height) and solve:

$A = ½(5)(15)$

$A = ½(75)$

$A = 37.5$

The correct answer is D.

Playing Four Square: Quadrilaterals

A quadrilateral is a four-sided polygon, and a polygon is any closed figure made of line segments that intersect. Your primary concern is to know how to find quadrilaterals' areas and perimeters. The measure of their perimeters is always the sum of their sides.

The sum of the angle measures of a quadrilateral is always 360°.

Drawing parallels: Parallelograms

Most of the GMAT quadrilaterals are parallelograms.

Parallelograms have properties that are very useful for solving GMAT problems:

- The opposite sides are parallel and equal in length.
- The opposite angles are equal in measure to each other.
- The measures of the adjacent angles add up to 180°, so they're supplementary to each other.
- The diagonals of a parallelogram bisect each other. In other words, they cross at the midpoint of both diagonals.

Figure 12-10 provides a visual representation of the very important properties of parallelograms.

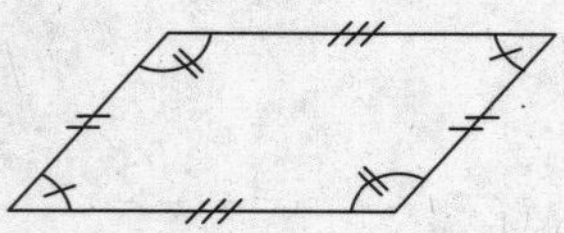

Figure 12-10: A parallelogram.

The area of any parallelogram is its base times its height ($A = bh$). You determine the height pretty much the same way you determine the height, or altitude, of a triangle. The difference is that you draw the perpendicular line from the base to the opposite side (instead of to the opposite angle, as in the case of a triangle). See Figure 12-11.

Figure 12-11:
Finding the
area of a
parallelo-
gram.

Figure 12-11:
Finding the
area of a
parallelo-
gram.

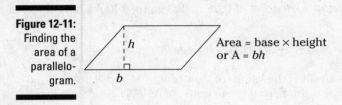

Area = base × height
or A = *bh*

You can use the Pythagorean theorem to help you find the height of a parallelogram. When you drop a perpendicular line from one corner to the base to create the height, the line becomes the leg of a right triangle. If the problem gives you the length of other sides of the triangle (or information you can use to determine the length), you can use the formula to find the length of the height.

Parallelograms come in various types:

- ✔ A *rectangle* is a parallelogram with four right angles. Because rectangles are parallelograms, rectangles have all the properties of parallelograms. Use $A = bh$ to find the area of a rectangle. The cool thing about rectangles, though, is that the height, or altitude, is the same as one of its sides.

- ✔ A *square* is a rectangle with four equal sides. It has four right angles, and its sides all have the same length. Because a square has four equal sides, you can easily find its area if you know the length of only one side. The area of a square can be expressed as $A = s^2$ or $A = s \times s$, where s is the length of a side. The perimeter of a square is $4s$.

  Here's a neat trick for finding the area of a square if the only measurement you know is the length of the diagonal. You can say $A = d^2/2$, where the diagonal is d. Remember that the diagonal of a square is the hypotenuse of an isosceles right triangle, and right triangles have some special formulas. This shortcut is just a way of using the Pythagorean theorem in reverse!

- ✔ A *rhombus* is a type of parallelogram. All four sides of a rhombus are equal in length, like a square, but a rhombus doesn't necessarily have four right angles. You can find the area of a rhombus by multiplying the lengths of the two diagonals (the straight lines that join opposite angles of the parallelogram, designated as *d*) and then dividing by 2, or $A = \frac{1}{2}d_1d_2$.

Raising the roof: Trapezoids

A *trapezoid* is a quadrilateral with two parallel sides and two nonparallel sides. The parallel sides are called the bases, and the other two sides are called the legs. Finding the area of a trapezoid is a bit tricky, but it can be done as long as you know the length of both bases and the height, or altitude. To find the area, you take the average of the two bases and multiply by the height or altitude. Thus, $A = \frac{1}{2}(b_1 + b_2) \times h$. See Figure 12-12 for a visual.

Figure 12-12:
The base
and height
of a
trapezoid.

b_1

h

b_2

In an *isosceles trapezoid*, the legs of the quadrilateral are the same length. It looks kind of like an A-frame with the roof cut off.

Here's how a question about quadrilaterals may appear on the GMAT:

In the following figure, square ABCD has sides the length of 4 units, and M and N are the midpoints of AB and CD, respectively. What is the perimeter, in units, of AMCN?

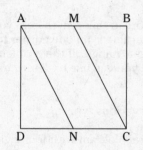

(A) 6

(B) $6\sqrt{5}$

(C) $2 + 2\sqrt{3}$

(D) $4 + 4\sqrt{5}$

(E) $8\sqrt{5}$

This question asks you to determine the perimeter of parallelogram AMCN, but it also incorporates what you know about triangles and simplifying radicals.

If M and N are the midpoints, then AM = 2 (which is ½) and NC = 2. Now you know the short sides of AMCN = 2. You can see that the long sides of the parallelogram are the hypotenuses of the right triangles within the square. The lengths of the legs of the right triangles are 2 and 4. These don't fit with any of the special ratios associated with right triangles, but you can use the Pythagorean theorem:

$$2^2 + 4^2 = c^2; 4 + 16 = c^2; 20 = c^2; c = \sqrt{20}$$

The perimeter = $(2 \times 2) + 2\sqrt{20}$, or $4 + 2\sqrt{20}$

This answer isn't available, so you must simplify the radical. (If you need to review how to simplify radicals, read Chapter 10.)

$20 = 4 \times 5$, and the square root of 4 is 2, so $\sqrt{20} = 2\sqrt{5}$. Now the perimeter = $4 + (2)2\sqrt{5}$. Multiply 2 and 2 to get 4, which leaves you with $4 + 4\sqrt{5}$, the answer provided by D.

Showing Their Good Sides: Other Polygons

The GMAT may throw in some other types of polygons to make things interesting. Here are some of the more common ones:

- **Pentagon:** A five-sided figure
- **Hexagon:** A six-sided figure (the *x* makes it sound like *six*)

- ✔ **Heptagon:** A seven-sided figure
- ✔ **Octagon:** An eight-sided figure (like *oct*opus)
- ✔ **Nonagon:** A nine-sided figure
- ✔ **Decagon:** A ten-sided figure (like *deca*thlon)

In general, GMAT polygons will be regular polygons, which means that all of the sides are the same length and all of the angles are equal. The rules for similar triangles apply to similar polygons: That is, if two polygons have exactly the same shape and the same angles, then the lengths of their corresponding sides are proportional to one another.

No set formula exists for determining the area of a polygon. You need to create quadrilaterals and triangles within the polygon, find their areas, and add them together to get the total area of the polygon.

You may remember how the sum of the angles of a triangle is 180° and the sum of the angles of a quadrilateral is 360°. Are you starting to detect a pattern here? Just add another 180° and you have the sum of the angles in a pentagon — 540°. But if you had to add the angles up like this, you'd soon run out of fingers to count on! Here's a formula for determining the sum of the interior angles of any polygon:

Sum of the angles = $(n - 2) \times 180°$, where n is equal to the number of sides.

Works every time! If the polygon's regular, you can also determine the measure of the angles. You divide the sum of the angles by the total number of angles. So each angle in a regular pentagon measures $540 \div 5 = 108°$.

The formula for determining the measure of an angle in a polygon works only if the GMAT tells you that the polygon is regular.

Eating Up Pieces of Pi: Circles

A circle, by technical definition, is a set of points in a plane that are at a fixed distance from a given point. That point is called the center. A circle is best drawn with the aid of a compass, but on the GMAT you'll just have your pencil.

Ring measurements: Radius, diameter, and circumference

Almost any GMAT problem regarding circles requires you to know about radius, diameter, and circumference.

The *radius* of a circle is the distance from the center of the circle to any point on the circle. Think of it as a *ray* going out from the center to the edge of the circle. The radius is usually indicated by the letter *r*, as shown in Figure 12-13.

The *diameter* of a circle is the length of a line that goes from one side of the circle to the other and passes through the center. The diameter is twice the length of the radius, and it's the longest possible distance across the circle. Diameter usually is indicated by the letter *d*, as shown in Figure 12-13.

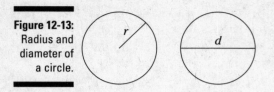

Figure 12-13:
Radius and
diameter of
a circle.

The *circumference* of a circle is the distance around the circle. You can think of the circumference as the perimeter of the circle, although this isn't quite true. It's really more technically accurate to say you're trying to find the perimeter of a regular polygon with an infinite number of sides as it gets rounder and rounder. Rather than taking the time to figure out how many sides add up to infinity, just use this formula:

$$C = 2\pi r$$

Or (because *d* = *2r*):

$$C = \pi d$$

You can manipulate this formula to find the diameter or the radius of a circle if you know the circumference:

- ✔ The formula for the radius is $r = C \div 2\pi$.
- ✔ The formula for the diameter is $d = C \div \pi$.

Another formula you need to know is for the area of a circle: $A = \pi r^2$.

You can manipulate this formula to find the diameter or the radius if you know the area:

- ✔ The formula for the radius is $r = \sqrt{A \div \pi}$
- ✔ The formula for the diameter is $d = 2\sqrt{A \div \pi}$

Blueprints for Noah: All about arcs

You should have a basic understanding of the following terms so you aren't running in circles on the GMAT math section:

- ✔ An *arc* of a circle is a portion along the edge of the circle. Because it runs along the circumference, an arc is actually a part of the circle. See Figure 12-14.
  - • A *minor arc* is less than 180°.
  - • A *major arc* is greater than 180°. In fact, the arc of the entire circle is 360°. You're more likely work with minor arcs than major ones on the GMAT.
- ✔ A *central angle* of a circle is an angle that's formed by two radii; it's called a central angle because its vertex is the center of the circle. The measurement of the central angle is the same as that of the arc formed by the endpoints of its radii. So a 90° central angle (like the one in Figure 12-14) intercepts one-quarter of the circle, or a 90° arc.

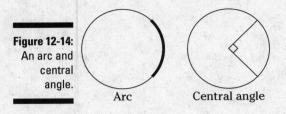

Figure 12-14:
An arc and central angle.

Arc   Central angle

In the following figure, A and B lie on the circle centered at C. CA is 9 units long, and the measure of ∠ACB is 40°. How many units long is minor arc AB?

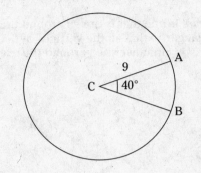

(A) π

(B) 2π

(C) 9π

(D) 18π

(E) 36π

First, determine how many degrees are in arc AB. Because CA and CB are radii of the circle, the degree measurement of the central angle ACB is the same measurement of the arc the ends of the radii form on the circle. So the minor arc AB is 40°. How does that help you determine the length of the arc? Well, you know that a circle is 360°. 40° is ⅑ of 360°. That means arc AB is ⅑ of the circumference of the circle. Determine the circumference and then figure out ⅑ of that length.

$$C = 2\pi r; \; C = 2\pi \times 9; \; C = 18\pi$$

$$\tfrac{1}{9} \times 18\pi = 2\pi$$

The correct answer must be B.

Line 'em up: Chords, inscribed and circumscribed figures, and tangents

The GMAT may toss in some extra lines and figures when it questions you about circles. The extra features may appear within or outside the circle.

Striking a chord

A *chord* is a line segment cutting across a circle that connects two points on the edge of a circle. Those two points at the end of the chord are also the endpoints of an intercepted arc. See Figure 12-15.

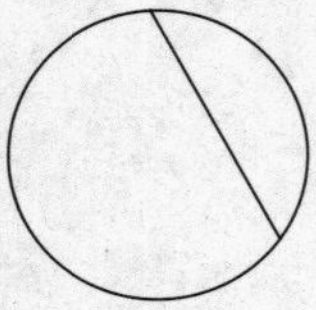

Figure 12-15:
A chord.

Moving in: Inscribed and circumscribed figures

An *inscribed figure* is any figure (angle, polygon, and so on) that's drawn inside another figure. For example, you could draw a triangle inside another circle so that all its vertices touch at points on the circle, just like Figure 12-16.

A *circumscribed figure* is one that is drawn around the outside another shape, such as a circle drawn around a triangle so that all the vertices of the triangle touch the circle. You'd say the circle in Figure 12-16 is circumscribed around the triangle.

Figure 12-16:
Inscribed and circumscribed figures.

The only difference between an inscribed and a circumscribed figure hinges on the reference. You refer to the figure on the outside of another figure as a circumscribed figure and the figure on the inside of another figure as an inscribed figure.

The GMAT may use circumscribed and inscribed figures to ask you to calculate the area of a shaded area. When you get a "shaded area" problem, it's often best to calculate the area of both figures and then subtract the area of one from another.

Going off on a tangent

A *tangent line* is one that intersects the circle at just one point. A good way to think of a tangent line in the real world is like a wheel rolling along a road. The road is tangent to the wheel. Figure 12-17 shows line AB tangent to the circle. The line is also perpendicular to the radius that touches the circle where the tangent intersects. To continue the wheel analogy, if that wheel had an infinite number of spokes coming from its center, only one spoke would touch (be perpendicular to) the ground at any one time.

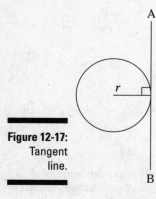

Figure 12-17:
Tangent line.

Here's how the GMAT may test you on circles within circles:

In the following figure, the circle centered at B is internally tangent to the circle centered at A. The smaller circle passes through the center of the larger circle and the length of AB is 4 units. If the smaller circle is removed from the larger circle, how many square units of the area of the larger circle will remain?

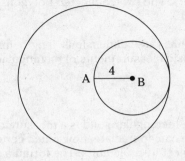

(A) 16π

(B) 36π

(C) 48π

(D) 64π

(E) 800π

Because the smaller circle passes through the center of the larger one, the radius of the larger circle is two times the radius of the smaller one: The radius of the larger circle equals 8. To find the area in question, you have to find the area of the larger circle and subtract the area of the smaller. To determine the area of the larger circle, apply the area formula:

$A = \pi(8^2)$

$A = 64\pi$

Determine the area of the smaller circle in the same way:

$A = \pi(4^2)$

$A = 16\pi$

Now subtract the two areas:

$64\pi - 16\pi = 48\pi$

The correct answer is C.

Getting a Little Depth Perception: Three-Dimensional Geometry

Three-dimensional geometry, or solid geometry, puts some depth to plane geometrical figures. Three-dimensional geometry is about as simple as plane geometry, and you can apply many of the same strategies. You'll most likely be asked no more than a handful of solid geometry questions on the GMAT, and they'll likely concern only rectangular solids and cylinders.

Chipping off the old block: Rectangular solids

You make a rectangular solid by taking a simple rectangle and adding depth. Good examples of a rectangular solids are bricks, cigar boxes, or boxes of your favorite cereal. A rectangular solid is also known as a *right rectangular prism* because it has 90° angles all around. *Prisms* have two congruent polygons on parallel planes that are connected to each other by their corresponding points. The two connected polygons make up the bases of the prism, as shown in Figure 12-19.

A rectangular solid has three dimensions: length, height, and width. You really only need to worry about two basic measurements of rectangular solids on the GMAT: total surface area and volume.

Finding volume

The volume *(V)* of a rectangular solid is a measure of how much space it occupies, or to put it in terms everyone can appreciate, how much cereal your cereal box holds. You measure the volume of an object in cubic units. The formula for the volume of a rectangular solid is simply its length *(l)* × width *(w)* × height *(h)*.

$$V = lwh$$

Another way of saying this is that the volume is equal to the base times the height *(V = Bh)*, where *B* is the area of the base. See what we mean in Figure 12-18.

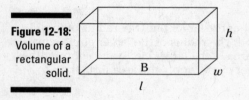

Figure 12-18: Volume of a rectangular solid.

Determining surface area

You can find the surface area *(SA)* of a rectangular solid by simply figuring out the areas of all six sides of the object and adding them together.

First you find the area of the length *(l)* times height *(h)*, then the area of length times width *(w)*, and finally width times height (see Figure 12-19). Now multiply each of these three area measurements times two (after you find the area of one side, you know that the opposite side has the same measurement). The formula for the surface area of a rectangular solid is

$$SA = 2lh + 2lw + 2wh$$

You can visualize the surface area of a rectangular solid, or any solid figure for that matter, by mentally flattening out all of the sides and putting them next to each other. It's sort of like taking apart a cardboard box to get it ready for recycling, only now you get to measure it. Lucky you!

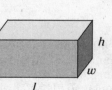

Figure 12-19: Surface area of a rectangular solid.

Sipping from soda cans and other cylinders

A *cylinder* is a circle that grows straight up into the third dimension to become the shape of a can of soda. The bases of a cylinder are two congruent circles on different planes. The cylinders you see on the GMAT are *right circular cylinders,* which means that the line segments that connect the two bases are perpendicular to the bases. Figure 12-20 shows a right circular cylinder. All the corresponding points on the circles are joined together by line segments. The line segment connecting the center of one circle to the center of the opposite circle is called the *axis*.

Figure 12-20:
A right
circular
cylinder.

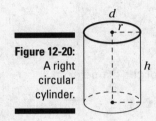

A right circular cylinder has the same measurements as a circle. That is, a right circular cylinder has a radius, diameter, and circumference. In addition, a cylinder has a third dimension, its height, or altitude.

To get the volume of a right circular cylinder, first take the area of the base (a circle), which is πr^2, and multiply by the height *(h)* of the cylinder. Here's the formula:

$$V = \pi r^2 h$$

If you want to find the total surface area of a right circular cylinder, you have to add up the areas of all the surfaces. Imagine taking a soda can, cutting off the top and bottom sections, and then slicing it down one side. You then spread out the various parts of the can. If you measure each one of these sections, you get the total surface area.

REMEMBER

When you measure the surface area of a right circular cylinder, don't forget to include the top and bottom of the can in your calculation.

Here's the formula for the total surface area *(SA)* of a right circular cylinder — the diameter *(d)* is 2 times the radius *(r)*:

$$SA = \pi dh + 2\pi r^2$$

EXAMPLE

If a 10 cm tall aluminum can that is a perfect right circular cylinder contains 250 cm^3 of soda, what is the diameter of the can in centimeters?

(A) $5/\sqrt{\pi}$

(B) $10/\pi$

(C) $10/\sqrt{\pi}$

(D) 10π

(E) $5\sqrt{\pi}$

Start with the formula for the volume of the right circular cylinder, where r is the radius of the base and h is the height of the can.

$$V = \pi r^2 h$$

You know that the volume is 250 cm³ and h is 10, so plug in these numbers:

$$250 = \pi r^2 \times 10$$
$$25 = \pi r^2$$
$$\frac{25}{\pi} = r^2$$
$$r = \sqrt{\frac{25}{\pi}}$$
$$r = \frac{5}{\sqrt{\pi}}$$

You're not done yet! You've found the radius, but the question asks for the diameter. In a sense, you're only halfway there:

$$2r = 2\left(\frac{5}{\sqrt{\pi}}\right) = \frac{10}{\sqrt{\pi}}$$

Look down the list of answers and you'll see that the correct choice is C. Choice A is the radius, not the diameter. Choice B is 10 divided by π rather than the square root of π. Choice D is 10 times π rather than 10 divided by the square root of π. Finally, although E resembles the radius, the square root of π appears in the numerator instead of the denominator.

Chapter 13

Keeping in Step: Coordinate Geometry

In This Chapter
▶ Taking off on the coordinate plane
▶ Using formulas to find slope, graph lines, midpoints, and distances
▶ Getting familiar with the graphs of functions

C oordinate geometry combines the study of algebra and planes with three-dimensional geometry. You can review geometry and algebra in Chapters 11 and 12; this chapter shows you how the concepts tie together. In this chapter, you figure out how equations and numbers relate to geometric forms and shapes, such as a straight line or a parabola.

You can expect to encounter coordinate geometry questions on roughly ten percent of the problems on the GMAT. If you're not particularly savvy about coordinate geometry, it won't significantly affect your GMAT math score.

Taking Flight: The Coordinate Plane

The coordinate plane doesn't have wings, but it does have points that spread out infinitely. You may not have encountered the coordinate plane in a while (it isn't something most people choose to deal with in everyday life), so take just a minute to refresh your memory about a few relevant terms that may pop up on the GMAT. Although you won't be asked to define these terms, knowing what they mean is absolutely essential.

Getting the line on some basic definitions

Here are some coordinate geometry terms that show up from time to time on the GMAT:

✔ **Coordinate plane:** The coordinate, or Cartesian, plane is a perfectly flat surface that contains a system in which points can be identified by their position using an ordered pair of numbers. This pair of numbers represents the points' distance from an origin on perpendicular axes. The coordinate of any particular point is the set of numbers that identifies the location of the point, such as (3, 4) or *(x, y)*.

✔ **x-axis:** The *x*-axis is the horizontal axis (number line) on a coordinate plane in which values or numbers start at the origin, which has a value of 0. Numbers increase in value to the right of the origin and decrease in value to the left. The *x* value of a point's coordinate is listed first.

- ✔ **y-axis:** The y-axis is the vertical axis (number line) on a coordinate plane in which values or numbers start at the origin, which has a value of 0. Numbers increase in value going up from the origin and decrease in value going down. The y value of a point's coordinate is listed second.

- ✔ **Origin:** The origin is the point (0, 0) on the coordinate plain. It's where the x- and y-axes intersect.

- ✔ **Ordered pair:** Also known as a coordinate pair, this is the set of two numbers that shows the distance of a point from the origin. The horizontal (x) coordinate is always listed first, and the vertical coordinate (y) is listed second.

- ✔ **Ordinate:** Ordinate is another way of referring to the y-coordinate in an ordered pair.

- ✔ **x-intercept:** The value of x where a line, curve, or some other function crosses the x-axis. The value of y is 0 at the x-intercept. The x-intercept is often the *solution* or *root* of an equation.

- ✔ **y-intercept:** The value of y where a line, curve, or some other function crosses the y-axis. The value of x is 0 at the y-intercept.

- ✔ **Slope:** Slope measures how steep a line is and is commonly referred to as *the rise over the run*.

Line dancing: Defining the coordinate plane

The coordinate plane extends infinitely in two directions and has no depth. It's a two-dimensional concept, having length and width. The coordinate plane provides an extremely helpful way to graphically work with equations that have two variables, usually x and y.

What's the point?

The coordinate plane consists of two perpendicular, intersecting number lines. The horizontal number line is called the x-axis, and the vertical number line is called the y-axis. The point where the two axes intersect is called the origin. The arrows at the end of the axes show that they go on infinitely.

You can identify any point on the coordinate plane by its coordinates (also known as an ordered pair), which designate the point's location along the x- and y-axes. For example, the ordered pair (2, 3) has a coordinate point that is located two units to the right of the origin along the horizontal (x) number line and three units up on the vertical (y) number line. In Figure 13-1, point A is at (2, 3). The x-coordinate appears first, and the y-coordinate shows up second. Pretty simple so far, huh?

On all fours: Quadrants

The intersection of the x- and y-axes forms four quadrants on the coordinate plane, which just so happen to be named Quadrants I, II, III, and IV (see Figure 13-1). Here's what you can assume about points based on the quadrants they're in:

- ✔ All points in Quadrant I have a positive x value and a positive y value.

- ✔ All points in Quadrant II have a negative x value and a positive y value.

- ✔ All points in Quadrant III have a negative x value and a negative y value.

- ✔ All points in Quadrant IV have a positive x value and a negative y value.

- ✔ All points along the x-axis have a y value of 0.

- ✔ All points along the y-axis have an x value of 0.

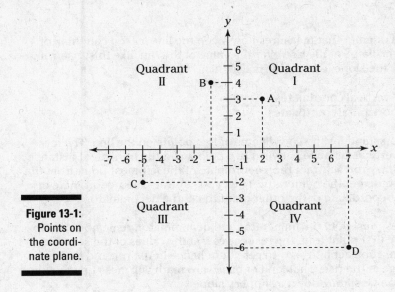

Figure 13-1:
Points on the coordinate plane.

Quadrant I starts to the right of the *y*-axis and above the *x*-axis. It's the upper-right portion of the coordinate plane. As shown in Figure 13-1, the other quadrants move counter-clockwise around the origin. Figure 13-1 also shows the location of coordinate points A, B, C, and D:

- Point A is in Quadrant I and has coordinates (2, 3).
- Point B is in Quadrant II and has coordinates (–1, 4).
- Point C is in Quadrant III and has coordinates (–5, –2).
- Point D is in Quadrant IV and has coordinates (7, –6).

The GMAT won't ask you to pick your favorite quadrant, but you may be asked to identify what quadrant a particular point belongs in.

Slip-Sliding Away: Slope and Linear Equations

One of the handiest things about the coordinate plane is that it graphs the locations of lines and linear equations. In fact, questions that expect you to know how to graph lines and equations are some of most common GMAT coordinate geometry questions. You should know the formula for finding the slope, the slope-intercept formula, and the formula for determining the distance between two points on the plane.

Taking a peak: Defining slope

Figure 13-2 gives you a visual definition of just what we mean by slope. You'll notice that if a line isn't parallel to one of the coordinate axes, it either rises or falls from the left-hand side of the coordinate plane to the right-hand side. The steepness of the line's rising or falling is its *slope*.

The formula for slope

The slope of the line is just a number that measures how steep the line is. You can think of the slope as a fraction with the value of the rise over the value of the run, like this: rise/run. In more mathematical terms, the slope formula looks like this:

$$\text{Slope}(m) = \frac{\text{change in vertical coordinates}}{\text{change in horizontal coordinates}} = \frac{y_2 - y_1}{x_2 - x_1}$$

The x's and y's in the equation stand for the coordinates of two points on the line. The formula is just the ratio of the vertical distance between two points and the horizontal distance between those same two points. You subtract the y-coordinate of the left-most point from the y-coordinate of the other point to get the numerator. Then you subtract the x-coordinate of the left-most point from the x-coordinate of the other point to get the denominator.

When you subtract the values present in the numerator and denominator, remember to subtract the x and y values of the first point from the respective x and y values of the second point. Don't fall for the trap of subtracting $x_2 - x_1$ to get your change in the run and then subtracting $y_1 - y_2$ for your change in the rise. That kind of backward math will mess up your calculations, and you'll very soon be sliding down a slippery slope.

The graph in Figure 13-2 shows how important it is to perform these operations in the right order.

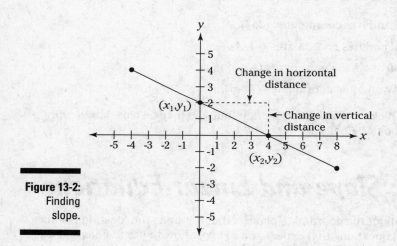

Figure 13-2: Finding slope.

In Figure 13-2, you'd use the coordinate point $(0, 2)$ as your (x_1, y_1), and the coordinate point $(4, 0)$ as (x_2, y_2). It may be tempting to subtract the 0 in each coordinate point from the corresponding greater number in the other coordinate point, but doing that switches the order of how you subtract the x and y values in the two coordinate points.

For the slope formula to work, you need to take 0 minus 2 for your $y_2 - y_1$ operation (which gives you −2), and then take 4 minus 0 as your $x_2 - x_1$ (which gives you 4). The resulting ratio, or fraction, is −²⁄₄, or −½. This gives you a slope of −½.

Positive and negative slope

You can see from Figure 13-2 that the line is falling from left to right. Aside from noticing the nice ski-slope effect, that's your visual clue that the line has a negative slope. Figure 13-3 shows how you can quickly eyeball a line to get a good idea of whether the slope is positive or negative.

In Figure 13-3, line *m* has a negative slope; line *n* has a positive slope.

✔ A line with a negative slope falls from left to right (its left side is higher than its right), and its slope is less than 0.

✔ A line with a positive slope rises from left to right (its right side is higher than its left), and its slope is greater than 0.

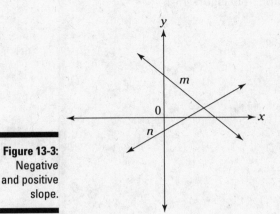

Figure 13-3:
Negative and positive slope.

Slopes of 0 and undefined slopes

Line *o* shown in Figure 13-4 has a slope of 0. Line *p* has a slope that's undefined; it has no slope.

✔ A horizontal line has a slope of 0; it neither rises nor falls and is parallel to the *x*-axis.

✔ The slope of a vertical line is undefined because you don't know whether it's rising or falling; it has no slope and is parallel to the *y*-axis.

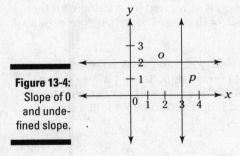

Figure 13-4:
Slope of 0 and unde-fined slope.

Using the slope-intercept formula to graph lines

The characteristics of a line can be conveyed through a mathematical formula. The equation of a line (also known as the *slope-intercept formula*) generally shows *y* as a function of *x*, like this:

$$y = mx + b$$

In the slope-intercept formula, the coefficient m is a constant that indicates the slope of the line, and the constant b is the y-intercept (that is, the point where the line crosses the y-axis). The equation of the line in Figure 13-2 is $y = -\frac{1}{2}x + 2$, because the slope is $-\frac{1}{2}$ and the y-intercept is 2. In Figure 13-4, the equation for line o is $y = 2$ and the equation for line p is $x = 3$.

A line with the formula $y = 4x + 1$ has a slope of 4 (which, as we said before, is a rise of 4 and run of 1) and a y-intercept of 1. The line is graphed in Figure 13-5.

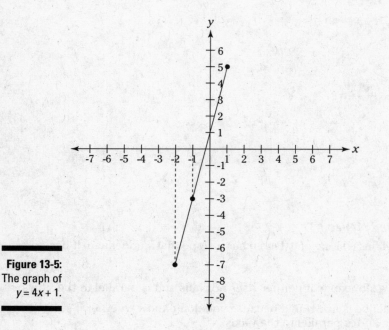

Figure 13-5:
The graph of
$y = 4x + 1$.

The GMAT may give you an equation of a line and ask you to choose the graph that correctly grids it. You can figure out how the line should look when it's graphed by starting with the value of the y-intercept, marking points that fit the value of the slope, and then connecting these points with a line.

Whenever you get an equation for a line that does not neatly fit into the slope-intercept format, go ahead and play with the equation a little bit (sounds fun, doesn't it?) so that it meets the $y = mx + b$ format that you know and love. For instance, if you saw the equation $\frac{1}{3}y - 3 = x$, you'd simply manipulate both sides of the equation and solve for y, like this:

$$\frac{1}{3}y - 3 = x$$

$$\frac{1}{3}y = x + 3$$

$$y = 3x + 9$$

Your new equation gives you the slope of the line, 3, as well as the y-intercept, 9. Pretty tricky!

Try these two sample questions to get a taste of how this information may be tested on the GMAT.

What is the equation of a line with a slope –¾ and a *y*-intercept of 8?

(A) $4x + 3y = 32$

(B) $-3x + 4y = 16$

(C) $3x - 4y = 32$

(D) $3x + 4y = 16$

(E) $3x + 4y = 32$

Because the slope-intercept formula for the line is $y = mx + b$, you know that *m* is the slope and *b* is the *y*-intercept. Plug these values into the slope-intercept formula:

$$y = (-\tfrac{3}{4})x + 8$$

All the answer choices have the same format:

$$ax + by = c$$

You need to convert your equation to the answers' format. Move the terms around by multiplying both sides by 4 and adding 3*x* to both sides, like this:

$$4y = -3x + 32$$
$$3x + 4y = 32$$

This means E is the correct answer.

Which quadrants would a line with the equation $y - 2x + 3 = 0$ for all real numbers pass through?

(A) I, II and III

(B) III and IV only

(C) I, II, III and IV

(D) I, III and IV

(E) II and IV only

You need to know where the quadrants are located on the coordinate plane. For reference, see Figure 13-1. You can immediately see that choice C is impossible. There isn't a straight line that can pass through all four quadrants, so cross out C.

The best way to start is to convert the linear equation into the slope-intercept form. You can convert the equation $y - 2x + 3 = 0$ to $y = 2x - 3$.

For this kind of question, you may want to draw on your notepad a coordinate plane graph and label the quadrants I, II, III, and IV. Nothing fancy, mind you, just enough to get your bearings. Now, draw a point below the origin on the *y*-axis representing –3, the *y*-intercept. Then draw a line that travels upward from left to right rising two units toward the top of the paper for every one to the right. Your figure doesn't have to be perfect. From your drawing, you can immediately see that the line passes through Quadrants I, III, and IV.

So D is your best choice. Choice A would be correct if you had a parallel line with a positive *y*-intercept. Choice B is possible for a line parallel to the *x*-axis with a negative *y*-intercept. Choice E would require a line with a negative slope passing through the origin.

Any line must travel through at least two quadrants, unless the line runs directly on top of either the *x*- or *y*-axis. A line that lies directly on top of an axis does not go *through* any quadrant. The lines that travel through only two quadrants are those that pass through the origin or are parallel to either the *x*- or the *y*-axis. All other lines must eventually travel through three quadrants.

Going the distance

Some of the questions on the GMAT may ask you to calculate the distance between two points on a line. You can solve these problems with coordinate geometry.

To answer these questions, use the *distance formula*. Assume you have two points, A (x_1, y_1) and B (x_2, y_2), on a line. The formula to find the distance between A and B is this:

$$AB = \sqrt{(x_2 - x_1)^2 + (y_2 - y_1)^2}$$

The graph in Figure 13-6 shows how the distance formula actually works.

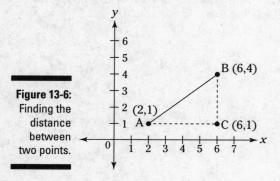

Figure 13-6:
Finding the distance between two points.

Notice that point A has coordinates (2, 1) and point B has coordinates (6, 4). To find the distance between these two points, you plug these numbers into the distance formula, like this:

$$AB = \sqrt{(x_2 - x_1)^2 + (y_2 - y_1)^2}$$
$$AB = \sqrt{(4)^2 + (3)^2}$$
$$AB = \sqrt{16 + 9}$$
$$AB = \sqrt{25}$$
$$AB = 5$$

If you're thinking that this formula looks familiar, you're absolutely right. It's another use for the good old Pythagorean theorem. (If this theorem is foreign to you, check out Chapter 6.) By connecting points A and B to a third point C, as shown in Figure 13-6, you get a right triangle, which in this case happens to be your tried and true 3:4:5 right triangle.

Here's a sample problem that asks you to find the midpoint and the distance between two points:

What is the distance of a line segment that connects the origin to the coordinate point (–2, –3)?

(A) $AB = \sqrt{13}$

(B) 5

(C) $\sqrt{5}$

(D) 8.94

(E) 13.42

Use the formula to figure out the distance between the coordinates of the origin (0, 0) and the endpoint (–2, –3):

$$AB = \sqrt{\left(x_2 - x_1\right)^2 + \left(y_2 - y_1\right)^2}$$
$$AB = \sqrt{\left(-2\right)^2 + \left(-3\right)^2}$$
$$AB = \sqrt{4 + 9}$$
$$AB = \sqrt{13}$$

Choice A is the answer. If you chose B, you simply took the coordinates for the endpoint, (–2, –3), and added them together to get distance, which, of course, isn't the proper method. Choice C results from failing to square the differences of the coordinates. You can guess that D and E are probably incorrect because uncovering their values would require using a calculator.

Notice that order doesn't matter when you subtract the x and y coordinate points from each other — you end up squaring their difference, so your answer will always be a positive number.

Keep in mind that, in the end, the distance between two points is always a positive number. If you ever see a negative number as an answer choice for a distance question, just let your mouse scoot on by.

Fully Functioning: Graphing Functions

Coordinate geometry and functions are connected. You can actually graph functions on the coordinate plane, and by looking at a graph of a function, you should be able to tell something about the function and its domain and range. The GMAT may give you a graph of a function and ask you to determine whether a statement about the function is true or false. We give you the information you need to know to get these questions right.

When you graph a function $f(x)$ on the coordinate plane, the x value of the function (the input, or the domain, of the function) goes along the x-, or horizontal, axis, and the $f(x)$ value of the function goes along the y-, or vertical, axis. Anytime you see a coordinate pair that represents a function, for example (x, y), the x value is the domain, or input, of the function and the y value is the output, or range, of the function. (If you need more info on functions, see Chapter 11.)

Passing the vertical line test

A function is a distinct relationship between the x (input) value and the y or $f(x)$ (output) value. For every x value, there is a distinct y value that is different from the y output value of any other x value. The vertical line test is one way to look at a graph and tell whether it's a graph of a function. This test says that no vertical line intersects the graph of a function at more than one point.

For example, the graphs in Figure 13-7 show two straight lines that pass the vertical line test and therefore represent functions.

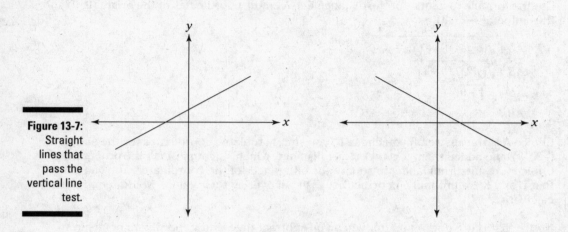

Figure 13-7: Straight lines that pass the vertical line test.

The two lines in Figure 13-7 go on infinitely in both directions. Any vertical line you draw on the graph would intersect the graphed line only at one point. For every x value along the line in each of these graphs, there's a separate and distinct y value that corresponds to it. These lines pass the vertical line test, which means they represent functions.

You probably already know that most lines are functions — after all, the equation of a line is $y = mx + b$. Now you can see it for yourself graphically.

Take a look at the line in Figure 13-8 to see a case where a straight line isn't the graph of a function.

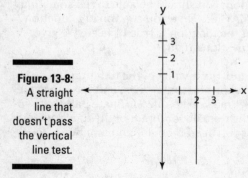

Figure 13-8: A straight line that doesn't pass the vertical line test.

The line in Figure 13-8 is vertical (its equation is $x = 2$), so it fails the vertical line test. There are bazillions of y values along the vertical line, but it has only one x value. Therefore, the vertical line in Figure 13-8 isn't a function.

Not all lines are straight. Sometimes you see graphs of curved lines. Take a look at the two graphs in Figure 13-9 and determine which of them graphs a function.

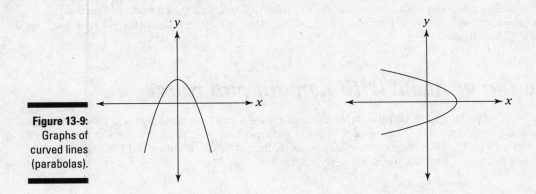

Figure 13-9:
Graphs of curved lines (parabolas).

The curves in Figure 13-9 look like parabolas, a shape we discuss in more detail in the upcoming section about graphing domain and range. The curve in the left graph opens downward, so it goes on infinitely downward and outward. For every *x* value on that curve, there's a separate and distinct *y* value. This curve passes the vertical line test and therefore graphs a function. The curve in the right graph is almost like the first one, except that it opens sideways. One vertical line *can* cross the path of this curve in more than one place. Therefore, this curve is not the graph of a function.

Questions that ask you to recognize the graph of a function appear rarely on the GMAT, but if you see one, you'll know what to do.

EXAMPLE

Which of the following graphs in Figure 13-10 is NOT a graph of a function?

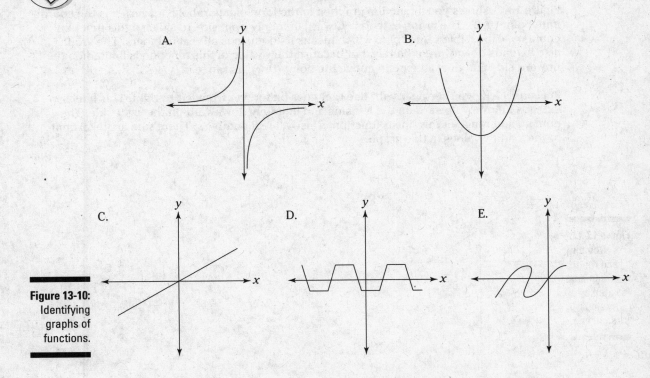

Figure 13-10:
Identifying graphs of functions.

This kind of question is relatively easy unless you're not familiar with the vertical line test. Choice E is the correct answer because it's a curve that sort of doubles back from right to left. It's possible for a vertical line to intersect that curve at more than one point. The other graphs in this question show curves, lines, or some other shape that a vertical line would never pass through at more than one point. All the graphs except E pass the test and are graphs of functions.

Feeling at home with domain and range

The GMAT expects you to be able to look at a graph of a function and have a pretty good idea of what the domain and the range of that particular function are. You may see a graph of a function and have to determine the effective domain and range. Figures 13-11, 13-12, and 13-13 are examples of what some of these graphs may look like.

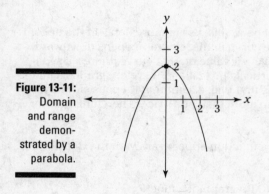

Figure 13-11: Domain and range demonstrated by a parabola.

Figure 13-11 shows you a function graphed in the form of a parabola. Its vertex is the coordinate point (0, 2). The graph extends outward infinitely from side to side, so this function contains all possible values of *x,* which means its domain is all real numbers. The graph also extends downward infinitely, but because the *y* value in this function is limited on the upward side and doesn't extend above the point (0, 2), its range is {*y*: *y* ≤ 2}

In Figure 13-12, you see a straight line that goes on forever from left to right. This line also extends infinitely upward on the left side and infinitely downward on the right side. The domain and range of this linear function is also all real numbers. There's no artificial limit to the *x* and *y* values in this graph.

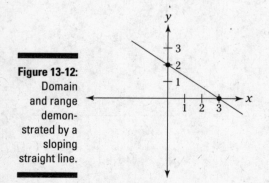

Figure 13-12: Domain and range demonstrated by a sloping straight line.

In Figure 13-13, the horizontal line extends infinitely from right to left, but it has only one value on the vertical axis, or *y*-axis. Its *y* value is limited to –3, so the equation for this line is $y = -3$ and the range is limited to simply $\{y: y = -3\}$. Because the line goes on forever from left to right, it includes every possible *x* value, which means the domain of this linear function is all real numbers.

That's really all there is to it. You'll be prepared for any GMAT question you face on test day:

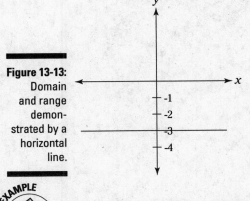

Figure 13-13:
Domain and range demonstrated by a horizontal line.

Which of the following answers could be the domain of the function of the figure below?

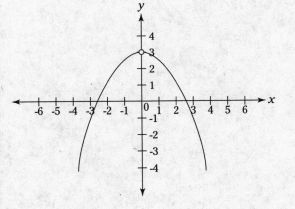

(A) $\{x: x \neq 0\}$

(B) $\{x: x \neq 3\}$

(C) $\{x: x = 0\}$

(D) $\{x: x \leq 3\}$

(E) $\{x: x < 0 > x\}$

This question asks for the *domain,* not the *range,* so don't let the fact that the upper limit of the *y* value is just shy of 3 distract you from looking for all the possible *x* values that make up the domain. You should toss out any answer choice that refers to the value 3 like a hot potato, so get rid of answers B and D right away.

The empty circle point (3, 0) means that you don't count that point in your answer. So, C is exactly the opposite of what you're looking for. Also, C limits your domain to only one value, 0. Because the value of 0 is actually *excluded* from the function, C simply can't be right. The way E is formatted doesn't make sense at all. Set your sights on A as the answer of the hour. The domain, or *x* value, is not equal to 0.

Chapter 14

Manipulating Numbers: Statistics and Sets

- -

In This Chapter

▶ Getting a grip on group problems

▶ Excelling with unions and intersections

▶ Arranging groups with permutations and combinations

▶ Managing means

▶ Solving standard deviations

▶ Prospering on probability problems

- -

From the time you mastered the ability to tie your shoes in kindergarten, you had to figure out how to work and play in groups. The GMAT tests what you know about groups of numbers, or sets. These question types are usually pretty easy, so you could probably work out the answers to most of the GMAT set questions given enough time. But of course, you don't have all the time in the world on the GMAT test. We provide you some sure shortcuts to help you answer set questions quickly.

You may find the statistics and probability questions a little more challenging. The GMAT test has more statistical questions than any other major standardized test. We guess they figure that if you're going to get an MBA, you should know some statistics. The science of statistics involves organizing, analyzing, and interpreting data in order to reach reasonable conclusions and to help in decision-making. You need to know how to determine probability and some type of statistical average and variations from the average. The statistics questions you'll encounter on the GMAT aren't particularly complex, but giving this subject your full attention will pay off.

Maneuvering through the Cliques: Groups

Group problems regard populations of persons or objects and the way these populations are grouped together into categories. The questions generally ask you either to find the total of a series of groups or to determine how many people or objects make up one of the subgroups.

You can find the answer to most group problems if you use your counting skills, but counting is time-consuming, and you want to work smarter, not harder, to solve these questions. Solving group problems comes down to applying simple arithmetic and nothing else.

The formula for solving group problems is

Group 1 + Group 2 – Both Groups + Neither Group = Grand Total

So if you're told that out of 110 students, 47 are enrolled in a cooking class, 56 take a welding course, and 33 take both cooking and welding, you can use the formula to find out how many students take neither cooking nor welding. Let Group 1 be the cooks and Group 2 the welders. The variable is the group that doesn't take either the cooking or welding class. Plug the known values into the formula and set up an equation to solve:

Group 1 + Group 2 – Both Groups + Neither Group = Grand Total

$$47 + 56 - 33 + \text{Neither Group} = 110$$
$$47 + 56 - 33 + x = 110$$
$$70 + x = 110$$
$$x = 40$$

Of the 110 students, 40 take neither cooking class nor welding class. Here's an example of how group problems may appear on the GMAT:

One-third of all United States taxpayers may deduct charitable contributions on their federal income tax returns. Forty percent of all taxpayers may deduct state income tax payments from their federal returns. If 55 percent of all taxpayers may not deduct either charitable contributions or state sales tax, what portion of all taxpayers may claim both types of deductions?

(A) 15%

(B) 18%

(C) 20%

(D) 28%

(E) $\frac{17}{60}$

Use the formula to determine the correct percentage of taxpayers who may claim both deductions. Group 1 can be the $\frac{1}{3}$ who claim charitable deductions, and Group 2 can be those who deduct state income tax payments. The unknown is those who make up both groups.

Even though most of the answer choices express the numbers as percentages, convert them to fractions, because you have to compare each answer to $\frac{1}{3}$. Converting percentages to fractions without using a calculator is easier than converting the other way around.

So 40 percent is the same as $\frac{40}{100}$, which reduces to $\frac{2}{5}$. Fifty-five percent is the same as $\frac{55}{100}$, which equals $\frac{11}{20}$. Plug in the values and solve the formula:

Group 1 + Group 2 – Both Groups + Neither Group = Grand Total

$$\tfrac{1}{3} + \tfrac{2}{5} - x + \tfrac{11}{20} = 1$$

To add and subtract fractions, you have to find a common denominator for all fractions and then convert the fractions so that all have the same denominator. The common denominator is 60 for this problem (see Chapter 10 for more about performing operations with fractions).

$$^{20}\!/_{60} + {}^{24}\!/_{60} - x + {}^{33}\!/_{60} = 1$$

$$^{77}\!/_{60} - x = 1$$

$$x = {}^{17}\!/_{60}$$

The correct answer is E.

Compute accurately. Don't be fooled into thinking that the one-third of the taxpayers who can claim charitable contributions equals 33 percent of taxpayers. Although one-third is very close to 33 percent, it isn't exactly that amount. If you used 33 percent instead of one-third, you may have chosen D, which isn't the right answer. If you convert ⅓ to 33 percent, you're sacrificing accuracy to save time.

Sharing the Road: Union and Intersection

Groups are related to sets. A *set* is a collection of objects, numbers, or values. The objects in a set are the *elements,* or *members,* of the set. Elements belong to the set. The symbol ∈ means "is an element of," while ∉ means an object or thing or value "is not an element of" a set.

When dealing with ways to combine sets, the terms *union* and *intersection* describe how two or more sets relate to one another through the elements they contain. An *empty set,* or *null set,* is represented by the symbol ∅, which simply means that there's nothing in that set.

Joining forces: Unions

A union is more inclusive than an intersection. The union of two sets A and B (written as $A \cup B$) contains the set of all elements of both set A and set B. For example, the union of sets $A = \{0, 1, 2, 3, 4, 5, 6, 7, 8, 9\}$ and $B = \{2, 4, 6, 8, 10\}$ is the set $A \cup B = \{0, 1, 2, 3, 4, 5, 6, 7, 8, 9, 10\}$.

Crossing paths: Intersections

An intersection of two or more sets is less inclusive than a union. The intersection of two sets A and B (written as $A \cap B$) is the set of all elements that appear in both sets, not just in either one. For example, the intersection of sets $A = \{0, 1, 2, 3, 5, 6, 7, 8, 9\}$ and $B = \{2, 4, 6, 8, 10\}$ is the set $A \cap B = \{2, 6, 8\}$.

If all the elements of set B also appear in set A, you'd say that set B is a *subset* of set A. So if set $A = \{0, 1, 2, 3, 5, 6, 7, 8, 9\}$ and set $B = \{2, 3, 5, 7\}$, set $B \subset A$. If none of the elements of two or more sets intersect, they are *disjoint* sets. For example, set A and set B are disjoint sets if set $A = \{0, 2, 6, 8\}$ and set $B = \{1, 3, 5, 7\}$.

Getting a visual: Venn diagrams

You can also illustrate the concept of sets with graphic diagrams. The classic Venn diagrams in Figure 14-1 give visual examples of how sets are related to one another using set terminology. You can draw Venn diagrams to help you answer GMAT questions about sets.

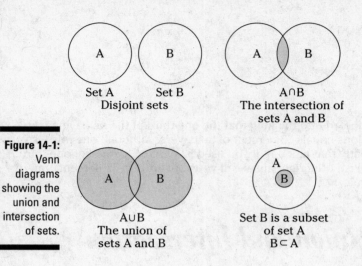

Figure 14-1:
Venn
diagrams
showing the
union and
intersection
of sets.

Set A   Set B
Disjoint sets

A∩B
The intersection of
sets A and B

A∪B
The union of
sets A and B

Set B is a subset
of set A
B⊂A

GMAT questions regarding sets are usually pretty straightforward. Here are a couple examples:

A = {a, b, c, d, e, f}

B = {c, e, g, i, k}

$C = A \cap B$

What are the elements of set C?

(A) {a, b, c, d, e, f, g, i, k}

(B) {c, e}

(C) ∅

(D) {a, b, c, d, e, f}

(E) {c, e, g, i, k}

You just need to correctly read the symbols that show the relationships between sets. Here, the set C is the intersection of sets A and B. Because the intersection of two sets includes only those elements that show up in both sets, the correct answer is B.

A = {5, 10, 15, 20}

B = {2, 4, 6, 8, 10}

$C = A \cup B$

What is the mean average of the elements of set C?

(A) 8.75

(B) 8.89

(C) 10

(D) ∅

(E) It cannot be determined from the information given.

Solving this problem requires two steps.

1. **Correctly interpret the ∪ symbol to determine the elements of set *C*.** Because ∪ means a combination of all of the elements of both sets, set C = {2, 4, 5, 6, 8, 10, 15, 20}.

    Don't count 10 twice, or you'll be double billing that number.

2. **Figure out the mean average of the numbers in set *C*.** Add up the numbers, and you get the grand total of 70. Now divide by the number of elements in the union of the two sets: 70 ÷ 8 = 8.75.

The correct answer is A. If you added the extra 10 to set *C*, you'd get answer B, which is 80 ÷ 9. Choice D is the mean average of the elements of the intersection of *A* and *B*. The other two choices are red herrings designed to throw you off when you're weary of taking the test.

> $L = \{s, t, u\}$
>
> $M = \{u, w, y\}$
>
> $N = \{v, w, y, z\}$

What is $|L \cup M|$?

(A) 6

(B) *{s, t, u, v, w, y}*

(C) *{u}*

(D) 5

(E) *{s, t, u, v, w, y, z}*

This question asks for the absolute value of the number of elements in a union of two sets — not the union of the two sets. (To find out more about absolute value, read Chapter 10.) The third set, *N*, is just thrown in as a distracter.

$L \cup M = \{s, t, u, w, y\}$, so $|L \cup M| = 5$, because 5 is the value of the number of elements in the set.

This means the correct answer is D.

You can eliminate B, C, and E because absolute value is a number, and these answer choices are sets rather than numerical values.

Making Arrangements: Permutations and Combinations

The GMAT tests you on how groups and sets may be arranged. When you calculate *permutations*, you figure out the number of ways the elements of a set can be arranged in specific orders. Determining *combinations* is similar to finding permutations, except that the order of the arrangements doesn't matter. To deal with permutations and combinations, you'll need to know about *factorials*. A factorial is the product of all natural numbers in the set of numbers, from one through the number of the factorial. Don't worry if you don't understand these concepts right away. We explain them more thoroughly, starting with permutations.

Positioning with permutations

Permutations problems ask you to determine how many arrangements of numbers are possible given a specific set of numbers and a particular order for the arrangements. For instance, the amount of possible telephone numbers you can develop given seven-digit numbers and ten possible values (the values between 0 and 9) to fill each of the seven places is huge, 10^7.

You can arrange the elements of the set {a, b, c} in six different ways:

$$a\,b\,c \quad a\,c\,b \quad b\,a\,c \quad b\,c\,a \quad c\,a\,b \quad c\,b\,a$$

You may think that because each group contains the same elements, these groupings aren't really different combinations. But with permutations, order matters. Even though two different phone numbers may have the same combination of numbers (like 345-7872 and 543-7728), the phone numbers ring two different lines because you input them into the phone in a different order.

 The number of permutations of *n* objects is *n!*. The ! is called a *factorial,* and the expression is read "*n* factorial." This means you take all the numbers in a series, starting with *n* and counting down by 1 until you get to the number 1, and then you multiply all those numbers together.

The factorial of 0 is written as 0!. 0! always equals 1.

Without writing out the arrangements for {a, b, c} like we just did, you can use factorials to figure out how many permutations exist for the three elements. Three different elements (the letters in the set) arranged in as many ways as possible goes like this: 3!, which is equal to $3 \times 2 \times 1$, which is equal to 6. So 3! = 6, and there are six permutations for three elements.

You follow the same procedure for more than three elements. Suppose that five people are in a wedding party. The photographer wants to photograph the wedding party in a row, one person right next to the other. How many different arrangements of the five wedding party members are possible?

$$5! = 5 \times 4 \times 3 \times 2 \times 1 = 120$$

As you can see, the greater the number of objects you're trying to find the number of permutations for, the more arrangements possible. That's all there is to your basic permutations. Here's a sample GMAT question:

How many ways can four different charms be arranged on a charm bracelet?

(A) 4

(B) 8

(C) 24

(D) 100

(E) 40,320

Write out the factorial for 4:

$$4 \times 3 \times 2 \times 1$$

Then just multiply the numbers to get the number of possible arrangements. The order you multiply them in doesn't matter. 4×3 is 12, and 12×2 is 24. Because 24×1 is 24, the correct answer is C.

You can eliminate A and B because they're too small. You know that more than four arrangements must exist, because you have four charms. Choice B is 4×2, which isn't much better. In permutations, you know the number gets pretty large in a hurry, but not as large as E, which is 8!.

The joy of permutations really begins when you have a fixed number of objects, *n*, to fill a limited number of places, *r*, and you care about the order the objects are arranged in.

For example, consider the predicament of the big-league baseball coach who has a 20-member baseball team and who needs to determine all the different batting orders that these 20 ball players can fill in a 9-slot batting lineup. You could work this out by writing out all of the factors from 20 back 9 places (because 20 players can only fill 9 slots in the batting order), like this:

$$20 \times 19 \times 18 \times 17 \times 16 \times 15 \times 14 \times 13 \times 12 = x$$

The coach doesn't have the luxury of figuring out all the possibilities in the heat of the game. Luckily, he has an easier way.

The number of permutations of *n* things taken *r* at a time is stated as $_nP_r$. (To help you remember the formula, you may even think of a certain public radio station that has these call letters.) The permutation formula for *n* objects taken *r* at a time looks like this:

$$_nP_r = n! \div (n - r)!$$

To use this formula to figure out the possible number of batting orders, calculate as follows:

$n!/(n - r)!$

$20!/(20 - 9)!$

$= 20!/11!$

The GMAT doesn't allow you to use calculators, so it won't expect you to calculate the permutation beyond this point. Here's an example of how permutations may appear on the GMAT:

A lawn care company has five employees, and there are ten houses that need care on a given day. How many different ways can the company assign the five employees to work at the different houses on that day if each employee works at two houses?

(A) 50

(B) $\frac{2!}{1!}$

(C) 120

(D) $\frac{10!}{5!}$

(E) 10!

This question may seem counterintuitive to the formula, which calculates n number of things taken r at a time to get the number of permutations. This problem appears to be taking a smaller number of things, r (the number of employees), and finding out how many times they can be spread around a greater number of places. That's what makes this a tricky question.

This problem may look backwards, but it really follows the same formula. Rather than thinking of how to spread five workers over ten houses, think of how many ways you can arrange the ten houses over the more limited number of workers.

$$_nP_r = n!/(n - r)!$$
$$_{10}P_5 = 10!/(10 - 5)!$$
$$= 10!/5!$$

The correct answer is D. With a calculator, you could figure out that 30,240 ways exist to assign employees. If you choose A, you're simply multiplying the number of workers times the number of houses. But that's not the correct calculation. Choice C is what you get if you calculated 5!, which isn't the complete answer. Likewise, E is incomplete.

Don't let B trip you up. You can't simplify factorials like you can common fractions. $\frac{10!}{5!}$ doesn't equal $\frac{2!}{1!}$.

If this problem was difficult for you, take heart: You won't see too many of these kinds of questions on the GMAT.

Coming together: Combinations

Combinations are a lot like permutations, only easier. A combination is the number of objects you can choose from a total sample of objects and combine when order doesn't matter. For instance, a combination problem may ask you to find out how many different teams, committees, or other types of groups can be formed from a set number of persons. Because the order doesn't matter with combinations, you get a lot fewer possibilities in your final calculation than you do with permutations.

If you're asked to select as many teams as you can from a set number of people and the order of the team members doesn't matter, you're finding the total number of combinations, as opposed to the permutations, of different teams.

The formula for combinations is the number of ways to choose r objects from a group of n objects when the order of the objects doesn't matter. The formula looks like this:

$$_nC_r = n!/r!(n - r)!$$

You can see right away that this formula is different from the one for permutations. Because you have a larger number in the denominator than you would have with a permutation, the final number will be smaller.

One way to think about combinations is to ask how many three-member committees can be formed by Tom, Dick, and Harry. The order of how you list the committee members doesn't matter, so you only have one possible combination of three-member committees from these three persons. A committee composed of Tom, Dick, and Harry is the same as a committee composed of Tom, Harry, and Dick or one composed of Dick, Tom, and Harry. A permutation would result in six different possible arrangements, but because order doesn't matter, you have only one possible committee makeup.

You can prove your calculation by using the combination formula:

$$_nC_r = n!/r!(n - r)!$$

$$_3C_3 = 3!/3!(3 - 3)!$$

The 3! in the numerator and denominator cancel each other out, so you're left with this:

$$1/(3 - 3)!$$

$1/(3 - 3)!$ is the same as $\frac{1}{0}!$. And $0! = 1$, so the answer is $\frac{1}{1}$, or 1. All three guys can form just one group.

Suppose a person taking a poll randomly selects a group of three people from a group of five available persons. To figure out how many possible groups of different persons will result, start with the combination formula, because the order of the persons in the group doesn't matter.

$$_nC_r = n!/r!(n - r)!$$

$$_5C_3 = 5!/3!(5 - 3)!$$

The factorial of 5 is 120 ($5 \times 4 \times 3 \times 2 \times 1$), and the factorial of 3 is 6 ($3 \times 2 \times 1$). So this is the resulting equation:

$$_5C_3 = 120/6(5 - 3)!$$

Subtract the values in the parentheses:

$$_5C_3 = 120/6(2)!$$

The value of 2! is 2 (because 2×1 is 2); $6 \times 2 = 12$:

$$_5C_3 = {}^{120}/_{12}$$

$$_5C_3 = 10$$

Therefore, the pollster could make ten different combinations of people to be polled.

Because you can't use a calculator, GMAT combination problems won't get too complex. The test makers won't make you do complex calculations on your notepad, even though it is erasable!

Some fourth graders are choosing foursquare teams at recess. What is the total possible number of combinations of four-person teams that could be chosen from a group of six kids?

(A) 6

(B) 15

(C) 120

(D) 360

(E) 98,280

Go ahead and apply the formula for combinations and see what happens:

$$_nC_r = n!/r!(n - r)!$$

$$_6C_4 = 6!/4!(6 - 4)!$$

$$_6C_4 = 6!/ 4! \times 2!$$

$$_6C_4 = {}^{720}\!/\!_{24} \times 2$$

$$_6C_4 = {}^{720}\!/\!_{48}$$

After you've done the calculations, you find that the correct answer is B.

If you went for D, you calculated a permutation instead of a combination.

Meeting in the Middle: Mean, Median, and Mode

In addition to arranging sets of numbers, on the GMAT you must evaluate them. To evaluate data correctly, you should know the central tendency of numbers and the dispersion of their values. A measurement of *central tendency* is a value that is typical, or representative, of a group of numbers or other information. Common tools for describing a central tendency include arithmetic mean, median, mode, and weighted mean.

Performing above average on arithmetic means

The most common of the tendency figures is the arithmetic mean, or simply the *mean*. The mean of a group of numbers is the same thing as their average. To find the mean of a set of numbers, add up the numbers and divide by the quantity of numbers in the group. The formula looks like this:

$$\text{Arithmetic Mean} = \frac{\text{Sum of all numbers}}{\text{Amount of numbers in the sum}}$$

You can use given values in this formula to solve for the other values. For instance, if the GMAT gave you the average and the sum of a group of numbers, you could figure out how many numbers were in the set by using the formula for arithmetic mean.

You'll probably see a bunch of questions on the GMAT that ask you to figure out the mean. Here's a sampling of just a couple of them:

George tried to compute the mean average of his 8 test scores. He mistakenly divided the correct sum of all of his test scores by 7 and got an average of 96. What is George's actual mean test score?

(A) 80

(B) 84

(C) 96

(D) 100

(E) 108

Because you know George's mean test score when the sum is divided by 7, you can determine the sum of George's scores. This information will then allow you to use the arithmetic mean formula to determine his mean average over 8 tests. Here's what you do:

1. **Apply the average formula to George's mistaken calculation.**

$$96 = \text{sum of scores}/7$$

$$96 \times 7 = \text{sum of scores}$$

$$672 = \text{sum of scores}$$

2. **Use George's test score sum to figure out his actual mean average.**

$$\text{Mean average} = {}^{672}\!/_{8}$$

$$\text{Mean average} = 84$$

You know that his average must be less than 96 because you're dividing by a larger number, so you can automatically eliminate C, D, and E. The correct answer is B.

What is the mean of these four expressions: $2n + 8$, $3n - 2$, $n + 4$, and $6n - 2$?

(A) $3n + 2$

(B) $3n + 8$

(C) $12n + 8$

(D) $48n + 32$

(E) $2n$

You figure the average by applying the formula. Divide the sum of the expressions by the number of expressions.

$$\text{Arithmetic Mean} = \frac{\text{Sum of all numbers}}{\text{Amount of numbers in the sum}}$$

$$\text{Arithmetic Mean} = \frac{2n + 8 + 3n - 2 + n + 4 + 6n - 2}{4}$$

$$\text{Arithmetic Mean} = \frac{12n + 8}{4}$$

Divide both terms in the numerator by 4: ${}^{12n}\!/_{4} = 3n$, and $\frac{8}{4} = 2$.

The mean is $3n + 2$, and A is the answer.

Mastering medians

Median is another tendency figure you may see tested on the GMAT. The median is the middle value among a list of several values or numbers. To find out the median, put the values or numbers in order, usually from low to high, and choose the value that falls exactly in the middle of the other values. If you have an odd number of values, just select the middle value. If you have an even number of values, find the two middle values and average them. The outcome is the median.

Managing modes

You may also encounter *mode* on the GMAT. The mode is the value that occurs most often in a set of values. Questions about mode may contain words like *frequency* or ask you how often a value occurs. For example, you may be asked what income occurs most frequently in a given population or sample. If more people in the population or sample have an income of $30,000 than any other income amount, the mode is $30,000.

Whizzing through weighted means

The GMAT may test you on *weighted means*. You determine a weighted mean by multiplying each individual value by the number of times it occurs in a set of numbers. Then you add these products together and divide this sum by the total number of times all the values occur. For example, suppose you're given Table 14-1 charting Becky's grades in all her classes and the amount of credits for each.

Table 14-1	The Weighted Mean of Grade Point Averages		
Class	*Number of Credits*	*Grade*	*Total Grade Points*
Statistics	5	3.8	19
English	5	1.9	9.5
Speech	4	2.3	9.2
Bowling	1	4.0	4
Total	15	2.78 GPA	41.7

First, you multiply the individual values (the grades) by the number of times they each occur (the credits) to get total grade points for each class. Then you add up the total grade points for all classes (41.7) and divide by the total number of times they all occur (which is the number of total credits, 15): 41.7 ÷ 15 = 2.78 GPA.

Straying from Home: Range and Standard Deviation

Besides knowing the main concepts of central tendency, you should also know about *variation* or *dispersion* of values in statistics. The mean, median, and mode can tell you something about the central tendency of a set of values, but the dispersion tells you how spread out the values are from the center. If dispersion is small, the values are clustered around the mean. But a wide dispersion of values tells you that the mean average isn't a reliable representative of all the values.

Scouting out the range

The easiest measure of dispersion is the *range*. The range is simply the biggest value minus the smallest value in the data. The range of values in statistics can either come from a population or a sample. The *population* is the set of all objects or things, that is, the total amount of all data considered. A *sample* is just a part of the population.

You can say that the range is the difference between the highest and lowest values in the set of data. For example, if the highest test score in the math class was 94 percent and the lowest was 59 percent, you'd subtract the low from the high to get the range.

$$94 - 59 = 35$$

The range of test scores is 35. Simple as that! Here's a sample problem:

EXAMPLE

From the set of numbers 47, 63, 53, 39, 72, 53, 54, and 57, what is the range?

(A) 8

(B) 53

(C) 39

(D) 72

(E) 33

The range of any set of numbers is the value of the greatest element minus the value of the least element. The biggest number here is 72 and the smallest is 39. The difference is 72 – 39, which equals 33.

The correct answer for the range is E. A is the number of the elements in the given set, not the range. Choice B is the mode for the set. Choice C is the least element, and D is the greatest element in the set.

Watching out for wanderers: Standard deviation

Another form of variation, or dispersion, you'll need to know about on the GMAT is *standard deviation*. The standard deviation expresses variation by measuring how spread out the distribution is from the mean. Although the range can give you an idea of the total spread, standard deviation is a more reliable indicator of dispersion, because it considers all the data, not just the two on each end. Standard deviation is the most widely used figure for expressing how much the data is dispersed from the mean.

For example, suppose you get a grade of 75 on a test where the mean grade is 70 and the vast majority of all the other grades fall between 60 and 80. Your score is comparatively better in this situation than if you get a 75 on the same test, where the mean grade is still 70, but most of the grades fall between 45 and 95. In the first situation, the grades are more tightly clustered around the central tendency. A standard deviation in this case is a small number. Getting a score that's a standard deviation away from the mean is harder. Your grade is higher compared to all the other test takers' in the first group than your grade would be in the second scenario. In the second scenario, the standard deviation is a bigger number than it is in the first group, and a grade of 75 isn't as good relative to the others.

You've probably had a statistics class by this time in your career, and you probably had to calculate standard deviation in that class. The GMAT won't ask you to actually calculate standard deviation, but it will expect you to know how to use standard deviation.

It's a good idea to be able to recognize that with a symmetrical bell curve, the relationship between the standard deviation and the mean is pretty scientific. Figure 14-2 shows a bell curve and the distribution of the standard deviations away from the mean. The mean appears as an X with a line over it, and it shows the average value is right in the middle of all the values. If you stray 1 standard deviation in either direction from the mean, you'll have netted 68 percent of all the values. Going another standard deviation away from the center, you pick up another 32 percent of all values, giving you about 95 percent of all values. Finally, when you go ± 3 standard deviations from the mean, you now have about 99.7 percent of all the values in your population or sample.

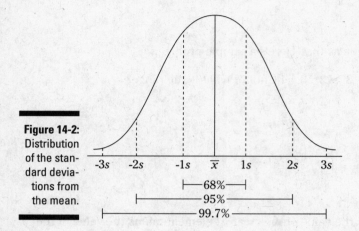

Figure 14-2: Distribution of the standard deviations from the mean.

If the curve in Figure 14-2 showed a group of test scores, it would mean that more than a majority of test-takers scored within 1 standard deviation of the mean (68 percent is more than 51 percent). The vast majority scored within 2 standard deviations, and virtually everyone scored within 3 standard deviations. Say that the mean test score is 80, and one standard deviation may be 10 points on either side. This means that 68 percent of the students scored between 70 and 90. If the second standard deviation was another 5 test points in either direction, you could say that 95 percent of the students scored between 65 and 95 on the test. Finally, you could say that the third standard deviation is another 4 points away from the mean. This means that 99.7 percent of the students scored between 61 and 99.

A small value for the standard deviation means that the values of the group are more tightly clustered around the mean. A greater standard deviation means that the numbers are more scattered away from the mean. The greater standard deviations a group has, the easier deviating from the center is. The less the standard deviation, the harder it is to deviate from the center.

Here's what a standard deviation question on the GMAT could look like:

I. 55, 56, 57, 58, 59

II. 41, 57, 57, 57, 73

III. 57, 57, 57, 57, 57

Which of the following orders sets I, II, and III from least standard deviation to greatest standard deviation?

(A) I, II, III

(B) I, III, II

(C) II, III, I

(D) III, I, II

(E) III, II, I

The set with the least standard deviation is the one that has the least amount of difference from the highest to the lowest values. The values in set III are all the same, so set III has the least standard deviation and should be listed first. Eliminate A, B, and C because they don't list III first.

There is a greater difference between the high and low values of set II (41 and 73) than there is between the high and low values of set I (55 and 59). So the set with the greatest standard deviation is set II, which means it should be listed last. Choice D lists the sets in their proper order from least standard deviation to greatest standard deviation, so it's the right answer.

Predicting the Future: Probability

Probability is the measure of how likely it is that a particular event will occur. It's a bit more scientific than telling fortunes and reading tarot cards. You express probability as a percentage, fraction, or decimal. You'd say that the probability of an event's occurring falls between 0 percent and 100 percent or between 0 and 1. If the probability of an event's occurrence is 0, or 0 percent, it's impossible for the event to occur. If the probability is 1, or 100 percent, the event is certain to occur. Few things in life are certain, other than death and taxes. For an event to be impossible is also rare. Therefore, the probability of the occurrence of an event usually falls somewhere between 0 and 1, or 0 and 100 percent.

Finding the probability of one event

Probability deals with *outcomes* and *events*. For situations where all possible outcomes are equally likely, the probability (P) that an event (E) occurs, represented by P (E), is defined as

$$P(E) = \frac{\text{The number of outcomes involving the occurrence of } E}{\text{The total possible number of outcomes}}$$

Because you express probability as a fraction, it can never be less than 0 or greater than 1. Getting both heads and tails with one flip of a coin is impossible, so the probability of that particular event occurring is 0. If you used a coin with heads on both sides, the probability of getting heads on one flip would be 1, because the number of possible outcomes is exactly the same as the number of outcomes that will occur.

Finding the probability of many events

You can find the probability of multiple events using several different formulas. In this section, we define the formulas first. Then we show you how to use them.

Consider a case in which there are two possible outcomes of events, A or B. You can represent the probability of one of the events, A or B, occurring as this:

P(A or B)

You can state the probability that (A or B) will occur in two ways, depending on whether the two events are mutually exclusive or not.

If the two events are mutually exclusive (which means they can't occur together, like rolling a 5 and 6 with one roll of one die), you use the *special rule of addition:*

P (A or B) = P A + P B

If the events aren't mutually exclusive (which means they can occur together, like drawing a playing card that displays clubs and a queen), you use the *general rule of addition:*

$$P \text{ (A or B)} = P\,A + P\,B - P \text{ (A and B)}$$

To find the probability of two events occurring together P (A and B), you use the rules of multiplication. If the two events are independent of one another, you apply the *special rule of multiplication:*

$$P \text{ (A and B)} = P\,A \times P\,B$$

If the outcome of the first event affects the outcome of the second event, you use the *general rule of multiplication.*

$$P \text{ (A and B)} = P\,A \times P \text{ (B\,|\,A)}$$

Applying the special rule of addition

You would use the special rule of addition to figure out the probability of rolling a die and coming up with either a 1 or a 2. You can't get both on one roll, so the events are mutually exclusive. Therefore, the probability of rolling a 1 or a 2 in one roll is P A + P B.

$$P \text{ (A or B)} = \tfrac{1}{6} + \tfrac{1}{6}$$

$$P \text{ (A or B)} = \tfrac{2}{6}$$

$$P \text{ (A or B)} = \tfrac{1}{3}$$

Applying the general rule of addition

To understand when you use the general rule of addition, imagine that three types of sodas are in a cooler. Colas are numbered consecutively 1 through 5, orange sodas are numbered 1 through 7, and grape sodas are numbered 1 through 8. Let event A stand for when a cola is taken out of the cooler and event B represent when a can with a number 2 is taken out. You want to know the probability of picking out *either* a cola *or* a can with the number 2 on it but *not* specifically a cola with the number 2 on it. The probabilities would be these:

$$P\,A = \tfrac{5}{20} \text{ (5 of the 20 cans are colas)}$$

$$P\,B = \tfrac{3}{20} \text{ (3 of the 20 cans are numbered 2)}$$

$$P \text{ (A and B)} = \tfrac{1}{20} \text{ (only 1 of the 20 cans is a cola can numbered 2)}$$

$$P \text{ (A or B)} = \tfrac{5}{20} + \tfrac{3}{20} - \tfrac{1}{20} = \tfrac{7}{20}$$

You can express this probability as 0.35 or as 35 percent. In the soda scenario, P (A and B) represents the chances of *both* A and B occurring. The probability of both events happening is called *joint probability.*

Applying the special rule of multiplication

The probability of multiple events occurring together is the product of the probabilities of the events occurring individually. For instance, if you're rolling two dice at the same time, here's how you'd find the probability of rolling a 1 and a 2:

$$P \text{ (A and B)} = \tfrac{1}{6} \times \tfrac{1}{6}$$

$$P \text{ (A and B)} = \tfrac{1}{36}$$

Applying the general rule of multiplication

Suppose the outcome of the second situation depends on the outcome of the first event. You then invoke the general rule of multiplication. The term $P(B|A)$ is a conditional probability, where the likelihood of the second event depends on the fact that A has already occurred. For example, to find the odds of drawing the ace of spades from a deck of 52 cards on one try and then drawing the king of spades on the second try — with the ace out of the deck — apply the formula like this:

$$P(A \text{ and } B) = P A \times P(B|A)$$

The line between the B and A stands for "B given A"; it doesn't mean divide!

$$P(A \text{ and } B) = \tfrac{1}{52} \times \tfrac{1}{51}$$

The probability of drawing the king of spades on the second draw is slightly better than the probability of drawing the ace on the first draw, because you've already removed one card from the deck on the first draw. Here's the answer:

$$P(A \text{ and } B) = \tfrac{1}{2,652}$$

We wouldn't bet against the house on that one! Here's a sample GMAT problem:

A bubble gum machine contains 3 blue, 2 red, 7 yellow, and 1 purple gumballs. The machine distributes one gumball for each dime. What is the chance that a child will get two red gumballs with two dimes?

(A) $\tfrac{2}{169}$

(B) $\tfrac{1}{13}$

(C) $\tfrac{2}{13}$

(D) $\tfrac{1}{156}$

(E) $\tfrac{1}{78}$

You need to treat getting the two red gumballs as two events.

Because the first event affects the outcome of the second event, apply the general rule of multiplication. The chance of getting a red gumball with the first dime is 2 (the number of red gumballs) divided by 13 (the total number of gumballs in the machine), or $\tfrac{2}{13}$. If the child tries to get the second gumball, the first red gumball is already gone. This leaves only 1 red gumball in the machine and 12 total gumballs remaining, so the chance of getting the second red gumball is $\tfrac{1}{12}$. The probability of both events happening is the product of the probability of each event occurring:

$$P(A \text{ and } B) = P A \times P(B|A)$$
$$P(A \text{ and } B) = \tfrac{2}{13} \times \tfrac{1}{12}$$
$$P(A \text{ and } B) = \tfrac{2}{156}$$
$$P(A \text{ and } B) = \tfrac{1}{78}$$

Choice E is the correct answer. Choice A is $\tfrac{2}{13} \times \tfrac{1}{13}$. It would look right if you didn't subtract the withdrawn red gumball from the total number on the second draw. Choice B is the chance of drawing one red gumball from a machine with 13 gumballs and only 1 red gumball. In this problem, $\tfrac{1}{13}$ would also be the chance of drawing the purple gumball. If you picked C, you found the chance of drawing the first red gumball. Choice D is $\tfrac{1}{156}$ instead of $\tfrac{2}{156}$, or $\tfrac{1}{78}$.

Chapter 15

It's All in the Presentation: GMAT Quantitative Question Types

In This Chapter
▶ Diving into data sufficiency questions
▶ Probing problem-solving questions

You need more than just math skills to excel on the quantitative section; you also need to know how to approach the questions. This chapter tells you what to expect from the math sections and how to work through the unique ways the GMAT presents the questions.

The kinds of math questions that appear on the GMAT test your ability to reason and think on your feet as you make use of the information you're given.

Two basic types of questions are intermingled throughout the quantitative section of the GMAT: data sufficiency questions and problem-solving questions. Both types of questions require similar skills, but they demand different approaches. In this chapter, we show you how to ace both kinds of questions.

Enough's Enough: Data Sufficiency Questions

The quantitative section has just 37 questions, and about half of them are presented in a unique form called data sufficiency. These questions aren't particularly hard if you understand how to approach them before you walk into the testing center. However, if you don't know much about these questions, getting confused and making careless mistakes are easy. Fortunately, you've decided to read this book to get a sneak peek. Your knowledge should be more than sufficient for data sufficiency!

You don't need the solution to find the answer

Unlike the traditional math problems you've seen throughout your life, data sufficiency questions don't actually require you to solve the problem. Instead, you have to evaluate two statements and determine which of those statements provides *sufficient* information for you to answer the question.

For each data sufficiency problem, you have a question and two statements, labeled (1) and (2). Your job is to decide whether each of the statements gives you enough information to answer the question with general math skills and everyday facts (such as the number of days in a month and the meaning of *clockwise*). If you need a refresher in the math concepts tested on the GMAT, read Chapters 10, 11, 12, 13, and 14.

Don't make foolish assumptions when you answer data sufficiency questions. Keep in mind that your job is to determine whether the information given is sufficient, not to try to make up for the lack of data! You're used to having to come up with an answer to every math problem, so if the statements lack just a little information, you may be tempted to stretch the data to reach a solution. Don't give in to temptation. For example, if a data sufficiency question provides a four-sided figure, don't assume that it's a square unless the data tells you it's a square — even if knowing that the figure is a square would allow you to solve the problem. Deal only with the information expressly as it's stated without making unwarranted assumptions.

The answer choices for data sufficiency questions are the same for each question:

(A) Statement (1) ALONE is sufficient, but statement (2) alone is not sufficient to answer the question asked.

(B) Statement (2) ALONE is sufficient, but statement (1) alone is not sufficient to answer the question asked.

(C) BOTH statements (1) and (2) TOGETHER are sufficient to answer the question asked, but NEITHER statement ALONE is sufficient.

(D) EACH statement ALONE is sufficient to answer the question asked.

(E) Statements (1) and (2) TOGETHER are NOT sufficient to answer the question asked, and additional data are needed.

The computer doesn't actually designate the answer choices with the letters A–E, but the choices appear in this order (you choose the right one with your mouse or keyboard), and we refer to them as A, B, C, D, and E to make the discussion simpler.

It's possible that just one of the statements gives enough data to answer the question, that the two statements taken together solve the problem, that both statements alone provide sufficient data, or that neither statement solves the problem, even with the information provided by the other one. That's a lot of information to examine and apply in two minutes! Don't worry. You can eliminate brain freeze by following a step-by-step approach to these questions.

Step-by-step: Approaching data sufficiency problems

Take a methodical approach to answering data sufficiency questions. Follow a series of steps:

1. **Evaluate the question to make sure you know exactly what you're supposed to solve, and if you can, decide what kind of information you need to solve the problem.**

2. **Examine one of the statements and determine whether the data in that one statement is enough to answer the question.**

   Start with the first one or whichever one seems easier to evaluate. Record your conclusion on the notepad.

3. **Examine the other statement and determine whether it has enough information to answer the question.**

   Record your conclusion on the notepad.

4. **Evaluate what you've written on your notepad.**

   - If you recorded *yes* for both statements, choose D.

   - If you recorded *yes* for (1) and *no* for (2), click on answer A.

   - If you recorded *no* for (1) and *yes* for (2), choose answer B.

   - If you've written *no* for both statements, go on to the next step.

5. **Examine the statements together to determine whether the data given in both is enough information to answer the question.**

   - If the answer is *yes,* choose answer C.

   - If the answer is *no,* choose answer E.

You can boil this method down to a nice, neat chart, like the one shown in Figure 15-1.

Data Sufficiency Answer Elimination Chart

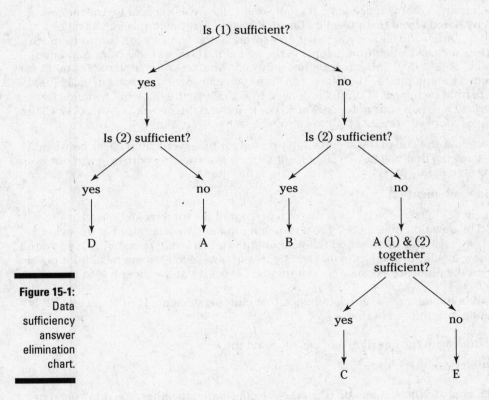

Figure 15-1:
Data
sufficiency
answer
elimination
chart.

Don't think *too* hard about whether an answer provides sufficient information to solve a problem. Data sufficiency questions aren't necessarily designed to *trick* you. In other words, you deal only with real numbers in these questions, and if a line looks straight, it is.

A statement is sufficient to answer the question if it provides only one possible answer for the question. If the information in a statement allows for two or more answers, the statement isn't sufficient.

Try the method on a fairly simple sample question:

David and Karena were among those runners who were raising money for a local charity. If David and Karena together raised $1,000 in the charity race, how much of the money did Karena raise?

(1) David raised ⅕ as much money as Karena did.

(2) David raised 5 percent of the total money raised at the event.

1. **Know what you have to solve for.**

   The question asks you to figure out how much money Karena raised for charity. The question gives you the total money raised by David and Karena together ($D + K = \$1,000$) but doesn't specify how much David raised. Check out the statements to see whether either or both of them let you know how much David came up with. If you have David's figure, you only need to subtract it from $1,000 to get Karena's figure.

2. **Consider statement (1) to determine whether it lets you solve for Karena's total.**

   You determined that you needed data that would allow you to separate the money raised by Karena from that raised by David. Knowing that David raised ⅕ as much money as Karena did allows you to set up a formula that you can solve for how much Karena raised. Just substitute $\frac{1}{5}K$ for D in the equation $D + K = \$1,000$. Your new equation is $\frac{1}{5}K + K = \$1,000$. This equation has only one variable, and that variable stands for how much Karena raised. Therefore, you know you can solve the problem using just the data from statement (1). You don't need to actually figure out what K stands for. Just write *1 = yes* on your notepad. You know that the right answer is either A or C, but you have to look at statement (2) to know which.

   If you were at the end of the section and pressed for time, you could guess between A and C, knowing that you have a 50 percent chance of answering correctly without even reading statement (2).

3. **Examine statement (2).**

   Statement (2) tells you that David raised 5 percent of the total money raised at the event. The question doesn't tell you how much total money was raised at the event, so you can't use this information to figure out how much David raised. And if you don't know how much David raised, you can't figure out how much Karena raised. Jot down *2 = no* on the notepad. Because (1) is a *yes* and (2) is a *no,* the answer has to be A.

If you've read both statements and determined that either statement (1) or statement (2) is sufficient alone, two things are true:

✔ You're done with the question and can move on the next one.

✔ The answer can't be C or E.

Both C and E apply to the statements when they're considered together. You don't need to consider the statements together if either statement is sufficient alone. Your only possible choices if *either* statement is sufficient are A if just statement (1) is sufficient, B if just statement (2) is sufficient, and D if each statement alone is sufficient.

Don't evaluate whether both statements together answer the problem unless you've determined that neither is sufficient alone. The only time you consider (1) and (2) together is if you've answered *no* to both statements. For instance, say the example question replaced statement (1) with this data: The event raised a total of $10,000. Statement (1) wouldn't be enough to answer the question. But because statement (2) tells you that David raised 5 percent of the total event money, you could answer the question using the data from both statements. Statement (1) provides the total amount, and statement (2) allows you to figure out how much David raised based on that amount. If you subtract that amount from $1,000, you'll have Karena's total.

Choice E would be right if statement (1) said, "The event raised more money this year than last year." In this case, neither statement, nor the two together, could answer the question.

Don't waste time trying to come up with the actual numeric answer if you don't have to. When you look at a question like the example, you may be tempted to solve the equation and figure out how much Karena raised. Don't give in! Finding the number just wastes precious time, and no one gives you extra credit for solving the problem! Instead, use your valuable time on other questions in the quantitative section.

Here's another example of a data sufficiency problem:

What's the value of the two-digit integer *x?*

(1) The sum of the two digits is 5.

(2) *x* is divisible by 5.

Apply the steps:

1. **Find out what to solve for.**

   This short question doesn't give you much of an idea about the kind of information you're solving for; you only know that *x* is a two-digit integer.

2. **Examine statement (1).**

   It tells you that the sum of the digits is 5. Several two-digit numbers are composed of digits that, when added together, equal 5: 14, 23, 32, 41, and 50. Statement (1) narrows the field of two-digit numbers down to just these possibilities, but that's not good enough. Because you don't have a single answer, statement (1) isn't sufficient. Write down *1 = no.* You've just eliminated answer choices A and D.

3. **Evaluate statement (2).**

   It says that *x* is divisible by 5. You probably realize immediately that every two-digit number ending in 0 or 5 is divisible by 5, so the possibilities are 10, 15, 20, 25, and so on. Clearly statement (2) isn't sufficient, because ⅕ of all two-digit numbers are divisible by 5. Write down *2 = no.* You've just eliminated B.

4. **Check out what you've written.**

   You have double *no's,* so you have to consider both statements together.

5. **Evaluate the two statements together.**

   Statement (1) narrows the two-digit numbers down to just five possibilities: 14, 23, 32, 41, and 50. Statement (2) narrows the list to those numbers that are divisible by 5. The only possibility from statement (1) that ends in 0 or 5 is 50. 50 is divisible by 5 and the digits add up to 5, so it answers the question. Because the two statements together provide enough information to answer the question, the answer is C.

You'll notice that, for this question, you did have to find the actual answer to the question to determine whether the information was sufficient. Sometimes doing so is the quickest way to determine whether statements provide enough data. An equation may exist that you could've set up (and not solved) that would have told you that you had sufficient information. However, on questions like this one, just applying the information to the question is often simpler and quicker. Solving the actual problem is okay *if it's the quickest way to determine that you have enough information.* Just remember to stop solving the problem as soon as you determine whether the information is sufficient!

Houston, We Have a Problem: Problem-Solving Questions

About half of the 37 math problems on the GMAT quantitative section are data sufficiency. The other half are problem-solving questions. As you may have guessed from the name, problem-solving questions require you to apply your mathematical skills to solve a problem. These questions are more like the ones you've seen on other standardized tests, like the SAT and ACT. They contain questions and provide five possible answer choices from which you select the correct answer.

The approach to regular old problem-solving questions is less clear-cut than the one for data sufficiency problems, but you should still follow an approach. Arriving at the test center with a practice problem-solving plan gives you a real edge for answering these standard math questions. These techniques apply more directly to some questions than others, but learn all of them so you're prepared for all types of problem-solving questions:

- **Examine all the data the question provides to make sure you know exactly what you're asked to do.** Some problems present you with figures, graphs, and scenarios, and some with just an equation with an equals sign. Don't jump into the answer choices until you've given the question a little thought.

- **Eliminate obviously incorrect answer choices if possible.** Before you begin solving a more complex math problem, look at the answer choices for any clearly illogical options. You can then focus your problem solving, and you won't pick these answers later through mistaken calculations. You can find tips for eliminating answer choices in Chapter 2.

- **Use the information in the problem.** The GMAT rarely presents you with the answer choice that states "It cannot be determined from the information." Almost every problem-solving question contains enough information for you to figure out the correct answer. But you need to use what you're given. Pull out the numbers and other terms in a problem and write them on your notepad in a way that makes the numbers meaningful. Depending on the problem, you may show relationships between quantities, draw simple diagrams, or organize information in a quick table.

- **Find the equation.** Some GMAT problems provide the equation for you. Others, like word problems, require you to come up with an equation using the language in the problem. Whenever possible, formulate an equation to solve from the information provided in the problem.

- **Know when to move on.** Sometimes you may confront a question that you just can't solve. Relax for a moment and reread the question to make sure that in your hurry you haven't missed something. If you still don't know what to do or if you can't remember the tested concept, eliminate all the answers you can and record your best guess.

Here are a couple examples of GMAT problem-solving questions:

A survey reveals that the average income of a company's customers is $45,000 per year. If 50 customers responded to the survey and the average income of the wealthiest 10 of those customers is $75,000, what is the average income of the other 40 customers?

(A) $27,500

(B) $35,000

(C) $37,500

(D) $42,500

(E) $50,000

Scan the question to get an idea of what it's asking of you. The word problem talks about surveys and averages, so it's a statistics question. It asks for the average income of 40 out of 50 customers and tells you that the average of the other 10 is $75,000 and that the average of all 50 is $45,000.

You can eliminate E off the bat because there's no way that the 40 customers with lower incomes have an average income more than the average income of all 50 customers. Choice D is probably wrong, too, because the top ten incomes carry such a high average compared to the total average. When you think about it, you have to balance ten incomes that are $30,000 above the overall average. Answer D, with $42,500, is only $2,500 below the overall average of $45,000. If you multiply $2,500 by 40 incomes, you get $100,000. But ten incomes times $30,000 is $300,000. Therefore, if $45,000 is the balancing point of the average total income, choice D tips the scales by $200,000. You know the answer is either A, B, or C, and you haven't even gotten down to solving yet!

Quickly eliminating answers before you begin can save you from choosing an answer that reflects a careless math error. Sometimes, the test makers are tricky; they anticipate the kinds of little mistakes you'll make, and they offer the resulting wrong answers as distracters in the answer choices. You may find yourself selecting an answer that you would have recognized as wrong if you just had more time. Eliminating answers that have to be wrong before you begin a problem keeps you from choosing answers that may come from faulty calculations and can't logically be right.

You can find the total income of all 50 customers and the total income of the wealthiest 10 customers by using the formula for averages. The average equals the sum of the values in a group divided by the number of values in the group. Apply the formula to find the total income for the group of 50. Then find the total income for the group of 10. Subtract the total income of the 10 from the total income of the 50 to find the total income of the 40. Then you can divide by 40 to get the average income for the group of 40. Here's how you do it:

Your calculations may be easier if you drop the three zeroes from the salaries. For this problem, shorten $45,000 to $45 and $75,000 to 75. Just remember to add the zeroes back on to your solution when you find it!

1. **Find the total income for the group of 50.**

   The average income is $45 and the number of group members is 50, so use the formula to find the sum (x):

   Average = Sum of values ÷ Number of values

   $$45 = \frac{x}{50}$$

   $$2,250 = x$$

2. **Find the total income for the group of 10.**

    The average income is $75 and the number of group members is 10, so use the formula to find the sum (y):

    Average = Sum of values ÷ Number of values

    $75 = y/10$

    $750 = y$

3. **Find the total income for the group of 40.**

    Subtract the total income of the group of 10 (y) from the total income for the group of 50 (x):

    $2,250 - 750 = 1,500$

4. **Find the average income of the group of 40.**

    The sum of the incomes in the group is $1,500, and the number of group members is 40, so apply the average formula:

    Average = Sum of values ÷ Number of values

    Average = $1,500 ÷ 40$

    Average = 37.5

Add three decimal places for the three zeroes you excluded in your calculations, and you have your answer. The average income of the 40 customers is $37,500, which is C.

An electronics firm produces 300 units of a particular MP3 player every hour of every day. Each unit costs the manufacturer $60 to produce, and retailers immediately purchase all the produced units. What is the minimum wholesale price (amount the manufacturer receives) per unit that the manufacturer should charge to make an hourly profit of $19,500?

(A) $60

(B) $65

(C) $95

(D) $125

(E) $145

Note what the question gives and what it's asking for. It provides units per hour and cost per unit. It also tells you the total desired profit. You're supposed to find the price per unit.

The first thing to do is eliminate obviously incorrect answer choices. Having read the question carefully, you know that you're looking for the wholesale price that will yield a profit (which results from price minus cost to produce) of $19,500 per hour. Because the answers given are wholesale prices, you can eliminate A and B. The cost to produce each unit is $60. If the company charged the same amount for the MP3 players as it spent to produce them, it would make no profit, so A is obviously incorrect. Choice B isn't much better. At a profit of just $5 per unit and 300 units per hour, the firm would make only $1,500 per hour.

You've eliminated two answer choices. Evaluate the data to find the correct answer from the remaining three. You know that 300 units are produced every hour and that those 300 units have to net a profit of $19,500. If you knew the amount of profit per unit, you could add that to the amount each unit costs to produce and get the minimum wholesale price. Set up an equation with x as the profit per unit:

$x = \$19,5000 \div 300$

$x = 65$

The firm needs to make a profit of $65 per unit. If you were careless and stopped there, you'd choose B. But because you've already eliminated B, you know you're not done yet.

You have to add profit to the per-unit production cost to get the final wholesale price:

$\$60 + \$65 = x$

$\$125 = x$

The answer is D.

You could use estimation to solve this problem by rounding $19,500 up to the nearest multiple of 300, which is $21,000, and then dividing 21 by 3 in your head and getting 7. This would tell you that you need a little less than $70 profit from each unit, or a little under $130 as the wholesale price (because $60 + $70 = $130).

Chapter 16

All Together Now: A Practice Mini Quantitative Section

In This Chapter

▶ Honing your GMAT math skills by taking practice questions

▶ Gaining greater insight through explanatory answers for each of the questions

Here's a chance to test your GMAT math skills before your embark on the real adventure of taking the test. This chapter contains only math questions of the types you'll see on the GMAT. If you want to time yourself, try to complete the questions in about 40 minutes. You can also choose to avoid the time pressure for now and focus on answering the questions. You'll have the opportunity to time yourself again when you take the practice tests in Chapters 17 and 19.

If the question is a data sufficiency type, choose

- ✔ A if statement (1) ALONE is sufficient to answer the questions but statement (2) isn't

- ✔ B if statement (2) ALONE is sufficient but statement (1) isn't

- ✔ C if BOTH statements (1) and (2) TOGETHER are sufficient to answer the question asked, but NEITHER statement ALONE is sufficient

- ✔ D if EACH statement ALONE is sufficient to answer the question asked

- ✔ E if statements (1) and (2) taken TOGETHER still aren't sufficient (in other words, you need more information to answer the question)

Read through all the answer explanations (even those for the questions you answered correctly), because something in the explanations may help you with other questions.

Here are 18 practice questions for the GMAT math section. Grab your pencil, set your timer for 40 minutes, and get started.

1. If $\left(\frac{3}{y} + 2\right)(y - 5) = 0$ and $y \neq 5$, then $y =$

   (A) $-\frac{3}{2}$

   (B) $-\frac{2}{3}$

   (C) $\frac{2}{3}$

   (D) $\frac{3}{2}$

   (E) 6

The GMAT usually starts out with a question of medium difficulty, and this one is in that range. If the product of two factors equals 0, then at least one of the factors must be 0 (because anything times 0 equals 0). Therefore, one of the factors in this equation must equal 0. You know it's not the second one, because y doesn't equal 5, and y would have to equal 5 for the second term to result in 0.

Therefore, you need to create an equation that sets the first factor equal to 0 and solve for y. Here's what you get for the first factor:

$$\left(\frac{3}{y} + 2\right) = 0$$

Subtract 2 from both sides:

$$\frac{3}{y} = -2$$

Cross-multiply (because $-2 = -\frac{2}{1}$):

$$3 = -2y$$

Divide both sides by -2:

$$-\frac{3}{2} = y$$

Correct answer: A.

2. If Esperanza will be 35 years old in 6 years, how old was she x years ago?

   (A) $41 - x$

   (B) $x - 41$

   (C) $35 - x$

   (D) $x - 29$

   (E) $29 - x$

If Esperanza will be 35 years old in 6 years, she is 29 right now $(35 - 6 = 29)$. Therefore, to determine how old she was x years ago, simply subtract x from her current age of 29: $29 - x$. *Correct answer:* E.

3. What is the value of $\frac{x}{3} + \frac{y}{3}$?

   (1) $\frac{x+y}{3} = 6$

   (2) $x + y = 18$

    (A)   (B)   (C)   (D)   (E)

The important thing to recognize is that $\frac{x}{3} + \frac{y}{3}$ is the same thing as $\frac{x+y}{3}$.

Statement (1) says that $\frac{x+y}{3} = 6$, and because $\frac{x}{3} + \frac{y}{3} = \frac{x+y}{3}$, $\frac{x}{3} + \frac{y}{3}$ must also equal 6. So you know that statement (1) is sufficient to answer the question and that the answer must be either A or D. To figure out which it is, consider statement (2). If it's sufficient, the answer is D. If not, the answer is A.

If $\frac{x}{3} + \frac{y}{3} = \frac{x+y}{3}$, then all you have to do with statement (2) is substitute 18 for $x + y$ in the expression, which gives you $\frac{18}{3}$. You know that $18 \div 3 = 6$, so statement (2) also provides sufficient information to answer the question. *Correct answer:* D.

4. Sofa King is having "a sale on top of a sale!" The price of a certain couch, which already had been discounted by 20 percent, is further reduced by an additional 20 percent. These successive discounts are equivalent to a single discount of which of the following?

   (A) 40%

   (B) 38%

   (C) 36%

   (D) 30%

   (E) 20%

The easiest way to solve this problem is to apply actual numbers to the circumstances. To simplify your life, use a nice, round figure like $100.

If the couch originally cost $100 but was discounted by 20 percent, you'd multiply $100 by 20 percent (0.20) and subtract that from $100 to find the discounted price ($100 \times 0.20 = 20$, and $100 - 20 = 80$). After the first round of discounts, the couch cost $80.

The couch, though, was discounted an additional 20 percent. Now you have to repeat the process, this time using $80 as the original price ($80 \times 0.20 = 16$, and $80 - 16 = 64$). The couch, twice discounted, cost $64.

But you're not finished yet. You need to calculate the total discount. The couch originally cost $100 and later cost $64. The discount, in dollars, is $100 - 64$, which is $36. To find out what the full discount is, simply divide that $36 by the original price of $100 ($\frac{36}{100} = 0.36$ or 36 percent). *Correct answer:* C.

5. If x is a member of the set {44, 45, 47, 52, 55, 58}, what is the value of x?

   (1) x is even.

   (2) x is a multiple of 4.

   (A)   (B)   (C)   (D)   (E)

Evaluate statement (1). Knowing that x is even doesn't help you much. There are three numbers in the set that are even: 44, 52, and 58. So statement (1) doesn't allow you to narrow down the value of x to one number. The answer can't be A or D.

Two numbers in the given set are multiples of 4: 44 and 52. Thus, knowing that x is a multiple of 4 doesn't give you a fixed value for x. Statement (2) by itself is not sufficient, so the answer can be only C or E. You still have one more evaluation: whether the two statements together provide sufficient information.

The two possible values created by knowing statement (2), 44 and 52, are also possible values provided by knowing statement (1). The two statements together don't enlighten you to the value of x. *Correct answer:* E.

6. In a given year, the United States census estimated that there were approximately 6.5 billion people in the world and 300 million in the United States. Approximately what percentage of the world's population lived in the United States that year?

   (A) 0.0046%

   (B) 0.046%

   (C) 0.46%

   (D) 4.6%

   (E) 46%

You need to know what millions and billions look like for the GMAT. One billion = 1,000,000,000, and one million = 1,000,000. In other words, one billion is 1,000 million.

6.5 billion is written 6,500,000,000. Writing out 6 billion is obvious, and 0.5 billion is one-half of 1,000 million, which is 500 million, or 500,000,000. You write out 300 million like this: 300,000,000. To solve for the percentage, simply divide 300,000,000 by 6,500,000,000, using the fraction form, like this:

$$\frac{300,000,000}{6,500,000,000}$$

Simplify things by canceling out eight zeros on the top and bottom. (This is legal because you're just reducing your fraction.) Then divide 3 by 65.

You don't actually have to complete the mathematical calculation, because all the answer choices are derivatives of 46. You do need to know, though, that when you divide 3 by 65, your answer will have three places after the decimal. If you can't figure this in your head, quickly set up the division problem on your scrap paper and mark where the decimal will be in your answer.

So 3 ÷ 65 = 0.046, but the question asks for a percentage. To convert the decimal to a percentage, move the decimal point two places to the right and add a percentage sign. The answer is 4.6%. *Correct answer:* D.

7. The symbol © represents one of the following operations: addition, subtraction, multiplication, or division. What is the value of 4 © 5?

   (1) 0 © 1 = 0

   (2) 0 © 1 = 1

   (A)   (B)   (C)   (D)   (E)

To determine the value of 4 © 5, you have to figure out which of the four operations the symbol represents. The way to do so is to plug each of the operations into the equations offered by each of the two statements and see whether either of them allows you to narrow the symbol down to just one operation.

Statement (1) gives you 0 © 1 = 0. Plug in each operation to see whether any make the equation true. You know addition and subtraction don't work because you can't add 1 to or subtract 1 from a number and end up with the same number. However, both multiplication and division work: 0 × 1 = 0, and 0 ÷ 1 = 0. Therefore, statement (1) isn't sufficient because it doesn't allow you to narrow the symbol down to just one operation. The answer, then, can't be A or D.

Statement (2) offers 0 © 1 = 1. The only difference between this equation and the one in statement (1) is the answer. You know that multiplication and division don't work, because they already produced an answer of zero. Subtraction results in −1, so the only operation that works is addition (0 + 1 = 1). This means that statement (2) alone gives you enough information to determine which operation the symbol stands for, which allows you to figure out the value of 4 © 5. *Correct answer:* B.

Data sufficiency questions don't ask for the actual numeric answer, so don't take the time to actually determine the value of 4 + 5 (not that it would take you long in this instance).

8. How many burritos did Dave's Wraps sell today?

   (1) A total of 350 burritos was sold at Dave's Wraps yesterday, which is 100 fewer than twice the number sold today.

   (2) The number of burritos sold at Dave's Wraps yesterday was 20 more than the number sold today.

   (A)   (B)   (C)   (D)   (E)

Evaluate each statement to determine whether it allows you to figure out the exact number of burrito sales for the day.

You can construct a mathematical equation from the language in statement (1). The unknown is the total number of today's burrito sales. Let b = today's burritos. *Fewer* means subtraction, so yesterday's sales equal $b - 100$. The equation then looks like this:

$$350 = 2b - 100$$

This equation has only one variable, so you know you can easily solve this equation to find out how many burritos left the shop today. (Don't take the time to actually figure it out, though!) Statement (1) is sufficient, and the answer is either A or D. To determine which it is, evaluate statement (2).

The second statement tells that the number of burritos sold at Dave's Wraps yesterday was 20 more than the number sold today, but this gives you two variables. You don't know how many burritos sold today *and* you don't know how many went yesterday. If y stands for yesterday's burrito sales, the equation would look something like this: $y = 20 + b$. You can't definitively solve an equation with two variables without more information, so statement (2) isn't sufficient. *Correct answer:* A.

(Oh, and if you won't be able to sleep unless we confirm for you the number of burritos sold today, it's 225: $450 = 2b$, so $225 = b$. You need your sleep for the GMAT!)

9. In the fictional country of Capitalistamia, to boost sales around holiday time the government dictates that a citizen may purchase goods up to a total value of $1,000 tax-free but must pay a 7 percent tax on the portion of the total value in excess of $1,000. How much tax must be paid by a citizen who purchases goods with a total value of $1,220?

   (A) $14.00

   (B) $15.40

   (C) $54.60

   (D) $70.00

   (E) $87.40

The first thing that should jump out at you is that the first $1,000 of purchases is tax-free, so you don't need to consider the first $1,000. Subtract $1,000 from $1,220 to get the value of purchases that will actually be taxed: $220.

To find the amount of tax due, you multiply 220 by 7 percent (or 0.07), but you don't have to take the time to fully work out the calculation. Estimate. 200 is close to 220, and 200×0.07 is 14.00, so the amount has to be just a little more than $14.

The only answer that's just a little more than $14.00 is B. If you take the time to multiply 220 and 0.07, you'll find that it's exactly $15.40. But because this is a test where saving time is crucial, avoid making full calculations whenever possible. *Correct answer:* B.

10. In the following figure, $\dfrac{a+b}{b} = \dfrac{5}{2}$, what does b equal?

$a°$

$b°$

(A) 108

(B) 99

(C) 81

(D) 72

(E) 63

The key to this problem is to recognize that a and b are supplementary angles, which means they add up to 180 degrees: $a + b = 180$. (Chapter 12 has more information on shapes and angles.)

Now all you have to do is substitute 180 for $a + b$ in the original equation and solve:

$$\frac{a+b}{b} = \frac{5}{2}$$

$$\frac{180}{b} = \frac{5}{2}$$

Cross-multiply:

$$360 = 5b$$

Divide both sides by 5:

$$72 = b$$

Correct answer: D.

11. Is the value of x closer to 75 than it is to 100?

    (1) $100 - x > x - 70$

    (2) $x > 85$

    (A)   (B)   (C)   (D)   (E)

    It helps to recognize that the halfway point between 100 and 75 is 87.5, so if x is greater than 87.5, it's closer to 100. If it's less than 87.5, it's closer to 75. (If it equals 87.5, it's the same distance from both.)

    If the difference between 100 and x $(100 - x)$ is greater than the difference between x and 70 $(x - 70)$, then x must be less than 87.5, because values greater than 87.5 would make $100 - x$ less than $x - 70$. Therefore, you absolutely know from statement (1) that x is closer to 75. It's sufficient to answer the question, and the answer is either A or D.

    Knowing that $x > 85$ doesn't help, because values of 88 and above would make x closer to 100 and values of 87 or 86 would make it closer to 75. Statement (2) isn't sufficient. *Correct answer:* A.

    For more about inequalities, consult Chapter 11.

12. How long did it take Ms. Nkalubo to drive her family nonstop from her home to Charlestown, West Virginia?

    (1) Ms. Nkalubo's average speed for the trip was 45 miles per hour.

    (2) If Ms. Nkalubo's average speed for the trip had been 1¼ as fast, the trip would have taken three hours.

    (A)   (B)   (C)   (D)   (E)

    This is a distance problem, so to determine the time of Ms. Nkalubo's trip, you have to use the distance equation, $r \times t = d$, which, as explained in Chapter 11, stands for *rate $\times$ time = distance*.

    Statement (1) is pretty easy to evaluate. Knowing that her average speed was 45 mph gives you the rate value for the equation but nothing more, so you're left with an unknown distance and an unknown amount of time. You can't solve an equation with two variables without more information. Therefore, you can't calculate her time. Statement (1) is not sufficient, so the answer can't be A or D.

    Statement (2) takes a little more thought. At first it may not appear to give you enough information to figure out time. But if you look further, you'll see that it enables you to set up two simultaneous equations. Here's how:

    The first equation is for Ms. Nkalubo's actual trip, which you can denote as Trip 1 (we've used a subscript 1 to show the values for Trip 1). Use the standard formula for distance:

    $$r_1 \times t_1 = d_1$$

    That's as much as you know about Trip 1 for now.

    The second equation is for the theoretical trip proposed in the problem, which you can call Trip 2 (which we've denoted with a subscript 2). Start with the standard distance formula:

    $$r_2 \times t_2 = d_2$$

Then develop this equation further with the information provided by statement (2). Begin with the easy value. Trip 2 would take 3 hours, so $r_2 \times 3 = d_2$. You also know that Ms. Nkalubo's speed for Trip 1 was 1¼, or ¾ the speed of Trip 2. Therefore, $r_2 = \frac{3}{4}r_1$. So now you have this equation for Trip 2:

$$\tfrac{3}{4}r_1 \times 3 = d_2$$

You should also recognize that d_1 and d_2 have the same value because the distances of the two trips are the same (it's the same trip!). Therefore, you can set the left side of the first equation equal to the left side of the second. At this point, you have an equation with only one variable, so you know you can solve for the exact length of Ms. Nkalubo's trip. Statement (2)'s information is sufficient to answer the question. *Correct answer:* B.

For those of you who hate to be left hanging and need to see how the equation turns out, we'll finish out the calculations. Just remember, you shouldn't do this part for the test; it's a waste of time. Here's what the equation looks like:

$$r_1 \times t_1 = \tfrac{3}{4}r_1 \times 3$$

Are you with us so far? (If not, see Chapter 11 for more about working with simultaneous equations.)

Divide both sides of the equation by r_1:

$$t_1 = \tfrac{3}{4} \times 3$$
$$t_1 = \tfrac{15}{4}$$

¹⁵⁄₄ of an hour is the same as 3¾ hours. The family was probably ready for some action after almost four hours in the car!

13. The arithmetic mean and standard deviation for a certain normal distribution are 9.5 and 1.5, respectively. What value is more than 2.5 standard deviations from the mean?

  (A) 5.75

  (B) 6

  (C) 6.5

  (D) 13.25

  (E) 13.5

Don't let the language of this problem scare you. You're really just applying basic operations.

The arithmetic mean is 9.5 and the standard deviation is 1.5, so you'll use a deviation of 1.5 to find values that stray from the mean. This means that the values that are one standard deviation from the mean are 11 and 8, which is the mean (9.5) plus or minus the standard deviation (1.5). The values two standard deviations from the mean are 12.5 and 6.5, which you get from adding and subtracting 3 (which is just 2×1.5) from the mean of 9.5. The values three standard deviations from the mean are 14 and 5, which you derive by adding and subtracting 4.5 (3×1.5) from the mean.

So to solve this problem, you find that the values that are 2.5 standard deviations from the mean are 13.25 and 5.75, because 2.5×1.5 is 3.75 (2.5×1.5). Look for an answer choice that's more than 13.25 or less than 5.75. The answer is 13.5. *Correct answer:* E.

14. What is the measure of ∠ABX in the following figure?

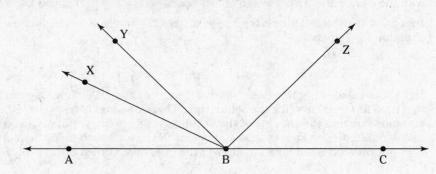

(1) *BX* bisects angle *ABY* and *BZ* bisects angle *YBC*.

(2) The measure of angle *YBZ* is 60 degrees.

(A)   (B)   (C)   (D)   (E)

It's important to recognize that because these four angles lie along a straight line, they add up to 180 degrees. (If you need a refresher on angles, read Chapter 12.)

Although it's lovely to know that *BX* bisects (which means cuts exactly in half) the two angles on the left side and that *BZ* bisects the two angles on the right side, without the measure of at least one of the angles, you have no way of knowing the measurements of any of the angles. So statement (1) isn't sufficient, and the answer has to be B, C, or E.

Statement (2) gives you only one of the angle measures, which by itself doesn't clarify the measure of ∠ABX any better than statement (1) does. Statement (2) isn't sufficient.

But remember that we said all we needed for statement (1) was a value for at least one of the angles. Well, statement (2) provides that value. Taken together, the two statements allow you to solve for the measure of ∠ABX. You can stop right there. *Correct answer:* C.

You don't actually have to figure out the measurement of the angle, but because we're so thorough, we go through the calculations for you anyway. This step is unnecessary on test day. Knowing that *BZ* bisects ∠YBC and that ∠YBZ measures 60 degrees allows you to deduce that ∠ZBC is also 60 degrees. Additionally, you've now accounted for 120 of the total 180 degrees allotted for the four angles, leaving 60 degrees to play with. Finally, because *BX* bisects angle *ABY,* two equal angles remain. Two equal angles that together equal 60 degrees must equal 30 degrees each, because $\frac{60}{2} = 30$.

15. On her annual road trip to visit her family in Seal Beach, California, Traci stopped to rest after she traveled ⅓ of the total distance and again after she traveled ¼ of the distance remaining between her first stop and her destination. She then drove the remaining 200 miles and arrived safely at her destination. What was the total distance, in miles, from Traci's starting point to Seal Beach?

    (A) 250

    (B) 300

    (C) 350

    (D) 400

    (E) 550

To solve this distance problem, set up an equation that represents adding up the three separate trip portions to get the entire distance. Let x equal the total distance in miles. Traci stopped to rest after she traveled ⅓ of the total distance, so the first part of the trip is ⅓x. She stopped again after she traveled ¼ of the distance remaining between her first stop and her destination, which is the total distance she traveled minus the first part of her trip. You can represent the second part of the trip mathematically like this: $\frac{1}{4}\left(x - \frac{1}{3}x\right)$. The third part of the trip is the remaining 200 miles. Add up the three parts of the trip to get the total distance:

$$\frac{1}{3}x + \frac{1}{4}\left(x - \frac{1}{3}x\right) + 200 = x$$

To solve the equation for x, first simplify:

$$\frac{1}{3}x + \frac{1}{4}\left(\frac{2}{3}x\right) + 200 = x$$

$$\frac{1}{3}x + \frac{1}{6}x + 200 = x$$

Multiply each expression on both sides by 6 to get rid of the fractions:

$$2x + x + 1{,}200 = 6x$$

Finish the solution:

$$3x + 1{,}200 = 6x$$

$$1{,}200 = 3x$$

$$400 = x$$

Correct answer: D.

16. In the fraction $\frac{a}{b}$, where a and b are positive integers, what is the value of b?

    (1) The lowest common denominator of $\frac{a}{b}$ and $\frac{1}{5}$ is 10.

    (2) $a = 3$

    (A)   (B)   (C)   (D)   (E)

This problem seems simple, but if you try to solve it too quickly, you may miss something. So consider all possibilities.

Statement (1) is the potentially tricky one. You may quickly jump to the conclusion that if the lowest common denominator (LCD) of the two fractions is 10, then $\frac{a}{b}$ must have a denominator of 10, which would mean that $b = 10$. However, b could also equal 2 and the two fractions would still have an LCD of 10. Because b has two possible values, statement (1) is insufficient. The answer is either B, C, or E.

Statement (2) is easier to evaluate. The value of the numerator has no bearing on the value of the denominator, so the fact that $a = 3$ is irrelevant to the value of b. Statement (2) is also insufficient, which means the answer is either C or E.

Knowing that $a = 3$ tells you nothing about whether the LCD is 10 or 2, so the two statements together are still insufficient to answer the question. *Correct answer:* E.

17. If n is a positive integer and $x + 3 = 4^n$, which of the following could NOT be a value of x?

    (A) 1

    (B) 13

    (C) 45

    (D) 61

    (E) 253

The easiest way to solve this problem is to plug each of the answer choices into the given equation and pick the one that doesn't make the expression true:

  ✔ Choice A gives you 1. Plug 1 into the equation: $1 + 3 = 4^n$. This would make $n = 1$, which is a positive integer, so A isn't right.

  ✔ If you substitute the 13 in B, you get $13 + 3 = 4^n$. $13 + 3$ is 16 and 4^2 is 16. The number 2 is a positive integer, so eliminate B.

  ✔ Choice C asks you to substitute 45 into the equation: $45 + 3 = 4^n$. The equation comes out to $48 = 4^n$, and although it may seem like 4 could be a root of 48, it's not. Choice C is the correct answer. You can choose C and go on, or you can check the last two answers just to be sure. Your decision depends on how much time you have remaining.

  ✔ If you plug 61, Choice D, into the equation, you get $61 + 3 = 4^n$. $61 + 3 = 64$, which is 4^3. But 3 is a positive integer, so D can't be right.

  ✔ Answer E is 253, and $253 + 3 = 256$. 256 is 4^4, which would make $n = 4$, a positive integer. Choice E makes the equation true, so it's the wrong answer.

Correct answer: C.

Be careful when you answer questions that ask you to find the answer that *can't* be true. In these cases, if an answer choice works, you have to eliminate it rather than choose it. Keep reminding yourself of your goal.

18. A downtown theater sells each of its floor seats for a certain price and each of its balcony seats for a certain price. If Matthew, Linda, and Jake each buy tickets for this theater, how much did Jake pay for one floor seat and one balcony seat?

    (1) Matthew bought four floor seats and three balcony seats for $82.50.

    (2) Linda bought eight floor seats and six balcony seats for $165.00.

    (A)   (B)   (C)   (D)   (E)

This is the last one, so it's probably tricky. At first, you may think that you can solve this with two simultaneous equations. When you look closer, this isn't the case. To get started, let f = the cost of a floor seat and b = the cost of a balcony seat. Then evaluate the statements.

If you write out Matthew's information in statement (1) mathematically, you get an equation with two variables, $4f + 3b = 82.50$. As we said before, you can't solve an equation with two variables without additional information. This statement alone isn't sufficient, so the answer's either B, C, or E.

Likewise, statement (2)'s information leads to an equation with two variables, $8f + 6b = 165$. This equation alone isn't enough to solve the problem, so the answer has to be C or E.

Here's where you may have gotten prematurely excited. You may have thought that statements (1) and (2) provided simultaneous equations that could be manipulated to give you the value of one of the variables. But if you look more closely, you'll see that the equations are exactly the same. When you reduce the second equation or expand the first, you have identical equations. Look at the second equation:

$$8f + 6b = 165$$

Divide both sides by 2:

$$4f + 3b = 82.50$$

It's the same as the first equation, so you don't have simultaneous equations at all, and the two statements together won't enable you to solve the problem. *Correct answer:* E.

Part V
Practice Makes Perfect

The 5th Wave   By Rich Tennant

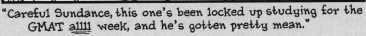

"Careful Sundance, this one's been locked up studying for the
GMAT a1111 week, and he's gotten pretty mean."

In this part . . .

The best way to prepare for any standardized test is to practice, and this part provides you with a bunch of questions to test your knowledge. We give you two complete GMAT practice tests, with tips on how to score yourself. Before you sit down with your pencil and scratch paper, though, make sure you have at least three and a half uninterrupted hours to devote to each test so you can get the full mind-numbing effect of plugging through the GMAT.

The chapters immediately following both of the tests provide explanations of the answer choices for each of the questions. You find out why the right answers are right and why the wrong answers are wrong. We provide a lot of valuable information in each of the explanations, so we suggest that you read through all of them, even the ones for questions you answered correctly.

Chapter 17

Putting the GMAT into Practice: Test #1

- -

In This Chapter

▶ Practicing analytical writing essays in a timed environment

▶ Carrying out a dress rehearsal for the GMAT quantitative section

▶ Putting into practice the techniques for mastering the GMAT verbal section

- -

*O*kay, you know your stuff. Now's your chance to shine. The following exam consists of two sections of multiple-choice questions and two analytical writing prompts. You have 75 minutes to complete 37 math questions, 75 minutes to complete 41 verbal questions, and an hour to write two essays.

To make the most of this practice exam, take the test under conditions similar to those of the actual test:

1. **Find a place where you won't be distracted. (Preferably as far from your neighbor's loud radio as possible.)**

2. **If possible, take the practice test at approximately the same time of day as the time you've scheduled your GMAT.**

3. **Use an alarm clock to time each section.**

4. **Take no more than one ten-minute break between the quantitative and verbal sections.**

5. **Mark your answers by circling the appropriate letters in the text.**

6. **Use a blank piece of paper or a small dry erase board for notes and figuring.**

7. **If possible, complete your essays on a computer with the grammar and spelling correction functions turned off.**

8. **When your time is up for each section, put down your pencil.**

After you've finished, you can check your answers to the quantitative questions using the answer key located at the end of this chapter. Complete explanations for the answers to this practice test are in Chapter 18.

Section 1: Analytical Writing Assessment

The analytical writing section consists of two tasks: analysis of an issue and analysis of an argument. You have 30 minutes to complete each of the two tasks. Try to write the two practice essays without taking a break between them. To best simulate the actual GMAT experience, compose your essays on a computer.

Analysis of an Issue

Time: 30 minutes

One essay

Directions: In this section, you need to analyze the issue presented and explain your views on it. There is no correct answer. You should consider various perspectives as you develop your own position on the issue.

Think for a few minutes about the issue and organize your response before you start writing. Leave time for revisions when you're finished.

You'll be scored based on your ability to accomplish these tasks:

✔ Organize, develop, and express your thoughts about the given issue.

✔ Provide pertinent supporting ideas with examples.

✔ Apply the rules of standard written English.

"None of the major problems currently confronting the world can be contained within the borders of a single country, and no country can, through its own efforts, be protected from these threats. Therefore, the United States must work, on an equal basis, with all other countries of the world to try to lessen the impact of the many global threats that confront us in the twenty-first century."

Discuss whether you agree or disagree with the opinion stated above. Provide supporting evidence for your views and use reasons and/or examples from your own experiences, observations, or reading.

Analysis of an argument

Time: 30 minutes

One essay

Directions: In this section, you're asked to write a critique of the argument presented. The prompt requests only your critique and does not ask you for your opinions on the matter.

Think for a few minutes about the argument and organize your response before you start writing. Leave time for revisions when you're finished.

You'll be scored based on your ability to accomplish these tasks:

✔ Organize, develop, and express your thoughts about the given argument.

✔ Provide pertinent supporting ideas with examples.

✔ Apply the rules of standard written English.

The following appeared as part of an editorial in a business magazine:

"Studies show that Americans with Ph.D.'s in the humanities and social sciences earn less than Americans with MBA degrees. The average amount of time that it takes to earn a Ph.D. in one of these fields is five years after college graduation, while an MBA can be earned in just two or three years. It is, therefore, a waste of time and resources to have some of America's brightest young people studying subjects such as literature and philosophy for five or more years when they are destined to earn less money, and pay less in taxes, than a person with an MBA. The government should discontinue all funds directed toward students pursuing Ph.D's in the social sciences and humanities since this a waste of taxpayer money."

Examine this argument and present your judgment on how well reasoned it is. In your discussion, analyze the author's position and how well the author uses evidence to support the argument. For example, you may need to question the author's underlying assumptions or consider alternative explanations that may weaken the conclusion. You can also provide additional support for or arguments against the author's position, describe how stating the argument differently may make it more reasonable, and discuss what provisions may better equip you to evaluate its thesis.

_____

_____

_____

_____

_____

_____

_____

_____

_____

Section 2: Quantitative

Time: 75 minutes

37 questions

Directions: Choose the best answer from the five choices.

Use the following answer choices to answer the data sufficiency questions:

(A) Statement (1) ALONE is sufficient, but statement (2) alone is not sufficient to answer the question asked;

(B) Statement (2) ALONE is sufficient, but statement (1) alone is not sufficient to answer the question asked;

(C) BOTH statements (1) and (2) TOGETHER are sufficient to answer the question asked, but NEITHER statement ALONE is sufficient;

(D) EACH statement ALONE is sufficient to answer the question asked;

(E) Statements (1) and (2) TOGETHER are NOT sufficient to answer the question asked, and additional data are needed.

1. The number $3 - 0.5$ is how many times the number $1 - 0.5$?

    (A) 4
    (B) 4.5
    (C) 5
    (D) 5.5
    (E) 6

2. If n is an integer, what is the greatest possible value for n that would still make the following statement true: $11 \times 10^n < \frac{1}{10}$?

    (A) -4
    (B) -3
    (C) -2
    (D) -1
    (E) 0

3. Michelle and Beth each received a salary increase. Which one received the greater dollar increase?

    (1) Michelle's salary increased 4 percent.

    (2) Beth's salary increased 6 percent.

    (A)   (B)   (C)   (D)   (E)

4. In which of the following pairs are the two numbers reciprocals of one another?

    I. $\frac{1}{15}$ and $-\frac{1}{15}$

    II. $\sqrt{2}$ and $\frac{\sqrt{2}}{2}$

    III. 4 and $\frac{1}{4}$

    (A) I only
    (B) III only
    (C) I and II
    (D) II and III
    (E) I and III

5. A high-end clothing store purchased a black leather jacket for x percent less than its list price and sold it for y percent less than its list price. What was the list price of the leather jacket?

    (1) $y = 10$

    (2) $x - y = 10$

    (A)   (B)   (C)   (D)   (E)

Go on to next page

6. Point (x, y) lies in which quadrant of the rectangular coordinate system shown in the figure below?

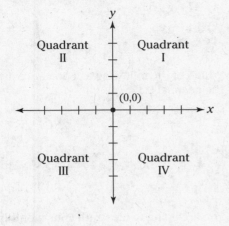

(1) $x = -2$

(2) $x + y < 0$

(A)　　(B)　　(C)　　(D)　　(E)

7. Which of the following is less than $\frac{1}{3}$?

(A) $\frac{8}{27}$

(B) $\frac{2}{5}$

(C) $\frac{18}{50}$

(D) $\frac{3}{8}$

(E) $\frac{4}{11}$

8. What was the total amount of money Eben and Emily invested to start their chocolate shop?

(1) Eben contributed 60 percent of the amount.

(2) Emily contributed $20,000.

(A)　　(B)　　(C)　　(D)　　(E)

9. What is the value of the positive integer x?

(1) $x^3 < 28$

(2) $x \neq x^3$

(A)　　(B)　　(C)　　(D)　　(E)

10. If basis points are defined so that 5 percent is equal to 100 basis points, then 7.5 percent is how many basis points greater than 5.5 percent?

(A) 0.04

(B) 40

(C) 400

(D) 4,000

(E) 40,000

11. Mr. Mulligan's $81,000 estate was divided among his spouse and two children. How much did the younger child receive?

(1) The younger child received $15,000 less than the older child and $30,000 less than the spouse.

(2) The spouse received 42% of the sum from the estate.

(A)　　(B)　　(C)　　(D)　　(E)

12. The value of $-2 - (-8)$ is how much greater than the value of $-4 - (-9)$?

(A) 2

(B) 1

(C) 0

(D) -1

(E) -2

13. In the figure below, the product of the three numbers in the horizontal row equals the sum of the three numbers in the vertical column. What is the value of $x + y$?

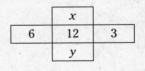

(A) 12

(B) 24

(C) 114

(D) 204

(E) 216

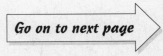

Go on to next page

14. If both a and b are nonzero numbers, what is the value of $\frac{a}{b}$?

    (1) $a = 5$

    (2) $a^2 = b^2$

    (A)   (B)   (C)   (D)   (E)

15. If x is an integer, is $\frac{24-x}{x}$ an integer?

    (1) $x < 5$

    (2) $x^2 = 36$

    (A)   (B)   (C)   (D)   (E)

16. The population of Growthtown doubles every 50 years. If the number of people in Growthtown is currently 10^3 people, what will its population be in three centuries?

    (A) $3(10^3)$

    (B) $6(10^3)$

    (C) $(2^6)(10^3)$

    (D) $(10^6)(10^3)$

    (E) $(10^3)^6$

17. Greg's Goosebumps produces Halloween items. Greg's production costs consist of annual fixed costs totaling $120,000 and variable costs averaging $4 per item. If Greg's selling price per item is $20, how many items must he produce and sell to earn an annual profit of $200,000?

    (A) 20,000

    (B) 15,000

    (C) 3,333

    (D) 5,000

    (E) 1,333

18. Adam works at a constant rate and stuffs 400 envelopes in 2 hours. How much less time would it take to stuff the same number of envelopes if Adam and Matt worked together?

    (1) Adam and Matt stuff envelopes at the same rate.

    (2) It takes Adam twice as long to stuff all of the envelopes as it takes Adam and Matt to stuff all of them together.

    (A)   (B)   (C)   (D)   (E)

19. Can the positive integer y be expressed as the product of two integers, each of which is greater than 1?

    (1) $47 < y < 53$

    (2) y is even

    (A)   (B)   (C)   (D)   (E)

20. Which of the following fractions is equal to the decimal 0.375?

    (A) $\frac{3}{7}$

    (B) $\frac{3}{8}$

    (C) $\frac{5}{6}$

    (D) $\frac{2}{5}$

    (E) $\frac{1}{3}$

21. You are going to illustrate your monthly budget using a circle graph. If the size of each sector is proportional to the amount of budget it represents, how many degrees of the circle would you use to represent rent, which is 35% of your budget?

    (A) 252

    (B) 189

    (C) 129.5

    (D) 126

    (E) 63

22. Is $x < 0$?

    (1) $x^3 < 0$

    (2) $-3x > 0$

    (A)   (B)   (C)   (D)   (E)

23. How many integers z are there such that $x < z < y$?

    (1) $y - x = 4$

    (2) x and y are not integers

    (A)   (B)   (C)   (D)   (E)

Go on to next page

24. 5.6 percent of the people in the labor force of Pretendville were unemployed in September, compared to 5.9 percent in October. If the number of people in the labor force of Pretendville was the same for both months, how many people were employed in October of 2005?

    (1) 10,000 more people were unemployed in October than in September.

    (2) In May of the same year, the number of unemployed people in the labor force was 135,000.

    (A)   (B)   (C)   (D)   (E)

25. In the figure below, what is the least number of table entries that is needed to show the product of each number and each of the other four numbers?

	1	2	3	4	5
1					
2					
3					
4					
5					

    (A) 0

    (B) 1

    (C) 4

    (D) 5

    (E) 10

26. If $(x - 4)$ is a factor of $(x^2 - kx - 28)$, then $k =$

    (A) −11

    (B) −7

    (C) −3

    (D) 3

    (E) 7

27. What is the radius of the circle below with center O?

    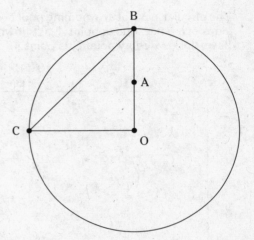

    (1) The ratio of OA to AB is 2 to 3.

    (2) Triangle OBC is isosceles.

    (A)   (B)   (C)   (D)   (E)

28. Is $ab < 12$?

    (1) $a < 3$ and $b < 4$

    (2) $\frac{1}{3} < a < \frac{2}{3}$ and $b^2 < 169$

    (A)   (B)   (C)   (D)   (E)

29. Angelo and Isabella are both salespersons. In any given week, Angelo makes $550 in base salary plus 8 percent of the portion of his sales above $1,000 for that week. Isabella makes 10 percent of her total sales for any given week. For what amount of weekly sales would Angelo and Isabella earn the same amount of money?

    (A) 23,500

    (B) 24,500

    (C) 25,500

    (D) 26,500

    (E) 27,500

Go on to next page ⟶

30. Two trains, FastTrain and SlowTrain, started simultaneously from opposite ends of a 900-mile route and traveled toward each other on parallel tracks. FastTrain, traveling at a constant rate, completed the 900-mile trip in 3 hours. SlowTrain, traveling at a constant rate, completed the same trip in 5 hours. How many miles had FastTrain traveled when it met SlowTrain?

    (A) 360

    (B) 540

    (C) 562.5

    (D) 580.5

    (E) 600

31. The circular base of a swimming pool lies in a level rectangular yard and just touches two straight sides of a fence, one at point *A*, as shown in the figure below. How far from the center of the pool's base, designated by point *C*, is point *A?*

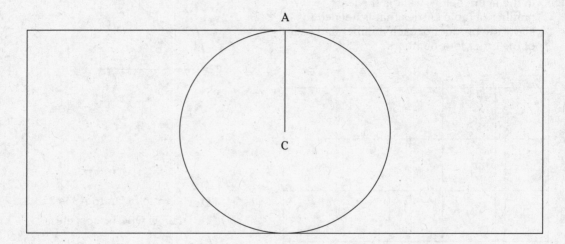

    (1) The base has an area of 1,000 square feet.

    (2) The length of the fence is 50 feet.

    (A)   (B)   (C)   (D)   (E)

32. If $a \neq 0$, is $b > 0$?

    (1) $ab = 14$

    (2) $a + b = 9$

    (A)   (B)   (C)   (D)   (E)

33. $\dfrac{1\frac{3}{5} - 2\frac{2}{3}}{\frac{1}{3} - \frac{2}{5}} = E$

    (A) −16

    (B) −15

    (C) 1

    (D) 14

    (E) 16

Go on to next page

34. If n is a positive integer and n^2 is divisible by 98, then the largest positive integer shown that must divide n is

(A) 2

(B) 7

(C) 14

(D) 28

(E) 56

35. Becky sets up a hot dog stand in her busy neighborhood and purchases x pounds of hot dogs for p dollars per pound. If she has to throw away s pounds of hot dogs due to spoilage and she sells the rest of the hot dogs for d dollars per pound, which of the following represents the net profit on the sale of the hot dogs?

(A) $(x - s)p - sd$

(B) $xp - (xd - sd)$

(C) $xd - sp$

(D) $(x - s)d - xp$

(E) $(s - p)d - xp$

36. What is the area of the rectangular region in the figure below?

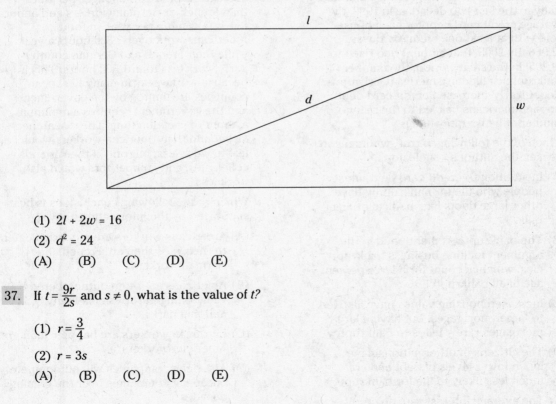

(1) $2l + 2w = 16$

(2) $d^2 = 24$

(A)   (B)   (C)   (D)   (E)

37. If $t = \dfrac{9r}{2s}$ and $s \neq 0$, what is the value of t?

(1) $r = \dfrac{3}{4}$

(2) $r = 3s$

(A)   (B)   (C)   (D)   (E)

STOP DO NOT TURN THE PAGE UNTIL TOLD TO DO SO.
DO NOT RETURN TO A PREVIOUS TEST.

Section 3: Verbal

Time: 75

41 questions

Directions: Follow these directions for each of the three question types:

✔ Sentence correction questions give you a sentence with an underlined portion. Choose the answer choice that best phrases the underlined words according to the rules of standard English. The first answer choice duplicates the phrasing of the underlined portion, so if you think the sentence is best as it is, choose the first answer. The other four answers provide alternative phrasings. Choose the one that rephrases the sentence in the clearest, most grammatically correct manner.

✔ Answer reading comprehension questions based on what the passage states directly or implicitly. Choose the best answer to every question.

✔ Critical reasoning questions present you with an argument and a question about the argument. Pick the choice that best answers the question.

1. The total debt owed by America's households and businesses has increased dramatically in the last two decades. In 1990, the average credit card debt for each household with at least one credit card was $2,966. By 2005, that amount had risen to $9,205. In the same period, the number of bankruptcies filed in America nearly doubled. Clearly, increased credit card debt among Americans has led to the rising number of bankruptcy filings.

   Which of the following, if true, would most weaken the author's conclusion?

   (A) In addition to credit card debt, most people who file for bankruptcy have other large debts like medical or legal bills.

   (B) The bankruptcies mentioned in the argument include business bankruptcies, which account for a large percentage of all bankruptcies.

   (C) Increased housing values have also led to larger mortgages, but having large mortgages rarely leads to bankruptcy.

   (D) The citizens of other nations have much lower levels of debt and are much less likely to file for bankruptcy.

   (E) The average interest rate on credit cards is nearly 20 percent per year, and many Americans can only afford to pay the interest.

2. A researcher found that Americans work an average of three hours longer per week than French or German workers and about five weeks more per year. In total, Americans work over 1,800 hours a year while their French and German counterparts work less than 1,500 hours. This is because workweeks in many European countries are limited by the government and the government requires a minimum amount of vacation time. The researcher also found that American workers would like to work less, but only if their friends, colleagues, and competitors would also work less.

   Which of the following conclusions is best supported by the information above?

   (A) Americans workers are more dedicated to their jobs than are French and German workers.

   (B) Americans are often outnumbered by vacationing Europeans in many U.S. national parks.

   (C) European workers are happier than are American workers.

   (D) American companies will outcompete European companies over the coming decades.

   (E) The best way to allow Americans to work fewer hours and take more vacation is through national legislation.

Go on to next page

Questions 3–4 are based on the following:

Allen: Our state has a ten-cent deposit on all carbonated beverage containers. This ensures that plastic and glass bottles and aluminum cans are recycled. Your state should have a bottle deposit program.

John: My state has a comprehensive recycling program that features curbside recycling and recycling bins at highway rest stops, parks, and other public places. Studies have shown that comprehensive recycling programs more effectively encourage recycling than do bottle deposit programs alone. Therefore, my state should not adopt a bottle deposit program.

3. John's conclusion would be most weakened by which of the following?

(A) Ten-cent bottle deposit programs are more effective than five-cent deposit programs.

(B) Americans in every state are much more likely to recycle now than they were in the 1970s when most deposit laws were passed.

(C) Beverage bottles, on average, account for only 8 percent of the litter along highways and 4 percent of the solid waste in landfills.

(D) Many states, including Allen's, have both a bottle deposit program and a comprehensive recycling program.

(E) Bottle deposit programs and comprehensive recycling programs are more effective at encouraging recycling than are ad campaigns.

4. John would also like to argue that the deposit laws are unfair because they don't apply equally to all industries. Which of the following, if true, best supports that contention?

(A) Citizens of some states pay bottle deposits while citizens of other states do not.

(B) The bottle deposit collected in Allen's state only applies to carbonated beverages, not uncarbonated sports drinks, juices, and ice tea.

(C) A two-liter bottle is counted as one container and is subject to only one deposit while a six-pack of cans requires six times the deposit.

(D) People living near a state border may drive across the border to buy their beverages in a state that doesn't collect a deposit.

(E) The deposit is charged on all carbonated beverages, including soft drinks from small, local companies, organic sodas, diet sodas, and even carbonated water.

5. Standing as monuments in the desert, <u>Native Americans used the saguaro cactus as a provider of food, water, and spiritual inspiration.</u>

(A) Native Americans used the saguaro cactus as a provider of food, water, and spiritual inspiration.

(B) Native Americans used the saguaro cactus to provide them with food, water, and spiritual inspiration.

(C) the saguaro cactus provided Native Americans with food, water, and spiritual inspiration.

(D) the saguaro cactus provided food, water, and spiritual inspiration needed by the Native Americans.

(E) food, water and spiritual inspiration were provided to the Native Americans by the saguaro cactus.

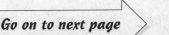

Go on to next page

6.   To Harry Truman, politics was a job just like any other, and during the Great Depression <u>we were glad to have any job at all</u>.

    (A) we were glad to have any job at all.

    (B) we was glad to have any job at all.

    (C) they were glad to have any job at all.

    (D) one was glad to have any job at all.

    (E) he was glad to have any job at all.

7.   A period of sixty days is <u>as much as even</u> the most patient homebuyers are willing to wait for the current owners to turn over a piece of property.

    (A) as much as even

    (B) even so much that

    (C) even as much as

    (D) even so much as

    (E) so much as even

Questions 8–12 refer to the following passage:

Line   The animal bones [found in a region of Africa by the anthropologists] exhibit numerous cutmarks, and they were often broken for the extraction of marrow. The implication is that the Klasies
(05) people consumed a wide range of game, from small, greyhound-size antelope like the Cape grysbok to more imposing quarry like buffalo and eland, as well as seals and penguins. The number and location of stone tool cutmarks and the rarity
(10) of carnivore tooth marks indicate that the people were not restricted to scavenging from lions or hyenas, and they often gained first access to the intact carcasses of even large mammals like buffalo and eland.
(15)   But the bones also show that the people tended to avoid confrontations with the more common—and more dangerous—buffalo to pursue a more docile but less common antelope, the eland. Both buffalo and eland are very large
(20) animals, but buffalo stand and resist potential predators, while eland panic and flee at signs of danger. The Klasies people did hunt buffalo, and a broken tip from a stone point is still imbedded in a neck vertebra of an extinct "giant" long-horned
(25) buffalo. The people focused, however, on the less threatening young or old members in buffalo herds.

The stone points found at Klasies could have been used to arm thrusting spears, but there is nothing to suggest that the people had projectiles (30) that could be launched from a distance, and they may thus have limited their personal risk by concentrating on eland herds that could be chased to exhaustion or driven into traps. The numerous eland bones in the Klasies layers represent (35) roughly the same proportion of prime-age adults that would occur in a living herd. This pattern suggests the animals were not victims of accidents or endemic diseases, which tend to selectively remove the very young and the old, but (40) rather that they suffered a catastrophe that affected individuals of all ages equally. The deposits preserve no evidence of a great flood, volcanic eruption, or epidemic disease, and from an eland perspective, the catastrophe was proba- (45) bly the human ability to drive whole herds over nearby cliffs.

This passage is excerpted from *The Dawn of Human Culture*, by Richard G. Klein (Wiley Publishing, 2002).

8.   The main argument advanced by the author of this passage is

    (A) It was easier for the Klasies people to hunt eland than buffalo.

    (B) The Klasies were unique among prehistoric people in that they consumed large land animals, such as buffalo, as well as smaller mammals from the sea.

    (C) The Klasies people were at least partially responsible for the catastrophic extinction of the prehistoric antelope called the eland.

    (D) Because the Klasies people lacked the use of projectile weapons and were therefore unable to hunt buffalo successfully, they diversified their diet to include smaller prey.

    (E) The prehistoric Klasies people had a diverse diet and advanced hunting skills and were probably not restricted to scavenging.

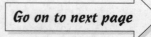
Go on to next page

9. What signs indicate to the anthropologists that Klasies people were not restricted to scavenging?

   (A) The number and location of stone tool cutmarks and the absence of carnivore teeth marks in the animal bones.

   (B) The fact that the animals consumed were not the victims of accidents or disease as would be expected from natural deaths.

   (C) The presence of a stone spear tip in the neck of a giant long-horned buffalo.

   (D) The variety of different species whose bones were found in the Klasies camp, such as penguins, seals, and antelope.

   (E) The lack of any evidence of a catastrophic event such as a flood, volcanic eruption, or epidemic disease.

10. According to the author's theory, why did the Klasies people focus on eland instead of buffalo?

    (A) The eland were more numerous than the buffalo.

    (B) The eland would stand and fight while the buffalo would usually panic and flee.

    (C) The buffalo would stand and fight while the eland would usually panic and flee.

    (D) The eland were more easily obtained from other animals through scavenging.

    (E) The eland were easily killed using the projectiles that the Klasies favored when hunting.

11. Which of the following game animals is NOT listed in the passage as a probable part of the Klasies diet?

    (A) penguins

    (B) hyenas

    (C) seals

    (D) giant long-horned buffalo

    (E) small, greyhound-sized antelope

12. Which of the following evidence does the author present to support the assertion that the catastrophe the eland suffered was caused by human beings?

    (A) The presence of bones from prime-age animals found in the Klasies site.

    (B) The broken tip of a stone point embedded in the neck of an eland skeleton.

    (C) The lack of any carnivore tooth marks on the eland bones at the Klasies site.

    (D) The number and location of tool marks found on the bones of a variety of animals at the Klasies site.

    (E) The lack of any signs of a flood, volcanic eruption, or epidemic disease.

13. The corporate strategic plan included provisions to expand operations, manufacturing would be streamlined, and introduce a new line of lower-priced items.

    (A) expand operations, manufacturing would be streamlined, and include a new line of lower-priced items.

    (B) create expanded operations, work to streamline manufacturing, and include a new line of lower-priced items.

    (C) expanded operations, streamlined manufacturing, and introduced a new line of lower-priced items.

    (D) expand operations, streamline manufacturing, and introduce a new line of lower-priced items.

    (E) expand operations, streamline manufacturing, and a new line of lower-priced items.

Go on to next page

14. People are usually quick to admit that they don't remember specific information such as names, dates or faces, <u>but they rarely acknowledge that these lapses may indicate the onset of significant memory problems.</u>

    (A) but they rarely acknowledge that these lapses may indicate the onset of significant memory problems.

    (B) yet rarely does one acknowledge the possibility of significant memory problems.

    (C) but not the possibility of serious memory problems.

    (D) still we don't usually acknowledge the fact that this may indicate possible serious memory problems.

    (E) and they don't seem to realize that this may indicate the onset of significant memory problems.

15. If you go on the game show and place first or second, <u>either you will receive the parting gift of a trip to Hawaii or the big money round.</u>

    (A) either you will receive the parting gift of a trip to Hawaii or the big money round.

    (B) either you will win the trip to Hawaii or the big money round.

    (C) you will either win the trip to Hawaii or go on to the big money round.

    (D) either you will go to Hawaii or the big money round.

    (E) your prize will be either a trip to Hawaii or you will go to the big money round.

16. <u>Many people contemplate leasing a car instead of buying one, they are unaware of both the large initial payment that is required and the possibility of another sizeable payment due at the end of the lease.</u>

    (A) Many people contemplate leasing a car instead of buying one, they are unaware of both the large initial payment that is required and the possibility of another sizeable payment due at the end of the lease.

    (B) Many people who contemplate leasing a car instead of buying one are unaware of both the large initial payment that is required and the possibility of another sizeable payment due at the end of the lease.

    (C) Many people contemplate leasing a car instead of buying one, and we are unaware of both the large initial payment that is required and the possibility of another sizeable payment due at the end of the lease.

    (D) Many people who contemplate leasing a car instead of buying one are unaware of both the large initial payment that are required and the possibility of another sizeable payment due at the end of the lease.

    (E) Many people contemplate leasing a car instead of buying one, since they are unaware of either the large initial payment that is required and the possibility of another sizeable payment due at the end of the lease.

Go on to next page

17. The newest trend in home buying is interest-only mortgages. These mortgages require a borrower to pay only the interest on the loan. This means that the principle (which is the amount borrowed) never gets any smaller. Buyers never accumulate any equity in their homes and often have to default. Therefore, these loans are bad for Americans and should be made illegal.

The argument in the above passage depends on which of the following assumptions?

(A) Homeowners can't afford to pay more than the interest on the loan.

(B) Some things that are bad for Americans should be made illegal.

(C) Interest-only mortgages don't require the buyer to pay more than the interest.

(D) Buyers with no equity in their homes often have to default on their loans.

(E) Owners won't accumulate equity based on the increasing value of their house.

18. The Earth's magnetic field has reversed a number of times in its history. Before the poles actually flip, the magnetic field weakens and the magnetic poles drift away from "true" north and south. On average, the magnetic north and south poles flip about once every 200,000 years. The last time the poles flipped was 780,000 years ago. Therefore, the poles are in the process of reversing.

Which of the following, if true, most strengthens the conclusion that the poles are reversing?

(A) Magnetic north has recently been moving toward closer alignment with "true" north.

(B) Sometimes the magnetic fields go for over one million years without reversing.

(C) The earth's atmosphere has warmed about one degree Celsius over the past century.

(D) The strength of the magnetic field has declined by over ten percent since 1845, the first year it was measured.

(E) The location of the magnetic poles has remained unchanged for as long as magnetic compasses have been in use.

Go on to next page

19. Obesity often leads to health problems, such as heart attacks, Type II diabetes, strokes, and cancer. A person who is considered clinically obese has a three-times-greater chance of heart trouble. Obesity is also responsible for as many as 90,000 cancer deaths per year. The earlier a person becomes obese, the greater the health problems and risk of death. By the year 2010, it is predicted that half the children in North and South America will be clinically obese compared to about one-third of children in 2000.

The above premises most logically lead to which of the following conclusions?

(A) Children will become more and more obese in the coming years.

(B) Children in North and South America are more obese than children in Europe or Asia.

(C) Obesity that begins in childhood poses a greater risk of health problems and death than does obesity that begins in adulthood.

(D) Today's children may be the first generation in centuries to have a shorter average life span than their parents.

(E) Parents should not be concerned about childhood obesity because kids have plenty of time to lose the weight.

Questions 20–23 refer to the following passage:

Line   It wasn't that long ago that entrepreneurs were considered to be mavericks, rebels, or even social deviants. They stood out because Corporate America was built on a foundation
(05) of loyalty and conformity. Big was better and economies of scale provided formidable barriers to entry. The last two decades, however, have placed a number of entrepreneurs in the limelight who have marched to the tune of a different
(10) drummer.
     Today's entrepreneurs have been heralded for having the same qualities exhibited by this country's first colonists. The colonists had contempt for the way things were done, and they
(15) weren't afraid to break away from the establishment. The entrepreneurs who are heralded by the media created their own firms so they could be free to pursue new opportunities and try new

approaches. They showed that bigger isn't always better and that the legacy systems and (20) bureaucratic practices of most established firms can be like anvils that keep them from keeping pace with changes in the marketplace. Each day, entrepreneurs create agile new ventures that change the way the game is played. (25)
     America is known as the "Land of the free and the home of the brave." This country encourages individuality and self-determination. It also encourages people to "go for it."
     Entrepreneurship has become an integral part (30) of this country's culture and economic system because it reflects the courage to break away from the pack and the desire to be the master of one's own destiny. Three statistics capture the entrepreneurial spirit in this country. First, 6.8 (35) million households (7.2 percent of the country's total) include someone who is trying to start a business. Second, between 700,000 and 1 million new businesses are created each year. Third, at least 90 percent of the richest people in the (40) United States generated their wealth through entrepreneurial endeavors.

This passage is excerpted from *Extraordinary Entrepreneurship: The Professional's Guide to Starting an Exceptional Enterprise,* by Stephen C. Harper (Wiley Publishing, 2004).

20. Which of the following statements best describes the main idea of the passage?

(A) Becoming an entrepreneur is very hard, considering that 6.8 million households are trying to start a business every year and, at most, 1 million succeed.

(B) Entrepreneurs were once considered to be trivial sideshows in an America dominated by corporations, but now entrepreneurs are recognized to be vital to the nation's economy.

(C) American entrepreneurs are chasing quick riches instead of contributing to the American economy through loyalty to the corporations that built this country.

(D) Entrepreneurs have demonstrated that in business smaller is now better.

(E) Big businesses can no longer keep pace with changes in the market, and entrepreneurs will dominate American business in the future.

Go on to next page

21. The author of the passage most likely includes the statistic concerning the richest people in the United States in order to

    (A) prove that everyone who starts a business is bound to succeed

    (B) contrast the conservative nature of today's entrepreneurs with the mavericks and rebels of past decades

    (C) show that entrepreneurs are "playing the game" better than big corporate America

    (D) highlight the challenges and difficulties that entrepreneurs face in an ever-changing marketplace

    (E) point out the absurdity of the statistic that 90 percent of America's richest people are entrepreneurs

22. According to the passage, how are today's entrepreneurs viewed compared to the entrepreneurs of the past?

    (A) Today's entrepreneurs are heralded for the things that got entrepreneurs of the past criticized.

    (B) Today's entrepreneurs are treated with much greater skepticism than entrepreneurs of the past.

    (C) Entrepreneurs of the past were "in the limelight" because they "walked to the beat of a different drummer."

    (D) It is much easier for today's entrepreneurs to get financing for their new projects.

    (E) Today's entrepreneurs are praised as "mavericks, rebels, and even social deviants."

23. Which of the following is NOT one of the phrases used by the author to praise entrepreneurship?

    (A) "the courage to break away from the pack"

    (B) "built on a foundation of loyalty and conformity"

    (C) "create agile new ventures that change the way the game is played"

    (D) "integral part of this country's culture and economic system"

    (E) "desire to be the master of one's own destiny"

24. Healthy human beings can't tickle themselves. This is because they anticipate the sensation and reduce their touch perception accordingly. Reducing the perception of completely predictable sensations allows the brain to focus on crucial changes in the environment not produced by the person's own actions. A person who tries to tickle himself and is simultaneously tickled by another person will have a heightened sense of the other person's touch compared to his own. Healthy people also can't mistake their own voice as coming from another person. Schizophrenics, however, may hear their own voices and, having not anticipated the sounds, not recognize the voice as their own.

    Which of the following statements can be correctly inferred from the passage above?

    (A) Human beings can't tickle themselves because they anticipate the sensation.

    (B) Further research in this area may lead to a better understanding of why certain people are more susceptible to tickling.

    (C) A healthy human hearing a tape of her own voice won't recognize the voice because she won't anticipate the sounds.

    (D) Tickling yourself as someone else is tickling you will reduce your sensory perceptions and cause you not to react to the tickling.

    (E) Healthy humans constantly anticipate the sound of their own voice and differentiate it from other voices.

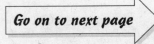
Go on to next page

25. One of the factors that the IRS considers when deciding whether to audit a tax return is the dollar amount of the deduction claimed for business travel. Salespeople and self-employed entrepreneurs often claim large deductions for mileage on their tax returns. If the IRS does decide to audit such a return, one of the things the auditors expect to see is a mileage log.

    Unfortunately, keeping mileage logs up-to-date can become a burden, and many busy people end up neglecting their mileage logs. The best solution to this problem is an electronic mileage log that runs on a personal digital assistant.

    Which of the following is an assumption made in drawing the conclusion above?

    (A) The cost of the electronic mileage log is not too much for salespeople or the self-employed.

    (B) Keeping electronic mileage logs up-to-date is less of a burden than traditional pen and paper logs.

    (C) The IRS expects to see a mileage log whenever a large mileage deduction is claimed.

    (D) Salespeople and the self-employed already have personal digital assistants on which to run the electronic mileage logs.

    (E) Electronic mileage logs are preferred by the IRS because they can't be falsified.

Questions 26–27 are based on the following:

Sara: Anthropologists estimate that diseases brought to the Western Hemisphere by the first Europeans, including smallpox, hepatitis, typhus, and measles, killed 95 percent of the Native American population and allowed Europeans to begin their conquest of the continent. If the Native American population had been twenty times greater, only 4.75 percent of the population would have died, and the Europeans would never have been able to conquer North and South America.

Michele: Those death rates are way too high. The average rate of death in Europe from the most virulent epidemic in recorded history, the Black Death of the 14th century, was only 33 percent. Even if the Native American populations were extremely vulnerable due to their never having been exposed to these diseases, the cumulative death rate of all of the diseases should not have been more than 50 to 75 percent on average.

26. Which of the following, if true, would most weaken Michele's conclusion?

    (A) Native Americans generally lacked the enzyme that would allow them to digest the sugars in milk.

    (B) Knowledge of medicine in Native America was much more advanced than in Europe at the time of Columbus.

    (C) At the time of Columbus, Native Americans were much less genetically diverse than Europeans, so there were fewer possibilities of natural immunity.

    (D) The death rates from the Black Death were higher than 33 percent in specific locations.

    (E) Diseases that quickly kill more than 75 percent of their infected hosts usually die off with their host's extinction.

27. Sara's argument relies on which of the following assumptions?

    (A) European technology was superior to the technology available to Native Americans at the time.

    (B) Diseases brought to the Western Hemisphere killed 95 percent of the Native American population.

    (C) The same number of Native Americans would have died of illnesses introduced by Europeans if the population of Native Americans had been twenty times greater.

    (D) Native Americans were the only people to be seriously affected by disease in the 1500s.

    (E) Diseases like smallpox, hepatitis, and measles were first brought to the Western Hemisphere by Europeans.

Go on to next page ⟶

28. Scientists have recently discovered that nearly all of the world's sharks live at ocean depths of 2,000 meters or less; leaving them well within reach of the deadly fishing nets of modern deep-sea trawlers.

    (A) leaving them well within reach of the deadly fishing nets of modern deep-sea trawlers.

    (B) they are, therefore, well within reach of the deadly fishing nets of modern deep-sea trawlers.

    (C) leaving us well within reach of the deadly fishing nets of modern deep-sea trawlers.

    (D) and this creates a danger zone within reach of modern deep-sea trawlers' deadly fishing nets.

    (E) which makes them well within reach of the deadly fishing nets of modern deep-sea trawlers.

29. Jason and Max founded an organic yogurt company, and he is now the largest employer in the county.

    (A) and he is now the largest employer in the county.

    (B) and they are now the largest employer in the county.

    (C) and it is now the largest employers in the county.

    (D) which is now the largest employer in the county.

    (E) that is now the largest employer in the county.

30. The best ways to store berries picked during the summer months is to either freeze them or have it made into jam.

    (A) is to either freeze them or have it made into jam.

    (B) is to either freeze them or make them into jam.

    (C) are to either freeze them or have them made into jam.

    (D) are to either freeze them or make them into jam.

    (E) is to either freeze them and have them made into jam.

31. Employers lose millions of work hours from employees every year during the NCAA basketball tournament known as March Madness. The men's and women's tournaments are conducted simultaneously, and tens of millions of American workers enter contests where they pick the winner of each game. Because some early round games actually take place during work hours, many employees are constantly checking basketball scores instead of working. Even employees who don't watch basketball at any other time of the year get caught up in the excitement.

    Which of the following is the most appropriate conclusion to the premises above?

    (A) The NCAA tournament is appropriately named because of the "madness" it creates among employees in March of every year.

    (B) Employees should not be allowed to check sports scores during business hours.

    (C) American businesses should indulge their employees during these two special weeks of the year.

    (D) The men's and women's NCAA tournaments combined form the world's most popular sporting event.

    (E) Everyone seems to have a different strategy for picking the winners, such as using team name, mascot, or uniform color.

Go on to next page ⟶

Questions 32–35 refer to the following passage:

Line   Human error is, by far, the most common and
most frequent cause of business disasters. By
definition, human errors are unintentional, and
because they occur randomly, we hope that the
(5) overall impact on your business operations will
be negligible. Each of us has had the experience
of developing a new document by revising an
older document or by using a template. When we
finish our work, we hit the "save" button and
(10) immediately realize that we have just written
over with new text an old document that we will
need again in the future. The same is true when
we reorganize our files to reduce the clutter we
made in the last month and unintentionally
(15) delete a whole folder of important documents.
     Unfortunately, there is no single simple solu-
tion. We have to expect that human errors will be
made, and we must be able to protect our businesses from ourselves to the extent possible. I
(20) often notice that managers hope that their
employees will be careful with important files,
and when they inadvertently delete a file, they
hope a backup file exists. I usually suggest keeping track of these events. If you do so, you will
(25) begin to realize that these errors occur with
greater frequency than you thought. A CD burner
is enthusiastically used for backing up data and
then forgotten after a few weeks have passed.
And the corrective action taken is most often less
(30) than satisfactory. In fact, we frequently have
observed that the loss of a file is either not even
realized or simply never reported, until someone
runs nervously through the company asking if
anyone still has a copy of a particular file. By that
(35) time, it is usually much too late to recover this
file from backup systems and it would require
more time to retrieve the deleted file than to
create a new one. IT managers often have busi-
nesspeople making requests of them such as
(40) "Could you see if we still have a backup file of the
presentation we gave to our most important
client last year? I don't remember the name of the
document, but I wrote it in the first quarter of the
year." This is not an efficient use of anyone's
(45) time, and as a small business owner or manager,
you know that experienced IT professionals are
too expensive to be used in this manner and you
have too many other important tasks for them.
     Small businesses need a solution that is a
(50) combination of user training and a backup mech-
anism from which users themselves can recover
unintentionally deleted files. It helps both the
users and the IT staff because the users no longer

have to request the IT staff to recover files for
them, which can be needlessly time-consuming.   (55)
And as a small business owner, you do not need
to hire someone to operate the backup system in
the event your staff needs to retrieve files.

This passage is excerpted from *Contingency
Planning and Disaster Recovery: A Small
Business Guide,* **by Donna R. Childs and Stefan
Dietrich (Wiley Publishing, 2002).**

32. The primary purpose of this passage is to

(A) inform small business owners of the
consequences of human error, the
most common and frequent of business
disasters

(B) advocate that small business owners
work toward a system of backing up
data that allows employees to recover
their own files in the case of human
error

(C) explain the futility of attempting to
recover data or documents that were
deleted more than a few hours ago

(D) recommend that small business owners
hire more IT staff so that employees
don't have to try to retrieve their own
documents in case of human error

(E) advise small business owners to train
employees to never delete files, reorganize files, or save any file and
thereby prevent the possibility of data
loss through human error

33. In the second paragraph, what do the
authors argue is a waste of an IT manager's
time?

(A) purchasing and installing a CD-burner
to back up data when the equipment is
soon forgotten

(B) training staff to use backup procedures
more efficiently to prevent the loss of
documents or data

(C) implementing a backup system that
allows users to quickly access backups
of their own data

(D) keeping track of human errors where
data is lost or backup files are used

(E) trying to recover a lost document from
a vague description months after it was
lost

Go on to next page ➡

34. Why do the authors suggest that managers keep track of events that result in data loss or data recovery?

    (A) to track which employees are most likely to make errors and use that information in their evaluations

    (B) so that the manager can determine how many IT staff members are needed to deal with data recovery

    (C) to prove that human errors resulting in data loss occur very infrequently

    (D) so that the manager can see that these events occur much more frequently than anticipated

    (E) because this information is very important to IT professionals seeking to establish data backup procedures

35. In the final paragraph, which of the following is NOT an advantage listed by the authors in their discussion of the preferred backup system?

    (A) Users themselves can uncover accidentally deleted files.

    (B) The backup system saves IT workers' time.

    (C) The backup system prevents human error.

    (D) Small business owners don't need to hire someone to run the backup system.

    (E) The backup system saves users' time.

36. Astronomers estimate that the new sunspot cycle will be 30 to 50 percent more active than the current cycle. Solar activity, including sunspots and solar flares, ejects huge quantities of charged particles into space. These particles are responsible for the phenomenon known as the *aurora borealis,* or "northern lights." The same particles also interfere with radio signals, disrupt satellite communications, and impede the transmission of power across high-voltage lines. Even though the new cycle of solar activity is predicted to be less intense than the peak cycle of a decade ago, the impacts will be felt by many more people around the world.

    Which of the following, if true, would provide the strongest reason for the paradox of the weaker solar activity's causing greater disruption?

    (A) Radio signals have become stronger and less likely to be disrupted, but many people rely on a satellite signal for the music and news they hear on their radios.

    (B) There are actually fewer high-voltage power lines in the Upper Midwest than there were a decade ago.

    (C) There has been an exponential increase in the number of people around the world with cell phones that could be disrupted by solar activity.

    (D) The northern lights are usually seen only in the very highest latitudes, but during periods of intense activity, they can be seen as far south as Chicago.

    (E) Fiber optic cables that supply the Internet connections for tens of millions of Americans are not affected by solar activity the way that radio and satellite signals are.

Go on to next page

37. The following advertisement appeared on behalf of a new breakfast cereal:

    "Healthy-Oh's breakfast cereal is one-of-a-kind good for you! Among breakfast cereals, only Healthy-Oh's has five grams of psyllium fiber. Psyllium fiber is good for your heart and helps you to lose weight. Doctors and nutritionists recommend at least twenty grams of fiber per day, so why not get twenty-five percent of your fiber the easy way with Healthy-Oh's cereal?"

    Which of the following, if true, would most weaken the product's claim to be "one-of-a-kind good for you"?

    (A) Healthy-Oh's is, in fact, the only cereal to use psyllium fiber.

    (B) Any fiber, including that found in many other cereals, has the same benefits to health as psyllium fiber.

    (C) Many doctors and nutritionists actually recommend at least twenty-five grams of fiber per day, and they base their recommendations on total calorie intake.

    (D) Another brand of cereal used to contain psyllium fiber, but it was not successful and is no longer on the market.

    (E) Psyllium fiber is also found in other products, such as powdered fiber supplements.

38. Many people who used to work crossword puzzles now prefer Sudoko, a type of puzzle that relies on logic instead of knowledge of obscure words.

    (A) Many people who used to work crossword puzzles now prefer Sudoko, a type of puzzle that relies on logic instead of knowledge of obscure words.

    (B) Many persons who used to work crossword puzzles now prefer Sudoko, one of the types of puzzle that rely on logic instead of knowledge of arcane words.

    (C) Many people who used to choose to work on crossword puzzles now choose to prefer Soduko, a type of puzzle that relies on logic instead of knowledge of obscure words.

    (D) Many who worked crossword puzzles now do Sudoko, it uses logic instead of obscure words.

    (E) Many people have chosen to try Sudoko, which uses logic instead of crossword puzzles, which relies on knowledge of obscure words.

39. Another interest rate increase was announced today, and along with the continued robust housing sales, this seems as if to indicate that the housing market remains strong.

    (A) as if to indicate that

    (B) indicative of

    (C) like an indication of

    (D) like it is indicative that

    (E) to indicate that

Go on to next page

40. The border between the United States and Canada is the longest undefended border in the world, and many lawmakers are starting to argue that <u>if parts of the border are not secured, the citizens of United States have faced an unknown threat.</u>

    (A) if parts of the border are not secured, the citizens of the United States have faced an unknown threat.

    (B) the citizens of the United States will always face an unknown threat if they did not secure it.

    (C) without securing it, the citizens of the United States will always face an unknown threat.

    (D) always would the citizens of the United States face an unknown threat if it is not secured.

    (E) if parts of the border are not secured, the citizens of the United States will always face an unknown threat.

41. Most Americans seem to think <u>that the Denver-Boulder area receives a lot of snow each year because they are so close to the mountains.</u>

    (A) that the Denver-Boulder area receives a lot of snow each year because they are so close to the mountains.

    (B) as the Denver-Boulder area receives a lot of snow each year because it is so close to the mountains.

    (C) that the Denver-Boulder area receives a lot of snow each year because it is so close to the mountains.

    (D) that the Denver-Boulder area receives a lot of snow each year because we are so close to the mountains.

    (E) that the Denver-Boulder area received a lot of snow each year because it is so close to the mountains.

STOP DO NOT TURN THE PAGE UNTIL TOLD TO DO SO.
DO NOT RETURN TO A PREVIOUS TEST.

Answer Key for Practice Exam 1

Section 2
Quantitative Answer Key

1. C	20. B
2. B	21. D
3. E	22. D
4. D	23. C
5. E	24. A
6. E	25. E
7. A	26. C
8. C	27. E
9. E	28. B
10. B	29. A
11. A	30. C
12. B	31. A
13. D	32. C
14. E	33. E
15. B	34. C
16. C	35. D
17. A	36. C
18. D	37. B
19. C	

Section 3
Verbal Answer Key

1. B	22. A
2. E	23. B
3. D	24. E
4. B	25. B
5. C	26. C
6. E	27. C
7. A	28. B
8. E	29. D
9. A	30. D
10. C	31. A
11. B	32. B
12. E	33. E
13. D	34. D
14. A	35. C
15. C	36. C
16. B	37. B
17. E	38. A
18. D	39. E
19. D	40. E
20. B	41. C
21. C	

Chapter 18

Explaining the Answers to Practice Test #1

⬤ ⬤

You've finished the test, but you're not done yet. It's time to check your answers. If you have time, read through all the answer explanations, even those for questions you answered correctly. Information that you hadn't thought of before may be conveyed in an answer explanation.

Explanations for the Analytical Writing Assessment

Scoring the practice analytical writing tasks is a little different than scoring the verbal and quantitative sections. Your job is to honestly analyze the essays you've written and assign yourself a score. You can also ask a writer friend or composition teacher to look over your essays and give you an opinion. To help you determine your score for this section, we've included a couple sample essays and an explanation of their strengths and weaknesses. Use these tools to identify your own essay's strengths and weaknesses and improve your essay responses before you take the real test.

Analysis of an issue

Your first task was to analyze an issue. Scores for this task range from 0–6. If you receive a 0 score, your essay is completely off topic, written in a foreign language, or is a copy of the essay prompt. If you receive a 2, your essay is disorganized, lacks reasons and examples, and contains numerous errors in grammar, usage, and mechanics. A score of 4 means your essay supports your position, organizes thoughts, and applies the conventions of standard written English adequately but not amazingly. A score of 6 indicates that you've written an outstanding essay that is well organized, eloquent, and persuasive; provides perceptive thinking and convincing examples; and demonstrates a command of the elements of standard written English.

Sample analysis of an issue essay

The analysis of an issue topic asked you to provide your opinion on the idea that the United States should work equally with other countries to lessen the impact of global threats. Here's an example of an essay:

It is certainly true that the problems facing the world are increasingly international, and the idea that America should work on an equal basis with all countries of the world seems noble. However, because the United States enjoys more abundant resources than most other nations, it has a responsibility to take on a larger role than other nations do when it comes to confronting global problems of the twenty-first century, like preserving the environment, maintaining international security, and combating disease.

Environmental issues such as global warming, deforestation, increased pollution of the air and water, and the threat of extinction of many species present difficult challenges. The United States is uniquely poised to take the lead on these issues. Developed countries create much more pollution and contribute more to global warming than do other countries. As the most developed large nation in the world, the United States creates more pollutants and greenhouse gases than any other country. The United States has a greater responsibility for the world's pollution and therefore must do more to lessen its impact. As the world's technological leader, the United States is most capable to develop pollution reduction technology to remove harmful contaminants throughout the world. Issues of deforestation and species' extinction are largely focused on developing nations like those in the tropical regions of the world. As the world's richest nation, the United States is in a better position to contribute the kind of economic assistance that allows for the preservation of species-rich areas like the tropical rain forests.

International security is another area of concern for the world in the twenty-first century. The United States spends about half of the total military spending in the entire world. With the most effective army in the world, the United States has to take the lead in international security. Combating terrorism, wars, and genocide will take effective leadership and cooperation from all nations, but the United States has the duty to assume greater responsibility because of its military might.

Technology has diminished the distances among nations, which exacerbates the spread of global diseases. The SARS virus spread through modern transportation networks from Asia to Canada in one week. New diseases constantly evolve and previously controlled infections, like strains of strep, can become immune to current antibiotics. The Aids virus spread from relatively contained roots in Africa to take over the whole world. And now the Avian Flu threatens to develop into pandemic the likes of which have not been experienced since the Spanish Flu epidemic almost a century ago. The United State's resources of money, food, and scientists make it one of the richest in the world, which therefore makes it the most logical source of assistance for the mounting threat of global disease.

Environmental concerns, international security, and disease present just three areas of potential calamity for the world in the twenty-first century. Because the United States possesses greater means to take on these global threats and others, it is not enough for the nation to play an equal role with other nations. The United States must assume a much larger role in defending the world against the widespread disasters that could destroy it.

This paper may earn a 5 because it combines logical, cogent analysis with a good command of standard written English. In addition:

- ✔ The writer begins the essay with a clear statement of the position and gives a reason for the position.

- ✔ The writer presents three global issues and provides convincing, detailed arguments as to why in each of these areas the U.S. must lead attempts to combat the problems. This essay demonstrates clear organization, moving clearly from point to point. Most of the essay serves to support the argument. The author doesn't fill space with unnecessary information.

✔ The author uses specific examples, such as SARS, AIDS, and the avian flu to show the impact of global disease and pollution to show the United States' responsibility for solving environmental concerns; however, the writer probably could have used more-specific examples to support the paragraph on international security.

✔ The essay doesn't contain any major grammatical, usage, or mechanical errors. Despite a few minor errors (like stating *Aids* instead of *AIDS*), the author presents a relatively clean essay for the time allotment. The essay contains varied sentence structure and precise vocabulary, and it is written mainly in active voice.

Analysis of an argument

Your second task was to analyze an argument. This essay has a slightly different scoring guide. Following the rules of standard written English and providing clear support for your position are still important, but including clear transitions between points takes on a more important role.

If your essay receives a 2, it may provide an unclear representation of the essay's position rather than a critique of the argument made in the prompt. If your essay receives a 4, you may provide a clear analysis for each of the elements of the argument but neglect to present clear transitions to link your points. An essay that receives a 6 identifies all the important elements of the argument and develops an organized position on their accuracy and reasonableness, using clear transitions between points.

Sample analysis of an argument essay

For this topic, you were supposed to analyze an argument about government funding of Ph.D.'s in the social sciences and humanities. Here's what a sample analysis of this topic may look like:

> The first impression of an argument supporting discontinued funding of Ph.D's that result in lower earning may be favorable, but a closer analysis of the issue demonstrates that the benefits of supporting Ph.D.'s in the social sciences and humanities actually outweigh the costs. What are the actual costs to state and federal government of helping a student earn a Ph.D. in social sciences and humanities? For the federal government the costs are actually quite minimal. Direct federal aid to students usually takes the form of guaranteed student loans or small need-based grants. Most Ph.D.'s repay their student loans and the cost to the federal government is a trivial amount. Need-based grants are generally very small, only a couple of thousand dollars, and have no real impact on the federal budget.

> State governments often contribute much more to Ph.D. students than does the federal government. This is especially true given that many of the biggest Ph.D. granting schools in America are state universities. The majority of Ph.D. students in the humanities and social sciences have graduate assistantships requiring them to either teach or research. In exchange their tuition and fees are waived and the student gets a stipend each month to cover rent, food, and the other costs of living. This arrangement usually costs the state around ten thousand dollars per year per student in stipend money as well as lost tuition. One other cost to both the state and federal government is lost taxes that students are not paying during the years they are in school. However, they can make up this amount by earning more after graduation.

What, then, are the benefits of having Ph.D.'s in the social sciences and humanities? Just as the primary costs are borne by the states, so the states also reap the most obvious benefits. Ph.D. students work for their tuition waiver and monthly stipend. These graduate assistants either teach classes or conduct research. In many cases the student is performing work that would otherwise have to be done by a professor. State universities get cheap labor from enthusiastic graduate students who happily perform duties that more experienced professors might shun. In addition, upon graduation the new Ph.D.'s become professors at state and private universities and educate future generations in English, literature, political science, philosophy, and all of the other social science and humanities courses. One final benefit of the graduate assistantship is that because Ph.D.'s often graduate with few loans, they can afford to work for much lower salaries than M.B.A.'s, M.D.'s, or J.D.'s.

Ph.D.'s in the social sciences and humanities cost the federal government very little and benefit the entire country. States contribute more to each new Ph.D. but they also reap more of the benefits. It is true that these Ph.D.'s make less than do holders or business or professional degrees, but this simply acts to keep college costs from rising any higher than they have already risen. This argument fails because the cost-benefit analysis on which it relies is flawed. The benefits that Ph.D.'s in the social sciences and humanities create for society, the government, and the economy are much greater than the costs.

Although this essay presents a well-reasoned argument in an interesting tone with descriptive examples, well-chosen words, clear transitions, and a variety of sentence structures, its author makes a fundamental error. The focus of this essay is on the issue of whether the government should fund social science and humanities Ph.D.'s and not on how well the creator of the original argument presented her position. This would be a pretty good essay if it were written for an analysis of an issue topic, but the focus of analysis of an argument essay must be on the argument itself rather than its topic.

The test taker should have introduced the essay with three reasons that the argument is unsound and should have discussed each of those reasons in detail in separate paragraphs. By failing to focus the essay on how the author of the prompt missed the mark in making the argument, the author of this essay missed the mark for this assignment. This failure may reduce the writer's score by two points for an otherwise pretty good essay.

Explanatory Answers to the Quantitative Questions

1. **C.** To solve this relatively easy basic operations problem, first subtract the two terms you need to compare:

    $3 - 0.5 = 2.5$

    $1 - 0.5 = 0.5$

    To find out how many times 0.5 goes into 2.5, just divide: You know that $25 \div 5$ is 5, so 0.5 goes into 2.5 five times, which means that $3 - 0.5$ is 5 times greater than $1 - 0.5$; the answer is 5.

2. **B.** It's probably easiest to approach this exponent question by substituting the answer choices for n in the inequality. Start with –2, because it's the middle value of the answer choices. If that makes the value too big, consider –3 and –4; if they make the value too small, consider –1 and 0.

    If n equals –2, you get 11×10^{-2}, or 0.11 (just move the decimal to the left two places).

Then you have to ask yourself whether 0.11 < 0.1 (¹⁄₁₀ = 0.1). 0.11 is actually ¹⁄₁₀₀ more than 0.1. Therefore, you have to move the decimal point one more place to the left, which means that n has to equal –3 to make 11×10^n less than ¹⁄₁₀. The answer is –3.

–4 also makes 11×10^n less than ¹⁄₁₀, but the problem asks for the *greatest* possible value, and –3 is greater than –4.

If you need to brush up on the basics of working with exponents, consult Chapter 10.

3. **E.** Here's your first data sufficiency problem. Refer to the chart in Chapter 15 to help you eliminate answers for data sufficiency questions.

The question asks you to evaluate the data you need to figure out whether Beth or Michelle received a greater dollar increase.

First evaluate statement (1), which tells you the percentage of Michelle's increase. However, you don't know Michelle's original salary, so you can't use the percentage to figure out the dollar amount of her increase. Statement (1) by itself isn't sufficient, which means that the answer can't be A or D.

Statement (2) offers the same kind of information about Beth's increase. Again, because you don't know Beth's original salary, knowing the percentage increase won't tell you how much her salary increased by dollars. Statement (2) isn't sufficient by itself, so the answer is either C or E. To figure which it is, consider whether you can figure out the greater dollar increase using both statements.

Because neither statement allows you to figure out the dollar amount, you can't use them together to answer the question, so you have to choose E.

On the GMAT, you can't assume information that isn't expressly stated. If you were tempted to choose C because the two statements together indicated that Beth received a greater percentage increase than Michelle, you assumed that both women had the same original salary.

4. **D.** For Roman numeral questions like this one, consider I, II, and III individually and eliminate answers based on your findings.

A reciprocal is the flip side of a fraction. Simply take the original fraction and invert the numerator and denominator to get its reciprocal. A way to test whether two values are reciprocals is to multiply them. If you multiply a fraction and its reciprocal, you always get 1.

You know the values in I aren't reciprocals of each other because they don't have a product of 1. ¹⁄₁₅ × – ¹⁄₁₅ = – ¹⁄₂₂₅. Instead, the two values are opposites (one is positive and the other negative).

Eliminate answers with I in them, which means A, C, and E. You're left with B and D, and both remaining choices contain III.

Just by evaluating the values in I and eliminating answer choices, you know the values in III are reciprocals without even looking at them. You only have to consider II to answer the question correctly.

Evaluating II may be a little tricky. The two values don't look like reciprocals at first glance, but they are. When you flip $\sqrt{2}$, you get $\dfrac{1}{\sqrt{2}}$. But you may remember from your math days (for some of you that was in the 1990s . . . or earlier!) that mathematicians hate to leave the radical (square root sign) in the denominator. Instead, they multiply the top and bottom of the fraction by the radical (in effect multiplying by 1):

$$\frac{1}{\sqrt{2}} \times \frac{\sqrt{2}}{\sqrt{2}} = \frac{\sqrt{2}}{2}$$

When you multiply the two values in II, you come up with a product of 1. Thus, the numbers in II are reciprocals, and the answer is D.

If you really wanted to consider III just in case, you'd see that the fact that III contains reciprocals jumps right out at you. 4 is the same as $\frac{4}{1}$, and the flipped fraction is $\frac{1}{4}$. Plus, $\frac{4}{1} \times \frac{1}{4} = 1$.

5. **E.** This data sufficiency question asks you to figure out what data you need to find the list price of a jacket.

    Statement (1) tells you the percentage less than the list price that the store sold the jacket for. But knowing this percentage without knowing the list price or more about the purchase price doesn't allow you to determine the list price of the jacket. Statement (1) by itself isn't sufficient, so you can eliminate A and D.

    Statement (2) gives you the difference of the percentage that the store paid off the list price and the percentage of the list price that the store sold the jacket for. Knowing this difference tells you what x is in terms of y, but that information won't get you the list price. Because statement (2) by itself isn't sufficient, you can eliminate B and consider whether both statements are sufficient to answer the question.

    The statements give you the percentage off the list price for purchasing and selling the jacket, but without knowing the other value, the purchase price, you have no way to determine the list price. You can eliminate C. Even together, the two statements don't help determine the answer. The answer is E.

6. **E.** This data sufficiency question concerns the quadrant plane of coordinate geometry fame. You need information that places the point in one specific quadrant of the plane. You can do that if you know whether each coordinate is negative or positive.

    Statement (1) tells you that x is negative, so you know that the point is to the left of the coordinate plane. But you don't know the value of y, so you don't know which of the left quadrants it is in. Eliminate A and D and check out statement (2).

    You could solve the equation in statement (2) to discover that either $y < -x$ or $x < -y$, but neither of those solutions tells you whether the values are definitely positive or negative. So eliminate B because statement II isn't sufficient. Now consider the two statements together.

    When you combine the information in the two equations, you get that $x = -2$ and that $y < 2$:

    $$x + y < 0$$
    $$-2 + y < 0$$
    $$y < 2$$

    You know the value of x, but you still have a range of values for y that could be either positive or negative. Therefore, you still don't know exactly which quadrant the point is in. The two statements together are insufficient to answer the question, so you can eliminate C. E is the correct answer.

7. **A.** If you've memorized the most common decimal values, you know that $\frac{1}{3}$ is 0.33, or 33 percent. So you're looking for fractions that are less than $\frac{1}{3}$, 0.33, or 33 percent.

    As you evaluate each answer choice, look for shortcuts to avoid wasting time doing long division. Start by manipulating the fractions.

    Look at A. $\frac{9}{27}$ is the same as $\frac{1}{3}$ ($\frac{1}{3} \times \frac{9}{9} = \frac{9}{27}$). $\frac{8}{27}$ is a bit smaller than $\frac{9}{27}$, so $\frac{8}{27}$ is less than $\frac{1}{3}$. At this point, you could choose the first answer and submit it. But if you have a little time, you may choose to run through the remaining answer choices just to make sure you haven't missed something.

    B's answer of $\frac{2}{5}$ is the same as $\frac{4}{10}$, which equals 40 percent, or 0.4, and is more than 33 percent, or 0.33.

    $\frac{18}{50}$ in C is the same as $\frac{36}{100}$, or 0.36, which is still more than 0.33.

    The fraction in D isn't so easily manipulated, but if you perform quick division, you'll see that $\frac{3}{8}$ is 0.375, which is over 0.33.

    When you divide 4 by 11 for E, you get just more than 0.36, a number higher than 0.33.

8. **C.** This question offers another data sufficiency problem. It asks you what you need to determine an amount of money invested in a business owned by Eben and Emily. To know the amount invested, you need to know how much both parties put in.

   Statement (1) tells you that Eben contributed 60 percent of the total amount, which means that Emily put in 40 percent. But because you don't know the total amount, you can't pin down the dollar amount they each contributed. Because statement (1) by itself isn't sufficient, you can eliminate A and D.

   Statement (2)'s information that Emily contributed $20,000 of the total amount tells you how much Emily put in but tells you nothing about Eben's investment. Statement (2) by itself doesn't give you enough information to know the total amount invested in the business. Eliminate B and consider the two statements together.

   After you know how much Emily put in, you can use what you know about her percentage of the investment to figure out the total amount. If Eben contributed 60 percent, then Emily contributed 40 percent, and her 40 percent equals $20,000. You can set up an equation to solve for the total amount, signified by T.

   $$40\% \times T = 20,000$$

   Because you can solve this equation for T, you know that the two statements together are sufficient to answer the problem. You can eliminate E. C is the correct answer.

   You don't have to actually solve the equation to answer this problem; don't waste time solving for T.

9. **E.** Here's a data sufficiency problem that's not presented as a word problem.

   Statement (1) tells you that $x^3 < 28$, which means that x can only be 1, 2, or 3, because when you cube each of these numbers you get 1, 8, and 27, respectively, and x can't be higher than 27. However, the statement still doesn't give one defined value for x. Therefore, statement (1) by itself isn't sufficient, and you can eliminate A and D.

   Statement (2) tells what x doesn't equal, but it doesn't let you know what it does equal. If $x \neq x^3$, then $x \neq 1$ because 1 is the only positive integer that's true for this equation. Thus, statement (2) isn't sufficient to tell you the value of x, and you can eliminate B.

   When you consider both statements together, you can narrow the values for x down to 2 or 3. Statement (1) tells you x is 1, 2, or 3, and statement (2) lets you know it isn't 1. You're still stuck with two values for x, which is one too many to solve the problem. Eliminate C. Your answer is E.

10. **B.** Don't spend a bunch of time worrying about what basis points are in this question. They're just units of measurement.

    This question really wants to see what you know about proportions. You know that 5 percent equals 100 basis points, and you can use a proportion to find out how many basis points 7.5 percent equals:

    $$\frac{5\%}{100} = \frac{7.5\%}{x}$$

    $$\frac{0.05}{100} = \frac{.075}{x}$$

    Cross-multiply:

    $$0.05x = 7.5$$

    $$x = 150$$

    You could follow the same process to figure out the basis points for 5.5 percent, but you don't have to take the time to do the calculations. All the answer choices begin with a 4, so you know that the basis points for 5.5 percent is a value that results in a number that begins with 4 when it's subtracted from 150. The value also has the same decimal placement as

150, because 7.5 percent and 5.5 percent have the same decimal placements. So you know that the number of basis points for 5.5 percent is 110 and that the difference between the two basis points values is 40 (150 − 110 = 40).

11. **A.** This data sufficiency problem concerns determining an amount of money again. (That's how you know the GMAT is a test for business school — all the questions about money!) You know the amount of the estate ($81,000) and that it was divided among three people. You need to determine what information allows you to figure out the younger child's portion.

Statement (1) gives you enough information to make an equation that allows you to solve for x, where x stands for the amount the younger child receives. So you can figure out the amount with just the information in statement (1). Here's how you'd set up the equation: If the younger child received $15,000 less than the older child and $30,000 less than the spouse, you can let x equal the amount that the younger child receives. This means that $x + 15,000$ equals the amount the older child got and $x + 30,000$ equals the amount the spouse got. The equation adds the three amounts to get the total estate, like this:

$$x + (x + 15,000) + (x + 30,000) = 81,000$$

You can solve for x, but don't take the time to do so. Statement (1) is sufficient, so you can eliminate B, C, and E and check the second statement to see whether it's sufficient, too. If it is, the answer is D; if it's not, the answer is A.

Statement (2) says the spouse received 42 percent of the sum from the estate. This information tells you what the spouse got, but you can't define how much each child received of the remaining 58 percent. You can't determine how much the younger child received from statement (2), so eliminate D. A is your answer.

After you've determined that one of the statements is sufficient, don't try to figure out whether both statements are sufficient together. Choice C is an option only if neither statement is sufficient by itself. Following the chart we give you in Chapter 15 helps you stay on track with data sufficiency problems.

12. **B.** You just need to know how to subtract negatives to solve this problem. When you subtract a negative, the negatives cancel out, so to speak, and you really just add a positive. So −2 − (−8) is the same as −2 + 8, and −2 + 8 = 6. −4 − (−9) is the same as −4 + 9, and −4 + 9 = 5. Because 6 is 1 greater than 5, the answer is B.

13. **D.** You can solve this problem by setting up an equation. The product of the three numbers in the horizontal row is 6 × 12 × 3. Without a calculator, it's probably easier to multiply 6 and 3 (which is 18) and then multiply that by 12. 18 × 12 = 216. So the sum of the three numbers in the vertical column is 216:

$$x + 12 + y = 216$$
$$x + y = 204$$

14. **E.** For this data sufficiency question, you need to have enough information to find the values of a and b.

Statement (1) gives you the value of a, but it tells you nothing about the value of b. You can eliminate A and D because statement (1) is not sufficient. Check the other statement.

Statement (2) doesn't tell you anything that allows you to define the values of a and b. So eliminate B and check to see whether both statements allow you to determine the two values.

With the knowledge that $a = 5$ and that $a^2 = b^2$, it would seem that you can find the value of b. You may think that you can just substitute 5 for a and solve the equation for b. At first glance, it appears that because $a = 5$, b must also equal 5. But be careful.

That $a^2 = b^2$ doesn't mean that $a = b$. If you substitute 5 for a in the equation, b could have two values. 5^2 is 25, and $25 = b^2$, so b could be either 5 or –5, because both equal 25 when they're squared.

The two statements are insufficient together, and you can eliminate C. Choose E.

15. **B.** Integers can't be decimals or fractions. They can be positive or negative or zero, though.

So $\frac{24-x}{x}$ is an integer if x is a positive or negative factor of 24, like 3 or –12. Just plug 3 into the equation to see what we mean:

$$\frac{24-3}{3} = \frac{21}{3} = 7$$

See whether statement (1) makes x a factor of 24. $x < 5$ means that x could be 4, 3, 2, or 1, all of which are factors of 24, but x could also be –5, –7, or –9, which aren't factors of 24. Therefore, this statement doesn't guarantee that x will be a factor of 24. Statement (1) isn't sufficient, and you can eliminate A and D.

Statement (2) lets you know that $x^2 = 36$, which means that x must equal 6 or –6. Both are factors of 24 and make the expression $\frac{24-x}{x}$ an integer. So statement (2) gives you enough information to answer the question. Eliminate C and E. B is your answer.

16. **C.** If the population doubles every 50 years, in 3 centuries (300 years) the population will double 6 times. You can express this value as 2^6. The 2 represents the doubling event and the 6 represents that it happens 6 times. So multiply the 10^3 people by 2^6 to find total population. You don't have to multiply the value because answer C states it simply as $(2^6)(10^3)$.

17. **A.** Think of this word problem in terms of algebraic equations:

profit = gross – production costs

gross = the number of items sold × the price per item

production costs = fixed costs + variable costs

Let y equal how many items Greg must produce and sell to earn an annual profit of \$200,000, set up an equation, and solve:

profit = gross – costs

$200,000 = (y \times 20) - (120,000 + 4y)$

$200,000 = 20y - 120,000 - 4y$

$200,000 = 16y - 120,000$

$320,000 = 16y$

$20,000 = y$

Your answer is A.

18. **D.** Here's a data sufficiency rate problem. You're seeking to determine how much less time it takes two people to stuff envelopes than it does one person. The problem gives you that Adam takes 2 hours to stuff 400 envelopes by himself. If you know how long it takes Matt to stuff envelopes, you can solve the problem

Statement (1) tells you that Adam and Matt stuff envelopes at the same rate, so you know how long Matt takes to stuff envelopes. The statement gives you the information you need to answer the problem, so you know the answer is either A or D. (You also know without doing too much thinking that it will take them both half the time to stuff 400 envelopes.) Now you need to determine whether the other statement is sufficient, too.

Statement (2) actually tells you how long it takes both men to stuff all of the envelopes, so it's also sufficient. If it takes Adam twice as long as when both of them stuff, the 2 hours are cut to 1. Because both statements are sufficient, the answer is D.

19. **C.** This question essentially asks you whether the positive integer y is any number other than a prime number, because a prime number can be expressed only as a product of 1 and itself.

Because the range provided by statement (1) contains a number that's prime (51), you can't determine whether y is a composite number from statement (1) alone. Statement (1) isn't sufficient by itself, and neither A nor D can be the answer. Consider statement (2).

At first, statement (2) may seem sufficient to you. Almost no even numbers are prime. But 2 is the one even number that's prime, so knowing that y is even doesn't allow you to say that it can be expressed as the product of 2 integers that are both greater than 1.

Because statement (2) isn't sufficient, the answer can't be B. Consider whether knowing both statements provides an answer to the question.

The two statements together narrow values for y to even numbers between 47 and 53. Those numbers are 48, 50, and 52, and none is a prime number. The information from both statements is sufficient to tell you that the possible values for y can be expressed as the product of two integers greater than 1, so the answer must be C.

20. **B.** If you don't happen to know that 0.375 is ⅜ from repeated exposure to home improvement shows or repeated work on your old house, you have to do a little math. You can try each answer by using long division, dividing the denominator into the numerator and eliminating obviously incorrect choices like ⅓ (you probably know that ⅓ = 0.33 repeating from years of math classes):

- ✔ 7 goes into 30 at least 4 times (7×4 is 28), so you know its decimal equivalent doesn't begin with 3. Choice A can't be right.

- ✔ 8 goes into 30 at least 3 times (8×3 is 24), so it's a possible answer choice because the decimal begins with 3.

- ✔ 9 goes into 40 at least 4 times (9×4 is 36), so its decimal equivalent begins with a 4, too. Eliminate C.

- ✔ Cross out D as well, because 5 goes into to 20 4 times, which means its decimal equivalent has to begin with a 4.

You've already eliminated E, so the answer has to be B.

Alternatively, you could approach the problem by changing 0.375 into a fraction. 0.375 is the same as $^{375}\!/_{1000}$. When you simplify this fraction, you get ⅜, which is B.

21. **D.** There are 360 degrees in a circle. To determine the number of degrees that represent rent, at 35 percent, just multiply 360 by 0.35:

$$360 \times 0.35 = 126.$$

22. **D.** This data sufficiency question requires you to deal with inequalities.

You don't have to define a value for x; you just have to know whether it's less than 0.

Statement (1) tells you that $x^3 < 0$, so x must be less than 0. Because x^3 is a negative number, its root has to be negative, because only a negative number results in a negative cube. For instance, -1^3 has to be negative, because $-1 \times -1 \times -1$ is -1. Given the information in this statement, x has to be negative. Statement (1) is sufficient, and the answer has to be A or D.

To determine whether statement (2) is also sufficient, first solve for x by dividing both sides of the given equation by -3.

REMEMBER

When you divide an inequality by a negative number, you have to flip the inequality sign so that it points the other way.

$-3x > 0$

Divide both sides by –3.

$x < 0$

Statement (2) gives you everything you need to know that $x < 0$, so it's sufficient as well. Eliminate A. Your answer is D.

23. **C.** For this problem, you need information to determine how many integers come between x and y.

Statement (1) may seem sufficient when you first look at it. If $y - x = 4$, you'd think that 4 integers fall between x and y.

You don't know whether y and x are integers themselves, so you don't know from statement (1) how many integers z will satisfy the expression. For example, if $x = 1$ and $y = 5$, z would equal 3 (2, 3, and 4), but if $x = 1.5$ and $y = 5.5$, z would equal 4 (2, 3, 4, 5). Statement (1) isn't sufficient, so the answer can't be A or D.

Statement (2) by itself tells you nothing. Any number of integers could be between two non-integers. The answer isn't B.

If you consider both statements, however, you know that $z = 4$. As we show in the earlier example, after you know that the difference between x and y is 4 and that both x and y are integers, you know that four integers are between them. The answer can't be E. Select C.

24. **A.** This problem deals with percentages. To know how many people were employed in October, you have to know something about the number of employed persons in either September or October.

Statement (1) gives you some information about the number of employed persons during the months of September and October. Given the difference in the unemployment rate (0.3 percent, because $5.9 - 5.6 = 0.3$) and that this difference amounted to 10,000 employed persons, you can easily set up an equation to solve for the total number of people in the labor force. Let y = the number of people in the labor force.

$0.3y = 10,000$

When you know the total number of people in the labor force (the value of y) and the percentage of people who were employed in October, which is 94.1 percent (100 percent – 5.9 percent unemployed), you can set up an equation to solve for the number of people employed in October. Let O stand for the number of employed in October.

$O = 0.9411y$

In this equation, y is a known value because you solved for it in the previous equation. You can solve this equation to find the total number of employed persons in October, so statement (1) is sufficient. The answer is either A or D.

Statement (2) tells you about the number of employed persons in May, but May figures have nothing to do with October figures. Statement (2) isn't sufficient, so you can eliminate D. Your answer is A.

25. **E.** Read the question carefully. You need only entries that "show the product of each number and each of the other four numbers." So as shown in the figure, starting from the top row, you need only four entries; in the second row, you need only three; in the third, two; and in the last row, just one. $4 + 3 + 2 + 1 = 10$, which is answer E.

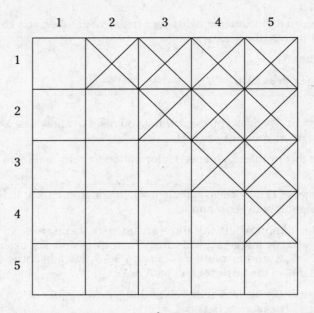

26. **C.** The quadratic expression in the problem ($x^2 - kx - 28$) has two factors, and the problem tells you that ($x - 4$) is one of them. To determine what the other factor is, focus on the last term in the expression (–28). Ask yourself what value multiplied by –4 produces –28. –28 ÷ –4 = 7, so the other factor has to contain a positive 7. ($x + 7$) has to be the other factor. If you use the FOIL method to multiply ($x - 4$) and ($x + 7$), the middle term of the expression turns out to be $3x$ ($7x - 4x$).

    Be careful when you choose a value for k. In the problem, the quadratic expression specifically shows that k is negative ($x^2 - kx - 28$), so k must be –3. Choose C.

27. **E.** This data sufficiency question tests your geometry knowledge. You try to find the length of the radius, which is line segment *OB* or *OC*. Statement (1) gives you the ratio of the two segments that make up *OB*, but this information doesn't help you figure out the line length because you don't have any line measurements to base the ratio on. Because statement (1) isn't sufficient, you can eliminate A and D.

    Statement (2) doesn't tell you anything you don't already know. *OB* and *OC* are the legs of triangle *OBC*, and they are both radii of the circle (which means they have to be equal in length). So the fact that triangle *OBC* is isosceles is nothing new. The second statement doesn't help you determine the length of the radius of the circle, so B can't be right.

    You don't have to consider the two statements together. Statement (1) was insufficient and statement (2) gave you no new information, so you know that the two statements together won't help you answer the question. Eliminate C, choose E, and go on to the next problem.

28. **B.** This data sufficiency problem asks you to draw a conclusion about an inequality. Data sufficiency questions often deal with inequalities because their solutions are often ambiguous. For this problem, you need to determine whether the product of a and b is less than 12.

    Statement (1) tells you that a is less than 3 and b is less than 4. If you didn't think about this statement thoroughly, you may have been tempted to say that it sufficiently determines that ab is less than 12 because 3 × 4 is 12 and the values are less than those.

    Consider all possibilities for a and b. If both a and b represent negative numbers that are less than –2 and –3, their product would actually be equal to or greater than 12.

    For instance, if a = –3 and b = –4, their product would be 12, which equals 12 and therefore isn't less than 12. Values for a and b of –9 and –10, respectively, would produce a product of 90, which is far more than 12. Statement (1) isn't sufficient to determine whether ab < 12, so eliminate A and D.

Consider statement (2). Start with the inequality it gives you for b^2. Solve the inequality by taking the square root of both sides, and make sure you consider both positive and negative possibilities:

$b^2 < 169$

$b < 13$ or -13

The other information in the statement tells you that a is greater than ⅓ of b but less than ⅔ of b. So when you multiply a and b, a will be at most ⅔ of b (which is 13). ⅔ × 13 is 8.67, so the product of a and b will certainly be less than 12 for all positive values of b. You don't need to worry about the negative values of b, because a negative multiplied by a positive is always a negative, which means the product is less than 12. Statement (2) give you enough information to answer the question, so you can eliminate C and E. Your answer is B.

29. **A.** The problem asks for the amount of weekly sales it takes for Angelo and Isabella to earn the same amount of money. You can write an equation that sets Angelo's and Isabella's weekly earnings equal to each other, with x representing weekly sales.

Weekly earnings for each salesperson equal base salary plus commission. So Angelo's earnings are $550 + (0.08)(x - 1,000)$, and Isabella's are $0.10x$. Set up the equation and solve:

$$550 + (0.08)(x - 1,000) = 0.10x$$

Distribute the 0.08:

$$550 + 0.08x - 80 = 0.10x$$

Combine terms and subtract $0.08x$ from both sides:

$$470 = 0.02x$$

Divide both sides by 0.02:

$$23,500 = x$$

Your answer is A.

30. **C.** This word problem is a distance problem.

The distance formula is *rate × time = distance*.

To find out how many miles FastTrain goes before it meets up with SlowTrain, first determine the rate of each train by modifying the distance formula and plugging in numbers.

rate = distance/time

FastTrain rate = ⁹⁰⁰⁄₃ or 300 miles/hour

SlowTrain rate = ⁹⁰⁰⁄₅ or 180 miles/hour

To continue with the solution, ask yourself which of the three elements of the formula (rate, time, or distance) both trains have in common when they meet in the middle. It's not rate, because you know from your calculations that the rates are different. It's not distance, because the faster train must travel more miles than the slower train. So it must be time. Don't let the 3 hour and 5 hour designations fool you. These tell you the total time each train took to travel the entire distance. But you're looking for the time it takes them to meet in the middle. Both trains travel the same amount of time before they meet.

Modify the distance formula to solve for time $(t = \frac{d}{r})$ and set up an equation that makes the two trains' times equal. You can let 1 stand for FastTrain and 2 stand for SlowTrain:

$$d_1/r_1 = d_2/r_2$$

Plug the values you know into the equation, with x standing for the distance FastTrain has traveled when the two trains meet. If FastTrain has traveled x miles when they meet, SlowTrain will have traveled $900 - x$ miles, or the difference between the total 900 miles and the x miles that FastTrain has traveled.

$$\frac{x}{300} = \frac{(900 - x)}{180}$$

Cross-multiply and solve:

$$180x = 300(900 - x)$$

Distribute the 300:

$$180x = 270,000 - 300x$$

Add $300x$ to both sides:

$$480x = 270,000$$

Divide both sides by 480:

$$x = 562.5$$

Your answer is C.

31. **A.** For this data sufficiency question, you need to know a little geometry.

Segment *CA,* the distance the question asks you to determine, is also the radius of the circular swimming pool. So if you can determine the radius of the circle, you're in business.

Statement (1) gives you the area of the base of the circular pool, which is the area of the circle. If you've memorized the formula for the area of a circle, you know that $A = \pi r^2$. Because you have the values for the area and π, you can solve for *r*. Don't actually solve for *r*. You know statement (1) is sufficient, so eliminate B, C, and E and consider statement (2).

Statement (2) gives you the length of a rectangular fence, which doesn't help you. Knowing the width of the fence would help, because that length is the diameter of the circle (and the diameter is twice the radius). But because you don't know the width, statement (2) isn't sufficient and you can eliminate D. Your answer is A.

32. **C.** Knowing that *a* isn't zero, you need to find out if can you determine whether *b* is greater than 0.

Statement (1) tells you that the product of *a* and *b* is 14. Given the rules of multiplication, you know that if *a* is positive, then *b* must be positive, and if *a* is negative, then *b* must be negative. But because you don't know what the value of *a* is, you can't determine whether *b* is greater than 0. So statement (1) isn't sufficient, and neither A nor D is the answer.

Statement (2) states that the sum of *a* and *b* is 9. Any number of combinations of positive and negative numbers could give you a sum of 9 (4 and 5, −10 and 1, 3 and 6, and so on). So statement (2) isn't sufficient. You can eliminate B and consider the two statements together.

The combination of the two statements provides you with two equations with two variables and two unknowns. If you solve one equation for a variable, you can plug that value into the other and solve for the other. The two statements seem sufficient, but you may want to do some calculations to make sure.

Solve the equation in statement (2) for *b:*

$$a + b = 9$$

$$b = 9 - a$$

Now, substitute the value for *b* into the first equation:

$$ab = 14$$

$$a(9 - a) = 14$$

Distribute the *a:*

$$-a^2 + 9a = 14$$

Multiply the whole equation by –1 to get a positive *a* term:

$$-1(-a^2 + 9a = 14)$$

$$a^2 - 9a = -14$$

Note you can formulate this equation as a quadratic:

$$a^2 - 9a + 14 = 0$$

Factor the quadratic:

$$(a - 7)(a - 2) = 0$$

$$a = 7 \text{ and } a = 2$$

As you figured out in your analysis of statement (1), because both values of *a* are positive, you know that *b* must be positive and greater than 0.

Both statements together are sufficient, so you can eliminate E. Choose C for your answer.

33. **E.** To solve this problem, you just need to know how to subtract and multiply fractions, like this (if you need a refresher, check out Chapter 10):

$$\frac{1\frac{3}{5} - 2\frac{2}{3}}{\frac{1}{3} - \frac{2}{5}}$$

Convert the mixed numbers in the numerator of the main fraction:

$$\frac{\frac{8}{5} + \frac{8}{3}}{\frac{1}{3} - \frac{2}{5}}$$

Find the common denominators in the fractions contained in the numerator and denominator of the main fraction:

$$\frac{\frac{24}{15} - \frac{40}{15}}{\frac{5}{15} - \frac{6}{15}}$$

Because all four denominators in the fractions in the numerator and denominator of the main fraction equal 15, they cancel each other out. When you subtract the values in the numerator and those in the denominator, you get this fraction:

$$\frac{-16}{-1}$$

So the answer is 16, or choice E.

34. **C.** You're looking for the square root of a number that 98 goes into. So consider multiples of 98 until you find one that is a perfect square: $98 \times 2 = 196$, and 196 is a perfect square, with a square root of 14. The largest integer in the answer choices that divides into 14 is 14. 7 and 2 go into 14, but they're not the largest integers that do so.

35. **D.** If you want to go to business school, this is a good problem to know how to solve.

profit = gross – costs

To use the formula for profit, you need to know how to figure out Becky's gross earnings: Becky's gross equals the pounds of hot dogs she sold times the selling cost per pound.

The pounds of hot dogs sold is represented by x (the number of pounds she bought) minus s (the number she threw out). The price per pound at which she sold the hot dogs is d. So you can find Becky's gross earnings using this formula:

Becky's gross = $(x - s)d$

Becky's costs represent how much she paid for all the pounds of hot dogs. The costs equal the amount of hot dogs she bought times the buying cost per pound. So the formula for how much she spent for the hot dogs looks like this:

Becky's costs = xp

Input the formulas for Becky's gross and costs into the formula for profit, which gives you this: profit = $(x - s)d - xp$. The answer is D.

36. **C.** To find area of the rectangle, you need to know its length (l) and width (w) because the formula for finding area is $l \times w$. So look for information in the statements that help you find the length and width of the rectangle.

With the equation you get in statement (1), you can solve for one of the variables. For instance, solving for l gives you $8 - w$. You can substitute the value for l into the equation for area, but you still have two variables, so you can't solve the problem:

$A = (8 - w)w$

Statement (1) isn't sufficient, so you can eliminate A and D and go on to statement (2).

Statement (2) provides you with the means to measure the diagonal of the rectangle.

The diagonal of the rectangle divides the rectangle into two right triangles and forms the hypotenuse for both. According to the Pythagorean theorem, in right triangles the square of the hypotenuse equals the sum of the squares of the two legs. The legs of the triangles are formed by the length and width of the rectangle, so you can build an equation for l and w in relation to the diagonal (or hypotenuse):

$l^2 + w^2 = d^2$

You know that d^2 is 24, so $l^2 + w^2 = 24$. But you don't have information to determine either of the two variables you have left, so statement (2) is insufficient and the answer is either C or E.

With the pieces of information you get from both statements, you have two equations and two similar unknowns. If you divide all the terms in statement (1)'s equations by 2 and then square both sides, you end up with some terms that match the terms you got from the Pythagorean theorem and statement (2):

$2l + 2w = 16$

$l + w = 8$

$(l + w)^2 = 8^2$ (Use FOIL to multiply the expressions on the left side.)

$l^2 + 2lw + w^2 = 64$

You should notice that $l^2 + w^2$ is present in the terms on the left side, and you figured out that $l^2 + w^2 = 24$ when you considered the second statement. So you can substitute 24 for $l^2 + w^2$ in the equation:

$l^2 + w^2 + 2lw = 64$

$24 + 2lw = 64$

$2lw = 40$

$lw = 20$

Because length times width (lw) equals area, both statements together do the trick. Eliminate E. The answer is C.

37. **B.** To solve for *t*, you need to know *r* in terms of *s* or *s* in terms of *r* so that one of the variables cancels out.

Statement (1) gives a numerical value for *r* but doesn't let you know its value in terms of *s*, so there are still two variables in the equation to solve for. Statement (1) isn't sufficient so neither A nor D can be right.

Statement (2) gives you a value for *r* in terms of *s*, so it's likely sufficient. You could choose B, but if you want to check to make sure, plug 3*s* in for *r* in the original equation:

$$t = \frac{9r}{2s}$$

$$t = \frac{9(3s)}{2s}$$

$$t = \frac{27s}{2s}$$

$$t = \frac{27}{2}$$

Statement (2) gives you enough information to solve for *t*. B is the correct answer.

Explanatory Answers to the Verbal Questions

1. **B.** This critical-reasoning question asks you to weaken the cause-and-effect argument.

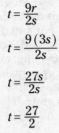

To weaken this cause-and-effect conclusion, you should select the answer choice that offers another logical cause for the effect or that calls into question whether the cause listed in the argument is actually responsible for the effect. Therefore, choose an answer choice that weakens the link between the evidence on increasing household credit card debt and increasing bankruptcies.

You can eliminate C because the premises don't mention housing values and C doesn't offer an alternative explanation for the increased bankruptcies. Get rid of D and E. Both strengthen the conclusion by providing more evidence for a link between credit card debt and bankruptcy. Choice A could be a possibility because it points out that people who file bankruptcy usually have other large debts, like medical bills and legal bills. However, Americans may have had medical and legal bills in the past and it may be the increased credit card debt that is actually causing people to have to file for bankruptcy. Choice B is the best answer. If many of the bankruptcies are business bankruptcies, they probably aren't related to household credit card debt.

2. **E.** This critical-reasoning question asks you to draw a conclusion, and the conclusion needs to address all the premises. So the best conclusion covers the fact that Americans work more because legislation in Europe requires more time off for Europeans and the fact that Americans would like to work less but will only do so if other Americans work less, too.

Begin by eliminating conclusions that aren't supported by the premises. Choice B doesn't work because the premises don't mention where the Europeans vacation (although it's true that they like to visit American national parks!). Eliminate D because the premises don't deal with the productivity of American companies versus European ones. Both A and C are wrong because although they seem to flow from the premises, it's not necessarily true that Europeans are happier because they have more vacation (maybe they feel guilty about all that free time) or that American workers are more dedicated because they take less vacation (they'd probably vacation freely if doing so were mandated by the government). Choice E is the best answer because it deals with all the premises and doesn't introduce information that the argument doesn't cover.

3. **D.** Questions 3 and 4 are based on John and Allen's discussion of a bottle deposit program proposed for the state where John lives. In this question, you're asked to weaken John's conclusion that his state shouldn't adopt the bottle deposit program. As evidence for his conclusion, John offers studies that show that the comprehensive recycling program currently in place in his state is better than a bottle deposit program.

   You need to choose an answer that disproves one of John's premises or that weakens the link between the premises and the conclusion.

   Eliminate A because the effectiveness of 5-cent versus 10-cent deposit programs is irrelevant to John's argument. You can eliminate C because the issue is recycling, not littering. Choice E discusses ad campaigns, which are not part of the argument and don't weaken the conclusion. Choice B seems to support John's conclusion that a bottle-deposit program isn't necessary, because it suggests that people in all states are recycling, even people in those states without a deposit program. Choice D damages John's conclusion by weakening the link between his evidence and his conclusion. If many states have both comprehensive recycling and a deposit program, this option is possible for John's state. That comprehensive recycling alone may be better than bottle deposits alone doesn't mean John's state shouldn't have both.

4. **B.** You're still working with John and Allen. Having lost the last argument (thanks to your correct answer choice!), John would now like to argue that bottle deposit programs are unfair because they don't apply equally to all industries. This time, it's your job to help John win the argument, so you need an answer choice that works with the premises you've already been given to support the new conclusion. The ideal answer choice bridges the gap between John and Allen's prior discussion and John's new conclusion.

   Eliminate A right away because citizens aren't industries, and treating citizens of different states differently doesn't lead to John's conclusion. Eliminate E as well, because E actually weakens John's conclusion; it tends to prove that all carbonated-beverage manufacturers are treated equally. Choices B, C, and D all seem like pretty good choices, but you can toss out choice C. Even though it holds more fluids, a two-liter bottle is just one container, as is each can in a six-pack. You can also eliminate D. Although it points to unequal treatment, it's unequal treatment of grocery and convenience stores based on location, not the unequal treatment of different industries. So B is the correct answer, because the bottle deposit applies only to the carbonated-beverage industry and not to the juice, tea, or sports-drink industries.

5. **C.** This sentence correction problem has some modifier issues.

   The way the sentence is written, it sounds like the Native Americans, rather than the saguaro cactus, are standing as monuments in the desert. That's because the beginning phrase always modifies the subject of the sentence. Because the subject is underlined, you know that you have to change the subject of the sentence to make this one right.

   Because the sentence has an error, eliminate A. Choice B fails to correct the error, because it still has Native Americans as the subject of the sentence. Choice E changes the subject from Native Americans and replaces it with food, water, and spiritual inspiration, so now these elements appear to be standing in the desert. Choice C and D each make the saguaro cactus the subject of the sentence, but C is a better choice because it's shorter, clearer, and more direct. Choice D uses passive voice to interject the unnecessary piece of information that Native Americans need food, water, and spiritual inspiration.

6. **E.** This sentence correction question features an error in pronoun use. The correct pronoun to replace the proper noun, Harry Truman, is *he,* not *we*. You can eliminate A, B, and C because they use a plural pronoun to refer to a single person. Choice D isn't good because *one* isn't a personal pronoun used to substitute for a proper noun. Choice E applies the correct singular pronoun.

7. **A.** This sentence doesn't contain any obvious errors. The underlined portion contains comparison language, but it seems to be idiomatically correct. Choice A is probably the correct answer, but check the other answers to make sure you haven't missed something. Choices B, C, and D incorrectly change the location of *even* in the expression, and B, D, and E use the idiomatically incorrect constructions of *so much that* and *so much as* to show similarity. The sentence is correct as written.

8. **E.** Questions 8–12 deal with a social science reading passage describing archeological finds in Africa. Before you answer the questions, read through the passage and organize the flow of information. The first paragraph introduces the scientists' assertions, justified by observing the animal bones, about the kinds of animals the Klasies people hunted. The next paragraph projects the idea that the bones show that the Klasies people hunted eland more than buffalo because eland were more docile. The passage ends with a description of how the people hunted the eland, which led to deaths in great numbers. The first question asks you to identify the main idea of the passage.

Try to discern the main idea for yourself as you're reading. Because most passages have a main idea question, you'll be ready for them. In this case, you know that the main idea has something to do with describing how the evidence that the anthropologists found reveals the hunting practices of the Klasies people.

Choice A deals with only a portion of the passage, whereas main ideas sum up the message of the complete reading. Choice B assumes knowledge concerning other prehistoric people that isn't found in the passage. Choice C focuses on a portion of the passage and draws a conclusion about eland extinction that isn't present in the reading. Choice D is a broad enough statement to be the main idea for the passage, but the passage states that eland are large animals, so saying that the Klasies people ate smaller prey doesn't make sense. Choice E best covers the descriptive elements that comprise the main idea, and it doesn't contradict information in the passage.

9. **A.** This specific-information question asks you about details described in a portion of the passage.

The computer may highlight the portion of the passage in which you can find specific information. For this question, this sentence in the first paragraph may be highlighted: "The number and location of stone tool cutmarks and the rarity of carnivore tooth marks indicate that the people were not restricted to scavenging from lions or hyenas." Choice A virtually duplicates the language of the passage.

10. **C.** The correct answer for this specific-information question isn't expressed as neatly as it was in the previous question. In the third paragraph, the author states that the Klasies people may have hunted eland to limit risk. In the second paragraph (where the passage discusses why the Klasies people hunted eland more than buffalo), you find that the people preferred to hunt eland because they fled in panic as opposed to the dangerous buffalo that stood and fought. So this must be what the author meant about avoiding risk.

The passage says that the archaeologists found numerous eland bones but doesn't state that eland were more numerous than buffalo. Instead, the second paragraph says eland were less common, so you can't make a case for A. The information in B directly contradicts the information in the passage. The passage doesn't mention scavenging in association with eland, and it suggests that the Klasies people had access to long-range projectiles. So, D and E aren't right.

11. **B.** This question asks for an exception. You're looking for the answer choice that *doesn't* fit.

Exception questions provide another situation in which you'll probably have to return to the text for the answer. After looking over the answer choices, skim the text and eliminate choices when you find them.

The passage mentions four of the five animals listed in the answer choices as a probable part of the Klasies' diet. In one sentence in the first paragraph, you find mentioned buffalo, eland, seals, and penguins. It looks like B, *hyena,* is the best answer.

12. **E.** Once again, you have to find specific information for a supporting idea. In this case, you're looking for the author's evidence that the catastrophe suffered by the eland was not natural but was caused by humans instead.

   From your initial reading, you probably remember that the author discusses the great demise of the eland in the third paragraph, so the answer is probably located in the last paragraph. The next-to-the-last sentence explains that the animals probably weren't victims of accident or endemic (common) disease because the strong adults were killed as well as the young and the old. The final sentence then provides the answer to the question by stating the evidence that this catastrophe was caused by humans. The author reasons that because there is no sign of the other possible catastrophes, like floods, volcanic eruptions, or epidemic diseases, humans must have driven the herds off of cliffs, which is the answer reflected in E. The author mentions the presence of bones as evidence that many eland died of something that affected all ages equally, but the bones alone don't explain how the eland were killed, so A is wrong. The stone tip point stuck out of a buffalo rather than an eland, so B's not it. Choices C and D don't work because the lack of carnivore tooth marks and tool cutmarks is explained in the first paragraph as evidence that the Klasies people hunted as well as scavenged.

13. **D.** This sentence correction problem contains a parallelism error. The three elements of the underlined list should be in the same format, but the second element (*manufacturing would be streamlined*) is a clause rather than an infinitive like the other two elements (*to expand* and *to include*). Because the sentence contains a mistake, A is wrong.

   Because *to* isn't included in the underlined portion and therefore initiates the list, you know the elements of the list are infinitives. So eliminate choices that don't begin each element with a verb.

   Expanded isn't in infinitive form, so you know C has to be wrong. The final element in E doesn't begin with a verb at all, so it's not right. Both B and D correct the error by beginning each element with the infinitive form of a verb, but B changes the meaning of the sentence slightly: to *create expanded operations* is different from to *expand operations*. B is also unnecessarily wordy.

14. **A.** This sentence correction question features a long, complex underlined phrase. This phrase is a subordinate clause with its own subject, verb, and third element, and it doesn't appear to have any obvious errors. Choice A may be the correct answer, but look at the other choices in case you've missed something. Eliminate B because it switches from the plural subject *people* in the first part of the sentence to the singular noun *one* in the second part, and both nouns refer to the same entity. The way C is constructed suggests that people don't remember the possibility that they may have memory problems, which doesn't make sense. Choice D switches from third person (*people*) to first person (*we*) to refer to the same entity, so it's wrong. And E introduces an unclear pronoun reference; you don't know whether *this* refers to the inability to remember or the quick admission. The sentence is best as written.

15. **C.** This sentence contains a couple problems with parallel construction.

   Either is misplaced; it should go immediately before the two entities separated by *or*. And because *receive* is the only verb in the *either/or* expression, the sentence literally states that you will receive the big money round. (Take out *either* and *the parting gift of a trip to Hawaii or* and you'll see what we mean.) Because the sentence doesn't make sense, you have to correct it.

   You already know you can eliminate A. Choice B just changes *receive* to *win,* and winning the big money round as a prize doesn't make sense. Choice D replaces *receive* with *go,* which could work with either *Hawaii* or *the big money round,* but it doesn't sound quite right and it doesn't address the problem with the placement of *either. Either* should go right before *Hawaii* to make this construction correct, because all the words before *Hawaii* apply to both of the entities connected by *or.* Choice E also fails to properly position *either.*

Proper construction requires that *either* be placed before *your prize* to make sense. The only answer that corrects the problems with parallel construction is C. *Either* properly introduces the two entities connected by *or*, and these two phrases maintain similar construction.

16. **B.** When you see two independent clauses joined by a comma, you're witness to a comma splice. You can rewrite this sentence into two sentences, include *and* after the comma, replace the comma with a semicolon, or subordinate one of the clauses.

    The sentence has an error, so A is gone. All the other choices correct the comma splice, but three of them create other errors. Choice C adds *and* after the comma, but it switches from third person to first person with the switch to *we*. Choice D subordinates a clause with the addition of *who* but introduces a subject/verb agreement problem between the singular noun *payment* and the plural verb *are*. Choice E contains the idiomatically incorrect construction of *either . . . and* instead of *either . . . or*. Choice B corrects the comma splice by subordinating a clause and doesn't introduce a new error.

17. **E.** This critical-reasoning question requires you to identify the assumption.

    You're looking for a statement that connects the premises to the conclusion. An assumption isn't directly stated in the premises. (You have to accept that the stated premises are true, even if the text doesn't provide evidence for them.)

    Eliminate B because it just restates part of the conclusion. Choice C can't be an assumption because it restates information from one of the premises. Choice D also essentially restates one of the premises. Choice A is a pretty solid choice; it seems reasonable that most people who take out interest-only mortgages do so because they can't afford to pay more than the interest. But the conclusion doesn't depend on this assumption. It does depend on the assumption in E that buyers who aren't paying down the principle on their loan won't accumulate value as their home value increases.

18. **D.** For this question, you need to strengthen the conclusion that the poles are currently in the process of reversing. Choice A actually weakens the conclusion because the magnetic pole's shifting *away* from true north would be a sign of the poles shifting. Choice B also weakens the conclusion, as 780,000, rather than a million, years have passed since the last reversal. Choice E weakens the conclusion as well, because it again suggests stability in the poles. Eliminate C because the warming of the atmosphere isn't relevant to the reversal of the poles. Choice D is the only answer choice that indicates a lessening of the strength of the magnetic field and a trend toward a reversal of the poles.

19. **D.** This question requires you to draw the logical conclusion from the given premises.

    You're looking for a conclusion that addresses all the premises but doesn't introduce outside information. Eliminate A because the premises don't address whether children will continue to become more obese after 2010. Choice B compares children in North and South America to those in Europe and Asia, and information about European and Asian children isn't present in the argument. Choice C is a restatement of the premise that childhood obesity is more dangerous than adult onset obesity. Choice E actually contradicts the premises and therefore can't be the conclusion. You're left with D, which addresses both the health problems associated with childhood obesity and the fact that such obesity has increased.

20. **B.** This business passage concerns entrepreneurs. The first paragraph compares the current perception of entrepreneurs with the perception two decades ago when entrepreneurs had unfavorable reputations. The second paragraph compares the entrepreneurial spirit with the characteristics of the colonists. The last paragraph provides statistical data to support the author's position that entrepreneurship is an important part of the culture.

    As usual, the first question for this passage is a main-idea question. The main idea of the passage concerns the way entrepreneurs are perceived as well as the importance of entrepreneurs in the society. Eliminate A because even though the idea may be true, the passage never actually discusses how hard becoming an entrepreneur is. Choice C isn't right, because it actually contradicts the author's claims that entrepreneurs are contributing to the nation's economy. Choice D seems like a logical choice, but although the author praises entrepreneurship, he doesn't go so far as to say that smaller is better. The author may hint at large corporations' being too slow, but he doesn't even imply that entrepreneurs will actually come to dominate American business, so E can't be right. Choice B is the best answer because it combines the changing perception of entrepreneurs with the role they play in the economy.

21. **C.** This inference question focuses your attention on why the author includes a specific statistic. You're asked why the author included the statistic that 90 percent of the richest people in the United States are entrepreneurs.

    Eliminate A because the passage in no way implies that every entrepreneur will succeed. In fact, the statistics seem to show that only 1 in 7 will actually start a business, and many of those businesses fail. The passage also doesn't provide support for B. Nothing in the reading claims that today's entrepreneurs are conservative.

    Don't make leaps of logic for inference questions. Stick to what's supported by information in the passage.

    Choice D may be good answer for other statistical data, but the use of the statistic that 90 percent of the richest people in America are entrepreneurs highlights success rather than difficulties. You may agree with the idea that it's absurd for so many of the richest people to be entrepreneurs, but the question doesn't ask you how you feel. Choice E isn't supported by the passage. Entrepreneurs must be playing the game better and the reward is that some entrepreneurs get very, very rich. Choice C is the best answer.

22. **A.** This specific-information question asks you to contrast how today's entrepreneurs are viewed compared to how entrepreneurs of the past were viewed. The passage makes this comparison in the first two paragraphs. First, you see that entrepreneurs used to be thought of negatively. Then you see that today's entrepreneurs are heralded for the qualities of nonconformity and risk-taking.

    Choice A looks pretty good, but check the other choices to make sure A is the best. Choice B opposes the idea expressed in the passage. Choice C misstates information in the passage. *Today's* entrepreneurs, not past entrepreneurs, are in the limelight for walking to the beat of a different drummer. Choice D contains information on financing that's not present in the passage. And E mistakenly applies the expression "mavericks, rebels, and even social deviants" to present-day entrepreneurs.

23. **B.** This specific-information question contains an exception, so you're looking for the choice that's not like the others. Skim the text and begin eliminating the phrases that the author uses to praise entrepreneurs.

    Phrases can be harder to skim for than single words, so consider each answer choice carefully.

    The statement in A appears in the third paragraph. The phrase in B doesn't sound like something the author of this passage would say. He seems to praise the nonconformity exhibited by entrepreneurs. The only time the author mentions loyalty and conformity is in the information about corporate America. Just to be sure, locate the last three phrases in the passage if you have time. Choice C is at the bottom of the second paragraph. Choices D and E are both in the third paragraph.

24. **E.** Have you noticed that you can't tickle yourself? Now you know why. The question asks you to make an inference that extends the reasoning in the argument. You're looking for a statement that logically flows from one of the premises but isn't stated directly. The passage states the information in A directly, so it can't be an inference. Eliminate B, because future research isn't alluded to in the argument. Choice C is an illogical extension of the argument.

The passage mentions what happens when a person is speaking, not what happens when a person hears a tape. Choice D contradicts the assertion in the passage that humans can't tickle themselves, so it's wrong. Choice E is supported by the premise that healthy humans can't mistake their voices and provides a reason that the passage suggests but doesn't state directly.

25. **B.** This was a taxing question, but we got a lot of mileage out of it! Look for an unstated assumption that the argument depends on.

    This type of question is a lot like an inference question except that instead of looking for a logical extension of the argument, you're looking for a premise that the author doesn't state but that's required to reach the conclusion. The correct assumption for this argument will bridge the gap between the difficulties of keeping a mileage log and the conclusion that an electronic mileage log is the solution.

    Eliminate C because the passage specifically states that the IRS wants to see mileage logs, so C's not an assumption. You can also eliminate E, which mentions the IRS but makes the unsupported claim that electronic logs are preferred by the IRS. Both A and D are clever distracters because they seem to be plausible assumptions. However, even if electronic mileage logs aren't expensive and salespeople and the self-employed do already have PDAs, that doesn't necessarily lead to the conclusion that the electronic logs are less of a burden to maintain. On the other hand, B states the precise assumption that the electronic logs are less of a burden, which means that busy people won't neglect them as often.

26. **C.** Questions 26 and 27 are based on a discussion between Sara and Michele concerning mortality rates of Native Americans during the 1500s. You are asked to weaken Michele's conclusion that the 95 percent death rate statistic is far too high and a rate of 50 percent to 75 percent would be the maximum. Because Michele relies on an analogy between the Black Death in Europe in the 14th century and the deaths among Native Americans, the best way to weaken her conclusion is to show that these phenomena really aren't analogous.

    Eliminate A immediately. The argument doesn't mention sugars in milk and presents no information to connect them to smallpox or the other diseases. Eliminate D, because even if death rates were high in specific locations during the Black Death, Michele's argument concerns averages. Both B and E actually strengthen Michele's argument. If Native Americans knew more about medicine than Europeans, they presumably should have died in fewer numbers. If most diseases can't kill more than 75 percent of their hosts or risk extinction, a rate of 95 percent would be too high. Choice C is the only choice that weakens the argument. Stating that Native Americans were genetically less diverse than Europeans shows that Michele isn't comparing analogous societies, which weakens her argument.

27. **C.** Sara concludes that if European diseases hadn't killed an estimated 95 percent of the Native American population, the Europeans couldn't have begun their conquest. You need to find the assumption that Sara relies on. Both B and E restate information already contained in the premises of Sara's argument, and stated premises can't be assumptions. The answer can't be A, because better European technology would support a European conquest of the New World with or without disease. Finally, D makes a statement that is irrelevant and not supported by the arguments. This leaves C, the correct answer. Sara assumes that even with 20 times more Natives Americans in the New World, the actual number of deaths from European disease would remain the same, which would mean that there would be many more Native Americans to defend against the Europeans invaders.

28. **B.** This particular sentence correction features an independent clause joined to a phrase by a semicolon. This punctuation would be correct if the phrase were an independent clause, but it's not. Only B and D provide answer choices that are independent clauses (complete sentences), so eliminate A, C, and E. Choice D contains an unclear pronoun reference; you're not sure whether *this* refers to the scientific discovery or where the sharks live. So B is the best answer.

29. **D.** This sentence correction question features a commonly tested pronoun reference problem.

    Because the sentence refers to two men, just whom *he* refers to is unclear. The proper pronoun to use to refer to a company is *it*. Choice B contains *they,* which could refer to Jason and Max, but *they* is plural and doesn't work with the singular noun *employer*. To use *they,* you'd have to change *employer* to *employers*. Choice C uses the proper pronoun, *it,* but doesn't work with the plural *employers*. This leaves you with D and E. *Which* is proper because it introduces a nonrestrictive clause (you know that because of the comma before it), so D is right and E is wrong.

30. **D.** The underlined portion of this sentence contains a lack of parallelism, a problem with subject/verb agreement, and a pronoun error. The most obvious error is that *it* is a singular pronoun used to refer to the plural *berries*. To correct this sentence, you need to change *it* to *them*. All choices but E correct this problem. The next error that stands out is that the singular verb *is* doesn't work with the plural subject *ways*. Only C and D correct this issue. Choice D is the better answer because C isn't parallel in the verb tenses in the elements connected by *either . . . or.*

31. **A.** This question asks you to choose the best conclusion for the premises. Remember that a conclusion encompasses all the premises and brings in no outside information. You can eliminate D because it talks about the NCAA basketball tournament being the world's most popular sporting event, which isn't in the premises. Choice E also relies on outside information, in this case about the way people pick winners. You may agree with B that employees shouldn't check sports scores, or with C that employers should just indulge their employees, but either way these statements are opinions and not appropriate conclusions. Choice A is the best answer. It covers all the premises without adding outside information.

32. **B.** This business passage deals with the problem of human error in computing. The first paragraph introduces and explains human computing errors. The second paragraph poses solutions and then dismisses them. The third paragraph provides a general solution to the problem.

    The first question asks you to determine the authors' primary purpose in writing the passage. The main idea is that human error is going to happen and the best way to minimize the damage is by developing a backup system that allows users to correct their own mistakes. In this passage, the authors do more than just inform — they argue in favor of such a system for small businesses.

    Eliminate A because the primary purpose is not merely to inform, and the fact that human error is a common disaster for businesses is a supporting idea and not the main idea. Choice C doesn't address the general purpose of the passage; it's way too specific. Choice D contradicts the recommendations of the authors, so it can't be right. The authors advocate the need for less IT personnel through backup systems that can be used by regular employees. You can also eliminate E, because the authors don't advise anything so radical as never deleting or reorganizing files. Choice B is the best answer; the authors' primary purpose is to advocate that small business owners develop a backup system that allows employees to retrieve their own files in case of human error.

33. **E.** This specific-information question focuses on the second paragraph of the passage. You're asked to determine what the authors feel is a waste of an IT manager's time. The best way to answer this question is to go to the text and skim the second paragraph. You'll find the answer in the last three sentences of the paragraph, where IT managers are asked to find deleted files based on very sketchy descriptions and the authors declare that "this is not an efficient use of anyone's time." The only answer choice that even comes close to fitting this part of the passage is the paraphrase in E.

34. **D.** This specific-information question doesn't point you to a specific paragraph, so the location of the information will probably be highlighted on your computer screen. You'll find the information toward the top of the long second paragraph. One sentence states

that if a manager does keep track, the manager will see that the events occur with greater frequency than the manager may have imagined. The answer choice that matches this information is D.

35. **C.** Your final specific-information question contains an exception. You know what to do: Find and eliminate answer choices until you have one exception left. This question directs you to the final paragraph, which is a short one. In that paragraph, you find all the answer choices except for C. Logically, C is the correct choice because nowhere does the author claim that any system can prevent human error.

36. **C.** For this critical-reasoning question, you're asked to provide a reason that would explain the paradox of weaker solar activity causing greater disruption in communications and power transmission. Despite the different wording, this is a basic strengthening-the-conclusion question. What you need to find is some reason why solar activity now would cause more of a problem than solar activity did ten years ago.

    You can begin by eliminating D. The argument mentions northern lights but not in the context of disruption. You can then eliminate B and E, because they both tend to lessen the impact of solar activity. Choice A seems like a possible choice because it mentions the increased use of satellite signals for radio reception. However, the answer also mentions that regular radio signals are stronger than they used to be, so the effect on communications may be balanced, neither stronger nor weaker than a decade ago. Choice C is the best answer, because a substantial increase in cell phone use would mean that solar flares cause more disruption than they did when cell phones were less popular.

37. **B.** This question asks that you weaken the claim of Healthy-O's that it is *one-of-a-kind good for you.* To do this, you could either show that Healthy-O's is not one-of-a-kind or that it's not good for you. Begin by eliminating C, which is irrelevant to the product's claims. Next, you can get rid of A and D, because both would strengthen the claim that Healthy-O's are unique. Choices B and E both seem to weaken the claim, but the claim of Healthy-O's unique goodness applies to breakfast cereals and E is talking about other products. Therefore, B is the best answer.

38. **A.** This entire sentence correction question is underlined, but the sentence appears to be fine as is. Check the other answer choices to be sure. Choice B introduces a subject-verb agreement error; the singular subject *one* requires the singular verb *relies.* Eliminate C because it includes unnecessary words, like *choose to.* Choice D is a comma splice, so it can't be right. Finally, E contains a problem with subject-verb agreement: *Relies* is a singular verb that refers to *puzzles,* a plural noun. The verb should be *rely.*

39. **E.** The underlined portion of this sentence includes the awkward and wordy phrase *as if to indicate that,* so A is probably wrong. Choice B is wrong because the preposition *of* doesn't correctly introduce the clause *the housing market remains strong.* Eliminate C because it's idiomatically incorrect; C should read *indication that* rather than *indication of.* Choice D adds an unnecessary clause — *it is indicative.* So E is the best answer. It clarifies the language in the phrase and doesn't create any new errors.

40. **E.** The underlined portion of this sentence contains an improper verb tense. The verb phrase *have always faced* is past tense, but the sentence speaks of what will happen in the future. Eliminate A. Choice B is also incorrect, because what the pronoun *it* refers to is unclear and the verb tense is still past tense. Answer C contains an awkward construction and a vague pronoun reference *(it),* as does D. Choice E corrects the verb tense problem in the original sentence without introducing new errors.

41. **C.** This final sentence correction question has one of those ever-popular pronoun errors. *Denver-Boulder area* is a singular noun, and it should be referred to by the singular pronoun *it* rather than the plural *they.* Eliminate A. Choice B is incorrect because it's not idiomatically correct to say *think as.* Choice D switches from third person to first person in the same sentence. This leaves you with C and E. Both correct the error, but E uses the past tense *(received)* when the remainder of the sentence is in present tense. Choice C is the best answer.

Chapter 19

Putting the GMAT into Practice: Test #2

- -

In This Chapter

▶ Giving analytical writing essays a try

▶ Rehearsing for the GMAT quantitative section

▶ Practicing the techniques for mastering the GMAT verbal section

- -

Here's another chance to strut your stuff. The following exam consists of two analytical writing prompts and two sections of multiple-choice questions. Give yourself one hour to write the two essays, 75 minutes to complete the 37 math questions, and 75 minutes to complete all 41 verbal questions.

To make the most of this practice exam, take the test under conditions similar to those of the actual test:

1. **Find a place where you won't be distracted. (Preferably as far as possible from your neighbor's nuclear science lab.)**

2. **Try to take the practice test at approximately the same time of day as the time you've scheduled your GMAT.**

3. **Use a timer to time each section.**

4. **Take no more than one ten-minute break between the quantitative and verbal sections.**

5. **Mark your answers by circling the appropriate letters in the text.**

6. **Use a blank piece of paper or a small dry erase board for notes and figuring.**

7. **When your time is up for each section, put down your pencil.**

After you've finished, you can check your answers to the quantitative questions using the answer key at the end of this chapter. Complete explanations for the answers to this practice test are in Chapter 20.

Section 1: Analytical Writing Assessment

The analytical writing section consists of two tasks: analysis of an issue and analysis of an argument. You have 30 minutes to complete each of the two tasks. Try to write the two essays without taking a break between them.

Analysis of an issue

Time: 30 minutes

One essay

Directions: In this section, you need to analyze the issue presented and explain your views on it. There is no correct answer. Instead, you should consider various perspectives as you develop your own position on the issue.

Think for a few minutes about the issue and organize your response before you start writing. Leave time for revisions when you're finished.

You'll be scored based on your ability to accomplish these tasks:

✔ Organize, develop, and express your thoughts about the given issue.

✔ Provide pertinent supporting ideas with examples.

✔ Apply the rules of standard written English.

"Graduate business courses with a technical component, such as accounting, marketing, or economics, should teach factual information and skills and should leave ethics to designated business ethics courses."

Discuss whether you agree or disagree with the opinion stated above. Provide supporting evidence for your views and use reasons and/or examples from your own experiences, observations, or reading.

_____

_____

_____

_____

_____

_____

_____

_____

_____

Analysis of an argument

Time: 30 minutes

One essay

Directions: In this section, you will be asked to write a critique of the argument presented. The prompt requests only your critique and does not ask you for your opinions on the matter.

Think for a few minutes about the argument and organize your response before you start writing. Leave time for revisions when you're finished.

You'll be scored based on your ability to accomplish these tasks:

✔ Organize, develop, and express your thoughts about the given argument.

✔ Provide pertinent supporting ideas with examples.

✔ Apply the rules of standard written English.

The following appeared as part of a letter to the editor in a local newspaper:

> "The growth of radio, television, movies, and other forms of mass media has led to the loss of intellectual creativity and curiosity among average Americans. A few writers now tell stories to tens of millions of Americans through songs played on the radio, television shows, and popular movies. Where one hundred years ago average Americans used to actively tell their own stories to countless small audiences, most Americans are now passive members of a much greater audience, all mesmerized by the same mass media offerings and reduced to commenting on the quality of various movies, sporting events, pop songs, and reality TV shows."

Examine this argument and present your judgment on how well reasoned it is. In your discussion, analyze the author's position and how well the author uses evidence to support the argument. For example, you may need to question the author's underlying assumptions or consider alternative explanations that may weaken the conclusion. You can also provide additional support for or arguments against the author's position, describe how stating the argument differently may make it more reasonable, and discuss what provisions may better equip you to evaluate its thesis.

Section 2: Quantitative

Time: 75 minutes

37 questions

Directions: Choose the best answer from the five choices.

Use the following answer choices to answer the data sufficiency questions:

(A) Statement (1) ALONE is sufficient, but statement (2) alone is not sufficient to answer the question asked;

(B) Statement (2) ALONE is sufficient, but statement (1) alone is not sufficient to answer the question asked;

(C) BOTH statements (1) and (2) TOGETHER are sufficient to answer the question asked, but NEITHER statement ALONE is sufficient;

(D) EACH statement ALONE is sufficient to answer the question asked;

(E) Statements (1) and (2) TOGETHER are NOT sufficient to answer the question asked, and additional data are needed.

1. Which of the following equations is NOT equivalent to $b^2 - 9 = 16a^2$?

    (A) $\dfrac{b^2 - 9}{16} = a^2$

    (B) $b^2 = 16a^2 + 9$

    (C) $b - 3 = 4a$

    (D) $2b^2 - 18 = 32a^2$

    (E) $(b - 3)(b + 3) = 16a^2$

2. How many multiples of 3 are there between 15 and 81, inclusive?

    (A) 22

    (B) 23

    (C) 24

    (D) 25

    (E) 26

3. If n is an integer, then n is divisible by how many positive integers?

    (1) n and 3^4 are each divisible by the same number of positive integers.

    (2) n is the product of two different prime numbers.

    (A)   (B)   (C)   (D)   (E)

4. If 80 percent of a rectangular park is covered by a rectangular football field that is 120 yards by 50 yards, what is the area of the park in square yards?

    (A) 4,800

    (B) 6,000

    (C) 7,200

    (D) 7,500

    (E) 10,000

5. Alison, the company CEO, wants to schedule a one-hour meeting on Monday for herself and three other managers, Bob, Colleen, and David. Is there a one-hour period on Monday available to all four people?

    (1) On Monday, Bob has an open period from 12:00 p.m. to 3:00 p.m. and David has an open period from 2:00 p.m. to 5:00 p.m.

    (2) On Monday, Alison and Colleen have an open period from 11:00 a.m. to 3:00 p.m.

    (A)   (B)   (C)   (D)   (E)

6. What is the ratio of a to b?

    (1) The ratio of $0.4a$ to $3b$ is 4 to 7.

    (2) a is 3 less than 4 times b.

    (A)   (B)   (C)   (D)   (E)

Go on to next page

7. Each of the three people individually can complete a certain job in 3, 4, and 5 hours, respectively. What is the lowest fraction of the job that can be done in 1 hour by 2 of the people working together at their respective rates?

(A) $\frac{1}{3}$

(B) $\frac{9}{20}$

(C) $\frac{8}{15}$

(D) $\frac{7}{12}$

(E) $\frac{2}{3}$

8. If x and y are two different integers, is $x + y$ divisible by 9?

(1) x and y are both divisible by 6.

(2) The digit(s) that make up both x and y, respectively, add up to 9.

(A)   (B)   (C)   (D)   (E)

9. What is the value of x?

(1) $1 - x = 2x + 21$

(2) $\frac{1}{3x} = -1$

(A)   (B)   (C)   (D)   (E)

10. In the rectangular coordinate system in the figure below, the shaded region is bound by straight lines. Which of the following is NOT an equation of one of the boundary lines?

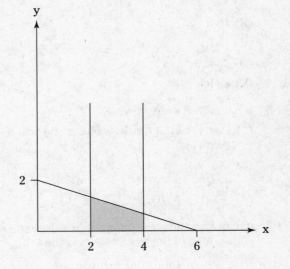

(A) $x = 2$

(B) $y = 0$

(C) $x = 4$

(D) $x + 3y = 6$

(E) $x + 2y = 6$

11. Is the prime number p equal to 5?

(1) $p = n^2 + 1$ where n is an integer greater than 1

(2) $p^2 < 26$

(A)   (B)   (C)   (D)   (E)

12. How many minutes does it take to travel 140 miles at 200 miles per hour?

(A) 1

(B) $1\frac{3}{10}$

(C) 14

(D) 21

(E) 42

Go on to next page

13. If the perimeter of a rectangular swimming pool is 40 feet and its area is 75 square feet, what is the length of each of the shorter sides?

    (A) 5 ft

    (B) 10 ft

    (C) 15 ft

    (D) 20 ft

    (E) 25 ft

14. What is Dori's age now?

    (1) Dori is now 3 times as old as she was 6 years ago.

    (2) Dori's sister Lauren is now twice as old as Dori was exactly 10 years ago.

    (A)   (B)   (C)   (D)   (E)

15. If a, b, c, d, and e are different positive integers, which of the five integers is the median?

    (1) $a < b < c$

    (2) $c + d < e$

    (A)   (B)   (C)   (D)   (E)

16. If the number of airline tickets sold per week (t) varies with the price (p) in dollars, according to the equation $t = 1,000 - 2p$, what would the total weekly revenue be from the sale of $200 airline tickets?

    (A) $600

    (B) $1,000

    (C) $1,400

    (D) $120,000

    (E) $280,000

17. Ethan has earned revenues of $230, $50, and $120 at his last three garage sales, and he plans to hold one additional sale. If Ethan earns an average (arithmetic mean) revenue of exactly $160 on the 4 sales, the revenue of the fourth sale must be:

    (A) $220

    (B) $230

    (C) $240

    (D) $250

    (E) $260

18. If $a + b = 27$, what is the value of ab?

    (1) a and b are consecutive integers

    (2) a and b are positive integers

    (A)   (B)   (C)   (D)   (E)

19. If X is a set of four numbers, a, b, c, and d, is the range of the numbers in X greater than 4?

    (1) a is the greatest number in X

    (2) $a - d > 4$

    (A)   (B)   (C)   (D)   (E)

Go on to next page $\Rightarrow$

20. In the triangle in the figure below, what is *a* in terms of *b?*

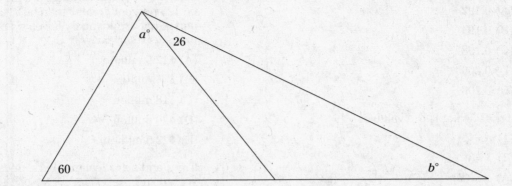

   (A) *b* + 94
   (B) 94 – *b*
   (C) *b* – 94
   (D) 70 – *b*
   (E) 70 + *b*

21. What is the maximum number of $1\frac{3}{4}$ foot pieces of wood that can be cut from 4 pieces of wood that are 12 feet in length?

   (A) 6
   (B) 14
   (C) 21
   (D) 24
   (E) 27

22. If *b* is greater than 120 percent of *a*, is *b* greater than 70?

   (1) *b* – *a* = 20
   (2) *a* > 70

   (A)　　(B)　　(C)　　(D)　　(E)

23. Hoses A and B simultaneously fill an empty swimming pool. If the flow of each hose is independent of the flow in the other hose, how many hours will it take to fill the pool?

   (1) Hose A alone would take 24 hours to fill the pool.
   (2) Hose B alone would take 30 hours to fill the pool.

   (A)　　(B)　　(C)　　(D)　　(E)

24. If the total price of *n* equally priced laptop computers was $13,000, what was the price per laptop computer?

   (1) If the price per laptop computer had been $3 less, the total price of the *n* laptop computers would have been 4 percent less.
   (2) If the price per laptop computer had been $2 more, the total price of the *n* laptop computers would have been $400 more.

   (A)　　(B)　　(C)　　(D)　　(E)

25. If 3 pounds of dried cherries that cost *x* dollars per pound are mixed with 4 pounds of dried apple chips that cost *y* dollars per pound, what is the cost, in dollars, per pound of the mixture?

   (A) 3*x* + 4*y*
   (B) $\dfrac{3x + 4y}{x + y}$
   (C) $\dfrac{3x + 4y}{xy}$
   (D) $\dfrac{3x + 4y}{12}$
   (E) $\dfrac{3x + 4y}{7}$

Go on to next page

26. $\dfrac{24}{125} =$

   (A) 0.192

   (B) 0.194

   (C) 0.198

   (D) 0.205

   (E) 0.209

27. If $a \neq 0$, what is the value of $\left(\dfrac{a^x}{a^y}\right)^3$?

   (1) $a = 2$

   (2) $x = y$

   (A)   (B)   (C)   (D)   (E)

28. What is the number of 360-degree rotations that Tashi's unicycle wheel made while rolling 50 meters in a straight line without slipping?

   (1) The diameter of the unicycle wheel, including the tire, was 0.25 meters.

   (2) The unicycle wheel made ten 360-degree rotations per minute.

   (A)   (B)   (C)   (D)   (E)

29. If $X = \{3, 4, 1, 0, 12, 10\}$, how much greater than the median of the numbers in X is the mean of the numbers in X?

   (A) 0.5

   (B) 1.0

   (C) 1.5

   (D) 2.0

   (E) 2.5

30. Joshua's Jewelry earned \$10 million last year. If this year's earnings are projected to be 125 percent greater than last year's earnings, what are Joshua's Jewelry's projected earnings this year?

   (A) \$12.5 million

   (B) \$15 million

   (C) \$18 million

   (D) \$20 million

   (E) \$22.5 million

31. If x, y, and z are real numbers, does $x = 24$?

   (1) The average (arithmetic mean) of x, y, and z is 8.

   (2) $y = -z$

   (A)   (B)   (C)   (D) .   (E)

32. If a and b are both integers, is a greater than b?

   (1) $a - 1$ and $b + 1$ are consecutive positive integers.

   (2) b is an odd integer.

   (A)   (B)   (C)   (D)   (E)

Go on to next page

33. The table in the figure below shows the amount of waste material in pounds thrown away by each of five different families in a single year and the amount of waste material in pounds recycled by each of the five families in that same year. According to the table, which family had the highest ratio of waste material recycled to waste material thrown away?

Family	Waste Material Thrown Away	Waste Material Recycled
A	100	30
B	50	22
C	20	7
D	55	30
E	10	4

(A) Family A

(B) Family B

(C) Family C

(D) Family D

(E) Family E

34. When 12 is divided by the positive integer x, the remainder is $x - 6$. Which of the following could be the value of x?

(A) 18

(B) 9

(C) 7

(D) 5

(E) 4

Go on to next page

35. On the number line in the figure below, the segment from 0 to 1 has been divided into fourths, as indicated by the large tick marks, and also into fifths, as indicated by the small tick marks. What is the least possible distance between any of the two tick marks?

(A) $\frac{1}{40}$

(B) $\frac{1}{20}$

(C) $\frac{1}{10}$

(D) $\frac{1}{9}$

(E) $\frac{1}{5}$

Go on to next page

36. In the figure below, segments *AB* and *CD* represent two different ways the same steel girder can support wall *EC*. The length of *AE* is how much greater than the length of *DE*?

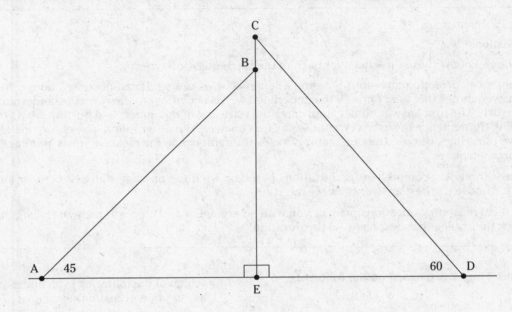

   (1) The length of *AB* is 20 meters.
   (2) The length of *DE* is 8 meters.

   (A)   (B)   (C)   (D)   (E)

37. If $xy \neq 0$, is $\dfrac{2}{x} + \dfrac{2}{y} = 8$

   (1) $x + y = 4xy$
   (2) $x = y$

   (A)   (B)   (C)   (D)   (E)

Section 3: Verbal

Time: 75 minutes

41 questions

Directions: Follow these directions for each of the three question types:

✔ Sentence correction questions give you a sentence with an underlined portion. Choose the answer choice that best phrases the underlined words according to the rules of standard written English. The first answer choice duplicates the phrasing of the underlined portion, so if you think the sentence is best as is, choose the first answer. The other four answers provide alternative phrasings. Choose the one that rephrases the sentence in the clearest, most grammatically correct manner.

✔ Answer reading-comprehension questions based on what the passage states directly or implicitly. Choose the best answer to every question.

✔ Critical-reasoning questions present you with an argument and a question about the argument. Pick the choice that best answers the question.

Questions 1 and 2 are based on the following passage:

Line

    Steve: Our company manufactures a device that stores and plays electronic music. Customers buy music over the Internet and download it using our software. The downloaded

(05) music can be played on only our devices. This is because we have incorporated technology that prevents the music from being copied, which is necessary to protect the rights of the artists.

    Justine: Music purchased and downloaded

(10) using your company's software should be compatible with other music devices manufactured by different companies. If a customer were to purchase a CD of the music, she would be able to play that CD in any brand of CD player. Your com-

(15) pany is trying to create an unfair advantage by forcing consumers who download music using your popular software to also buy one of your electronic devices rather than another manufacturer's device.

1. Which of the following is an underlying assumption of Justine's conclusion?

(A) Copyright protections are no longer necessary in the twenty-first century.

(B) The electronic devices manufactured by Steve's company are not as well-made as the devices made by other companies.

(C) Other manufacturers of electronic music players don't also have popular software that customers could choose.

(D) Customers who buy and download electronic music files using the Internet no longer purchase CDs.

(E) Forcing customers who use the popular software created by Steve's company to also buy an electronic device from that company would create an unfair advantage.

Go on to next page

2. Which of the following, if true, would most weaken Steve's argument?

   (A) If Steve's company didn't protect musical copyrights, it would be responsible to compensate artists for their lost revenues.

   (B) Effective copyright protections that would still allow music to be played on other manufacturers' devices could be employed.

   (C) Customers are extremely loyal to Steve's company and don't usually even consider buying other manufacturers' devices.

   (D) A single copy of a song downloaded using Steve's company's software can only be stored on one of his company's devices at any time.

   (E) No copyright protection is completely foolproof, and illegal software exists that can override the copyright protections used by Steve's company.

Questions 3–7 refer to the following passage:

Line

Plant injury resulting from high light intensity is due not to the light per se but to an excess of light energy over that utilized by photosynthesis. When light reaching the leaves is not used for (05) photosynthesis, the excess energy triggers production of free radicals that can damage cells (oxidative damage). This often occurs when light intensity is high but photosynthesis is inhibited due to stress from temperature extremes, (10) drought, or excessive soil water. When light intensity is at a low level where photosynthesis and respiration reach equilibrium and the net carbon gain is zero, no plant growth will occur. This light level is the light compensation point (15) (LCP). Leaves exposed to light levels below the LCP for an extended period of time will eventually senesce. Both LSP and LCP vary among turfgrass species and with temperature and CO_2 concentration.

(20)   Under high irradiance, warm-season grasses maintain a higher rate of photosynthesis than cool-season grasses. However, cool-season grasses have a lower LCP and exhibit higher photosynthetic rates under low light levels compared (25) to warm-season grasses. Photosynthetic rates of both warm-season and cool-season grasses exhibit a diurnal pattern on clear, sunny days,

increasing from sunrise, reaching a maximum around noon, and then decreasing to the lowest levels by sunset. (30)

Photosynthesis is affected by light duration because it occurs only during daylight. Increasing light duration may not increase the rate of carbon fixation, but the total amount of carbon fixed by photosynthesis will increase due to (35) increased light exposure. Sunlight has all the colors of visible light and is composed of different wavelengths. Not all wavelengths are equally effective in driving photosynthesis, however. Most photosynthetic activity is stimulated by (40) blue and red wavelengths — chlorophylls absorb blue and red light and carotenoids absorb blue light. Green light is reflected, thus giving plants their green color. Green-yellow and far red are transmitted through the leaf. (45)

This passage is excerpted from *Applied Turfgrass Science and Physiology,* **by Jack Fry and Bingru Huang (Wiley Publishing, 2004).**

3. The authors of the passage are primarily concerned with

   (A) discussing the impacts of light energy and photosynthesis on warm-season and cool-season grasses.

   (B) arguing in favor of warm-season grasses, which are less prone to oxidative damage than cool-season grasses.

   (C) exploring the important role of photosynthesis in sustaining turfgrass production.

   (D) comparing different kinds of turfgrasses according to their responses to various levels of light energy.

   (E) clarifying the scientific details of recent research into the photosynthesis of turfgrass.

4. In the context of the passage, which of the following is the best definition for the word *senesce* (used in the next-to-last sentence of the first paragraph)?

   (A) Grow faster

   (B) Grow slower

   (C) Turn darker green

   (D) Die back

   (E) Evolve

Go on to next page

5. According to the passage, which of the following is an important difference between warm-season and cool-season grasses?

    (A) Cool-season grasses can better withstand higher light intensities such as those found nearer the equator, while warm-season grasses are better suited to northern climates.

    (B) Warm-season grasses can handle the higher light levels of summer, while cool-season grasses can grow during the lower light conditions of winter.

    (C) Most of the photosynthesis in warm-season grasses takes place during the day, while cool-season grasses usually photosynthesize at night.

    (D) Warm season grasses use only the blue and red spectrums of light for photosynthesis, while reflecting harmful green light.

    (E) Excess light reaching cool-season grasses can be responsible for damage to the plant's cells, while warm-season grasses are unharmed.

6. Which of the following can be inferred from the discussion on oxidative damage (in the first paragraph)?

    (A) Oxidative damage most frequently occurs about one hour after sunrise and one hour before sunset.

    (B) Homeowners should water their lawns as often as possible because damage to grass is caused by drought and not simply by light intensity.

    (C) Oxidative damage to grass occurs when light reaching the leaves is not used for photosynthesis and, therefore, forms carbon fixation.

    (D) Damage to grass occurs because of the high intensity of light and homeowners can do nothing to preserve their lawns.

    (E) Both overwatering and underwatering a lawn can inhibit photosynthesis and damage grass.

7. According to the passage, each of the following is true of turfgrass photosynthesis EXCEPT

    (A) Its rate depends only on the amount of light energy.

    (B) It occurs only during daylight.

    (C) It is stimulated by blue and red wavelengths of light.

    (D) It is inhibited by temperature extremes.

    (E) It peaks around noon on clear, sunny days.

8. The ivory-billed woodpecker has been considered extinct for the past several decades. Recently, researchers claim to have found a pair of ivory-billeds in Arkansas. Their best evidence is a video that shows a large woodpecker flying away from the camera. The bird has the characteristic large white patches on the trailing edge of the wings. This is one of the factors that distinguishes ivory-billeds from the closely related pileated woodpecker. However, skeptics of the discovery argue that some abnormal pileateds can have extra white on the wing and that the bird in the video is most likely an abnormal pileated. They conclude that the ivory-billed has not been found and is still extinct.

    Which of the following, if true, would most strengthen the skeptic's conclusion that the ivory-billed woodpecker is still extinct?

    (A) Before this discovery, the last reported ivory-billeds were seen in Louisiana.

    (B) In the same area where the video was shot, researchers also heard the distinctive double-tap used by ivory-billeds.

    (C) The first person to discover the ivory-billeds was not a specialist, but professional ornithologists were soon brought in to confirm the identification.

    (D) Of the five key fieldmarks that identify ivory-billeds, only the extra white on the wing has been seen and this is also the only feature that occurs on abnormal pileateds.

    (E) The bird in the video is clearly seen using the shallow wing beats of the ivory-billed rather than the deeper wing beats of the pileated.

Go on to next page

9. The following is a concept plan developed by the Men's and Women's Professional Tennis Tour:

"Television viewers around the world are becoming more interested in reality TV. In America, viewers flock to shows about people stranded on a deserted island, racing around the world, auditioning to become singing stars, or trying to find a spouse. Reality TV has caught on in other countries around the world as well. Tennis players are already popular for their appearance and personalities as well as for their tennis ability. Therefore, the Tennis Tour can become even more popular with TV viewers if we add some elements of reality TV to our broadcasts. As a first step, we will begin interviewing players before the matches and having coaches wear microphones during the matches."

Which of the following, if true, would most strengthen the conclusion that adding reality television elements will increase the popularity of tennis on TV?

(A) TV viewers who occasionally watch tennis would be more interested if they knew more about the players.

(B) The reality television elements will actually alienate much of tennis's current TV audience.

(C) Personal information about the players is already widely available on the Internet and some of the websites of women's tennis stars are extremely popular.

(D) The tennis stars are very enthusiastic about the changes because they feel like the increased exposure could lead to endorsements, modeling, and even movie roles.

(E) The summer and winter Olympics have been using reality TV elements for many years.

10. The interior Western United States is sinking. The area of the U.S. between the Sierra Nevada mountains and the Colorado Plateau is known as the *Basin and Range*. This area has been sinking for millions of years due to expansion of the Earth's crust. The lowest point in North America, Death Valley, California, is part of the Basin and Range. Since the southern portion of the region is sinking much faster than the northern portion, places like Phoenix, Arizona, at just over 1,100 feet of elevation, are very low, and places farther north, like Reno, Nevada, at almost 4,500 feet of elevation, are higher. The fact that the elevation of the southern part of the region is getting progressively lower allows more moisture from the Gulf of California to bypass places like Phoenix and penetrate farther into the northern part of the region.

Which of the following is the most appropriate conclusion to the premises above?

(A) Therefore, the region known as the *Basin and Range* will continue to expand into areas currently part of the Colorado Plateau.

(B) As the northern portion of the region continues to sink, the southern areas of the region will receive more moisture.

(C) Therefore, the drier climate of places like Phoenix is attributable to the compression of the Earth's crust.

(D) The southern portion of the region includes areas that are very dry and well below sea level.

(E) As the area continues to sink, Phoenix, Arizona, will become drier and drier, while areas to the north will receive more moisture.

Go on to next page

11. <u>Hurry and get your special eclipse-viewing glasses, the United States is due for a total solar eclipse in 2017!</u>

   (A) Hurry and get your special eclipse-viewing glasses, the United States is due for a total solar eclipse in 2017!

   (B) Hurry to get your special eclipse-viewing glasses, the United States is due for a total solar eclipse in 2017.

   (C) Hurry to get your special eclipse-viewing glasses, because the United States is due for a total solar eclipse in 2017!

   (D) Hurry and get your special eclipse-viewing glasses, because the United States is due for a total solar eclipse in 2017.

   (E) Hurriedly get your special eclipse-viewing glasses, the United States is due for a total solar eclipse in 2017.

12. Some movie producers have tried to offer their movies on DVD and in the movie theaters simultaneously, <u>but theater operators has refused to cooperate.</u>

   (A) but theater operators has refused to cooperate.

   (B) theater operators have refused to cooperate.

   (C) but theater operators have refused to cooperate.

   (D) but theater operators' cooperation has been refused.

   (E) but theater operators hasn't cooperated.

13. Historically, the stock market frequently loses money during the summer months and generally gains value over the winter, <u>so serious investors often withdraw from the stock market in the spring and reinvest in the fall.</u>

   (A) so serious investors often withdraw from the stock market in the spring and reinvest in the fall.

   (B) so the serious investor often withdraw from the stock market in the spring and reinvest in the fall.

   (C) so serious investors often withdraw from the stock market in the spring and then usually decide to reinvest in the fall.

   (D) so serious investors often withdraw from the stock market in the spring and do their reinvesting in the fall.

   (E) so serious investors often withdraw from the stock market in the spring and reinvest in the fall, if they are serious.

14. <u>Cautioning against taking excessively high doses of certain vitamins and minerals, Americans are being warned by nutritionists.</u>

   (A) Cautioning against taking excessively high doses of certain vitamins and minerals, Americans are being warned by nutritionists.

   (B) Nutritionists are cautioning Americans against taking excessively high doses of certain vitamins and minerals.

   (C) Cautioning against taking doses of certain vitamins and minerals that are too high, Americans are warned by nutritionists.

   (D) Nutritionists caution and warn Americans against taking doses of certain vitamins and minerals that are too high.

   (E) To caution against taking excessively high doses of certain vitamins and minerals, Americans are being warned by nutritionists.

Go on to next page

Questions 15–18 refer to the following passage:

Line   One obvious goal of any public relations cam-
paign is to stand out from the crowd. And when
it comes to nonprofits, there is always a crowd.
     People in the nonprofit world often don't like
(05) to think of themselves as being in competition in
the way that businesses are. But the competition
is there just the same, and it can be ferocious.
     No matter what your organization's field
of activity — health care, community service,
(10) education, the arts, environmental protection,
promotion of cultural activities, historical preservation, or any other worthwhile cause — you are,
in effect, in competition with all the other organizations that specialize in the same area. And not
(15) only are you competing with your sister organizations, but you are also in de facto competition
with organizations that operate in other areas.
Despite the focus of your efforts, the odds are
that you and your competitors are reaching out
(20) to many of the same people.
     The reality is that people usually don't sup-
port just one organization. More typically, they
support concerns ranging from the local to the
global. It is not unusual for one person to support
(25) his local library, homeless shelter, and symphony
orchestra while being involved with organizations that protect whales in the Pacific or support medical research in the Amazon or care for
orphans in Africa. And then there is your organi-
(30) zation, trying desperately to be heard above the
clamor. That one individual may receive letters,
appeals, and newsletters from literally dozens of
organizations, all asking for attention and support. Therefore, one obvious job that your public
(35) relations efforts should accomplish is to help
your organization stand out from the background
noise by making a personal connection. In more
hard-nosed terms, public relations can be a tool
to help you beat the competition.

**This passage is excerpted from *The Public
Relations Handbook for Nonprofits: A
Comprehensive and Practical Guide,* by Art
Feinglass (Wiley Publishing, 2005).**

15. Which of the following statements best
describes the main idea of the passage?

(A) Nonprofit organizations don't compete directly with each other for donor
dollars.

(B) Individuals who donate to nonprofits
often help a number of different organizations, from the local to the international level.

(C) The nonprofit world is crowded with
organizations that are all appealing to
same set of generous donors.

(D) Making your nonprofit organization
stand out from the crowd through
effective public relations is vital to its
success.

(E) Sending letters soliciting support is no
longer an effective way to raise funds
for nonprofit organizations.

16. What does the article imply when, in the
first sentence of the second paragraph,
it says, "People in the nonprofit world
often don't like to think of themselves as
being in competition in the way that businesses are"?

(A) Those who work in nonprofits think
of competition for donor dollars as
more cutthroat than normal business
competition.

(B) People who work for nonprofits think
that the pot of donor dollars from
which they draw is endless.

(C) Nonprofits' public relations managers
don't have the business skills necessary to compete for a limited supply
of donations.

(D) Workers at local nonprofits recognize
that they are competing against other
local nonprofits but don't see that
they are also competing against sister
organizations.

(E) Many who work for nonprofits think
that because they are doing something
good, they don't also have to compete.

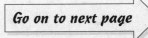
Go on to next page

17. Which of the following is NOT listed in the passage as a type of nonprofit that people support?

    (A) Medical research in the Amazon

    (B) Food banks

    (C) Symphony orchestra

    (D) Protecting whales in the Pacific

    (E) Local library

18. According to the passage, what is the "obvious" way that public relations efforts can help an organization stand out from the crowd?

    (A) By making a personal connection with the donor who receives dozens of other requests for support.

    (B) By encouraging donors to support more than one type of nonprofit organization.

    (C) By undermining the credibility of sister organizations that are competing for the same donor dollars.

    (D) By helping the organization to beat the competition.

    (E) By focusing the organization's efforts on donors who have a natural affinity for the group through location, personal history, or interests.

19. Hearing loss is sometimes called a loss of intimacy <u>because the more hearing ability declines</u>, the ability to pick out a voice over background noise is one of the first things to go.

    (A) because the more hearing ability declines

    (B) as hearing ability declines

    (C) because as hearing ability declines

    (D) because hearing ability declines as

    (E) because when hearing abilities declines

20. The powerful Medici family, <u>that dominated the Italian Renaissance, used chocolate as a political tool,</u> only serving a special kind of chocolate flavored with Jasmine to important allies.

    (A) that dominated the Italian Renaissance, used chocolate as a political tool,

    (B) was able to dominate the Italian Renaissance, using chocolate as a political tool,

    (C) that dominated the Italian Renaissance by using chocolate as a political tool,

    (D) who dominated the Italian Renaissance, used chocolate as a political tool,

    (E) who's domination of the Italian Renaissance was based on the use of chocolate as a political tool,

Go on to next page

21. <u>Alumni that earn bachelor's degrees from a large state institution are more likely to attend its alma mater's sporting events,</u> while alumni from smaller liberal arts colleges frequently show their allegiance by donating money.

    (A) Alumni that earn bachelor's degrees from a large state institution are more likely to attend its alma mater's sporting events,

    (B) Alumni that earn bachelor's degrees from large state institutions are more likely to attend their alma maters' sporting events,

    (C) Alumni that earn bachelor's degrees from large state institutions are more likely to attend their alma maters sporting events,

    (D) Alumni, who each earn a bachelor's degrees from a large state institution, are more likely to attend their alma maters' sporting events,

    (E) Alumni who's bachelor's degrees come from a large state institution are more likely to attend its alma mater's sporting events,

22. Scientists have recently analyzed glass spherules that were created by the meteor impact near the Yucatan Peninsula in Mexico <u>and have concluded that the infamous meteor arrived 300,000 years too early to have killed the dinosaurs.</u>

    (A) and have concluded that the infamous meteor arrived 300,000 years too early to have killed the dinosaurs.

    (B) but have concluded that the infamous meteor arrived 300,000 years too early to have killed the dinosaurs.

    (C) having concluded that the infamous meteor arrived 300,000 years too early to have killed the dinosaurs.

    (D) and have concluded that the infamous meteor arrived 300,000 years too early to kill the dinosaurs.

    (E) and concludes that the infamous meteor arrived 300,000 years too early to have killed the dinosaurs.

23. The U.S. Forest Service manages the National Forests for the American people, <u>yet they often sell timber below cost to private business and, in a recent year, it lost more than $2 billion of taxpayer money on these "sweetheart deals."</u>

    (A) yet they often sell timber below cost to private business and, in a recent year, it lost more than $2 billion of taxpayer money on these "sweetheart deals."

    (B) yet it often sell timber below cost to private business and, in a recent year, it lost more than $2 billion of taxpayer money on these "sweetheart deals."

    (C) yet the Service often sells timber below cost to private business and, in a recent year, it lost more than $2 billion of taxpayer money on this "sweetheart deals."

    (D) yet it often sells timber below cost to private business, in a recent year, it lost more than $2 billion of taxpayer money on these "sweetheart deals."

    (E) yet it often sells timber below cost to private business and, in a recent year, lost more than $2 billion of taxpayer money on these "sweetheart deals."

Go on to next page

24. Many names that people think of as Irish were actually brought to Ireland by the Anglo-Norman invasion of Ireland in the 12th century. Names like Seamus, Patrick, and Sean are so widespread because of the Catholic Church's requirements that Irish sons and daughters be named after saints. *Seamus* is the Gaelic version of *James,* and *Sean* is the Gaelic version of *John.* Criminal laws in Ireland from the 1500s to the 1900s forbade parents from giving their children traditional Irish names like Cathal, Aodh, and Brian. Now that parents are free to do so, they should give their children these long-forgotten, traditional names that are truly Irish.

Which of the following inferences can be drawn from the above argument?

(A) The author of the argument considers names like Aodh and Brian that were used in Ireland since before the 12th century to be "traditional."

(B) Irish parents prefer to give their children names that are as traditionally Irish as possible.

(C) Parents in Ireland are now free to give their children any name that they choose.

(D) The author of the argument feels that, even after hundreds of years of use, names like Patrick, Seamus, and Sean are still not "truly Irish."

(E) The author of the argument is still bitter about the introduction of non-Irish names into Ireland in the 12th century.

Questions 25 and 26 are based on the following:

Linda: You should bring a reusable mug. Foam plastic never decomposes. That cup you're drinking your coffee from will still be in the landfill in two hundred years!

Jane: I usually bring my own reusable plastic mug, but in the future, I might not have to feel so guilty about forgetting it. I just read that scientists have discovered that they can heat foam plastic to make liquid styrene, which is a certain kind of plastic that bacteria can eat. The bacteria store the carbon from the foam plastic in a form that ordinary bacteria in the soil can break down. The result is that less foam plastic ends up in the landfill; therefore, it's just as environmentally friendly for me to use this foam plastic cup as it is to bring my own mug.

25. If Linda wanted to weaken Jane's conclusion, which of the following, if true, would be her best response?

(A) This special recycling process you describe requires energy, so the reusable mug is still more environmentally friendly.

(B) Many coffee shops switched from foam plastic to coated paper cups long ago, even though the coated paper cups provide less insulation.

(C) You should still bring your own mug with you because your mug provides superior insulation and keeps your coffee hot at least twice as long.

(D) The real environmental problems associated with drinking coffee are in the tropics, where forests are continually being cleared to grow more coffee.

(E) Most coffee shops and convenience stores consider it a refill if you bring your own mug and, therefore, charge only about half as much.

Go on to next page

26. Jane's assertion that she may not have to feel so guilty about forgetting her mug in the future relies on which of the following assumptions?

    (A) She usually brings her reusable plastic mug with her, leading to a sense of guilt when she forgets it.

    (B) The recycling process will take place in America and create good jobs for moderately skilled workers.

    (C) The process discovered by the scientists will turn out to be practical and cost-effective enough to become widespread.

    (D) Linda feels just as guilty when she forgets to bring her reusable cloth shopping bag when she goes to the grocery store.

    (E) There will be no additional advances in material technology that even further reduce the impact of using a disposable cup.

27. The standard computer keyboard, called QWERTY because of the arrangement of the first six letters, is very inefficient. The letters were arranged in this odd but familiar manner when the first typewriters were being designed in the 1800s. When keys were arranged logically, typists could strike the keys very quickly. Early typewriters were so slow the fast typists caused mechanical problems in the machines. In order to slow down the typists, the keys were rearranged in a seemingly random order. If a manufacturer of computer keyboards were to arrange the keys in the most efficient manner, everyone would want to buy a new, improved keyboard.

    If true, which of the following would most seriously weaken the above conclusion?

    (A) Modern computer word-processing systems are much faster than the most accomplished typist and there is no reason to use the slower keyboard.

    (B) Americans have universally adapted to the QWERTY keyboard and aren't interested in learning an entirely new system.

    (C) Discovering the most efficient arrangement of keys would require extensive tests on typists and non-typists alike.

    (D) The human brain is incredibly adaptable and can adapt to any arrangement of the keyboard, even if it is less efficient.

    (E) Computer keyboards include many keys that were not needed on manual or electric typewriters.

Go on to next page

Questions 28–32 refer to the following passage:

Line

Immediately after the execution of Socrates, Plato and his companions relocated to nearby Megara, where a small school of Socratic thought was established. During the next nine years (from
(5) 399 to 390 B.C.E.), Plato committed his first works to writing, a body of works that included *Laches, Protagoras,* and *Apology.* These works are collectively known as Plato's Socratic dialogues, because they are heavily focused on and influ-
(10) enced by his late teacher.

During this same period, it is speculated that Plato did a two-year stint (between 395 and 394 B.C.E.) with the military, possibly fighting in the Corinthian War, in which Athens and a collection
(15) of other city-states banded together to overthrow Spartan rule. It is not known for sure if he did indeed fight in this war, though there are some legends that he fought well enough to gain some decorations. During this time, Plato is also sup-
(20) posed to have journeyed to Egypt, where he visited Alexandria and possibly learned the secrets of the water clock, which he would bring back to Greek society. Again, this information is not well documented, so it may fall under the category of
(25) apocrypha.

What is known for sure is that Plato traveled to southern Italy for the first time in 390 B.C.E., at the age of 37. There he met Archytas of Tarentum, who was leading a resurgence in the
(30) study of the works of Pythagoras. This exposure to Pythagoreanism had very profound effects on Plato; it formed the foundation of the notion that mathematics was the truest way of expressing the universe that Man could use. These ideas
(35) showed up in many of his later works, including *Republic,* as Plato used mathematical concepts to describe the nature of the universe and the human mind.

This passage is excerpted from *Plato Within Your Grasp,* by Brian Proffitt (Wiley Publishing, 2004).

28. The primary purpose of this passage is to

(A) argue for a new interpretation of Plato's early works that are collectively known as the Socratic dialogues.

(B) explain the profound influence that Archytas of Tarentum had on Plato's view of man as described in the *Republic.*

(C) chronicle Plato's military exploits as he fought for Athens during the Corinthian War.

(D) detail the circumstances surrounding the establishment of a Socratic school of thought in Megara following Socrates' execution.

(E) describe what is known of Plato's life from the time of Socrates' execution until Plato's visit to southern Italy in 390 B.C.E.

29. It can be inferred from the passage that the phrase "category of apocrypha" at the end of the second paragraph means:

(A) Intentional lies meant to harm a reputation

(B) Histories well-documented by ancient historians

(C) Unnecessary information that detracts from historical truth

(D) Stories of questionable authenticity

(E) Tales of horror designed to impart fear

Go on to next page

30. According to the passage, which of the following best describes the impact that Plato's visit to southern Italy in 390 B.C.E. had on his later works?

    (A) It injected into his writing the Pythagorean concept of mathematics as the truest way of expressing the universe.

    (B) It allowed him to bring back to Greece the secrets of an accurate water clock, which greatly impacted his view of time.

    (C) It forced him to get past the stifling influence that the execution of Socrates had on his works of the previous decade.

    (D) It had virtually no influence on his work, and the journey itself cannot even be confirmed.

    (E) His later works are infused with tragedy based on his military experience in southern Italy.

31. Which of the following books is NOT attributed to Plato in the passage?

    (A) *Apology*

    (B) *Phaedo*

    (C) *Laches*

    (D) *Protagoras*

    (E) *Republic*

32. It can be logically inferred from the passage that Sparta

    (A) was overthrown during the Corinthian War because of Plato's involvement.

    (B) ruled over Athens for some period of time prior to 395 B.C.E.

    (C) lacked the important philosophical schools found in Athens.

    (D) was responsible for the execution of Socrates.

    (E) was a military state constantly at war with its neighbors.

33. Almost the whole of Yellowstone National Park is located in one of the world's largest volcanic craters; the question is <u>if the recent increased activity of the park's geysers and hot springs indicate that the volcano has become active.</u>

    (A) if the recent increased activity of the park's geysers and hot springs indicate that the volcano has become active.

    (B) if recently observed increases in the activity of the park's geysers and hot springs indicate that the volcano has become active.

    (C) whether recently observed increases in the activity of the park's geysers and hot springs indicate that the volcano is becoming active.

    (D) whether recently observed increases in the activity of the park's geysers and hot springs indicate that the volcano has become active.

    (E) whether recently observed increases in the activity of the park's geysers and hot springs indicate they are becoming active.

34. On the Australian island of Tasmania, bulldog ants, known as *jack-jumpers,* kill more people each year <u>than the total number of people that are killed by the various snakes, spiders, and other venomous creatures combined.</u>

    (A) than the total number of people that are killed by the various snakes, spiders, and other venomous creatures combined.

    (B) than the total number of people who are killed by the combination of the various snakes, spiders, and other venomous creatures.

    (C) than all the various snakes, spiders, and other venomous creatures combined.

    (D) than people that are killed by the other creatures with venom, such as snakes and spiders.

    (E) than do the various snakes, spiders, and other venomous creatures.

Go on to next page

35. The day, lunar month, and solar year all have natural, astronomical reasons for existence, <u>while the two units of time that most tyrannize modern workers, the hour and the week, are artificial constructs.</u>

    (A) while the two units of time that most tyrannize modern workers, the hour and the week, are artificial constructs.

    (B) while the two units of time most especially responsible for tyrannizing modern workers, the hour and the week, being constructed artificially.

    (C) whereas the two units of time that most tyrannize modern workers, the hour and the week, are artificial constructs.

    (D) whereas the two units that most tyrannize modern workers on the basis of time, the hour and the week, are artificially constructed.

    (E) while the hour and the week where constructed artificially, so that they are now the two units of time that most tyrannize modern workers.

36. In order to raise funds, the Copper Country Land Trust hosts a musical concert and potluck dinner in the fall, <u>a family ski race in the winter, and puts together a trail run in the summer.</u>

    (A) a family ski race in the winter, and puts together a trail run in the summer.

    (B) organized a family ski race in the winter, and puts together a trail run in the summer

    (C) a family ski race in the winter, and a trail run in the summer.

    (D) puts together a family ski race in the winter, and a summer trail run.

    (E) a winter ski race, and it puts together a trail run in the summer.

37. Snakes exist on every continent except for Antarctica, which is inhospitable to all cold-blooded animals. The continent of Australia is home to many of the deadliest snakes in the world. However, the nearby island nation of New Zealand has no snakes at all. Scientists estimate that snakes originated about 100 million years ago when the continents were joined and the snakes stayed on the main land masses of the continents when they split apart. Snakes are absent from New Zealand because they are unable to swim and therefore could not make the journey.

    Which of the following, if true, would most strengthen the conclusion of the above argument?

    (A) Snakes are found in South America at latitudes farther south than New Zealand.

    (B) Islands like Hawaii and New Zealand are very aggressive about preventing an accidental introduction of snakes.

    (C) Sea snakes can swim and are present in the warmer oceans of the world.

    (D) Snakes are also absent from other major islands, such as Hawaii, Ireland, and Greenland.

    (E) Snakes are found on many other islands of the Pacific Ocean.

Go on to next page ⟶

38. Major airlines claim that the fares they charge haven't increased in recent years. However, the various fees that used to be included in the quoted fare are now charged separately. The fees added to the quoted fare now include the 9/11 security fee, the fuel surcharge, and the airport departure fee. The airlines are just following the example of other travel-related industries that have added on fees and taxes for years. The rental car and hotel industries usually quote a rate that is 20 percent less than the actual bill. In major cities, restaurants and bars usually have an additional tax rate that is included on the bill with the sales tax. In fact, there isn't one aspect of traveling where the quoted price is the final price.

If true, which of the following facts concerning the costs of travel would most weaken the above conclusion?

(A) Many items ordered through the mail include shipping and handling fees that are more than the cost of the actual item.

(B) The price of a gallon of gasoline that is quoted at the pump and on the gas station signs already includes all the fuel taxes and is the actual, final price.

(C) When traveling outside of the United States and Canada, Americans should remember that the quoted price is often just the starting point for negotiations and that the final price is usually much lower.

(D) The quoted price for travel on most cruise ships doesn't include a variety of fees, including fees for excursions, beverages charges, and gratuities for the staff.

(E) The price quoted for a new car usually doesn't even include the destination charge, which is the cost of getting the car to the dealership.

39. The graduated income tax is the most progressive form of tax because people who make less money pay a lower percentage of their earnings in taxes, while those who earn more pay a higher percentage. The sales tax is more regressive because it is collected when people spend money rather than earn it. Since the same percentage tax is collected from everyone, regardless of income, and because people who make less money must spend a larger percentage of their income on necessities, the effective sales tax rate that people pay actually increases as they earn less money. Therefore, in order to be fair to all of its citizens, this state should increase income tax rates and eliminate the sales tax.

The conclusion drawn above is based on the assumption that

(A) a progressive tax is one that collects more money from people who make more money.

(B) a flat income tax would be fairer to all taxpayers because everyone would pay the same rate regardless of income.

(C) a higher sales tax rate actually encourages people to save more of their income because they aren't taxed until they spend the money.

(D) a regressive tax hits poor people the hardest.

(E) sales taxes are collected on all purchases, including necessities such as food and clothing.

40. In the year 2005 alone, about one-third of the coral reefs in the Caribbean died. The Caribbean coral are more fortunate than those in the Indian and Pacific Oceans, where death rates are near 90 percent. Scientist say that warm ocean temperatures are the cause of the unprecedented devastation. Coral may appear to be a hard, rocky substance, but coral reefs are actually huge colonies of living animals. Living reefs teem with fish and provide areas for fish and other sea life to reproduce. Living reefs are colorful and vibrant, while dead reefs are bleached white and devoid of life. Coral reefs grow only a fraction of an inch per year. Once a reef dies, it will probably never recover. Ocean temperatures are expected to continue to rise, and most of the remaining coral reefs in the world will probably begin to die within the next decade.

    Which of the following is the most appropriate conclusion for these premises?

    (A) Therefore, if you ever want the chance to see a healthy coral reef, go soon.

    (B) Thus, rising ocean temperatures will have no impact on fish populations.

    (C) Once the coral dies, it will be bleached white and devoid of life.

    (D) SCUBA and snorkeling tourism is big business for many Caribbean nations.

    (E) Coral reefs in the cooler waters at the edge of the tropics will probably survive the longest.

41. The following is taken from an advertisement for a new prescription drug:

    "Are you one of the millions of Americans who have occasional trouble sleeping? Do the stresses of modern life prevent you from getting enough exercise and keeping to a regular sleep schedule? Do you find yourself lying awake worrying about the sleep you're not getting? New Nocturna can help you get a full night's sleep every night. Ask your doctor about Nocturna. When nature needs a little help, try Nocturna."

    Which of the following is implied by the above argument?

    (A) Many people wouldn't need to use a prescription drug if they got more exercise and kept to a regular sleep schedule.

    (B) Nocturna is more effective than similar sleep aids on the market.

    (C) Millions of Americans have occasional trouble sleeping.

    (D) Overuse of caffeine is one of the factors contributing to sleep problems among Americans.

    (E) The only way for you to get a good night's sleep is by taking Nocturna.

Answer Key for Practice Exam 2

Section 2
Quantitative Answer Key

1. C	20. B
2. B	21. D
3. D	22. B
4. D	23. C
5. C	24. D
6. A	25. E
7. B	26. A
8. B	27. B
9. D	28. A
10. E	29. C
11. C	30. E
12. E	31. C
13. A	32. A
14. A	33. D
15. E	34. B
16. D	35. B
17. C	36. D
18. A	37. A
19. B	

Section 3
Verbal Answer Key

1. C	22. A
2. B	23. E
3. A	24. D
4. D	25. A
5. B	26. C
6. E	27. B
7. A	28. E
8. D	29. D
9. A	30. A
10. E	31. B
11. C	32. B
12. C	33. C
13. A	34. E
14. B	35. C
15. D	36. C
16. E	37. D
17. B	38. B
18. A	39. E
19. C	40. A
20. D	41. A
21. B	

Chapter 20

Explaining the Answers to Practice Test #2

∙ ∙

This chapter gives you the opportunity to check your answers. If you have time, read through all the answer explanations, even those for questions you answered correctly. An answer explanation may contain information that you haven't considered before.

Explanations for the Analytical Writing Assessment

Scoring the practice analytical writing tasks is a little different from scoring the verbal and quantitative sections. Your job is to honestly analyze the essays you've written and to assign yourself a score. You can also ask a writer friend or composition teacher to look over your essays and give you an opinion. To help you determine your score for this section, we've included a couple sample essays and an explanation of their strengths and weaknesses. Use these tools to identify your own essays' strengths and weaknesses and to improve your essay responses before you take the real test.

Analysis of an issue

Your first task was to analyze an issue. Scores for this task range from 0–6. If you receive a 0 score, your essay is completely off topic, written in a foreign language, or is a copy of the essay prompt. If you receive a 2, your essay lacks organization, fails to provide persuasive reasons and examples, and contains numerous errors in grammar, usage, and mechanics. A score of 4 means your essay supports your position, organizes thoughts, and applies the conventions of standard written English adequately but not amazingly. A score of 6 indicates that you've written an outstanding essay that is well organized, eloquent, and persuasive; that provides perceptive thinking and convincing examples; and that demonstrates a command of the elements of standard written English.

Sample analysis of an issue essay

The analysis of an issue topic asked you to provide your opinion on whether ethics should be taught as part of the curriculum of substantive business courses or whether it should be confined to designated business ethics courses. Here's an example of an essay that discusses the issue:

Ethics is a key word in business today. Corporate scandals have repeatedly rocked the public's faith in business leaders. In fact, some business people such as those at Enron, Tyco, WorldCom and other infamous corporations, do seem to have low ethical standards. It would seem, therefore, that business schools should take every possible chance to discuss ethics, regardless of the official subject matter of the course. Even technical courses like accounting, marketing, and economics seem to be good places for ethics training, especially given the fact that each individual subject has its own ethics challenges. However, because business ethics is too important to be the subject of occasional mention in substantive courses, business ethics is best left to designated ethics courses.

Courses with a technical component have little spare time to properly explore ethics. Courses in accounting, marketing, and economics include complex subject matter, and professors often have difficulty finding the time necessary to teach the fundamentals of the course. Any discussion of ethics in these courses would be as an aside. Certainly business ethics deserves more than just a brief mention in between discussions of accounting practices.

A second reason that ethics instruction should be the domain of specific ethics courses is that teachers of subjects with a technical component are not used to teaching ethics courses. Business ethics teachers are experts in the subject and are used to fostering class discussion and helping students understand personal ethics. Ethics are more than a simple list of rules, but a teacher who is used to teaching economics may present ethics in the same way as the laws of supply and demand. Maybe ethics could be discussed in less technical general management classes, but not in the classes with technical component. Business ethics should be left to professional ethics teachers that can do justice to its importance.

Some have argued that people involved in more technical areas, particularly accounting, have had their own ethics problems recently and, therefore, ethics should be included in the instruction of these subjects. Although it is true that ethical violations have recently occurred in all areas of business, including accounting, this does not mean that a different version of ethics needs to be taught in accounting class. The ethical violations in the accounting scandals follow the same pattern as they do in other areas of business: lack of public disclosure, actual lies, insider trading, violation of the fiduciary duty to stockholders, and abuse of public trust. Aside from these general business ethics violations, the accountants involved in the recent scandals were also guilty of bad accounting. So, while business ethics needs to be taught in business ethics classes, accounting practices should be taught in accounting classes.

Some business schools have recently scaled back their offerings or requirements in the area of business ethics. Now is the wrong time to be reducing the emphasis on ethics in business. Graduate business schools need to make sure that every student gets a foundation in ethics before graduating. This will not be accomplished with the occasional mention of ethics in the middle of a marketing class. Schools should retain designated ethics courses in their MBA curriculum.

While businesses ethics should be emphasized as often as possible, business courses with a technical component are best place to education students on ethics. Business ethics is too important to be the subject of perfunctory mention in substantive courses. Business ethics is best left to designated ethics courses.

No paper written in 30 minutes will be perfect. Certainly this essay would benefit from another round of editing. However, the essay is well organized, precise, and insightful. The essay applies specific and well-chosen examples. The author provides persuasively reasoned support for each of the points.

The writer begins by laying out why this issue is important. With all the ethics scandals that have "repeatedly rocked" the business world, it's no wonder graduate business schools may consider adding ethics components to every class. The introduction skillfully acknowledges the complexities of the issue and then ends in a clear position: Ethics should be left to designated ethics courses and not included in subjects with a technical component.

The next three paragraphs provide specific reasons why ethics shouldn't be included in marketing, economics, and accounting courses. These reasons are clearly stated and firmly supported. The examples used are specific and concrete. The list of ethical violations by accountants is particularly detailed, and the conclusion that accountants need to be taught best accounting practices in order to avoid further scandals is insightful. The author also acknowledges and rebuts points that the opposing view may bring up. This sort of rebuttal should be a component of any well-written essay on an issue.

The writer uses the fifth paragraph to again bring out the particular relevance of the issue. Graduate business schools are reducing ethics courses and the analysis that adding ethics components to non-ethics courses could speed up this process is very astute. The essay then concludes with a simple restatement of the thesis.

The essay is probably worth a score of 4 or 5. For the most part, it demonstrates a command of written English. The author applies a variety of sentence structures while maintaining clarity. Precise word choices make the essay more interesting to the reader. The essay may have a very few minor grammatical and mechanical errors, but it has no major flaws. The essay is well organized and employs effective transitions, but it doesn't try to be flamboyant or to impress the reader with complicated jargon. Anyone can achieve this level of writing with practice.

Analysis of an argument

Your second task was to analyze an argument. This essay has a slightly different scoring guide. Following the rules of standard written English and providing clear support for your position are still important, but including clear transitions between points takes on a more significant role.

If your writing receives a 2, it may provide an unclear representation of the essay's position rather than a critique of the argument made in the prompt. If your essay receives a 4, you may provide a clear analysis for each of the elements of the argument but neglect to present clear transitions to link your points. An essay that receives a 6 identifies all the important elements of the argument and develops an organized position on their accuracy and reasonableness, using clear transitions between points.

Sample analysis of an argument essay

For this topic, you were asked to analyze an argument that mass media has contributed to a lack of creativity and curiosity. Here's what an analysis of this topic may look like:

> The author of this letter argues that the prevalence of mass media in American society today has led to a great lack of intellectual creativity and curiosity among the average citizen. The author's statement that mass media permeates American culture is sound; the assumption he makes that the average American spends countless hours every day watching television and movies and listening to music is probably accurate. Very

few American families live in a TV-free home, and anyone who has ridden in a car has probably listened to the radio. However, the conclusion that mass media exposure has contributed to a diminishment in creativity and curiosity is flawed. The author doesn't provide adequate proof that the prevalence of mass media has led to the demise of creativity, nor does the author prove that a lack of creativity actually exists.

In making his argument that mass media has resulted in a lack of creativity, the author does not consider that there may be other causes for the alleged demise of originality and imagination. For example, people today are much busier than they were a hundred years ago. Americans work long hours and take fewer vacation days in an attempt to realize the American dream. Society's emphasis on "having it all" has contributed to Americans taking on more activities than they have time to accomplish. So, it could be the stress and exhaustion of modern living that contributes to a lack of creativity or curiosity at the end of the workday rather than the predominance of mass media. By failing to address other causes for the author's perceived diminishment of American ingenuity and inquisitiveness, the author does a disservice to his argument. If he had acknowledged and refuted the likelihood of other causes for the American creative sloth, the author's argument would have made a bigger impact.

Furthermore, the author argument would have been stronger if he had proven that a lack of modern American creatively actually exists. He tries to promote the idea that before the prevalence of mass media in American culture, more people told stories. Although it's true that watching television has replaced singing around the campfire as a primary source of entertainment, his evidence does not support his assumption that modern Americans lack creativity. His only support for this argument is that before mass media more people told stories to a small audience and now a few people tell stories to a large audience. He offers no concrete evidence or specific examples to prove that the old way of communicating was more original than the current mode. And, again, he fails to address the opposing viewpoint. It could be that Americans have been inspired by pop culture to compose songs of their own, develop their own idea for a screen play or novel, or try out for a part on a reality TV show. Ideas that may not have occurred to Americans living one hundred years ago without exposure to other's ideas.

The writer of this letter to the editor attempts to make a cause and effect argument, but he fails to prove that the cause he puts forth is the one and only cause for the effect. Nor does he prove that the effect even exists. The argument would have been much stronger if the author had provided clear evidence to support that mass media has ruined creativity in America and had show how no other cause promoted this lack. Similarly, it would have been much easier to jump on the bandwagon with the author if he had provided some clear examples of how Americans are less creative than they were before the prevalence of mass media. Without strong supporting evidence and an acknowledgment of the opposing viewpoint, this argument fails to convince.

This essay fulfills the requirement of taking on the reasoning methods of the original argument. It shows knowledge of what makes an argument well reasoned: strong supporting examples and acknowledgement and rebuttal of an opposing viewpoint. And it uses good reasoning skills to show the lack of reasoning in the original argument. Notice that the author doesn't go into detail about how she feels about the topic. She presents an opinion about the topic only when it's necessary to show where the writer of the letter failed to consider a point. The essay fulfills the assignment because it's well written, well organized, and focused. It would probably receive at least a 5, possibly a 6.

Explanatory Answers to the Quantitative Questions

1. **C.** For this exception question, eliminate each answer choice that's the same as $b^2 - 9 = 16a^2$. All but one of the answer choices are simple manipulations of the original equation. Choice A divides both sides of the original equation by 16, B subtracts 9 from both sides, D multiplies both sides by 2, and E just factors the left side of the equation, which is the difference of two squares.

   On the surface, C appears to be the result of taking the square root of both sides of the equation. However, although $4a$ is the square root of $16a^2$, $b - 3$ isn't the square root of $b^2 - 9$. You can't find the square root of a sum or difference by finding the square root of each of the terms. If you thought C was the same as $b^2 - 9 = 16a^2$, you've claimed that $(b - 3)^2 = b^2 - 9$. But when you multiply $(b - 3)(b - 3)$, you get $b^2 - 6b + 9$, not $b^2 - 9$. C is the correct answer.

2. **B.** You can answer this question by simply counting the multiples: 15, 18, 21, 24, 27, 30, 33, 36, 39, 42, 45, 48, 51, 54, 57, 60, 63, 66, 69, 72, 75, 78, 81. (The *inclusive* means you include 15 and 81 in your total.) There are 23 multiples.

   Alternatively, you can save time by subtracting 15 from 81, which results in 66. Then, because you're counting by threes, divide 66 by 3 to get 22. You're not finished, though. Add 1 because the set is inclusive of 15 and 81. The answer is 23, choice B.

3. **D.** For this data sufficiency question, keep in mind that integers don't include fractions or decimals.

   Statement (1) claims that n and 3^4 are each divisible by the same number of positive integers. Because you can definitively find the value of 3^4 (81), you can figure out how many positive integers go into it. Because n has the same number of divisors, this statement gives you all you need to solve the problem. Don't spend precious time actually figuring out how many divisors 81 has.

   Because statement (1) is sufficient, you can eliminate B, C, and E and check out the second statement. If it's sufficient, the answer is D; if it isn't, the answer is A.

   Statement (2) tells you that n is the product of two different prime numbers, which means that the positive integers that divide into n are 1, the two different prime numbers you multiply together to get n, and n itself (a total of 4). Statement (2) is sufficient, so you can eliminate A. Your answer is D.

4. **D.** You can set up an equation from this word problem. Make x equal to the area of the park in square yards. Eighty percent of the park is comprised of a field measuring 120 yards by 50 yards, which means the area of the football field is 6,000 square yards ($A = lw$, so $A = 120 \times 50$). Now you just need to find the area of the total park. Eighty percent of the total is expressed as $0.80 \times x$:

   $$0.80x = 6,000$$

   $$x = 7,500$$

5. **C.** This data sufficiency problem doesn't require much math skill. You just have to try to synchronize schedules.

   Statement (1) tells you about Bob and David's schedules (they can meet from 2:00–3:00) but tells you nothing about Alison and Colleen. Statement (1) isn't sufficient, so you can eliminate A and D.

   Statement (2) tells you about Alison and Colleen's schedules (they can meet between 11:00 and 3:00), but it doesn't mention Bob and David. Statement (2) isn't sufficient, but you've probably already figured out that because statement (1) gives you Bob and David's times and statement (2) gives you Alison and Colleen's times, the two statements together can answer the question. Eliminate B and E. C is the correct answer.

6. **A.** To solve the ratio, you need to know values for a and b.

   Statement (1) allows you to set up a simple proportion that you can use to solve for $\%$ $(\frac{0.4a}{3b} = \frac{4}{7}; \frac{a}{b} = \frac{4}{7} \div \frac{0.4}{3})$. Statement (1) is sufficient, so the answer is A or D.

   Statement (2) allows you to set up the equation $a = 4b - 3$, but this equation allows you to solve for only $^{(a+3)}\!/\!_b$ and not $\%$. Statement (2) isn't sufficient, so you can eliminate D. A is correct.

7. **B.** To solve for the lowest portion of the job that can be done by two people in an hour, you have to choose the two slowest people, who are the two who complete the job in 4 and 5 hours.

   The person who takes 5 hours completes $\frac{1}{5}$ of the job in 1 hour (it takes him 5 hours total, so in 1 hour he completes 1 out of 5 hours, or $\frac{1}{5}$ of the job). Similarly, the person who works 4 hours to complete the job finishes $\frac{1}{4}$ of the job in 1 hour. Add $\frac{1}{5}$ and $\frac{1}{4}$ and you get $\frac{9}{20}$ ($\frac{1}{5} = \frac{4}{20}$; $\frac{1}{4} = \frac{5}{20}$; $\frac{4}{20} + \frac{5}{20} = \frac{9}{20}$). The answer is B.

8. **B.** This data sufficiency problem concerns divisibility.

   If you check statement (1) by substituting small numbers for x and y, you find that the information is insufficient. If x and y are 6 and 12, $x + y = 18$, which is divisible by 9. But if x and y are 12 and 18, they would add up to 30, which isn't divisible by 9. Eliminate A and D and check the second statement.

   Statement (2) tells you that the digit(s) that make up both x and y, respectively, add up to 9 (so x could be 18 and y could be 81), which means that x and y are divisible by 9.

   If two terms are divisible by a number (in this case, 9), their sum is divisible by that same number.

   Statement (2) is sufficient, so you can eliminate C and E and choose B.

9. **D.** You just need to know whether you can solve for x to figure out if the statements are sufficient. Statement (1) provides an equation with just one variable (x), so you know that you can solve it for x ($x = -\frac{1}{3}$) and that the first statement is sufficient. Eliminate B, C, and E.

   The same holds true for statement (2). The equation has just one variable (x), so you know you can solve it for x ($x = -\frac{1}{3}$). Because statement (2) is sufficient, you can eliminate A and choose D as your answer.

10. **E.** The boundary lines of the shaded shape are the vertical lines $x = 2$ and $x = 4$, so eliminate A and C. Horizontally, the shape is bound on the bottom by the x axis, which has an equation of $y = 0$. So eliminate B. You know that the equation of the topmost horizontal line is either $x + 3y = 6$ or $x + 2y = 6$ because those are the two remaining choices.

    An easy way to determine which graph of a line is right is by using the slope-intercept formula ($y = mx + b$) and plugging in what you know.

    From the graph, you can see that the y-intercept (the point where the line intercepts the y-axis) is 2 and that the slope (the rise over run) is equal to $-\frac{2}{6} = -\frac{1}{3}$. Plug these values into the appropriate places in the equation:

    $$y = -\tfrac{1}{3}x + 2$$

    To get rid of the fraction, multiply the terms on both sides of the equation by 3:

    $$3y = -x + 6$$

    Then manipulate the equation into standard form by adding x to both sides:

    $$x + 3y = 6$$

    The only equation that is NOT an equation of one of the boundary lines is answer E.

11. **C.** This problem tests your knowledge of prime numbers.

    Statement (1) doesn't give enough information to designate one value for the prime number p. It could be 5 (if n = 2), 17 (if n = 3), and so on. So p could be a variety of prime numbers. Statement (1) isn't sufficient, so eliminate A and D.

    Statement (2) doesn't allow for as many possibilities as the first statement does, but it doesn't narrow p to one value. If p were 2, p^2 would be 4, which is less than 26. Or p could equal 3, which would make p^2 = 9 and less than 26. And if p were 5, p^2 would be 25, which is less than 26. (Larger values for p wouldn't result in a value less than 26 for p^2.) Eliminate B and consider the two statements together.

    The two statements together narrow the field. The lowest value p can equal given the information in statement (1) is 5, which eliminates 2 and 3 as possibilities for p in statement (2). If $p^2 = n^2 + 1$ where n is greater than 1 and if $p^2 < 26$, p can only be 5. The two statements together are sufficient, and you can eliminate E. C is correct.

12. **E.** The key to this problem is noticing that it asks for how many *minutes* the travel takes, not *hours*. The distance formula is *rate* × *time* = *distance,* so *time* = *distance/rate.*

    Substitute the known values into the equation:

    $t = \frac{d}{r}$

    t = 140 miles/200 hours

    t = $\frac{7}{10}$ hours

    But the question asks for minutes, so you're not done. Multiply $\frac{7}{10}$ hours times 60 minutes/1 hour: $\frac{7}{10} \times \frac{60}{1} = \frac{420}{10}$, or 42 minutes.

13. **A.** To solve this problem, set up two equations with two unknowns: one for perimeter and one for area. Here's the perimeter equation:

    $2l + 2w = 40$

    And here's the area equation:

    $lw = 75$

    Solve the perimeter problem for l:

    $2l + 2w = 40$

    $l + w = 20$

    $l = 20 - w$

    Now substitute $20 - w$ for l in the area equation and solve for w:

    $lw = 75$

    $(20 - w)(w) = 75$

    $20w - w^2 = 75$

    $0 = w^2 - 20w + 75$

    Factor the quadratic expression:

    $0 = (w - 15)(w - 5)$

    Solve for w in each factor, which results in w = 15 and w = 5. Because the problem asks you for the length of the shorter side, you know the answer is 5 feet, or A.

14. **A.** Set up equations for the statements in this word problem to see whether they allow you to determine Dori's age.

    Statement (1) allows you to set up an equation with just one unknown (Dori's age now). If you let D = Dori's current age, the information in the first statement results in this equation:

    $D = 3(D - 6)$

You don't have to actually solve this equation to know that it's enough to give you Dori's age. Eliminate B, C, and E and look at the second statement.

Statement (2) allows you to set up an equation with two unknowns: $L = 2(D-10)$. Because you don't know Lauren's age, there's no way to solve the problem given just statement (2). Statement (2) isn't sufficient, so eliminate D. A is the correct answer.

15. **E.** The median is the middle value of a set of data points that are ordered from lowest to highest. So you're seeking information that allows you to put a through e in order and determine the middle value.

Statement (1) indicates the order of a, b, and c, but it doesn't tell you about their relationship to d and e. This statement isn't sufficient, so eliminate A and D.

Statement (2) indicates that c and d come before e, but you don't know whether c or d comes first, and the statement doesn't indicate their relationship to a or b. Statement (2) isn't sufficient, so B isn't right.

The two statements together get you close. They narrow the orders to either a, b, c, d, e or a, b, d, c, e. The orders you can't determine directly concern the median values, so the two statements together aren't sufficient. Eliminate C. Your answer is E.

16. **D.** Use the given equation to solve this problem. First, substitute 200 for p to see how many airlines tickets were sold:

$$t = 1,000 - 2p$$
$$t = 1,000 - 2(200)$$
$$t = 1,000 - 400$$
$$t = 600$$

Finally, multiply the 600 tickets by \$200 per ticket to get \$120,000.

17. **C.** The formula for arithmetic mean is

mean = (sum of the values) ÷ (number of values)

Let x equal the revenue of the fourth sale, set up an equation, and solve:

mean = (sum of the values) ÷ (number of values)
$$160 = (230 + 50 + 120 + x) \div 4$$
$$160(4) = 230 + 50 + 120 + x$$
$$640 = 400 + x$$
$$240 = x$$

18. **A.** Look for information that allows you to determine the value of at least one of the variables, because you already know that the sum of the variables is 27.

Statement (1) tells you that a and b are consecutive. If a and b are consecutive integers that add up to 27, one of them has to be 13 and the other 14. This statement provides you with values for both variables, so you can easily determine the product ab. Statement (1) is sufficient, and the answer is either A or D.

Statement (2) tells you that a and b are limited to only positive integers, which leaves open a number of possibilities for both variables (like 1 and 26, 2 and 25, 3 and 24, and so on). Statement (2) isn't sufficient, so eliminate D. The answer is A.

19. **B.** To solve this problem, you have to be able to say with certainty that the range is greater than 4.

range = largest value − smallest value

Statement (1) tells you nothing to help you determine the range. It tells you which variable is largest, but you don't know its value or the value of the lowest variable. Statement (1) isn't sufficient, so the answer isn't A or D.

Statement (2) tells you that the difference between two of the values, *d* and *a,* is more than 4. This is helpful because if any of the two numbers in the set have a difference of more than 4, the range, at the very least, has to be greater than 4. Statement (2) is sufficient, and you can eliminate C and E. Choose B.

20. **B.** Knowing that the two unlabeled angles in each triangle are supplementary (add up to 180 degrees) helps you solve for "*a* in terms of *b,*" as does knowing that the three angles of a triangle always add up to 180 degrees.

Solving for "*a* in terms of *b*" means that you find out what *a* equals without finding a definitive value for *b*.

The value of the unlabeled angle in the left triangle is equal to $180 - 60 - a$, or $120 - a$. The value of the unlabeled angle in the right triangle is $180 - 26 - b$, or $154 - b$. Set up an equation that adds the two values to equal 180 and solve for "*a* in terms of *b*":

$$(120 - a) + (154 - b) = 180$$
$$274 - a - b = 180$$
$$94 - a - b = 0$$
$$94 - b = a$$

21. **D.** To calculate how many $1\frac{3}{4}$ pieces can be cut from four 12-foot long wood pieces, divide 12 by $1\frac{3}{4}$ — ignoring the remainder (scrap wood) — and then multiply by 4. Start by converting $1\frac{3}{4}$ to $\frac{7}{4}$ and solve:

$$\frac{12}{\frac{7}{4}} = 12 \times \frac{4}{7} = \frac{48}{7} = 6\frac{3}{4}$$

Ignore the ¾ remainder. You can get 6 pieces from one length of wood. Because there are 4 lengths of wood, multiply 6 and 4 to get 24.

22. **B.** This data sufficiency problem concerns percentages. The problem tells you that $b > 1.2a$, and it asks you to determine whether *b* is greater than 70. So you have to find out something about the value of *a*.

Statement (1) tells you that there's a difference of 20 between *a* and *b*. Being told that $b - a = 20$ and that $b > 1.2a$ doesn't provide conclusive data to state that $b > 70$. For example, $a = 10$ and $b = 30$ satisfies both conditions but doesn't result in $b > 70$; $a = 60$ and $b = 80$ satisfies both conditions and does result in $b > 70$. Statement (1) isn't sufficient to answer the question, so the answer is B, C, or E.

Statement (2) tells you that $a > 70$. If *a* is greater than 70, then *b* is greater than 120 percent of 70 (which, of course, is greater than 70). So given statement (2), *b* is greater than 70. Statement (2) is sufficient; eliminate C and E. Your answer is B.

23. **C.** To solve this problem, you need to know the rates for each of the two hoses.

Statement (1) tells you only the rate of hose A and therefore isn't sufficient. Eliminate A and D.

Likewise, statement (2) gives you only the rate of hose B and isn't sufficient. B can't be right.

But if you know the rate of hose A from statement (1) and the rate of hose B from statement (2), you can assume that you can figure out how long the two hoses will take to fill the pool together from the information in both statements. Eliminate E. C is the correct answer.

Don't take the time during the test to solve the problem, but here's how you would do it if you had to:

If A takes 24 hours to fill the pool, then A fills ¼₄ of the pool every hour. If B takes 30 hours to fill the pool, then B fills ⅟₃₀ of the pool every hour. Together, the two hoses fill ¾₀ of the pool every hour: ¼₄ + ⅟₃₀ = ⁹⁄₁₂₀ = ¾₀. The last step is to set up an equation to solve for *t*:

¾₀ × *t* = 1 (1 equals the total job)

t = 1 ÷ ¾₀

t = 1 × ⁴⁰⁄₃

t = 13⅓ hours

24. **D.** If you know *n*, you can solve for the price per laptop. When you let *p* = the price of each laptop computer, you know from the problem that *np* = 13,000.

Statement (1) allows you to set up two equations with two unknowns to solve for *n*. You already know that *np* = 13,000. With this statement, you also know this:

$$n(p - 3) = 13{,}000 - (13{,}000 \times 0.04)$$

When you have two equations with two unknowns, you can solve for either variable. In this case, when you multiply out the equation from the first statement, you get a value for *np*. Then you can substitute 13,000 for *np* and solve for *n*. Statement (1) is sufficient, and the answer is either A or D.

Statement (2) also allows you to set up two equations with two unknowns to solve for *n*:

$$np = 13{,}000$$

$$n(p + 2) = 13{,}000 + 400$$

Again, when you multiply out the second equation, you end up with a value for *np*. When you substitute 13,000 for *np*, you can solve for *n*. Statement (2) is also sufficient, so you can eliminate A. Your answer is D.

25. **E.** Read the question carefully. It asks you to figure the cost *per pound* of the mixture. To calculate per pound, you have to eventually divide the cost by the number of pounds.

Set up an equation to determine the cost of the total mixture. The cost of the mixture is 3*x* (total cost of dried cherries) + 4*y* (total cost of dried apples).

The total number of pounds is 7 (3 pounds cherries + 4 pounds apples). So the final equation is the cost divided by number of pounds: $\dfrac{3x + 4y}{7}$.

26. **A.** This problem is simply a matter of long division. After you determine that 125 goes into 240 only one time, you can eliminate D and E because they both begin with 2 instead of 1. You know the next digit is 9 because all remaining answer choices begin with 0.19. When you multiply 125 by 9, you get 1,125. 1,150 − 1,125 is 25. Add a zero to the end to get 250. 125 goes into 250 twice, so you know the answer is 0.192.

27. **B.** You have to know something about the values of *x* and *y* to solve this problem.

Statement (1) tells you what *a* equals, but you don't know anything about *x* or *y*. The most you can come up with is this: $\left(\dfrac{2^x}{2^y}\right)^3$. Because you can't solve this equation, statement (1) is insufficient, and A and D are out.

Statement (2) gives you information about *x* and *y*. Because *x* and *y* equal each other, you can rewrite the expression like this: $\left(\dfrac{a^x}{a^x}\right)^3$. The expression in parentheses equals 1, and 1^3 = 1. You can solve the equation given statement (2), so C and E are wrong. The answer is B.

28. **A.** To determine the number of 360-degree rotations (once around) that Tashi's wheel turned in the 50 meters, you have to know the circumference of the circle in meters. Then you can divide 50 by the circumference to arrive at your answer. To determine the circumference, you need to know the radius, because $C = 2\pi r$.

    The diameter is double the radius, so statement (1) gives you enough information to determine the radius and solve the problem. The first statement is sufficient, so the answer is either A or D.

    The initial question provides no information on total time, so the number of rotations per minute doesn't help solve the problem. Statement (2) is insufficient, so the answer can't be D. Choose A.

29. **C.** To solve this problem, you need to know the mean and median of the set of numbers. Find the mean by applying the formula:

    mean = (sum of values)/(number of values)

    $^{30}\!/_6 = 5$

    The median is the middle value for an odd number of values and the arithmetic mean of the two middle values for an even number of values.

    Order the values in the set from lowest to highest: 0, 1, 3, 4, 10, 12.

    Find the two middle values: 3 and 4.

    Find their mean to get the median: (3 + 4)/2 = 3.5

    After you know the mean and median, subtract them to get the final answer: 5 − 3.5 = 1.5. C is correct.

30. **E.** If this year's earnings are projected to be 125 percent greater than last year's earnings, and last year's earnings were 10 million, this year's earnings will be an additional 10 million and then some. Multiply last year's 10 million by 125 percent, or 1.25:

    10 million × 1.25 = 12.5 million

    Add 12.5 million to 10 million to get 22.5 million. Your answer is E.

31. **C.** The only information this problem gives you is that x, y, and z are real numbers, which means that they could be just about any value you think of as a number.

    Knowing that x, y, and z have an average mean of 8 doesn't help you at all to determine what x equals. You'd have to know the value of at least two of the values to make a determination about the value of one of the others. Statement (1) alone doesn't give you enough information to answer the question, so eliminate A and D.

    Statement (2) just tells you that y and z are opposites, and this information alone doesn't help you to conclude that $x = 24$. You can eliminate B, but check out the two statements together: The second one gives you the information you need to solve for x in the first one.

    If the mean of x, y, and z is 8, the sum of the three variables must be 24 (24 ÷ 3 = 8). If y and z are opposites, their values cancel each other out when you add them together. So x must be 24. Eliminate E. The correct response is C.

32. **A.** This data sufficiency problem deals with an inequality. You're trying to figure out whether $a > b$.

    Statement (1) tells you that $a - 1$ and $b + 1$ are consecutive positive integers, which means that in all instances a is bigger than b. Try some substitution to check this out. If a is −1 or 0, $a - 1$ would be negative, so a can't be −1 or 0. If a is 1, $a - 1$ would be 0. 0 is neither negative nor positive, so you can't say it's a positive integer. So a must be 2 or greater. If a is 2, $a - 1$ would be 1. For $b + 1$ to be a positive consecutive integer, b would have to be 0 (0 + 1 = 1), which is less than a (2). Try another. If a is 23, $a - 1$ would be 22. So b would have to be either 20 (20 + 1 = 21) or 22 (22 + 1 = 23). 23 is greater than both 20 and 22, so a is greater than b. Statement (1) is sufficient, and the answer is either A or D.

Whether b is odd or even has no bearing on whether it's less than or greater than a, so statement (2) isn't sufficient. You can eliminate D. A is correct.

33. **D.** You don't need to calculate each ratio to answer this question. Glance through the figures for recycled waste and eliminate any families that recycle less than 50 percent of what they throw away.

    The only family with a value for recycled material that is more than half of its value for tossed material is Family D (30 is more than half of 55).

34. **B.** Quickly try each answer choice at a time to see which satisfies the requirements of the problem — except don't bother trying A (18) because it's already more than 12. Try B, which is 9. It goes into 12 once, with 3 left over, and 9 – 6 = 3. You don't need to look any further.

35. **B.** The small ticks are placed at $\frac{1}{5}$, $\frac{2}{5}$, $\frac{3}{5}$, and $\frac{4}{5}$. The large ticks are placed at $\frac{1}{4}$, $\frac{2}{4}$, and $\frac{3}{4}$. The least common denominator for all ticks is 20, so the tick marks in ascending order are placed at $\frac{4}{20}$, $\frac{5}{20}$, $\frac{8}{20}$, $\frac{10}{20}$, $\frac{12}{20}$, $\frac{15}{20}$, and $\frac{16}{20}$. The least distance between tick marks on this number line is $\frac{1}{20}$.

36. **D.** Recognize that the two triangles in the figure are both special right triangles. One is a 45:45:90 right triangle with sides in the ratio $1:1:\sqrt{2}$ and one is a 30:60:90 with sides in the ratio $1:\sqrt{3}:2$. Also, recognize that their hypotenuses, AB and CD, are equal because they represent the same steel girder. Given these valuable tidbits of information, all you need is the length of one side of one of the triangles to discover all sides of both triangles. When you know the length of one side, you can solve for the length of its hypotenuse, which is the same length as the hypotenuse of the other triangle. Then you solve for the other side lengths and find the requested difference between AE and DE.

    Statement (1) gives you the length of AB, so you can solve for AE. Plus, the length of AB is also the length of CD, because they represent the same girder. You can use the length of CD to solve for DE and then find the difference between AE and DE. Statement (1) is sufficient to answer the question, so the answer is either A or D.

    Statement (2) gives you the same valuable information as statement (1). You know the length of DE, so you can solve for CD. You know the length of CD is the same as the length of AB, so you can use that information to solve for AE. Then you can find the difference between AE and DE. Statement (2) is also sufficient, so the answer can't be A. Choose D.

37. **A.** Here's your final data sufficiency question (and final math question overall!).

    Convert the original equation into something that looks more like the equation in statement (1). Start by finding a common denominator:

$$\frac{2}{x} + \frac{2}{y} = 8$$

$$\frac{2y}{xy} + \frac{2x}{xy} = \frac{8xy}{xy}$$

$$2y + 2x = 8xy$$

$$x + y = 4xy$$

Because the equation in statement (1) looks exactly like this one, statement (1) is sufficient to determine that $\frac{2}{x} + \frac{2}{y} = 8$. The answer is either A or D.

Statement (2) says that $x = y$, but without knowing their actual values, like $x = y = 1$ or $x = y = 2$, you can't determine whether $\frac{2}{x} + \frac{2}{y} = 8$ is true. For example $x = y = \frac{1}{2}$ would make it true, but $x = y = 1$ would not. Statement (2) isn't sufficient. Eliminate D. Your answer is A.

Explanatory Answers to Verbal Questions

1. **C.** Questions 1 and 2 are based on a discussion between Steve and Justine concerning electronic music devices. Question 1 asks you to identify the underlying assumption of Justine's conclusion that Steve's company is trying to create an unfair advantage and force customers to purchase electronic devices made by Steve's company.

   You can eliminate choice A because it goes way beyond the scope of the argument. Just because she doesn't address the issue of copyrights doesn't mean she thinks they're no longer necessary. The argument doesn't mention the quality of Steve's device, so B isn't pertinent. Choice D isn't relevant to the argument; Justine's statement about CDs isn't meant to imply that CDs are obsolete. And E can't be an assumption because it's specifically stated in the passage. Choice C must be the correct choice. Justine's argument that Steve's company has an unfair advantage relies on the assumption that Steve's company is the only one that offers popular download software and that other manufacturers don't have popular software of their own.

2. **B.** This question asks you to weaken Steve's cause-and-effect argument that his company's specific software is necessary to protect the right of musicians. Find an answer that shows that other ways to prevent copying exist.

   The presence of an exception to an otherwise general premise doesn't refute the argument, so you can eliminate E.

   Choice C doesn't directly relate to Steve's conclusion because his argument is based on the need for copyright protection, not the absence or presence of customer loyalty. Choices A and D actually seem to strengthen Steve's conclusion. Choice A provides a legal reason for the company to have to include strict copyright protection. Choice D indicates that the copyright protections are in place on Steve's company's devices. Choice B is the correct answer, because if another type of protection could be used that also allows for competition, Steve's argument that limiting competition is necessary for copyright protection is questionable.

3. **A.** Questions 3 through 7 deal with a *fascinating* science passage that describes the impacts of light energy on turfgrass. This somewhat difficult passage contains some technical concepts and several challenging scientific terms. Even if you didn't comprehend the entire passage on the first reading, you should've been able to discern what the passage was generally about. The first paragraph discusses general plant injury resulting from an excess of light energy and ends with a specific application to turfgrass. The second paragraph compares and contrasts the photosynthesis rates in warm-season and cool-season grasses. And the third passage goes on to more specifically describe how light duration affects photosynthesis.

   The first question asks you to identify the author's primary concern in writing the passage. This question type extends the main idea to relate to why the author wrote the passage. As is typical for science passages, the author is mainly concerned with putting out some information, not advancing a position, so you can eliminate B right off the bat just based on its first word, *arguing*. The author doesn't argue for anything in this passage.

   You know that the passage is discussing light energy, photosynthesis, and turfgrass. On closer inspection, you'll find that the author is primarily concerned with educating people so that they know the difference between warm-season and cool-season turfgrass and so that they understand the factors that damage grass. Choices C, D, and E deal with specific parts of the passage but not the passage as a whole. Neither C nor E deals with light energy (and the passage doesn't mention anything about the research being recent), and D neglects photosynthesis. The only answer that encompasses all these ideas is A.

4. **D.** When a GMAT reading question asks you to define vocabulary, determine the definition from the context of the passage rather than from your prior knowledge about the word.

Going with a definition of the word that you already knew probably wasn't a big issue in this question, because *senesce* isn't a word that normally graces everyday conversation. Read the sentence that contains the word and the surrounding ideas. The passage talks about senesce occurring in plants that are exposed to light below the light compensation point. This means that the grass isn't getting enough light to carry on the photosynthesis necessary to simply sustain the current height. This indicates that the definition of *senesce* is "to wither" or "to shrink." Go through the answer choices and find the one that best matches your definition.

Eliminate A and B because the passage indicates that in senesce no growth occurs, fast or slow. Neither C nor E has anything to do with shrinking or withering. Choice D is the best answer because it's the only one that conveys the idea of withering.

5. **B.** This specific-information question asks you to identify an important difference between cool-season and warm-season grasses. The second paragraph discusses the two kinds of turfgrasses. Warm-season grasses do better in the summer because they can withstand higher light intensities. Cool-season grasses don't die back as much in the winter because they can survive on a lower amount of light energy. Eliminate C because the passage says that all plants that photosynthesize do so during the day. Choice D is also incorrect because the third paragraph indicates that all green plants use the same light levels. Choice E isn't right because the first paragraph suggests that both cool-season and warm-season grasses are harmed by excess light levels. That leaves you with A and B. Both address the important difference in light level tolerance between the two types of grasses, but A states that cool-season grasses can withstand higher light intensities, and the opposite is true. Choice B is the answer that properly states the actual difference between the two grasses.

6. **E.** The question asks you to make an inference regarding the discussion of oxidative damage. In the first paragraph, you find out that oxidative damage occurs not only because of high light intensity but also because more light energy arrives than photosynthesis can use. Anything that hinders photosynthesis can contribute to oxidative damage.

Choose an answer that you can logically deduce from the information in the passage without making wild assumptions.

Choice A is incorrect because light intensity is greatest at noon, not at sunrise and sunset. And because overwatering can impede photosynthesis and damage grass, B is out. Eliminate C because oxidative damage results from the formation of free radicals, not carbon fixation. Choice D is wrong because light intensity alone doesn't damage grass; temperature change, drought, and excessive water can also inhibit photosynthesis. Because the passage lists these preventable impediments to photosynthesis, you can logically reason that homeowners can do something to prevent oxidative damage to their lawns (like watering them), which makes E the best answer.

7. **A.** To answer this exception question, simply return to the text and eliminate the answer choices that fit the description. In this case, eliminate the choices that are mentioned in the passage as being true of photosynthesis. You can locate the information in B and C in the third paragraph, so eliminate them. Choice D comes from the first paragraph, and E from the second paragraph, so eliminate those choices as well. You're left with A, which isn't found in the passage and actually contradicts information in the passage.

8. **D.** This question concerns the reported discovery of ivory-billed woodpeckers in Arkansas. The argument is most like an analogy. Because the sighted birds have large white patches on their wings and ivory-billed woodpeckers have large white patches, the sighted birds are ivory-billed woodpeckers. Skeptics weakened the analogy by stating that an abnormal pileated woodpecker may also have the distinctive white patches. You're asked to strengthen the skeptic's conclusion, so you want an answer choice that strengthens the comparison between the pileated woodpecker and the sighted birds.

Choice C seems to weaken the conclusion rather than strengthen it, and the skeptics don't have an issue with the credentials of those who confirmed the identification. So C is wrong.

Choices B and E each weaken the conclusion. Choice B indicates that researchers heard the audio sign of the ivory-billed, the distinctive double-tap, and E indicates that the wing beats on the video are indicative of the ivory-billed rather than the pileated. You're left with choices A and D. You can eliminate A because Louisiana borders Arkansas and the fact that an ivory-billed was last seen in Louisiana doesn't mean one couldn't be in Arkansas. Choice D is the best answer. If the only one of the five fieldmarks seen also happens to be the only one that's a feature of an abnormal pileated, this would support the skeptic's conclusion that the bird is probably an abnormal pileated woodpecker.

9. **A.** This question involves a concept plan from the professional tennis tour. You're asked to strengthen the conclusion that adding some reality TV elements to tennis will also add viewers.

Your job is not to determine whether the information in the answer choices is true. You're to assume that each answer choice contains true information and to evaluate the ability of each to strengthen the conclusion based on that assumption.

You can eliminate D and E because they don't speak directly to the conclusion. The fact that tennis stars think they can use the exposure to further their careers doesn't mean additional viewers will watch the tour, and the simple fact that the summer and winter Olympics have used reality TV elements for years is meaningless without a discussion of the impact these elements have had on TV ratings. Choice C tends to question (or weaken) the effectiveness of the plan. If any information fans want is already available on the Internet, they may not be interested in the extra interviews. Choice B clearly weakens the conclusion. If the reality elements alienate current fans, ratings may actually decrease as a result. Choice A is the only choice that strengthens the specific conclusion of the argument.

10. **E.** You're asked to draw a conclusion from the premises. An appropriate conclusion covers all the information in the premises and doesn't include any outside information. The argument isn't about the expansion of the region but rather its sinking, so A isn't right. Choice C addresses the compression of the Earth's crust, while the passage says that *expansion* causes the region to sink, so C can't be a conclusion. There isn't enough information in the paragraph to draw the conclusion in D. It says Phoenix is low but still states that its elevation is 1,100 feet, which is more than 1,000 feet above sea level. Choices B and E come up with opposite conclusions, but the one that's supported by the passage is E, so eliminate B. Passage E implies that the sinking will continue in the southern area and that sinking makes the climate drier; therefore, you can conclude from the premises that the southern area will continue to get drier.

11. **C.** The problem with this sentence is that it's a comma splice. The clauses on both sides of the comma are independent, so you can't join them with just a comma. To correct the problem, either change the punctuation or make one clause subordinate to (or dependent on) the other.

The sentence also contains an idiomatically incorrect construction, *hurry and get.* Find an answer choice that corrects both errors without creating any new problems. Because the sentence contains an error, you can immediately eliminate A. Choices B and E both fail to correct the run-on sentence problem. They still join two independent clauses with a comma. Get rid of them. Choice D corrects the run-on sentence problem but doesn't change *hurry and get* to the more proper *hurry to get.* Choice C corrects both errors, so it's the best choice.

12. **C.** The underlined portion of this sentence contains an error in subject-verb agreement. The noun is plural, *theater operators,* but the verb is singular, *has refused.* There are no other errors, so choose the answer choice that makes the verb plural without creating other errors. Because the sentence contains a mistake, eliminate A. Choice E fails to fix the subject-verb agreement error. Choice B fixes the verb problem but creates a new error by dropping *but* and creating an independent clause and therefore a run-on sentence. Choice D fixes the error but changes the clause to passive voice, which changes the meaning of sentence. Choice C is the only answer that simply fixes the error without creating any new errors.

13. **A.** The underlined portion doesn't appear to have any errors. Choice A may be the right choice, but you should quickly look at the other choices just to be sure they don't reveal an error you didn't catch. Choice B creates a new error in subject-verb agreement. Choices C and D are needlessly wordy. Choice E adds a redundant clause. The sentence is indeed correct as written.

14. **B.** This sentence contains a beginning phrase, which is your clue that the sentence may have a modifier problem. The way the sentence is written, Americans are cautioning against taking high doses of vitamins, but the real cautioners are the nutritionists.

REMEMBER

A beginning phrase always refers to the subject of the sentence, so make sure the reference is appropriate.

Find an answer choice that conveys that the nutritionists are the ones doing the cautioning. Choice C maintains the same construction as A, so you can eliminate both of these choices. Choice E changes the beginning phrase, but it doesn't correct the problem of the phrase's modifying *Americans* rather than *nutritionists*. Eliminate E. That leaves B and D. Both change the structure of the sentence so that the nutritionists are the ones doing the cautioning, but D is redundant because it uses two verbs (caution and warn) to convey the same message. And it changes *high doses* to the wordier phrase *that are too high* and moves the phrase farther away from the noun *(doses)* that it refers to. Choice B is the only option that corrects the initial modifier problem without creating a new error.

15. **D.** This business passage deals with the fact that nonprofit organizations aren't "noncompetition organizations" and promotes public relations as a way of allowing nonprofits to stand out in the crowd.

As usual, the first question asks you for the main idea of the passage. As you were reading the passage, you probably noted that the passage emphasized the need for effective public relations to help a nonprofit overcome the competition. The main idea statement should convey this information.

Choice A directly opposes the message of the passage, so you can eliminate it. And the passage doesn't go into specific detail about what types of money-raising methods are ineffective, so E doesn't convey the main idea. Choice B at least states information that is included in the passage, but it conveys only a part of the message (the topic of the third paragraph) and not the overall idea. Choice C also focuses on just one small portion of the passage, the idea found in the second paragraph. Choice D encompasses all the information covered in the passage and conveys the author's emphasis on the need for public relations.

16. **E.** This question asks you to make an inference based on a particular sentence in the passage. The sentence states that people who work in nonprofits don't really see themselves as being in competition. The correct answer extends this reasoning to its logical implication. You can eliminate A. It's too much of a leap of logic to say that nonprofit workers think of nonprofit competition as more cutthroat than competition in for-profit ventures. To make the inference in B, you have to go beyond the information that the passage states or implies. And whether nonprofit workers think the pot of donor dollars is bottomless is irrelevant to what they think about the level of competition. The author of the passage makes a case for using public relations to promote nonprofits, so C doesn't make sense. Choice D may be possible, but the passage doesn't mention any difference in the way workers view competition with sister organizations as opposed to competition with unrelated nonprofits. D also seems to imply that nonprofits know they're competing with their sister organizations even while working for the same cause. Choice E is the best answer. It's logical to say that nonprofits don't think about competition because they're doing good work and aren't trying to make a profit like businesses.

17. **B.** Look through the passage to find each of the choices for this exception question. Cross a choice off when you find it in the passage. The list of nonprofits is in the last paragraph. There you find A, medical research in the Amazon; C, symphony orchestra; D, protecting whales in the Pacific; and E, local library. Only B, food banks, isn't found in the passage. Although food banks are fine nonprofit organizations, they aren't part of the text.

18. **A.** This specific-information question requires you to refer to the passage to look for a way that public relations efforts can help an organization stand out from the crowd. You're given the word *obvious* in quotation marks, so scanning the passage for the word *obvious* or the phrase *stand out from the crowd* may save you time. You find *obvious* in the next-to-last sentence of the passage. You also find *stand out from the background noise.* According to the passage, making a personal connection is what helps your organization stand out. Choice A mentions a personal connection and is probably the right answer. The passage mentions beating the competition but not in direct association with a way to make the organization stand out in a crowd, so D isn't as good an answer as A. The passage makes no case for B or C, and E sounds warm and fuzzy, but focusing on donors with natural affinities to the organization isn't addressed in the passage.

19. **C.** The underlined portion of this sentence has an error in diction. The idiomatically correct phrasing is "the more . . . , the more. . . ." This sentence doesn't complete the thought, so you can eliminate A. Choice B seems to correct the error with a better word, *as,* but introduces a new error, because without *because,* the second clause becomes independent, creating a run-on sentence. Choice D moves *as* to the end of the phrase, which makes the sentence logically unsound. Choice E introduces a problem with subject-verb agreement when it pairs the plural noun *abilities* with the singular verb *declines.* Choice (C) corrects the phrasing and doesn't create new errors.

20. **D.** The pronoun *that* is used to begin a restrictive clause and doesn't need a comma before it. Because the comma isn't part of the underlined portion, you have to replace *that* with *who,* which is the pronoun used when discussing people. Eliminate A. Choice B doesn't fix the error because the comma improperly separates the subject, *family,* from its verb, *was.* Choice C doesn't change *that* and therefore retains the original error. Choice E solves the original problem but includes a needlessly wordy and redundant clause. Choice D corrects the error by replacing *that* with *who* and doesn't cause any additional errors.

21. **B.** This sentence contains a pronoun-reference error. The singular pronoun *its* seems to refer to the college, but the pronoun should refer to *alumni* (which is plural). A third-person plural pronoun is needed in this circumstance. As usual when the sentence has an error, eliminate A. Choice E doesn't fix the error and creates an additional error by using an improper form of the possessive *whose.* Choice D corrects the error but unnecessarily includes *each* in the nonrestrictive clause. Choice C corrects the error but creates a new problem by removing the possessive form from *alma maters.* Choice B is the correct answer because it corrects the pronoun error and doesn't create any new errors.

22. **A.** This sentence doesn't appear to need correcting. The underlined portion has no obvious errors and works well with the rest of the sentence. Choice A is probably the correct answer, but check the other answers to be sure. Choice B is wrong because the proper conjunction for this sentence is *and* rather than *but.* The second part of the sentence doesn't contrast the first. Choice C eliminates the conjunction altogether and makes it sound as though the Yucatan Peninsula is doing the concluding. Choice D seems like a reasonable alternative. However, the change in verb form creates an error. The proper verb form is the past perfect *to have killed.* This shows that the meteor's arrival took place before the scientists' discovery of the evidence. Choice E introduces a verb error with *concludes.* The subject *scientists* is plural, while the verb *concludes* is singular. The verb also needs to be past tense (or past perfect tense) to fit with the other verbs in the sentence. The answer is A.

23. **E.** This sentence correction question features another pronoun error. Because the U.S. Forest Service is a singular entity, the correct form of the first pronoun in the underlined portion is *it* instead of *they.* Choice A is not the correct answer. Choice B corrects the error but creates a problem with subject-verb agreement (the verb should be *sells* rather than *sell*). Choice C also creates a new error when it changes *these* to *this.* Choice D doesn't use a conjunction with the comma to join the two independent clauses, which makes the sentence a comma splice. Choice E corrects the pronoun reference without making new errors.

24. **D.** This critical-reasoning question provides reasons for the choosing of Irish boys' names. The argument explains that many "Irish" names were actually imposed on the Irish by Anglo-Norman invaders. The question asks you to make an inference based on the argument.

You usually make inferences based on one of the premises rather than the conclusion, and inferences aren't explicitly stated in the argument.

Choice A just reiterates information that the author states directly, so it can't be an inference. Choice C also mentions a fact that is stated directly in the premises. Choices B and E have the opposite problem; their information isn't stated in the premises, but you also don't have enough information to infer them from the premises. Concluding that Irish parents prefer the most traditional name available is too far-fetched, as is concluding that the author is actually bitter about the introduction of non-Irish names to Ireland. The only answer choice that works is D. If the author of the argument speaks of traditional names as those that were Irish before the 12th century, the author must think that Seamus, Sean, and Patrick are not traditional names.

25. **A.** Questions 25 and 26 are based on a discussion between Linda and Jane that takes place over a cup of coffee. But the discussion is over the cup more than the coffee. Linda reminds Jane that her foam plastic cup will outlast both of them, and Jane responds with some impressive scientific discoveries. In the first question of the two, you're required to provide Linda with a response that will weaken Jane's conclusion that it's just as environmentally friendly to use the foam plastic cup now that bacteria will dispose of it for her. You're looking for a response that acknowledges the science that Jane is quoting but also reasserts the eco-superiority of the reusable mug.

You can eliminate choice B. It's nice that coffee shops are trying to use less foam plastic, but it doesn't apply to Jane's conclusion that bacteria can eat her cup. Choice C names another nice feature of the reusable mug (better insulation). But the cup's insulation abilities don't address whether it's environmentally friendly. Choice D is irrelevant to the argument because it points out an environmental problem that applies to the way coffee is grown, not to the material in the cup that's used to drink coffee. Choice E states a financial advantage of a reusable mug, but it has no bearing on the eco-friendly argument. Choice A is the correct answer; if the foam cup uses up energy in the recycling process, the foam cup has more of a negative impact on the environment than the reusable mug.

26. **C.** The second question involving Linda and Jane asks you to identify the assumption that Jane relies on when she talks about not feeling guilty for using a foam plastic cup in the future. The assumption that you're looking for is something that isn't stated but that is required to help Jane reach her conclusion. Choice A is specifically stated in the premises and can't be an assumption. Whether the recycling takes place in America is an economic question and is not related specifically to guilt over environmental concerns, but B is a reasonable choice if you don't find anything better. You can eliminate D because how Linda feels about forgetting her shopping bag isn't relevant to Jane's guilt over her foam plastic cup. If you choose E, you're saying that Jane assumes there won't be any more advances in materials technology; however, if further advances do reduce the impact of a disposable cup, Jane would feel even less guilt. Choice C is the best answer because Jane's guilt would be alleviated by the recycling of her disposable cup, and for that to happen, the foam plastic-eating bacteria solution has to spread at least to her own town.

27. **B.** The question asks you to weaken the conclusion that everyone would buy more efficient keyboards if they were available. To weaken this conclusion, you need to choose an answer that gives a reason that people wouldn't want the more efficient keyboard. Choice C neither strengthens nor weakens the argument. It may take a lot of testing to develop the new keyboard, but that doesn't prove that people won't want it. Choice E is similarly off base. There may be more keys on the computer keyboard, but that doesn't mean the keyboards can't be arranged efficiently and that people wouldn't want to use the resulting efficient arrangement. Choice A actually strengthens the conclusion somewhat by arguing that the justification for the QWERTY keyboard no longer exists, so it's not the right answer. Choice D

moderately weakens the conclusion by implying that the human brain is capable of adapting to the QWERTY keyboard, but check B to see whether it's better. Choice B provides the strongest rebuttal to the notion that everyone will want the new keyboard. If people have used the QWERTY system for their entire lives, they aren't likely to want to learn a whole new keyboard arrangement and therefore won't buy the new keyboards.

28. **E.** This humanities passage gives you a little history about Plato, the ancient Greek philosopher. As usual, the first question is a main idea question. You may say that this particular question asks you to pick out the primary purpose of the passage on Plato (a little alliteration to clear the air!). To find the primary purpose, simply identify the main idea and then use clues in the writing to figure out why the author wrote the passage. In this case, the author's style is didactic, so his general purpose is to inform rather than to argue a point.

Each of the answer choices mentions something that's included in the passage, but choices A, B, C, and D focus on subtopics and not the main idea. Choice A also doesn't work because the author doesn't talk about an interpretation of Plato's early works. Choice B provides more-accurate information but focuses on only the last paragraph of the passage. Choice C isn't accurate because the passage briefly questions the authenticity of tales of Plato's military exploits but doesn't go so far as to chronicle them. Choice D just focuses on a topic from the first paragraph. Therefore, E must be the best choice. The primary purpose of the passage is to describe Plato's early life.

29. **D.** This question focuses on a single phrase and asks you to infer its meaning in the passage. Earlier in the same sentence, the author mentions a lack of documentation for the information, which means that *the category of apocrypha* probably refers to something that isn't well supported by evidence. The answer choice that reflects that meaning is D.

30. **A.** This specific-information question asks about the impact that Plato's visit to Italy had on his later works. The Italian travels appear in the last paragraph, which emphasizes the importance of Plato's exposure to Pythagoreanism, including its influence on the *Republic*. Choice A mentions Pythagoreanism, so it's probably correct, but check the others just to be sure. The passage mentions the water clock in its description of Plato's travels to Egypt, not Italy, so B isn't right. There's nothing in the passage to suggest that Socrates' influence on Plato was stifling, so eliminate C. Choice D confuses earlier tales of military exploits with the confirmed trip to southern Italy, so it can't be right. Choice E is also wrong because Plato's military service was to have taken place earlier in Greece, not Italy. Stick with A.

31. **B.** Exception questions are easier to answer on the computerized test because the passage lines up side-by-side with the question.

Simply locate the titles of the works and eliminate them as you find them. In this case, the works are italicized, so this question should be quick and easy. Three works, *Laches, Protagoras,* and *Apology,* are in the first paragraph, and the *Republic* is listed in the last paragraph. That leaves the *Phaedo,* which is one of Plato's works but isn't listed in the passage.

32. **B.** This inference question doesn't point you to a specific part of the passage, so you have to work a bit harder than you did in the last question. The author mentions Spartan rule in the second paragraph, so concentrate your effort there. Eliminate any obviously wrong choices and then return to the passage as necessary. You can eliminate A, because the author questions whether Plato was involved in the war at all.

Don't answer questions based on what you know about a reading topic from other sources. Even though you may have learned in history class that Sparta was constantly at war and that Sparta controlled Athens when Socrates was executed, you can't use outside knowledge to answer a reading question.

The passage doesn't mention anything about Sparta's warring propensities or control of Athens, so eliminate E and D. Nor does the passage compare the philosophical education available in Athens to that available in Sparta, so choosing C isn't warranted. The only information you can infer is found in B. If Athens overthrew Sparta in 395 B.C.E., you can infer that Sparta controlled Athens at some point before that time.

33. **C.** You can eliminate answer choice A because the underlined portion of this sentence correction problem contains at least three errors:

   ✔ When only two possibilities exist, as in this case, you use *whether* rather than *if*.

   ✔ The second error concerns subject-verb agreement. The subject of the clause is *activity*, which is singular, so you need to use the singular verb *indicates* rather than the plural form, *indicate*.

   ✔ Because the volcanic activity is in the process of becoming active, saying *is becoming active* is better than saying *has become active*.

   Get rid of B because it uses *if* rather than *whether* and doesn't correct the verb form at the end of the sentence. The remaining choices solve the problem with subject/verb agreement and word choice, but D fails to correct the error in verb form. Choice C is the only answer to correct all errors.

34. **E.** This sentence construction literally states that "jack-jumpers" kill more people than the total number of people. What it means to say is that the ants kill more people than other creatures do. Eliminate A. Eliminate B because it's just as poorly constructed as A. Choice C makes it sound like the number of people killed by ants is greater than the number of snakes, spiders, and other creatures killed by ants, and that isn't what the original sentence means. Choice D still says that the ants kill more people than people do. Choice E is the best answer because it clarifies the comparison.

35. **C.** This sentence correction question underlines the entire dependent clause. The sentence may at first appear to have no errors. However, when you glance through the possibilities, you notice that some of the options begin the clause with *whereas,* which is a better word choice for the context of this sentence. *While* usually means *at the same time* and shouldn't be used to convey the idea of *although* or *but*. So A is incorrect. Choices B and E maintain the use of *while,* so you can eliminate both of them. This leaves you with C and D. Choice D corrects the word choice issues but substitutes the words *on the basis of time* for the clearer *of time* and moves the phrase farther away from the noun it modifies. Choose C over D.

36. **C.** This sentence has a problem with parallelism. The verb *hosts* relates to the first two elements in the list (hosts a musical concert and hosts a family ski race), but the third element interjects a new verb phrase *(puts together)*. To promote parallel structure, *hosts* has to go with all three elements or each element needs its own verb. You know you can get rid of A. Neither D nor E fixes the parallelism issue, so you can eliminate them. Choice D initiates the second element with a verb but not the third element. Choice E introduces a subject *(it)* into the third element of the list, which makes it a clause instead of a phrase like the other elements. Choice B fixes the parallelism error by initiating each element with a verb, but *organized* is past tense and the other two verbs are present tense, so B isn't right. Choice C fixes the problem with parallelism by allowing *hosts* to introduce each of the phrases in the list, so it's the best answer.

37. **D.** This critical-reasoning question discusses the fact that no snakes live on the island nation of New Zealand. It asks you to strengthen the conclusion that the inability of snakes to swim is responsible for their absence. To strengthen the cause-and-effect argument, find an answer that promotes the lack of swimming as the primary cause of a lack of snakes. Choice A doesn't address the snake-swimming issue, so it doesn't strengthen the argument. There isn't a question of whether snakes exist in the areas around New Zealand. Choice B helps explain why snakes haven't been accidentally introduced in New Zealand but doesn't say anything about why they weren't on the island in the first place. Choice C discusses sea snakes, which are different from the land snakes the paragraph concerns, so their characteristics aren't applicable to the author's conclusion. Choice E weakens the conclusion; if snakes appear on other islands, they must have gotten there somehow, regardless of whether they could swim. Choice D is best answer of the five choices, because if snakes are absent from other large islands, the reason would seem to be that they can't swim.

Don't allow your knowledge that snakes exist on islands like Hawaii to stop you from choosing D. Remember that you're supposed to assume the answer choices are true regardless of whether you know otherwise.

38. **B.** This critical-reasoning question requires you to weaken the conclusion that the quoted price for travel fees isn't the final price. In order to weaken this conclusion, you should find an area of travel that doesn't include hidden fees. Choices A and E point out that hidden fees exist (and may be higher) in other industries, but comparing travel fees to fees in other industries doesn't weaken the conclusion that the travel industry hides fees that aren't quoted. Choice D actually shows an instance in the travel industry where the final price isn't the quoted price, so it can't be right. Choice C points out the fact that some final prices are actually lower that the quoted price, but the final price is still different from the quoted price, so C actually strengthens the argument. Choice B points out one instance in the travel industry in which the final price is the same as the advertised price. This finding weakens the conclusion that there isn't "one aspect of traveling where the quoted price is the final price." Choice B is the best answer of the five.

39. **E.** For this question, you need to identify the assumption underlying the conclusion. The argument concludes that the state should raise the income tax and lower the sales tax in order to be fairer to all of its citizens. Choice A can't be an assumption because its premise is actually stated in the argument. Because the argument doesn't discuss a flat tax, B can't be an assumption the author makes. Likewise, the argument isn't about encouraging citizens to save money, so C is irrelevant and not an assumption the author makes. You could choose D if the question asked you to make an inference, but it's asking for an assumption. Choice E is the best answer. In order for the sales tax to be truly regressive, it must tax necessities as well as luxuries. In making the argument that sales tax burdens the poor, the author must be assuming that sales tax applies to essential purchases. Otherwise, the sales tax would not apply to those who can afford only necessities.

40. **A.** The question asks for you to draw a conclusion from the premises discussing the devastation of coral reefs worldwide. The conclusion should tie together the premises rather than focus on a single premise. Choice B isn't supported by the premises; fish populations will certainly be affected by the loss of breeding habitats. Choice C is a restatement of one of the premises; dead coral is bleached white and devoid of life, so C can't be a conclusion. Choice D may be a true statement, but it doesn't conclude the argument that coral reefs are dying. Choice E is another true statement, but it doesn't bring together the author's premises. It is another premise to the argument. Choice A is the correct answer; the author argues that the reefs are dying worldwide, so they probably won't last long.

41. **A.** For this question, you need to choose the statement that's implied by one of the premises of the prescription-drug advertisement. Choice B may be something the manufacturer wants you to believe, but the ad doesn't compare Nocturna and other sleep aids, so this inference isn't warranted. Choice C is actually stated in the premises and therefore, by definition, isn't an implication. The creator of the prescription sleep aid doesn't choose to imply that a chemical like caffeine could be responsible for disrupting people's sleep, so D is out. Choice E may be a conclusion for the argument, but it's not an implication of a specific premise. It concerns people in general rather than just those who have trouble sleeping, so it's not a precise implication. Choice A is the best answer because the second sentence of the argument clearly implies that two of the causes for sleep problems are lack of exercise and an irregular sleep schedule; with this information, you can infer that exercise and a regular sleep schedule would enhance sleep.

Part VI
The Part of Tens

The 5th Wave   By Rich Tennant

Brad felt foolish letting a fly on the wall distract him from his GMAT.

In this part . . .

We give you quite a lot of information in the review chapters of this book. This part synthesizes some of that information into nice, neat lists. We provide you with ten question types that are easiest to master, ten errors to avoid in your analytical writing essays (and to look for in the sentence correction questions), and ten of the most important math formulas to remember for the test. Memorizing the information in these lists can get you ready for many of the GMAT questions you'll encounter.

Chapter 21

Ten Questions You've Got a Good Shot At

In This Chapter

▶ Revealing questions you've got a good chance to get right

▶ Taking advantage of the easier questions

With all that math, grammar, and logical reasoning, you could develop a headache just thinking about the GMAT. And it doesn't help that you have to pull off two essays in one hour! Why can't the GMAT cut you some slack? Well, it does . . . sort of. You see, certain GMAT questions may be a little easier for you than the others. You can answer these questions correctly with greater consistency and buy a little time to use on the tougher questions in each section.

Main Theme Reading Questions

In general, reading-comprehension questions are a little easier than critical-reasoning questions. For reading-comprehension questions, the answers are right there on the screen; you just need to find them. One reason main theme questions in particular are easier is that 90 percent of the passages present you with one. Identifying the main theme should become automatic, so you don't even have to refer back to a passage to answer a question. And usually three of the five answer choices are clearly off topic or too specific, so you only have to choose the best answer of the remaining two.

Specific-Information Reading Questions

Specific-information questions appear in every reading-comprehension passage, so you'll get used to them. You have a great shot at these questions because the computer highlights the text that contains the answer. Just read the highlighted part of the passage (and maybe the text around it) to find the right answer. As long as you stay focused, you should bat a thousand on these beauties!

Sentence Corrections

Although sentence correction questions may not seem easy at first, they become easier with practice. The GMAT tends to focus on the same sentence errors, so practice tests help you get familiar with the errors you need to know about. You'll notice the same kinds of errors appearing frequently, so you'll be able to give the right answers frequently, too.

Exception Questions for Reading Passages

Exception questions ask you to choose the answer that *isn't* stated in the passage. All you have to do is eliminate each answer choice that appears in the text. The choice left standing is the correct answer.

Strengthening or Weakening Critical Arguments

Strengthen-the-argument and weaken-the-argument critical-reasoning questions tend to rely on cause-and-effect relationships or analogies. If an author reaches a conclusion by cause and effect, you choose an answer that either shows other causes for the effect (to weaken the argument) or that emphasizes that there are no other causes for the effect (to strengthen the argument). To weaken analogy arguments, choose an answer that shows the compared entities are dissimilar. An answer that highlights similarities strengthens the argument.

Data Sufficiency Math Questions

Data sufficiency questions usually take less time to answer than problem-solving math questions. You don't have to actually solve the problem to answer the question correctly. Just follow the step-by-step process outlined in Chapter 15 to stay focused.

Math Problem Solving with Figures

One of the hardest parts of a problem-solving question is getting started. You may have trouble sifting through the information you get from word problems, but a figure presents known information clearly. Examine the information in the figure and solve the problem.

Math Problems Involving Basic Operations

Some problem-solving questions present you with an equation or a simple word problem involving arithmetic, exponents, or other basic operations. You've been applying these basics since childhood, so all you have to do is read carefully!

Substitution Math Problems

Problem-solving questions that ask you to substitute values for symbols can be simple after you understand what you're supposed to do. In most cases, you just need to exchange a value for a symbol in an otherwise simple equation.

Interpreting Graphs and Charts

Graphs and charts usually provide clear answers to an accompanying math question. Just don't make these questions harder than they are by reading too much into them.

Chapter 22

Ten Writing Errors to Avoid

Chapter 8 gives you what you need to know to develop a good writing style for the analytical writing assessment, but becoming a better writer takes practice. Fortunately, you can rapidly improve your writing style (and your analytical writing assessment score) if you avoid these ten common writing mistakes!

Composing Complicated Sentences

The chances of making multiple grammar and punctuation errors increase with the length and complexity of your sentences. If you need to improve your writing in a hurry, concentrate on simplicity. Make your point, end your sentence, and move on. Remember that the readers have to grade many exams. Don't make your reader work too hard to understand your sentences. You can (and should) use a variety of sentence structures, but keep them simple.

Presenting Your Text in Passive Voice

Active voice is clearer and more powerful than the passive voice. Passive voice uses more words than are necessary and clouds the main action. You're much more likely to make errors in verb usage with a passive sentence. Remember that the passive voice is only really appropriate when the doer of the action is unknown or unimportant, such as in scientific writing. For business writing and the GMAT, use active voice. (See "Building a Solid Foundation: Grammar Basics" in Chapter 3 for more about active and passive voice.)

If you need a quick refresher on the difference between active and passive, consider these two sentences: *Active voice should be used on the GMAT* is passive, because no one is doing the action. *You should use active voice on the GMAT* is active.

Wasting Time with Unfamiliar Words

Trying to impress the essay readers with your advanced vocabulary is tempting. But if you aren't completely familiar with a word's meaning, don't use it on the GMAT. GMAT readers focus more on how you organize and support your thoughts than on the reading level of your essay. And they'll take points off your score if you misuse words. You have only 30 minutes to develop your argument, so don't waste time coming up with five-syllable words unless you just happen to use them in your normal conversation.

Using Unclear (or Zero) Transitions

Tell your reader where your argument is going by including clear transitions. With just one or two words, you can tell the reader whether the next paragraph continues the current idea, refutes it, or moves in a new direction. Using transition words and phrases can really improve your assessment score.

Going Overboard with Generic Terms

To clarify your points and excite your reader, pack your sentences with lively and unambiguous descriptions rather than fuzzy generalities (like *interesting, great,* and *awful*). Your writing makes a greater impact and will receive a higher score when you fortify it with expressive language.

Writing in Informal English

Save slang and creative capitalization and punctuation for the e-mails you send to your friends and coworkers. For the GMAT, apply the rules of standard written English you learned in grammar class.

Giving a Laundry List of Examples

Satisfy essay readers with a few clearly developed examples to back up your points rather than a list of undeveloped examples. Readers are more concerned with the depth of your supporting evidence than they are with its quantity. In fact, you could earn a 6 with just one example if you develop it well.

Succumbing to Sentence Fragments

Your essay shouldn't read like an outline. Fully develop your thoughts with properly punctuated complete sentences and well-organized paragraphs.

Announcing a Position

Both essay prompts require you to adopt a position. But merely stating your position and jumping into your argument is insufficient. Introduce your essay with a brief analysis of the argument or issue that shows the readers you understand what you're writing about.

Putting Aside Proofreading

Leave yourself enough time at the end of the 30 minutes to quickly read through your essay and correct any obvious errors. Plan on using about three minutes to proofread and eliminate careless errors. Doing so could raise your score a complete point.

Chapter 23

Ten Formulas You Need to Know on Test Day

In This Chapter

▶ Putting the formulas you'll want to remember in one convenient place
▶ Filling your head with information you'll no longer remember the day after the test

This chapter provides you with a rundown of many of the equations you should know for the GMAT quantitative section.

Doing Algebraic Work Problems

Production stands for the amount of work that gets done. Here's how you calculate it:

Production = rate of work × time

This formula works well for word problems. For instance, perhaps two bricklayers, Sarah and Joe, are working on a wall. Sarah lays 16 rows per day, and Joe lays 20 rows per day. If they each work 8-hour days, how many rows can the two of them lay in 1 hour, assuming they maintain a steady rate? You can use the formula to find out how many rows each of them lays per day and then divide that by 8 hours.

Handling Distance Problems

The formula for figuring out distance or speed problems in algebra is

Distance = rate × time

You can solve any problem involving distance, speed, or time spent traveling with this equation.

FOIL Expressions

Memorizing these expressions makes FOILing (multiplying binomials) much easier:

$$(a + b)^2 = a^2 + 2ab + b^2$$
$$(a - b)^2 = a^2 - 2ab + b^2$$
$$(a + b)(a - b) = a^2 - b^2$$

The Slope-Intercept Formula

The characteristics of a line can be demonstrated with a formula. The equation of a line generally shows y as a function of x.

$$y = mx + b$$

In the slope-intercept formula, m is a constant that indicates the slope of the line, and b is a constant that indicates the y-intercept $(0, y)$. So a line with a formula $y = 3x + 4$ has a slope of 3 and a y-intercept of 4.

The Formula for Slope

Given two points (x_1, y_1) and (x_2, y_2), you can find slope using this handy formula:

$$\frac{y_2 - y_1}{x_2 - x_1}$$

Special Right Triangles

If you memorize these ratios for special right triangles, figuring out side lengths of right triangles should come naturally. Here are some common ratios of side lengths:

- 3:4:5
- 5:12:13

And here are the ratios of side lengths of triangles with special angle measures:

- **45°:45°:90° triangle:** $s:s:s\sqrt{2}$ (where s = the length of one of the legs) or $\frac{s}{\sqrt{2}}:\frac{s}{\sqrt{2}}:s$ (where s = the length of the hypotenuse)
- **30°:60°:90° triangle:** $s:s\sqrt{3}:2s$ (where s = the length of the shortest side)

Equation for Average Mean

To find the average, or mean, of a set of values, use this formula:

$$A = \frac{Sum\ of\ all\ numbers}{Amount\ of\ numbers\ that\ make\ up\ the\ sum}$$

Formula for Groups

Here's the formula for solving problems that involve classifying people or objects in groups:

Group 1 + Group 2 – Both Groups + Neither Group = Grand Total

Finding the Probability of One Event

To find the probability of an event in which all possible outcomes are equally likely, use this formula:

$$P(E) = \frac{\text{The number of outcomes involving the occurrence of } E}{\text{The total possible number of outcomes}}$$

Finding the Probability of Multiple Events

You can use two ways to figure out the probability that two events (A and B) will occur, depending on whether the events are mutually exclusive.

If the two events are mutually exclusive, you use the *special rule of addition:*

P (A or B) = P (A) + P (B)

If the events aren't mutually exclusive, you use the *general rule of addition*:

P (A or B) = P (A) + P (B) − P (A and B)

To find the probability of two events occurring together, you use the rules of multiplication. If the two events are independent of one another, you apply the *special rule of multiplication:*

P (A and B) = P (A) × P (B)

If the outcome of the first event affects the outcome of the second event, you use the *general rule of multiplication,* in which (B I A) means *B given A:*

P (A and B) = P (A) × P (B I A)

Index

BUSINESS, CAREERS & PERSONAL FINANCE

Grant Writing FOR DUMMIES
A Reference for the Rest of Us!
0-7645-5307-0

Home Buying FOR DUMMIES
A Reference for the Rest of Us!
0-7645-5331-3 *†

Also available:
- Accounting For Dummies †
  0-7645-5314-3
- Business Plans Kit For Dummies †
  0-7645-5365-8
- Cover Letters For Dummies
  0-7645-5224-4
- Frugal Living For Dummies
  0-7645-5403-4
- Leadership For Dummies
  0-7645-5176-0
- Managing For Dummies
  0-7645-1771-6

- Marketing For Dummies
  0-7645-5600-2
- Personal Finance For Dummies *
  0-7645-2590-5
- Project Management For Dummies
  0-7645-5283-X
- Resumes For Dummies †
  0-7645-5471-9
- Selling For Dummies
  0-7645-5363-1
- Small Business Kit For Dummies *†
  0-7645-5093-4

HOME & BUSINESS COMPUTER BASICS

Windows XP FOR DUMMIES
A Reference for the Rest of Us!
Andy Rathbone
0-7645-4074-2

Excel 2003 ALL-IN-ONE DESK REFERENCE FOR DUMMIES
9 BOOKS IN 1
Greg Harvey
0-7645-3758-X

Also available:
- ACT! 6 For Dummies
  0-7645-2645-6
- iLife '04 All-in-One Desk Reference
  For Dummies
  0-7645-7347-0
- iPAQ For Dummies
  0-7645-6769-1
- Mac OS X Panther Timesaving
  Techniques For Dummies
  0-7645-5812-9
- Macs For Dummies
  0-7645-5656-8
- Microsoft Money 2004 For Dummies
  0-7645-4195-1

- Office 2003 All-in-One Desk Reference
  For Dummies
  0-7645-3883-7
- Outlook 2003 For Dummies
  0-7645-3759-8
- PCs For Dummies
  0-7645-4074-2
- TiVo For Dummies
  0-7645-6923-6
- Upgrading and Fixing PCs For Dummies
  0-7645-1665-5
- Windows XP Timesaving Techniques
  For Dummies
  0-7645-3748-2

FOOD, HOME, GARDEN, HOBBIES, MUSIC & PETS

Feng Shui FOR DUMMIES
A Reference for the Rest of Us!
0-7645-5295-3

Poker FOR DUMMIES
A Reference for the Rest of Us!
0-7645-5232-5

Also available:
- Bass Guitar For Dummies
  0-7645-2487-9
- Diabetes Cookbook For Dummies
  0-7645-5230-9
- Gardening For Dummies *
  0-7645-5130-2
- Guitar For Dummies
  0-7645-5106-X
- Holiday Decorating For Dummies
  0-7645-2570-0
- Home Improvement All-in-One
  For Dummies
  0-7645-5680-0

- Knitting For Dummies
  0-7645-5395-X
- Piano For Dummies
  0-7645-5105-1
- Puppies For Dummies
  0-7645-5255-4
- Scrapbooking For Dummies
  0-7645-7208-3
- Senior Dogs For Dummies
  0-7645-5818-8
- Singing For Dummies
  0-7645-2475-5
- 30-Minute Meals For Dummies
  0-7645-2589-1

INTERNET & DIGITAL MEDIA

Digital Photography FOR DUMMIES
A Reference for the Rest of Us!
Julie Adair King
0-7645-1664-7

Starting an eBay Business FOR DUMMIES
A Reference for the Rest of Us!
Marsha Collier
0-7645-6924-4

Also available:
- 2005 Online Shopping Directory
  For Dummies
  0-7645-7495-7
- CD & DVD Recording For Dummies
  0-7645-5956-7
- eBay For Dummies
  0-7645-5654-1
- Fighting Spam For Dummies
  0-7645-5965-6
- Genealogy Online For Dummies
  0-7645-5964-8
- Google For Dummies
  0-7645-4420-9

- Home Recording For Musicians
  For Dummies
  0-7645-1634-5
- The Internet For Dummies
  0-7645-4173-0
- iPod & iTunes For Dummies
  0-7645-7772-7
- Preventing Identity Theft For Dummies
  0-7645-7336-5
- Pro Tools All-in-One Desk Reference
  For Dummies
  0-7645-5714-9
- Roxio Easy Media Creator For Dummies
  0-7645-7131-1

* Separate Canadian edition also available
† Separate U.K. edition also available

SPORTS, FITNESS, PARENTING, RELIGION & SPIRITUALITY

0-7645-5146-9

0-7645-5418-2

Also available:
- Adoption For Dummies
  0-7645-5488-3
- Basketball For Dummies
  0-7645-5248-1
- The Bible For Dummies
  0-7645-5296-1
- Buddhism For Dummies
  0-7645-5359-3
- Catholicism For Dummies
  0-7645-5391-7
- Hockey For Dummies
  0-7645-5228-7

- Judaism For Dummies
  0-7645-5299-6
- Martial Arts For Dummies
  0-7645-5358-5
- Pilates For Dummies
  0-7645-5397-6
- Religion For Dummies
  0-7645-5264-3
- Teaching Kids to Read For Dummies
  0-7645-4043-2
- Weight Training For Dummies
  0-7645-5168-X
- Yoga For Dummies
  0-7645-5117-5

TRAVEL

0-7645-5438-7

0-7645-5453-0

Also available:
- Alaska For Dummies
  0-7645-1761-9
- Arizona For Dummies
  0-7645-6938-4
- Cancún and the Yucatán For Dummies
  0-7645-2437-2
- Cruise Vacations For Dummies
  0-7645-6941-4
- Europe For Dummies
  0-7645-5456-5
- Ireland For Dummies
  0-7645-5455-7

- Las Vegas For Dummies
  0-7645-5448-4
- London For Dummies
  0-7645-4277-X
- New York City For Dummies
  0-7645-6945-7
- Paris For Dummies
  0-7645-5494-8
- RV Vacations For Dummies
  0-7645-5443-3
- Walt Disney World & Orlando For Dummies
  0-7645-6943-0

GRAPHICS, DESIGN & WEB DEVELOPMENT

0-7645-4345-8

0-7645-5589-8

Also available:
- Adobe Acrobat 6 PDF For Dummies
  0-7645-3760-1
- Building a Web Site For Dummies
  0-7645-7144-3
- Dreamweaver MX 2004 For Dummies
  0-7645-4342-3
- FrontPage 2003 For Dummies
  0-7645-3882-9
- HTML 4 For Dummies
  0-7645-1995-6
- Illustrator CS For Dummies
  0-7645-4084-X

- Macromedia Flash MX 2004 For Dummies
  0-7645-4358-X
- Photoshop 7 All-in-One Desk Reference For Dummies
  0-7645-1667-1
- Photoshop CS Timesaving Techniques For Dummies
  0-7645-6782-9
- PHP 5 For Dummies
  0-7645-4166-8
- PowerPoint 2003 For Dummies
  0-7645-3908-6
- QuarkXPress 6 For Dummies
  0-7645-2593-X

NETWORKING, SECURITY, PROGRAMMING & DATABASES

0-7645-6852-3

0-7645-5784-X

Also available:
- A+ Certification For Dummies
  0-7645-4187-0
- Access 2003 All-in-One Desk Reference For Dummies
  0-7645-3988-4
- Beginning Programming For Dummies
  0-7645-4997-9
- C For Dummies
  0-7645-7068-4
- Firewalls For Dummies
  0-7645-4048-3
- Home Networking For Dummies
  0-7645-42796

- Network Security For Dummies
  0-7645-1679-5
- Networking For Dummies
  0-7645-1677-9
- TCP/IP For Dummies
  0-7645-1760-0
- VBA For Dummies
  0-7645-3989-2
- Wireless All In-One Desk Reference For Dummies
  0-7645-7496-5
- Wireless Home Networking For Dummies
  0-7645-3910-8

HEALTH & SELF-HELP

0-7645-6820-5 *†

0-7645-2566-2

Also available:
- Alzheimer's For Dummies
  0-7645-3899-3
- Asthma For Dummies
  0-7645-4233-8
- Controlling Cholesterol For Dummies
  0-7645-5440-9
- Depression For Dummies
  0-7645-3900-0
- Dieting For Dummies
  0-7645-4149-8
- Fertility For Dummies
  0-7645-2549-2
- Fibromyalgia For Dummies
  0-7645-5441-7

- Improving Your Memory For Dummies
  0-7645-5435-2
- Pregnancy For Dummies †
  0-7645-4483-7
- Quitting Smoking For Dummies
  0-7645-2629-4
- Relationships For Dummies
  0-7645-5384-4
- Thyroid For Dummies
  0-7645-5385-2

EDUCATION, HISTORY, REFERENCE & TEST PREPARATION

0-7645-5194-9

0-7645-4186-2

Also available:
- Algebra For Dummies
  0-7645-5325-9
- British History For Dummies
  0-7645-7021-8
- Calculus For Dummies
  0-7645-2498-4
- English Grammar For Dummies
  0-7645-5322-4
- Forensics For Dummies
  0-7645-5580-4
- The GMAT For Dummies
  0-7645-5251-1
- Inglés Para Dummies
  0-7645-5427-1

- Italian For Dummies
  0-7645-5196-5
- Latin For Dummies
  0-7645-5431-X
- Lewis & Clark For Dummies
  0-7645-2545-X
- Research Papers For Dummies
  0-7645-5426-3
- The SAT I For Dummies
  0-7645-7193-1
- Science Fair Projects For Dummies
  0-7645-5460-3
- U.S. History For Dummies
  0-7645-5249-X

Get smart @ dummies.com®

- **Find a full list of Dummies titles**
- **Look into loads of FREE on-site articles**
- **Sign up for FREE eTips e-mailed to you weekly**
- **See what other products carry the Dummies name**
- **Shop directly from the Dummies bookstore**
- **Enter to win new prizes every month!**